W9-ATD-777

French Lovers

ALSO BY JOSEPH BARRY:

Left Bank, Right Bank

Contemporary American Architecture

The People of Paris

Passions and Politics: A Biography of Versailles

Infamous Woman: The Life of George Sand

French Lovers

FROM
HELOISE AND ABELARD
TO
BEAUVOIR AND SARTRE

by
JOSEPH BARRY

ARBOR HOUSE
New York

TO LILIANE, ALWAYS

 Published in the United States of America by Arbor House Publishing Company and in Canada by Fitzhenry & Whiteside Ltd.
Manufactured in the United States of America

10 9 8 7 6 5 4 3 2 1

Library of Congress Cataloging in Publication Data

Barry, Joseph Amber, 1917–
French lovers.

Translation of: A la française.
1. Love. 2. Courtship—France—History. 3. Biography.
I. Title.
HQ801.A2B3313 1987 306.7'092'2 86-20601
ISBN 0-87795-844-0

CONTENTS

PREFACE

THE great French dress designer Paul Poiret—who yielded to an even greater *couturière,* Coco Chanel—relished a mistress who not only modeled his creations to perfection, but was also a gourmet cook. Frequently she would rise at five in the morning to begin preparations for lunch, then return to Poiret in bed, "smelling deliciously," he said, "of thyme, fennel and chives."

Early in his career, Poiret had also captured the exquisite relationship between love and fashion, as Nina Epton recounts with some awe in *Love and the French.* "You must take a lover," he told his leading sales lady, since her loveless life, he remarked, "prevented her from feeling the sensual charm that is the hallmark of a superb gown."

Seemingly the only thing lacking in this syndrome of French culture is the wine—but it was certainly poured at Poiret's lunch. "If God forbids wine," Cardinal Richelieu once observed, "why would He have made it so good?"

We might add French painting, music, and architecture. And conversation. At their best the French are lucid, literate, and tolerant, and they are blessed with an unguilty sense of pleasure—the happy products of a temperate climate. They have the proper latitude, and attitude, for love.

The plurality of life styles is a consequence, as well, of a great country's gift of privacy. Avid of their own privacy, the French give you yours. Actually Gertrude Stein, expatriate, expressed it best. "It is not what France gives you," she said, "it's what it doesn't take away." Perhaps that is the essence of French tolerance, whose offspring is variety, the daily assurance, the daily *miracle,* of individuality. Sin is not confused with crime, immorality with illegality. Adults are assumed to be grownup keepers of their own consciences.

The French are frivolous, too, if that means taking serious things lightly and delightful things seriously. In fact, in their frivolity they are faithful to one thing—change. True, they say, *plus ça change, plus c'est la même chose*—the more things change, the more they are the same—but you must know change to know *that!* For centuries they have been noted as a nation endowed with extraordinary curiosity. Anything new in style or life will draw from them sparkling Cartesian—French-logical—conclusions. At the same time they have a passion for simple distractions, that refuge of complicated natures.

French taste is rightly famous, and I have been attending it for forty years. To savor is French. So is to flavor. But to each constant of French culture and civilization, one must add French sensibility, French *esprit.* If I had to hazard a definition of French sexuality—and now we are touching the flesh and fiber of this book—I would say it is sensuality sharpened by intellectuality. You can see it in a Monet painting, you can hear it in Debussy's *Pelléas,* and of course you savor it in French cuisine. It is as if the mind had taste buds, taste buds and nerve endings a mind. French *volupté* is not our *voluptuousness,* Edith Wharton said, "it is the intangible charm the imagination extracts from things tangible." It is that and more.

Henry James finally chose England over France as his dwelling place, despite English cooking. You cannot, he said, choose a country for that "ignoble thing, food." So he left Paris for London and Rye. But then, Henry James was not among the world's greatest lovers.

What land has contributed more to the ways and means, the lore and language, of love than the nation Henry James left behind? Not Italy. Think of all those cafés with men only, or of Casanova's memoirs, which he wrote in French. Not India, despite the *Kama Sutra.* An Indian friend, when asked whatever happened to the wonderful eroticism of Indian sculpture, glumly responded, "British occupation" (though one wonders how long that will serve as an excuse). As for the land of the geisha, I'll take the land of the Frenchwoman. There is no love, for this American, like the love between peers, and one can savor that in the story of Voltaire and the lady scientist Mme. du Châtelet.

"How fortunate," our Frenchman exclaimed, "to admire her whom I adore!"

It is the superiority of the woman relative to her man that determines the quality, certainly the equality, of the good French couple. Heloise, said Henry Adams, was worth a dozen Abelards. Marie Antoinette, said Mirabeau, was the man of the couple, not Louis XVI.

There is a lovely paradox here. The Frenchman demands a great deal of his wife, and he gets it. The Frenchwoman demands less of her husband, and she gets it. The one gets what he likes, the other likes what she gets. She does not ask him to be handsome. He does not have to be a genius, simply witty. For this, "no woman in the world can compete with the Frenchwoman"—it is Englishman William Shenstone speaking—"her power of intellectual irritation. She will draw wit out of a fool." She will even have the support of her husband's mother.

Two hundred years ago French academician Joseph Droz doubted whether love would be inspired by a husband. He concluded that a woman should not marry before her love had been won. Far earlier, women were stating the same proposition in stronger terms. "Love," the Countess of Champagne ruled at a medieval Court of Love, "is for lovers, not for married couples." Today Frenchmen take pride in a kind of "elegant sufficiency," treating their wives as they once treated their mistresses and ministers. They take shame only in constancy.

For almost a millenium the French have been reflecting on the ways and arts of love, four centuries before the discovery of America. Drawers upon drawers of catalog cards, many of them handwritten, are devoted to *amour* and its practices at the National Library of Paris. Had Ovid never existed, it is most likely that a Frenchman would have invented him.

What would Bartlett, Stevenson, or the *Oxford Dictionary of Quotations* do without the aphorisms of La Rochefoucauld, Stendhal, Rabelais, Balzac, Molière, Montaigne, Mme. de Staël, La Fontaine, et al., on Love? They would be left with Shakespeare and Oscar Wilde. The oldest, possibly the most haunting, love story in English concerns the adulterous passion, reciprocated, of Lancelot for his queen, Guinevere. Sir Thomas Mallory transcribed it from French manuscripts and titled the English version *Le Morte d'Arthur.* That story finds its place in my chapter on courtly love, the finest contribution of France to the intricate history of love.

The *ménage à trois* is assumed, perhaps rightly, to be another French contribution to that design for living among the varieties of love's arrangements. Was there ever a more flagrant, royal example set before the people than the conduct of the Sun King? In one wing of Louis XIV's great palace at Versailles, the queen and her ladies-in-waiting; in the other, his mistress of the moment. But Louis, too, had his precedent in the Renaissance trio of Henri II, Diane de Poitiers, and Queen Catherine de Medici. For my part, however, if multiple arrangements are in order, my preference goes to a *ménage à quatre:* a quartet is more equitable and fair. The examples, alas, are rare, but one might begin with the story of Voltaire and Mme. du Châtelet, then skip to Beauvoir and Sartre.

The very language of love seems to fall into French idiom, not so much as a matter of chic as of French origins: liaison, libertine, gallantry; chivalry, sadism, even chastity; alliance, dalliance, misalliance; ardor, passion, jealousy; paramour, fiancé, cuckold; desire, admire, embrace; fervor, folly, cherish, charm. Short stories à la Maupassant spring from the groupings. Couple worldly cynicism and romantic yearnings and you have the very image of the French spirit. *Romance* is a French word; *sophistication* should be. The land of *mesure* is also the country of extremes:

STENDHAL: "Half, the most beautiful half, of life is hidden from the man who has not loved passionately."
A CERTAIN DR. FÉRÉ: "One can only fall madly in love if one is mad."
CHAMFORT: "Love is the contact of two epiderms."
CLAUDE ANET: "In the last resort, civilization, art, thought—everything—stem from love."

How did France get that way? What is the reality of its legendary couples, the true story of its famous, myth-wrapped lovers? Indeed, of its civilization, art, thought, everything, for is not the history of a nation to be sought in the entwined lives of its people? In this sense, I have tried to make Emerson's remark my own: "There is properly no History; only Biography." That is, the lived experience of human societies. Here, then, is a chronicle of couples through nine centuries of French history, a story of strong, unusual personalities joined by passion or circumstance, sometimes caught in the power relationships of the couple. Those of the twentieth century I have known personally, several intimately. The longer I live, the less inclined I am to generalize; wherefore this approach to the evolution of French attitudes, behavior, and morals: a story of couples in which all couples, I believe, can find something of their own story—for nothing human is completely alien to any of us.

I chose each couple as revelatory of its age but also for its relevance to our own. However remote in time, love is in the present tense; all lovers are remarkably contemporary, their concerns strikingly similar to our own: the friction of the sexes, the problem of fidelity, power, love, jealousy, of personality, of simply living together. Can a couple have two centers? Must a *ménage à trois,* so often conceived as the French way, mean a humiliated wife? How should one cope with one's own jealousy, knowing that to love passionately is to experience it? How does one confront differences of age, aging itself? Are love and freedom compatible?

We have a privileged view of past lives, past couples: we know how they end. We are led to reassess their beginnings and to modify their developments so as to bring couples and lives to a happier ending. The wisdom of hindsight? Certainly. It is how we learn from the past, so as to learn how to look with some perspective at our own improvable lives. The couples before us have the diversity of our own individual particularity, pushed to an extreme most of us have fantasied or dreamed, but rarely dared. The individuality they have won is universality enough.

For many years and for a number of reasons, I have been preoccupied with the couple, past and present and future, most often my own, but also with the couplings and uncouplings of my French friends, their intimate, incessant dialogues, their strivings, often their struggles, to live together in a modern mode that is still defining itself. I have come to believe that a prime indicator of a civilization is the one-to-one relationship of its people—man to man, woman to woman, woman to man; in short, its couples. Exploring the past, I have found myself on an inevitable voyage of self-discovery, examining at each stage my own experiences and the conclusions I have been drawing from them.

Each generation needs new translations, new readings of the old classics, new performances of the old plays, whether the writer is Montaigne or the playwright Shakespeare, Sophocles or Molière. In this study of love and the couple through French history, the translations are predominantly mine; so are the interpretations. First published in France for its severest test, my study, its constructs, and interpretations have been found by French critics—despite their inbuilt suspicion of a foreign intruder and however upsetting for received ideas—to be new, challenging, even disturbing, but textually unassailable, since they were buttressed with precise notes and sources. All quotations are attributed.

Thus the dialogue with the dead need not be less alive and pertinent than the interviews with the living; or old materials, re-viewed, less yielding of fresh insights than those that appear here for the first time. The approach I took is a kind of mixture of Freud and Marx—each is essential in the explanation of the other—with a touch of Einstein, for the observer is also moving and evolving in the moving account of human relationships. I might add, finally, a pinch of Nietzsche, which allows for that drive of a strong personality to lift itself bodily out of the drag of its condition.

THE story of the medieval couple Abelard and Heloise, at the beginning of our voyage, startles with immediate implications, but we are struck more pungently by these two at the voyage's end, with Beauvoir and Sartre. What pair has symbolized more widely the modern, liberated couple, wherever people read, than this dyad of existentialist, Left Bank lovers? As did Beauvoir, Heloise denounced marriage and children as fetters for her philosopher-lover. Why should he not take her as his concubine and thus be untroubled by her as his wife? She would rather be his whore, she told Abelard, than the empress of Rome.

There is, too, the clash of the nobleman's principle of love as pleasure and the Church's Paulian view of woman as the devil in the flesh. Abelard, born a nobleman, died a priest. But in the lovely period that followed, courtly love predominated and noblewomen ruled through Courts of Love. The ideal of gallantry and refinement, brooding in the hopes and dreams of the feminine imagination, became a reality, briefly, to reappear whenever romanticism reoccurs.

With Henry II and twenty-year-older mistress Diane de Poitiers, the Renaissance emerged from the Middle Ages and the aristocratic pleasure principle again triumphed. But the middle class was also emerging, and with it Monsieur and Madame de Montaigne. He has been called the bourgeois philosopher par excellence for his advocacy of moderation—passion is destructive of marriage; seek love elsewhere. What might Madame de Montaigne have thought of this?

As for Molière, was he the bourgeois playwright—of eminent common sense—as is taught? He was not. He was the Sun King's entertainer, as was his twenty-year-*younger* wife (some said his daughter), actress Armande Béjart, whom noblemen took to bed, her husband knowing. How did this supremely lucid man, who was love's prisoner, respond to that? How did the dramatist resolve the dramatic conflict in his own life, for "not to be jealous," he recognized, "is to love coldly"—and he loved passionately? "You will tell me I must be crazy to love like this," he confessed to a friend, "but I believe there is only one kind of love, and that those who do not feel the same as I have never really loved."

With Voltaire and Madame du Châtelet, love and the Enlightenment, we come close to the ideal couple—a pair of equals. Not to be confused with a *happy* couple. (We all know one or two happy couples, rarely more and increasingly less, where *he* is gently dominating and *she* is greatly loving and quite happily serving.) Voltaire regarded his meeting with Emilie, married, mother of three, and a mathematician who would structure his own thinking, as the turning point in his life. They had both had previous lovers and would both have lovers concomitantly, a *ménage à quatre,* sometimes *cinq.* The odd number belonged to Emilie.

As for the Marquis and Marquise de Sade, the two played out their life roles to such an extreme that if it were fiction, the account would be caricature. Never, perhaps, was the pleasure principle conducted so far, nor the concept of the "dutiful wife," which transcended even the age's notion of the wife's duty. One recalls here the monastic devotion of Juliette Drouet, literally cloistered by her lover Victor Hugo, and no less of the oversung devotion of the Marquise de Lafayette to the rather fatuous Marquis. But Sade, too, has his complexity. One may kill for pleasure, he said during the Reign of Terror, but not guillotine someone in the name of an abstraction, such as justice. Should we finally condone Sade, even canonize him, as his apologists—Beauvoir oddly among them—seem to wish to do?

With Marie, Comtesse d'Agoult, we have a flowering and fading of the Romantic movement, acidly reflected upon by one of the most fascinating women of the nineteenth century. In fact, a subtitle with which I toyed for the story of her liaison with Franz Liszt went like this: "What if Anna Karenina had Lived to Write her Own Novel, rather than Throw Herself under a Train?" For Marie d'Agoult, as for Anna K., it was all for love, but Liszt, à la Count Vronsky, could not forswear society; his profession as a pianist demanded it. (How many men sacrifice their careers for love, or do not suddenly find that love fades as the career is threatened?) "I hate your tears," said Liszt when he left. "I hate music," Marie would say in turn. "I loved it too long." Marie went on to become Daniel Stern, writer, but she was the one of the couple who never wholly recovered.

Gertrude Stein was born two years before Marie d'Agoult died, in 1876; Alice B. Toklas was buried in the Père Lachaise cemetery, alongside Gertrude, in 1967. Gertrude and Alice were an American couple who initiated the twentieth century in France. No account of the School of Paris Painting could omit its foreigners, if only to mention Picasso. We cannot speak of Paris writers without noting the names of Joyce, Hemingway, or Stein. As Gertrude's "adopted nephew," I observed the two lovers until Gertrude's death and remained close to Alice until hers. Gertrude, as the creative writer, was the center of their couple. *Can* there be two centers?

This exploration of artist and artist's companion continues with Jean Cocteau and Jean Marais. Surprisingly, perhaps, the story of the two Jeans is not so much to be compared with that of Gertrude and Alice as to be contrasted with the sad story of Marie d'Agoult and Liszt, for the two Jeans', I believe, is essentially a happy romantic love story. It is, in large part, because they had come to terms with their nature and each other and with a society that on the whole was tolerant and understanding and now, after Jean Marais's forthright and touching memoirs, largely sympathetic. It is also because the two Jeans were complementary—playwright and actor, moviemaker and leading man—and were thus a working couple. They had the grace as well, like the ancient Greeks, to end their idyll before it turned sour—a lesson, however paradoxical, for an enduring couple.

With Sartre and Simone de Beauvoir we are fully in our time, closing the twentieth century. But opening toward what? For many they have been the very emblem of the liberated couple. Their famous *pacte* permitted them "contingent love affairs." Yet there is now explosive evidence that the arrangement was tailored for Sartre, not for both; that in their "perfect" relationship of the "modern" couple there was the age-old pattern of dominant male–subordinate female. Whatever, one asks, led a woman who would write the basic statement for modern feminists, *The Second Sex,* to accept second place to a man? And why does she weep on every second page of her autobiographical novels? Has not Beauvoir been rent by her impassioned drive for autonomy and independence at the same time as she strained for oneness with the man she loved, who, she tells us, "was not made for monogamy"—or for love?

And what might be our own conclusion as we stumble on the steps and feel for the door to the future?

A great circle seems to have been drawn from Abelard and Heloise to Beauvoir and Sartre. I confess that when I began I had thought I would be chronicling the birth and death of the couple, because, I believed, we were witnessing its last agonies as our century came to an end. However, as the research and the writing progressed over the years, coincident with my own errant experience, I discovered something else: couples draw their own circles within the great circle of French history and civilization. Together they form a great, unending spiral in which succeeding couples return, at another level, in another time.

In any event, an unpredicted pattern became apparent. Instead of a disheartening, descending line or, for that matter, a recomforting ascending curve in the chronology of the French couple, there were ups and downs in unexpected places and times. Fabulous, exemplary, or way out, the couples, in all their diversity, demonstrate one thing: to an extraordinary extent two people can create a world within a world, though the outside world can come crashing through with wars, plagues, sickness, or more mundane disasters.

First, our couples instruct us, we must find ourselves, assume our natures. If pleasure is a problem, we will have little pleasure in pairing.

If we cannot live with ourselves, it is unlikely we can live with any other. If two people are lonely or unhappy, they can double the unhappiness, the loneliness, by marriage. We must thus first unburden the couple of the responsibility of our being or not being happy in order to give it a chance to give us that happiness.

One by one, then two by two, we *can* rise above our pasts—infancy, childhood, conditioning—to form pairs of equals. We have no blueprints. But there are examples, and France provides us with some of the finest.

J. B.
Paris, 1977–1986.

1

THE COUPLE AND THE CROSS: HELOISE AND ABELARD

> What honor could she win, [Heloise] protested, from a marriage which would dishonor me and humiliate us both? . . . Nature had created me for all mankind—it would be a sorry scandal if I should bind myself to a single woman and submit to such base servitude. . . . Along with the loss to my reputation she put before me the difficulties of marriage [and cited] the apostle Paul.
>
> —Peter Abelard, *Historia Calamitatum* (circa A.D. 1133)

> I must say that not for a moment was I tempted by [Sartre's] suggestion of marriage. Marriage multiplies by two the obligations of family and society. . . . Concern about my own independence scarcely weighed for me . . . rather, I could see how much it would cost Sartre to say good-bye to his travels, his freedom, his youth, in becoming a teacher somewhere in the provinces and settling down as an adult. To settle down as a married man would have been yet one more renunciation.
>
> —Simone de Beauvoir, *La Force de l'Age* (1960)

IT was a time, as we begin, when not simply the couple but even marriage was suspect, when the demonic carnality of woman, whether concubine or wife, was scarcely questioned and her transformation from Eve into Mary was deemed a miracle hardly to be hoped for. It was the Middle Ages.

The pagan exuberance of the Celts and the Franks, when France was still Gaul, had long since been dampened, then extinguished. "Thou has conquered, O pale Galilean," the famous line of Swinburne reads, "the world has grown grey from thy breath."[1] However, it was not Christ, compassionate uplifter of fallen women, but rather his apostles and the Church fathers who had equated sexuality with Satanism and had condemned women as the Devil's ally.[2]

Soon noblewomen to the south—in a Provence closer to a cultivated Moorish Spain than to a comparatively provincial Paris—would impose courtly love or the conception of woman as someone who must be courted and whose love must be earned.[3] It would be women's most enduring triumph down to the present.

But it was a time before this, before Gothic architecture was born or the cathedral we know as Notre Dame was even begun. It was the year 1100, when a comely youth of twenty who called himself Abelard—no one is sure why[4]—came to storm Paris "by force of reason"[5] as others of his generation had gone on the First Crusade to wrest Jerusalem from the Saracens by pure force.

He had been born in 1079, the first child of a noble Breton, Lord Berengar of Le Pallet, a small fief twelve miles east of Nantes, when Brittany was an independent dukedom not yet incorporated into France. His father had "smiled" upon Peter and had encouraged him in his studies, before preparing him for knighthood and eventual lordship of the feudal domain. Sieur Berengar himself, Abelard tells us in *Historia Calamitatum (The Story of My Calamities)*,

> had acquired some knowledge of letters before he buckled on the sword of knighthood, and later on his passion for learning became such that he determined to have all his sons instructed in letters before they were trained in arms.[6]

Peter's father and mother would retire from the world in their last years and enter a religious life, as was a fairly common procedure then—one prepared for eternity as one approached one's death. Pleasure may have been the nobleman's pursuit, but piety and prayer overtook him as his days diminished, and the Church had the last word with absolution. So, too, in a capsule, one might describe the life of Abelard.

"I was my father's firstborn," says Abelard, "and being of special dearness to him, the greatest care was taken over my education." That tutoring consisted largely of the writings in Latin of pagan philosophers and the Church fathers—Plato (but little Aristotle), Virgil, Cicero, Seneca, and Ovid, St. Paul, St. Jerome, and St. Augustine. Elements of the faith were drummed into the child before he could read or even understand them. Later Ovid would become, and remain, Abelard's favorite poet, especially his *Metamorphoses* and *Art of Love.* Quotations from them would sprinkle his own writing with their wit, cynicism, and conceits. The lines had a special relevance to the attitude toward life of the younger Abelard; Heloise, too, had read Ovid.

The period, in a word, was awash with amorality, despite the Church's damming constraint. It may have been a time of hellfire, but it was not that of middle-class hypocrisy—confessional manuals of the age dealt with fornication and adultery in blunt, explicit language.[7] As for medieval assumption of male superiority, it was no more questioned than the story of Eve's creation from one of Adam's lower ribs.

These fragments from Ovid's *Art of Love* are clothed in the seventeenth-century dress of Dryden's translation:

> Perhaps she calls it force, but if she 'scape,
> She will not thank you for th' omitted rape.
> The Sex is cunning to conceal their fires;
> They would be forc'd e'en to their own desires.
> They seem t'accuse you, with a downcast sight,
> But in their souls confess you did them right.
> Who might be forc'd, and yet untouch'd depart,
> Thank you with their tongues, but curse you
> with their heart.
>
> Be cautious lest you overact your part,
> And temper your hypocrisy with art. . . .
> If pale and meagre, praise her shape and youth,
> Active when small, when gross she's plump and smooth.
>
> Such to the town my fam'd instructions prove,
> So much am I renown'd for arts of love.
> Me ev'ry youth shall praise, extol my name,
> And o'er the globe diffuse my lasting fame.[8]

Fame was Peter Abelard's impassioned goal: Ovid's proud cry echoes throughout *Historia Calamitatum.* But which road to fame, the red or the black, the military or the religious, the only paths to glory down to Stendhal's Napoleonic time? The Church was a power—survivor, successor and heir of the Roman Empire—second to no other. In France it was virtually a state, with a wealth far greater than the king's—entire villages and thousands of serfs, accumulated treasure and vast revenues from obligatory tithes. And a love of learning could only be satisfied by the Church.

As a lad Peter was quick and bright, soon exhausting his tutors and going on to a cathedral town, Angers, for more advanced studies. Here he acquired a bit of astronomy, geometry, and arithmetic, more Latin poetry, and a great deal of scholastic logic. He shone so brilliantly as a scholar that he foreswore knighthood and his rights as firstborn to give himself entirely to philosophy. He preferred "exercises of the intelligence and triumphs of logic to the trophies of battle." Clearly the path to fame lay through the Church.

The weapon for forcing that road, Abelard early discovered, was dialectics, "the discipline of disciplines,"[9] especially when wielded with a flashing eloquence. So he learned the skills of rhetoric in the art of argument, still the most admired faculty in France. He practiced dialectics as other youth practiced swordsmanship, and went with the blessing of his father and a retinue of servants from school to cathedral school, contending with his teachers in scholastic jousts. Finally, at the age of twenty, not entirely unknown, Peter Abelard arrived in Paris.

The spiritual center of France, Paris then was a small medieval town cupped on an island in the Seine, spilling across one bridge to the right bank, with its fields, and across the other to the left bank and the quarter where Latin was the lingua franca of some five thousand students who had swarmed there from all corners of Europe. The great cloister school on the island, just outside the early Romanesque basilica of Notre Dame, was their lodestone. At its head was Master William of Champeaux, famous at thirty. At his feet now sat—or more likely stood —the young, ambitious Abelard, restlessly.

> Though welcomed at first, I soon became a nuisance to him, because I persisted in refuting certain of his ideas, and, unafraid of engaging frequent argument against him, sometimes got the better. This boldness also aroused the wrath of leading fellow students, because I was the youngest and the latest comer. Thus began the series of my misfortunes, which still continue. As my reputation daily increased, envy was kindled against me on every side.

Briefly—scholasticism is not our first concern—William of Champeaux was a *realist;* young Abelard professed *nominalism.* The first held with Plato that ideas, or universals, had existence in the mind of God and therefore enjoyed a reality independent of their worldly manifestations. The second argued that universals were but names given to classes of similar things, a notion elaborated by Aristotle. For a long time the Church espoused realism because it implied greater faith in the omnipotence and omnipresence of God. Eventually Abelard would combine the two doctrines in *conceptualism,* which proposed that universals were *necessary* creations of the intellect, since they corresponded to realities in the mind of God.

In the heat and passion of those debates, long since dropped by the Church, lives and careers could be at stake: battles of faith versus reason were involved, and Church authorities had good grounds for fearing where reliance on reason could lead. Wherefore the watchful eye on the disputatious Abelard. In *Sic et Non,* he would write: "Through doubting we arrive at inquiry, and through inquiry we perceive the truth."

The youthful Abelard may have sought only to prove his dialectical mastery rather than "truth" in the embarrassment of his master, pressing William with relentless *reductio ad absurdum* into a logical corner and there harrying him before his students. Abelard's original sin was arrogance; he would pay for it dearly. It led, however, to the exhilarating recompense of forming a school of his own. Despite William's opposition, possibly without the Church's permission, Abelard, age twenty-two, opened a school at Melun. Did powerful friends or kinsmen at court permit the risk of affronting the local bishop? It could, in part, explain his lifelong boldness.

Though Abelard's school was twenty-eight miles southeast of Paris, hundreds of students found their way to it, gladly paid for his teaching, and numbered themselves among his followers. His was surely the most rational, stimulating, and provocative teaching of that turbulent period.

Soon Abelard moved school and students north to Corbeil, which was closer to Paris and to his target, William. Shortly, however, the nights spent in study and preparation for the day's lectures and dialectical debates so exhausted him, he left France for his parents' home in Brittany, there to rest and recuperate for several years—"grievously missed," he informs us, "by those eager for instruction in dialectics." When he returned to Paris, he discovered that William of Champeaux had taken religious vows and joined the regular clergy, giving an indispensable boost to his career in the Church. Within a few years, in fact, William was made Bishop of Châlons. In the interim he had founded the Abbey of St. Victor, slightly upstream from the Cathedral of Notre Dame—and Abelard pursued him *there:* "I went to study rhetoric under him, and among other controversial battles, I succeeded by irrefutable argument to make him change, ruining his old doctrine of universals."

Thus Peter Abelard went from triumph to triumph, discomfiting the great Anselm himself at Laon, where he had gone for the master's lectures on theology. Then, once again, he returned to Paris, this time to fill William's place at the cloister school of Notre Dame, "the chair long since destined for me." He had unhorsed all his opponents. As head of the school, he was made canon of the Cathedral. He was already a tonsured clerk, or *clericus,* and wore black clerical robes, but he was not ordained as a priest and consequently was not part of the regular clergy. This meant he could marry, but *that* certainly would mean a constraint on further advancement in Church circles. (Though many priests of the time and even a few bishops had wives or concubines, a Paulian celibacy was preached for the clergy, and marriage itself had long been disapproved, then was finally forbidden by Pope Gregory VII shortly before Abelard's arrival in Paris. The practice lingered nonetheless in France until well into the thirteenth century.)

Peter Abelard now erected his own philosophical system of conceptualism and made it theologically appealing; his school in Paris became the most popular in Europe. Three thousand students, for a fee, crowded his classes. Even Rome sent him pupils, and from his renowned school would come a pope, nineteen cardinals, and more than fifty bishops and archbishops.[10] He was brilliant, lucid, and eloquent, handsome, wealthy, noble, and more arrogant than ever, "regarding myself as the only philosopher of standing on the earth." Men admired him; women adored him, but, he says, he did not return their sidelong glances. He had enemies—his hauteur assured him that—but the patriarchs of the Church might well have considered the prodigal son as recuperated and, once ordained priest, as one of their own, an ecclesiastical prince.

Then, as he himself might have put it, Abelard met Eve.[11] For "there was in Paris at this time a young girl [*adolescentula*] named Heloise, the niece of Fulbert, one of the canons of the Cathedral."

Heloise was sixteen or seventeen; Abelard was almost forty. She lived with her uncle Fulbert in one of the numerous houses within the walled cloister of Notre Dame. We know nothing of her father, little of her mother, or why she lived with her maternal uncle (if uncle he were: in view of the violence of his later behavior, some suspect that he may have been her father[12]). We know only what Abelard tells us: she had been educated in the excellent convent school of nearby Argenteuil, receiving instruction that young women would not generally receive in France until the twentieth century—that is, a fair equivalent of a young man's (which we have described in Abelard's case). Furthermore, like young Abelard's, Heloise's education was reinforced at home, by a doting uncle: "he did everything in his power to develop it." Stories of her scholarship and intelligence were recounted on the crowded island, and echoed beyond—"throughout the kingdom," according to Abelard. We might dismiss his comment entirely as conventional Latin hyperbole if Peter the Venerable, Abbot of Cluny, were not to say the same thing of the young Heloise many years later.

Was it possibly a striking beauty that made the erudition ("so rare in a woman," Abelard said) something to be remarked? Heloise was "tall and well-proportioned," an admirer informs us, after having viewed her disinterred bones six centuries later, "with a high, rounded forehead and very white teeth."[13] "She was not," says Abelard, "the least of women in looks. As for the extent of her learning," he adds, "she stood supreme."

That Abelard had noticed Heloise we know from him; that Heloise had earlier remarked the handsome, erudite Abelard we shall hear later from her: "What king or philosopher could match your renown? . . . When you appeared in public, who did not rush to catch sight of you, or crane his neck and strain his eyes to see you as you departed? What wife, what young girl did not burn for you in your absence or become inflamed by your presence?"[14] More Latin rhetoric, further proof of Heloise's acquaintance with classical Latin expressions? Perhaps.

Was Master Abelard, then, as much seduced as seducing? The plot, the initial strategic approach, he confesses, was his:

> Having reflected on all her qualities appealing to a lover, I judged her worthy of a liaison of love, and thought I should reach my goal very easily. I had such celebrity at that time and possessed such graces of youth and body that I feared no refusal from any woman I found worthy of my love. I thought moreover that this young girl would yield all the more readily because she was cultivated and loved her studies. Even when we were separated, we could be in contact by letters, writing things too bold to be uttered, and thus our delicious relations would never be broken.

Is Abelard, in retrospect, mortifying himself for what subsequently happened? Is there a penitent irony in these cold statements? "Pride and lechery," he ruefully remarks before introducing Heloise into his autobiographical account, "will bring me toppling down from my pedestal," as they had been the cause of the downfall of "the greatest of men." Nevertheless, the younger Abelard, the preautobiographical, unwounded Abelard, "inflamed with passion for this young girl," sought out her uncle and proposed lodging with them, cunningly offering to tutor Heloise (women were not allowed to attend his classes) as well as to pay richly for his lodging. "Fulbert," he had informed himself, "was avaricious and also wanted to help his niece progress with her studies." (Was marriage to the technically eligible Abelard not too remote a possibility?) Master Abelard, as we have said, was wealthy, no one was more learned, and few were reputed to be more chaste. Gladly Fulbert accepted. He solicited Abelard to give his niece lessons at any time, day or night, his school duties permitted. He could beat her if she resisted his instructions or proved too lazy. "And so was confided"—the words are always Abelard's—"a tender lamb to a famished wolf."

In the days and weeks that followed, "the pretext of study gave way entirely to love." The books lay open, but Abelard's hands "sought her breasts more often than the pages." To allay suspicion, he beat Heloise, but the beating as disguise became a delight. "The blows were sweeter than any balm," he says with the bluntness of the age. "In our ardor we traversed all phases of love. We exhausted whatever refinement passion could imagine. Since we were inexpert, the more novel the pleasure, the more deliriously we engaged in it and the less restrained we were by fastidiousness."

Are we witnessing the birth of *l'amour-passion* in the Western world? The first version of *Tristan and Isolde* will be written eight decades later. Are we noting as well the first recorded inklings of a self-aware sadomasochism, though it would be grossly misleading to couple Abelard and Heloise with the later Marquis and Marquise de Sade? Sufficient for the moment may be Henry Adams's comment that Heloise was "a Frenchwoman to the last millimetre of her shadow . . . worth a dozen Abelards."[15]

Then Master Abelard became mortally bored . . . with classes and teaching. He who had been so vibrant and provocative now taught by rote from memory. He was dead tired from the long white nights of lovemaking, too fatigued or drained of interest to continue working on his study of the prophet Ezekiel or his awaited commentary on Aristotle. Rather, he composed lyrics and music for love songs heard throughout the land. So he tells us, though the songs have never been found. And the name of Heloise, of whom the songs sang, "was on the lips of all"—all but the willfully deaf, dumb, and blind Fulbert. "Lamenting students" were the first to suspect the cause of their master's decline, and they dared to warn him that he was dangerously subject to a woman, "the preoccupation," Abelard agreed, "nay, worse, the disturbance of my mind and spirit."

Finally even Fulbert was made to see. He discovered the lovers *in flagrante delicto,* "like Mars and Venus," together in bed. What "disillusion and pain" for the uncle! What "pain and shame" for the lovers! "What sorrows she suffered at the thought of my dishonor!" Abelard was expelled from the house, "but soon afterward Heloise sensed motherhood with transports of joy" (says Abelard). One night during Fulbert's absence, he stole her from the house, dressed her as a nun, and took her to his sister in Brittany, where she gave birth to a son who was named Astrolabe. (Hail and farewell to Astrolabe; we shall hear very little more of him.)

Before the birth, however, Abelard had hurried back to Paris and his classes, resuming his teaching of philosophy and theology. He found a half-crazed Fulbert, and feared for his life or "some foul injury." He set his servants on guard, then took compassion on the poor devil's obvious misery.

> I went to him, confessed my deceit, pleaded with him, begged his forgiveness, promised whatever reparations he might require. I affirmed that my conduct would not surprise anyone who had experienced the power of love and knew to what depths, since the beginning of the human race, women had brought down the greatest of men. And the better to appease him, I offered a satisfaction that surpassed all his hopes: I proposed marrying her whom I had seduced, on the sole condition that my marriage be kept secret, so as not to injure my reputation. He consented.

Since marriage meant a religious ceremony, the "secrecy" could not conceivably extend to the Church hierarchy: it would almost immediately be made known to Abelard's superiors, and his career would at best be held in abeyance. His concern was for his reputation with the public, commencing with his students—the ridicule invoked by the spectacle of a married philosopher, of a man devoted to study and the "higher verities" subject to the whims of a wife and the servitudes of domesticity. For the medieval scholar, matrimony summoned not only the admonition of St. Paul about women and marriage, but the vision of Socrates hectored by his wife, Xantippe.

In any event, Abelard's promise of marriage, secret or public, seemed to satisfy Fulbert's bourgeois soul.

But not Heloise's, which was neither middle class nor mediocre, but rather a soul stoically her own and therefore Abelard's—such was her selfless love—to do with as he would.

"I immediately went to Brittany," says the latter, "to fetch *mon amante* [*amicam*] and make her my wife."

The remarkable Heloise would hear naught of it. She pointed out both the peril and the scandal that their marriage would create: the peril that her uncle would not keep it secret—since marriage is principally aimed at public opinion, must it not logically be made public?—and the scandal that would as surely occur after it became public knowledge. What honor would be hers, she asked, if it brought dishonor and humiliation to him? She quoted St. Paul, St. Jerome, Cicero, and Seneca: the wise man, the philosopher, the man dedicated to God, should not be married; he must not divide his time between his studies and devotions and his wife. What should Abelard have to do "with the squawlings of infants, the lullabies of nurses . . . ?"

Heloise's arguments will resound through the ages, to be admiringly quoted by Nietzsche in his own misogynist *Human—All Too Human* and unconsciously echoed in Simone de Beauvoir's renunciation of marriage in the name of a bachelor's freedom for the young philosopher Jean-Paul Sartre.

Heloise, that scarcely believable teenager, was as great a casuist for love as Abelard for God, but she, no less than he, held to the medieval view of continence and celibacy as the ideal for philosopher and cleric. "He for God only," as Milton wrote, "she for God in him." Heloise may have been the first of the brilliant women to have accepted what they had been schooled to be, and in the process become eloquent advocates of the system denigrating them. She presents the case against herself with Portia's skill, proving a love from whose bonds she would release Abelard. Her erudition, recall, and logic as she argues against Abelard's marrying her—not once does she mention her mothering his child—still forces a reluctant admiration. Hers is a masterful exposition of the medieval attitude toward the couple, as formulated by the Church and assimilated by the women, even such women as Heloise—or were less educated women less indoctrinated, less impressed, despite the great reach of the Church? (One anonymous woman is said to have stood up during a typical Sunday sermon belittling women to protest.)

Blandly Abelard repeats Heloise as saying to him, "Nature itself had created me for the whole world. It would be a scandal if I should bind myself to a single woman and bow under such a yoke." She had cited St. Paul: "Art thou loosed from a wife? Seek not a wife. But and if thou marry, thou hast not sinned. Nevertheless such shall have trouble in the flesh: but I would spare you." And if Abelard would heed neither the apostle nor the Church fathers concerning the burden of marriage, at least he might listen to the philosophers, said Heloise. For instance St. Jerome—Abelard's own model for himself—who approvingly related the story of Cicero's example: "After he had divorced Terentia and was asked by Hirtius to wed his sister, he sternly refused, saying, he could not devote himself alike to a wife and to philosophy." Immediately Heloise followed with the famous description of the dreariness of married life—the messy, crying infants; the silly, inescapable nurses—all squalid distractions for the philosopher.

Repeatedly Heloise cites the pagan Stoics, with the consequence that she herself has been called "an enlightened pagan."[16] And she reminds Abelard that Seneca, whom she regards as greatest of the Roman philosophers, had given this advice to Lucilius: Don't neglect philosophy, do not think you can do it in your time of leisure. "Interrupt it but for an interval"—could Heloise possibly have been thinking of child care?—"and you might as well give it up, for once interrupted it will come to an end." This single-minded devotion to intellectual pursuit Heloise compared to that of a monk serving God, whose vow of chastity kept women at an undisturbing distance.

Think, too, of your dignity as a philosopher, Heloise exhorted Abelard. Recall the marriage of Socrates and Xantippe and the penalty he paid for that lapse from philosophy. Recall that day "when he had undergone an endless stream of invective from Xantippe in the window above [as he stood below in the street, and] he suddenly felt a douse of filthy water poured on his head. All he could manage to say as he wiped his head was, 'I knew rain would follow such thunder.' "

Think of your reputation, Heloise implored. How could Abelard impress the world as a teacher of theology or a devoted philosopher, if he failed to practice what he taught? Heloise went further, perhaps as far as any woman of any time. Her love for Abelard, she said, was pure love, freely given—the very essence of friendship described by Cicero—and not to be compromised by the obligations of marriage. Why should not Abelard take her as his concubine rather than be troubled by her as his wife? If that meant separations, so much the sweeter would be the occasions they came together.

None of Heloise's arguments or proposals, says Abelard, dissuaded him from his determination to marry her. For his, unlike Heloise's, was "an exclusive, jealous love which rendered insupportable the thought that she might belong to another"! This last is a persuasive observation of Étienne Gilson, and the Catholic philosopher continues:

> The only means of holding Heloise forever was to marry her. "Because [as Abelard will later reveal in a letter to Heloise] I loved you beyond measure and longed to hold you forever." Sure of the present, he was jealous of the future—scarcely a noble sentiment, and even base and mean for one who knew Heloise as Abelard must have known her, but one he experienced nevertheless, as so many other men would have done in his place, and which he never afterwards denied.[17]

Moreover, keeping the marriage secret, Abelard must have thought, made it possible for him to have his cake and eat it—that is, preserve his "reputation" and have Heloise to himself.

Whatever Abelard decided, Heloise accepted. Thus he entrusted their child to his sister in Brittany and took Heloise with him to Paris. No contemporary criticism has come down faulting Heloise or Abelard for not even mentioning infant Astrolabe in their discourse or decision. ("Maternal indifference to infants"—not to mention the father's—"characterized traditional society" until well into the nineteenth century.[18]) Leaving their child, then, with Abelard's sister—his parents were now in monasteries—the two lovers returned "secretly" to Paris and were "secretly" married at dawn several days later—which is to say, "in the presence of Heloise's uncle and a few of his friends." And "secretly" bride and groom went to their separate residences, to see each other "rarely and furtively."

For all the world they were as they were before, unmarried, which was hardly what Fulbert had hoped for; a secret wife was scarcely more than a concubine. As Heloise had foreseen, Fulbert almost immediately set friends and servants to divulging the marriage. Vigorously Heloise denied it, whereupon she was so abused by her uncle that Abelard had her stealthily removed to the convent of her childhood, at Argenteuil. "I also had her made a religious habit worn by novices, except for the veil, and obliged her to put it on"—which did not prevent his discreetly visiting Heloise at the convent and there, one holy day, making love to her in the refectory.

The fury of Fulbert, when he discovered Heloise's absence, can easily be imagined. Convinced Abelard had spirited her away to be rid of her (and who could easily gainsay that?), Fulbert conceived a most diabolical revenge with the aid of friends or relatives. The account is Abelard's:

> One night as I lay sleeping in my chamber, one of my servants, corrupted by gold, delivered me to their vengeance, which the world would learn of to its stupefaction: they cut off those parts of my body with which I had committed the offense they deplored. Then they fled.

(Two would be arrested—one of them the servant—their eyes torn out and their genital organs, fitting the punishment to the crime, removed. Sentenced, Fulbert would be let off with the confiscation of all his worldly goods—and disappear from our story.)

The morning of his castration, Abelard continues,

> the entire city assembled outside my house. The astonishment, the general stupor, the moaning, wailing, and crying with which they tortured me would be difficult, if not impossible, to describe. The clerks above all and especially the students tormented me with their lamentations and unsupportable sobs. Their pity was infinitely more cruel than my wound. I suffered more from my humiliation than from my pain.

Abelard dwells bitterly on his humiliation. "What glory I had enjoyed but a moment before, how with the stroke of an instant it was lowered and destroyed! . . . What a triumph for my enemies . . . what an affliction for my relatives and friends! . . . Where to go now? What face to show the world? I would be pointed at by everyone, torn apart by all tongues, become a monstrous spectacle." He was haunted by passages in the Old Testament, scorning the eunuch as "an abomination to the Lord, forbidden entrance to church as if a stinking, unclean monster." Castrated animals could not be offered as sacrifices, for fear of offending God.

The stricken Abelard sought refuge. It was "the feeling of shame," he confesses, "rather than that of a religious calling," that brought him to the Abbey of St. Denis and a religious life. Before he committed himself to the monastery, however, he ordered Heloise to take the veil and vows of a nun at Argenteuil. "It was your command," she would remind him, and she would reproach him for distrusting one who would willingly have followed him "to Hell itself."

Friends and family tried to dissuade Heloise from renouncing the freedom of the world at so young an age (she was not yet twenty) for the "yoke of convent rule" (the phrase is Abelard's own). But Heloise unhesitatingly obeyed, quoting the words of Cornelia, Roman heroine, as she prepared to kill herself on hearing of her husband Pompey's death: " 'My august spouse, so little made for marriage, have I brought this on your noble head? Criminal that I am for having married you and caused your misfortune! Take then in expiation this punishment I now go forth to receive.' "

Pronouncing these words, "she marched to the altar [at Argenteuil] and received the blessed veil from the hands of the bishop," inspiring Pope's lines:

> Yet then, to those dread altars as I drew,
> Not on the cross my eyes were fix'd, but you.

Then only did Abelard follow, entering the quasi-royal Abbey of St. Denis as a monk. And for ten years there was no communication, no letter, from Abelard to Heloise, nor even mention of her during this period in *Historia Calamitatum.* Is it not the story of *his* calamities? With the passage of time Abelard recovered from his wound, even to his pride, a recuperation considerably aided by the large number of students who pleaded with him and the Abbot of St. Denis that he resume his lecturing. And so he did, a year later, determining to become the "philosopher of God" as he had been the "philosopher of the world," now that God, with "divine surgery," had removed his worldly desires.

Soon the priory at nearby Maisoncelle, where he had gone to teach, overflowed with students, whom he instructed in his brand of theology —one based on "true philosophy"; that is, rational inquiry. His students "did not want mere words," says Abelard, "since one can believe only what one understands, and it would be ridiculous to preach to others what one understood no better than they." Boldly Abelard attempted to bring a similarly rational approach to the tangled theme of Unity and the Trinity, and he even risked a book on the delicate subject. Stung, the Church declared that a myth was best left as a mystery. Without hearing his defense, a council at Soissons in 1121 condemned Abelard's work, obliging him to throw it publicly into a bonfire and to shut himself up once more in a monastery.

Newly named head of the St. Denis monastery, the justly celebrated Abbot Suger—he would first employ the Gothic arch in church architecture—had Abelard released from his restriction and permitted to resume his teaching, but at a greater remove from Paris. Near Nogent-sur-Seine, "upon a desert spot which I knew," a piece of ground given him by certain persons, "I built a sort of oratory of reeds and thatch," says Abelard. And once again students flocked to him despite the distance from Paris, erecting huts for themselves and rebuilding the oratory in stone. Daringly identifying it with the Holy Ghost, Abelard named the oratory the Paraclete (the Comforter).

Churchmen attacked his choice, accusing him, not without reason, of defying the Council of Soissons by stubbornly continuing to separate the Persons of the Trinity. Abelard's success at the Paraclete—"I was hidden, in body, in this spot, but my renown overran the whole world and filled it with my word"—increased their discontent as well as Abelard's danger—"I never heard of the convocation of ecclesiastics without thinking it had my condemnation as its object."

Such was his despair that Abelard desultorily "thought of abandoning the realm of Christendom and going over to the heathen"—to the Saracens—who would readily believe he "could be won to their pagan beliefs," because of the accusations of the Church. Several years later, in fact, he was "offered" the Abbey of St. Gildas de Ruis, which meant effective banishment to the ocean's edge in Brittany—"the very end of the earth."

It was indeed, for him, a wretched change from the Paraclete. "I found a barbarous land, a brutal and savage people, shameless, rebellious monks" with concubines and offspring. As abbot, however, Abelard was now in the fortunate position of being able to come to the aid of Heloise, suddenly in need of it. For in 1129 her convent at Argenteuil, of which she was prioress, was closed to nuns and she and her sisters had to find a new home. Hearing of it, Abelard turned his own deserted Paraclete over to them and went himself to assist Heloise to settle in with her charges. It was the first meeting of the lovers in a decade, and a tender pride informs Abelard's lines, which describe Heloise's first years as abbess at the Paraclete: "The bishops loved her like a daughter, the abbots like a sister, the laymen like a mother, and all were astonished equally by her religion, prudence, and the incomparable gentleness of her patience."

Abelard's visits during those years, however, were looked upon with suspicion; indeed, viewed as evidence that carnal desire for his wife had never abandoned him—he who, of all men, should have been thought "beyond such suspicions." Bitterly Abelard remarks that "Christ Himself would not have been spared the malice of my enemies!"

Among his enemies was now the powerful Bernard of Clairvaux, guardian of Church orthodoxy and the faith. Pressure increased upon Abelard, and he yielded. He ceased his visits to the Paraclete and resigned himself to the horrors of Brittany and St. Gildas. He had expelled or had had excommunicated the most rebellious of his monks, but those who had remained "were even worse than the others." Ambushes awaited him inside and outside the cloister—"how many times have they not tried to poison me!" One day at Nantes, a poisoned dish had been set for him, but it was a monk who had accompanied him "who partook of it in ignorance, succumbing on the spot." Finally,

> it was no longer a question of poison; it was the dagger they were sharpening against my breast, which I barely escaped, thanks to a powerful, neighboring lord. The same perils menace me still and every day I see the sword raised above my head. Even at table I can scarcely breathe. . . . This is the torture I undergo at every moment; I, a poor monk, raised to the prelacy, become more miserable in becoming more rich, so that by my example the ambitious may learn to curb their greed.

A new Abelard now speaks, a man whose conversion began after the Council of Soissons with the experience at the Paraclete. He no longer seeks worldly fame, but rather salvation for himself and Heloise—"now my sister in Christ rather than my wife." The glory he now seeks is God's, and with the same passionate energy as he had sought his own. He has gone through his purgatory on earth and has emerged, it suddenly seems to the reader, a profoundly religious man. *Historia Calamitatum,* one feels, written entirely at this time at St. Gildas, must be entirely reread in the light of this repentance; then the references to "fame" and "wordly reputation," seemingly so boastful, acquire a restored irony: he has deliberately provoked our scorn for what he has since learned himself to depreciate, a *tour de force* so subtle, with a *dénouement* so sudden, it almost escapes us. Abelard has given himself completely to God. With the words "Thy will be done" he closes the account of his life.

Historia Calamitatum is, in the convention of the time, in the form of a "letter to a friend," whom Abelard is attempting to console with the story of his own more sorrowful lot. It was read, as intended for medieval manuscripts many times copied, by others. One copy "fell" into the hands of Heloise at the Paraclete. It moved her to the first of the love letters, the first authentic sound of the voice, the cry, that has stirred eight centuries of poets, among them Villon, Petrarch, and Pope.

"Domino suo, imo patri," Heloise begins, *"conjugi suo, imo fratri; ancilla sua, imo filia; ipsius uxor, imo soror; Abelardo Heloissa.* To her master, no, her father; to her husband, no, her brother; from his servant, no, his daughter; from his wife, no, his sister; to Abelard, from Heloise." There is the opening cry of anger, touched by fear, for the dangers Abelard faces from the very monks he calls his children. She and her sisters would gladly share the risks with him, would he but write to them. Alas, he does not even write to her—she who has been linked to him by destiny and marriage, she who is above all his dearest *friend,* that tender, holy word. Does he not also have a special duty to the Paraclete, which he alone created, and to an entire community of women he helped dedicate to God?

The tone of Heloise's letter sharpens, pain and anger rise:

> You know, my beloved, the whole world knows, how in losing you I lost all. . . . You alone can cause me sadness or bring happiness and comfort. You alone have a great debt to repay me: I have obediently carried out all your commands. Powerless to oppose you in anything, I had the courage, on a single word from

> you, to destroy myself. Even more, strange to say: my love was transformed into such madness that it sacrificed beyond hope of recovery that which it most ardently desired. When you commanded it, I changed myself, not only my dress, but my mind, to prove you were master of my soul, as of my body. God knows, I sought nothing of you save yourself; I wanted nothing of yours, simply you. The name of *wife* may seem more holy, more valuable, but sweeter to me is the word *friend,* or even—if it does not offend you—the word *concubine* or *whore.* I believed that the more I humbled myself on your account, the more grace you would acquire in the eyes of God and the less damage I should do to the splendor of your reputation.

In the "letter to a friend," adds Heloise, Abelard had recounted some of her reasons for opposing their marriage, but he had kept silent concerning most of her arguments for "preferring love to matrimony, freedom to chains." As he knew, she would rather be his whore than the empress of Augustus, for she would be choosing him for himself, not for his wealth or power: a woman who marries a man for his money "is offering herself for sale." Marriage as prostitution—this may be the first time the feminist theme sounded in the mouth of a woman, one pledged paradoxically to self-sacrifice.

The very thought of their first meetings, however, their first clandestine discoveries of the ways of love, warms Heloise's mood. "What queen, what great lady, did not envy me my joys and my bed!" she exclaims. *She* is the Abbess of the Paraclete, we have difficulty in recalling. A cry for companionship, even if only epistolary, now springs to her lips. "Tell me, if you can, why after our entry into religion, which you alone decided, you have so neglected and forgotten me that neither by word nor by letter, when you were present or absent, you offered me the slightest consolation?" Was it because, as the world suspects and she herself believes, desire having been removed, Abelard no longer experienced love? Now, at least, could he not give some semblance of himself through *words*—"of which you have more than enough to spare"?

To the contrary, Heloise repeats, she has loved Abelard for himself: carnal pleasure had not joined her to him (so much for the Church's admonition about the "carnality" of women), but rather a love so pure that on a word from him, and for *his* sake, she had removed herself from "all pleasure." She had not entered a convent for love of God, but from love of Abelard: she knew "there would be no reward from God for this." Abelard, on the other hand, had had so little faith in her that he had obliged her to take the veil before he himself entered a monastery, "though, God knows, I would have unhesitatingly followed you, at your bidding, into the flames of Hell."

The flames are not literary metaphor; they are literal belief. The blasphemous choice of human over divine love at the risk of damnation is the essence of Heloise's dilemma, though she does not speak of any doubt. How beyond the philter-induced love of Iseult for Tristan is the love of Heloise for Abelard, how beyond simple adultery her self-immolation. And how ideal a middle-class drama is Wagner's *Tristan and Isolde,* with its satisfying story of adultery enjoyed, adultery punished, though it has been elevated to the very symbol of "Western preoccupation with love and death."[19] If we must reach for a modern comparison with Heloise, we might find it in a fictional heroine of a Graham Greene or a François Mauriac, who knowingly risks her soul for love of another, unworthy of her sacrifice; at the same time, as we read, we are persuaded to believe, thanks to the believing author, that God in His divine grace will understand the depth of her love and raise the fallen woman up to heaven, where she may rejoin her redeemed lover.

"Remember what I have done," Heloise implores with a dignity she never loses; "think how unjust you would be, if now that I merit more you give me less—or even nothing—when I ask so little"—no more than a letter—"so that I might devote myself to the service of God with more joy. . . . Adieu, my only love."

Abelard replied—one is tempted to write as Mark Twain—"from the North Pole of his frozen heart."[20] We would be as unfair to Heloise, however, as to Abelard, were we to belittle her beloved in this cold fashion. He has his own *angoisse* and fiery dilemmas and, in his profound faith, a higher, if more remote, aspiration for Heloise, as selfless now as hers for him—nothing less than the salvation of her soul for eternity. "To Heloise, his very dear sister in Christ, from Abelard, her brother in Christ," he begins his reply. "If I have not addressed you a letter of consolation or exhortation since we left the world for God, you must not attribute it to my negligence, but to the absolute confidence I have in your wisdom. I did not think it necessary for one to whom God has given all the gifts of his grace," to one who herself is now an abbess, watching carefully over the strayed and consoling the weak with wisdom. Abelard thanks Heloise and her daughters for their concern. He asks that they pray for him, encloses a prayer he would like them to recite, and entreats Heloise, "my sister once dear in the world, now dearest in Christ," should his enemies triumph or an "accident" occur, to bury his body at the Paraclete. "But your main concern," he ends his letter, "must be for the salvation of my soul. You will thus prove to the dead man the love you bore the living. . . . Live in peace and health, live and remember me in Christ, I pray you."

Heloise replies: Do not, if you love us, speak of your death. She can only pray that she die before him (and we shall hear Beauvoir say of Sartre that the only harm he could do her would be to die first). Has she not already suffered enough? Heloise asks. "O God," she cries, "if I dare say it, Thou art cruel to me in everything!" He had lifted her above all women only to cast her down. The indignation at the injustice of their fate becomes Promethean in its defiance: "When we delivered ourselves to fornication, divine punishment was spared us; but when we legitimatized our illicit love and covered the shame of our fornication with the veil of marriage, only then did the Lord's anger fall upon us!"

Is it the fate of women, asks Heloise, to be the cause of the fall of men, as was the case at the very beginning with the first woman—Eve? To Adam she adds the litany of fallen men: Samson, Solomon, David, Job—and Abelard. Then, as diabolically as Dostoievsky's Inquisitor, Heloise argues the possibility of the devil's having struck Abelard through marriage since he failed through fornication. "Denied the power to do evil through evil, he did evil through good." Thus Heloise poses the problem of evil in a world created entire by God. And if it was through her—innocent and unconsenting—that the Lord had struck Abelard, then Heloise "can never cease accusing Him of the greatest cruelty"; and she will forever further offend Him with indignation rather than appease Him with a gesture of penitence.

For how can she be called truly repentant, however great her mortification of the flesh, "if the mind holds tight to the will to sin and is aflame with its old desires"? She is the innocent sinner, Heloise insists: she speaks with love of that which she is supposed to lament—the sweet pleasures they had tasted together as lovers. They still haunt her, tantalizing her thoughts, tormenting her sleep—if torment it can be called! "Even during celebration of Mass, when prayer should be its purest, lewd visions of those pleasures take possession of my poor soul so completely that I yield to their voluptuousness rather than to the piety of prayer. I who should tremble for the sins I have committed, can only sigh for what I have lost." Even in sleep Heloise knew no respite, her plaint inspiring Pope's fine lines:

> When at the close of each sad, sorrowing day,
> Fancy restores what vengeance snatch'd away,
> Then conscience sleeps, and leaving Nature free,
> All my loose soul unbounded springs to thee!

Oh curst, dear horrors of all-conscious night!
How glowing guilt exalts the keen delight!
Provoking demons all restraint remove,
And stir within me every source of love.
I hear thee, view thee, gaze o'er all thy charms,
And round thy phantom glue my clasping arms.
I wake:—no more I hear, no more I view,
The phantom flies me, as unkind as you.
I call aloud; it hears not what I say:
I stretch my empty arms; it glides away.
To dream once more I close my willing eyes;
Ye soft illusions, dear deceits, arise!

Heloise closes her letter with despair: "Men say I am chaste, because they do not perceive the hypocrite!" God, who searches hearts and loins and sees in the darkness, sees better.

Abelard was appalled. This was the passionate *adolescentula,* the nineteen-year-old Heloise, he had known, not the widely respected Abbess of the Paraclete, the converted bride of Christ. "The entirety of your last letter," he replied with rebuke, "is given over to a listing of the wrongs you have suffered!" Point by point he considers and refutes them, bearing down with the full force of his dialectical powers as if wrestling with the devil for Heloise's soul. Do not praise me for a wisdom I do not possess, she had written. Her refusal to accept his praise, he counters, merely proves its truth. Similarly he disposes, or attempts to dispose, with the points she has raised, until finally he comes to the heart, the crux, of Heloise's plaint, "[her] old, eternal complaint against God for the manner of [their] conversion."

The pursuit of Abelard's argument becomes an adventure into the medieval mind. His very castration, he says, was "an act of divine mercy." The argument quickly becomes personal. You claim you will do anything for my sake, he continues, yet you know how tormented I am by your "eternal complaint" against God's justice. You say you would follow me into the very fires of Hell, yet you seem willing to risk cutting yourself off from me, I who you yourself believe am hastening toward God. So cease your plaint, lest "the goal we must come to" —death—will find us separated or unblessed and miserable. Would it have been easier to endure, if what had happened to me had been unjust? Think how my enemies would have rejoiced at my greater disgrace! Who could possibly be stirred to pity for one rightly punished? "However"—the dialectical twist is delicious—"it might ease your bitterness if I do prove that what befell us both was just, as well as for both our benefits, and that God had more cause to punish us when we were married than when we were in a state of fornication." You will recall that after our marriage I had visited you in the convent at Argenteuil and such was my uncontrollable lust, we had taken our pleasure "in a corner of the refectory in the very place dedicated to the most holy Virgin, the Mother of God." Then God, in His wisdom and mercy, had made use of evil itself by striking through Fulbert "that organ which alone was guilty," thus purging the body and purifying the spirit and "healing two souls at the same stroke," preparing us for a greater mission. Think of the depths in which we had wallowed, of the times I had forced you "with threats and blows" to consent to my lovemaking, and of the pleasures we had placed above God Himself, now that the "contagion of carnal impurity," the "heavy yoke of carnal desire," have been graciously and pityingly removed.

Join me, *my inseparable companion,* Abelard pleads, join me in thanksgiving to God, who wisely joined us in indissoluble marriage when I wanted jealously to keep you to myself. Had we not been united in wedlock, you might have clung to the world even as I withdrew from it, "either from the influence of your relatives or the enjoyment of carnal pleasures." But the Lord had already planned to use our wedlock for our joint conversion to Him.

> What a terrible loss and grievous misfortune if you had given yourself to the degradation of carnal pleasure only to give birth in pain to a few children for the world when now you foster so many offspring in exultation for heaven! Nor would you have been anything more than a woman, you who now rise even above men and have transformed the curse of Eve into the blessing of Mary.

How unseemly and unfitting it would have been to devote those now-holy hands to the degrading concerns of a woman's usual drudgery! (How modern feminist our medieval Abelard.)

"Do not, my sister, be unjust to a Father who paternally sets us on the right path," he adjures Heloise. Weep for the cruelty done to Christ, your spiritual bridegroom, not for that done to your husband on earth, for His was the supreme grace for us both. He wounded the body to heal the soul, He punished once so that there would not be eternal punishment—"two were guilty, one paid the penalty." Abelard closes with a truly moving prayer that he asked Heloise to offer God in both their behalf. It ends thus:

> Thou hast joined us, O Lord, and Thou hast parted us when and as it pleased Thee. Now, Lord, what Thou hast mercifully begun, mercifully end, and those whom Thou hast parted for a time in this world, unite forever in heaven.

Was Heloise convinced by Abelard's arguments, however moved she was by his prayer? It seems not. She did not in her next letter give in; she made a series of statements, then grew silent. She did not record submission, but rather withdrawal of her eternal—and perhaps unassuaged—plaint. She would not, she replied to Abelard, give him any cause for finding her disobedient: she will henceforth bridle her words as he would have her do. Fortunately she can moderate her writing as she could never moderate her speech, so overflowing and compulsive is her heart. However—the Stoic reappears—"as one nail drives out another, a new thought an old," she will no longer give expression to her old complaint, but rather turn her mind as wholly as humanly possible to the Paraclete and its direction.

With this Heloise poses a series of questions that are impersonal, practical, and often revealing. How did the order of nuns commence and what authority is there for it? Would Abelard prescribe a Rule for her charges, "suitable for women"? How should they dress, taking into account the "menstrual purging of their superfluous humours *(humoris superflui menstruae purgationes)*"? What should be the regulation for meat or wine "which leads to lechery" (meat was thought to kindle fleshly desires)? Should she entertain male visitors at her table, as does an abbot regularly, for does not Ovid in his *Art of Love* describe "the occasion for fornication provided especially by banquets"? What about the gathering of the harvest? Are nuns to work as monks do? What Rule applies equally to them? Surely it is not "reason or good sense for both women and men to be bound by a common Rule—that is, to have the same burden laid on the weak as on the strong." Though sometimes women's weakness can match men's virtue, and when it comes to meat and wine, "our sex is protected by greater soberness," since, as Aristotle has said, "a woman's body is pierced with holes for purgings," thus "the fumes of wine are speedily released."

In like manner Heloise, fully the abbess, learnedly and extensively quotes from the Evangelists, St. Jerome, St. Augustine, St. Gregory, Chrysostom, Macrobius Theodosius, St. Benedict, Cicero, St. Peter, the Proverbs, *The Lives of the Fathers,* and, of course, *The Art of Love.* She contributes eruditely to answers for her own questions; if a tendency is to be noted, it might be called rationalist-humanist or simply "Abelardian" (unsurprisingly). Thus excessive fasting and abstinence are dismissed with an effective quotation from St. Paul: " 'Everything that God created is good and nothing is to be rejected, if taken with thanksgiving.' " And from St. Augustine: " 'So that it may truly be better understood how virtue may be in natural habit though not in works, I will quote an example of which no Catholic is in doubt. That the Lord Jesus, in the truth of the flesh, was hungry and thirsty and ate and drank, no one can fail to know who is faithful to his Gospel. Yet surely the virtue of continence was as great in him as in John the Baptist? "For John came neither eating nor drinking and men said he was possessed. The Son of Man came eating and drinking and they said, 'Look at him, a glutton and a drinker, a friend of taxgatherers and sinners!' " ' " (The final quotation is from Matthew 11: 18–19.)

In closing, Heloise writes that it is for Abelard, their master and creator of their community, "to lay down the Rule for us to follow." After him, there might be another to direct them, "and so, we are afraid, less likely to feel concern for us, or less likely to be listened to; or if he is no less willing, less able. Speak to us, then, and we shall listen. Farewell."

Farewell, my lover, my husband, Heloise is in effect saying, *hail, my spiritual adviser.* There will be no more letters from Heloise to Abelard: the series has come to at least an *aesthetic* end. Heloise has put the questions whose answers will thereafter regulate her life. The rest is silence—on her part.

There are two more letters from Abelard, longer than all the others together, lending substance to the theory that *Historia Calamitatum* and the correspondence, when issued along with the *Rule for the Paraclete* in the thirteenth century, were intended for the guidance of its later abbess and nuns. As for the authenticity of the letters (that of *Historia* has been unchallenged) in view of their posthumous appearance as copies of the original manuscripts (which have never been found), we might say that no demonstration to date of forgery has been quite convincing.[21] One version, for example, has Abelard composing all the letters; a second, Heloise; and a third, a third person—of the thirteenth century. Even were the third version accurate, the letters would still serve our purpose: to explore the beliefs, attitudes, and behavior of the most famous couple of the Middle Ages on the basis of an *authenticated manuscript of almost the same period.* Whether it was Shakespeare, Bacon, or Sir X who wrote *Hamlet,* we should still be reading, reacting to, and interpreting the same Renaissance play. And finally, if indeed there had been a thirteenth-century forger of the Abelard-Heloise correspondence, he or she would doubtless have been "one of the most powerful creative writers known to any literature," as Étienne Gilson wisely concluded. "We could no more find his (or her) like than we could find another Heloise and Abelard."[22]

Returning, then, from this discursion to consideration of Abelard's response to Heloise's questions, one is struck in the first of his two letters by the repeated reference to the "dignity of women" as a basis for the "authority and dignity of the order of nuns." Since his contemporaries lingered singularly over the "dignity of man," who was created "in the image of God," and engaged, as if in an obligatory seesaw, in an accompanying lowering of woman, Abelard's view has such a novel ring that a woman Latinist of our time has called it "evangelical feminism" and Abelard himself "a feminist of a rather special kind."[23] (One might better term it "of a *theoretical* kind.")

For his authority on the dignity of women, Abelard characteristically went back to the very origin of Christianity; his clearest statement is in one of the sermons he wrote for the Paraclete (Sermon XIII):

> Who is so unique and singular in dignity as Christ, in whom, the Apostle says, there is "neither male nor female" [Gal. 3:28]? In the body of Christ, which is the Church, difference of sex, therefore, confers no dignity. For Christ looks not to the condition of sex, but to the quality of merits.

In perfect harmony with his opinion, Abelard had, as his personal seal, the androgynous insignia of two heads, one of a man, the other of a woman.

Continuing his letter to Heloise, Abelard writes: as Christ had declared both sexes equal in dignity, so He gave them both authority for a monastic calling. Moreover, He granted women, who had been among the favored of His first followers, a parity with men in the religious life and in the grace of God.

Despite this egalitarian point of view, this "evangelical feminism," traced to the most impeccable of sources, Abelard did *not* escape the enduring ambivalence of Christian practice (any more than Heloise)—that is, the inconsistency verging on contradiction between the teachings and behavior of Christ regarding women and the denigrating antifeminism of the Church fathers. St. Paul, in fact, made doctrine out of the contradiction by declaring women equal to men in the order of God's grace, "where there is no sex," but subordinate to them in the order of nature, which included the visible Church and society. (Equality in heaven but not on earth.) Though Abelard went somewhat further in asserting women's equal *dignity* in the Church, he did not proclaim their *equality*—a woman could be an abbess but never a bishop, which meant first being ordained as a priest. As for equality (or dignity) in society, Abelard was as categorical as any ecclesiastic: women were to be subservient to their husbands, as decreed in the very order of creation—"man in the image of God, woman only in His likeness," he directly, she from his rib. Moreover, as Eve, woman first tasted the forbidden fruit and seduced man into the same sin. Abelard adds, with his "special kind of feminism," that Adam partook out of love for Eve and his desire not to cause her sorrow.

In conformity with his view, Abelard proposed a not-uncommon solution to the problems raised by Heloise—a double, or twinned, monastery, one for monks, the other for nuns (the Paraclete). The outside labor of the convent—field work and the like—would be performed by the monks; the inside labor—baking bread and similar "feminine" activities—by the nuns, who, furthermore, were never to leave the precincts. Final authority over both communities would be exercised by the monks' abbot, but Abelard follows immediately with a few caveats. The abbot was not to dominate, but rather serve the abbess (Heloise): "He should be like a steward in a king's palace, who does not bear down on the queen with his powers but treats her sagaciously, obeying her at once in necessary matters but paying no heed when it might be harmful, and performing all his services outside the bedchamber without ever entering its privacy unbidden [!]" He was to make no decision about the nuns of the Paraclete without consulting its abbess, or give them instructions, or even speak to them, except through her. The monks, too, were never to impose anything against the abbess's will, but rather comply with her wishes, professing their vows to her like the nuns and promising obedience.

For discipline within the Paraclete, Abelard resorted to a military simile. As a lord over his army, Heloise should rule over her nuns, appointing several to serve under her "like dukes or counts, while the rest act as soldiers or infantry under the direction of others, and fight willingly against the Devil and his hordes." The feudal order is not merely evoked; it is assumed to be the divine order. A later churchman put it this way in a sermon: "Who would cultivate our fields, if you were all lords?" God the All Powerful, he continued, had accordingly divided humanity into ten groups: "The first three were *les grands* of the earth whom God Himself had chosen and established, with the seven others to serve and be subject to them."[24] (A contemporary historian states it succinctly: "The nobles fought, the clergy prayed and the rest of the population provided them with the means of doing so."[25]) Abelard cites the Scriptures to the same purpose, with approval. One could hardly expect otherwise.

For the lesser, practical details of convent life, Abelard referred more often to reasonableness than to custom. The nuns were to be permitted meat—three times a week. Little was forbidden except excess, whether in drinking wine or in fasting. No mortification of the flesh. Abelard showed more concern for moral intention and inward piety than outward display. Clothing was to be sensible and sanitary ("a full change"), bedding adequate ("pillows and mattresses"). The nuns were to be educated according to their ability to learn: God was to be worshiped with understanding.

Was Abelard's a "compassionate sensitivity" not only for women,[26] but for other underprivileged (a sensitivity to be measured, as always, against his time)? His concern for the poor was unshared by a Church still consolidating its power vis-à-vis the crown, the nobles, and a residual paganism among the people. In his last "Letter of Direction," Abelard laid down that the wretched custom of wiping dirty hands and knives on the bread for the poor (rather than on their garments) was to be forbidden nuns at the Paraclete. He struck even more strongly, in a sermon written for Heloise's convent, at those who engaged in the "plunder of the poor," whether Churchmen, noblemen, or middlemen. Furthermore, he declared, giving to the poor was not to be regarded as charity, but simply as restoration of what had been stolen from them.

Does this explain in part the Abelard an Heloise could love?

PETER Abelard returned to teaching—on the heights of Sainte Genevieve in Paris's Latin Quarter—with a dogged, persistent pursuit of a rational road to understanding God. "All that God does," he continued to assert, "He wills necessarily and does necessarily. Therefore it is of necessity that God willed and created the world." Within inescapable medieval limits, it was as close to the modern, rational doctrine best expressed by Einstein—"God does not play dice with humanity"—as any man of the time came. It was, in any event, centuries too soon for Abelard's time.

Two men of the Church followed his writings with sniffing attention —Bernard of Clairvaux, who had reaffirmed his role as the watchdog of Christian orthodoxy and was eventually canonized, and his disciple William, recently Abbot of St. Thierry. The works of Abelard, William wrote to Bernard, with a copy to the Bishop of Chartres, had spread dangerously beyond the Alps, affecting Rome herself: "I tell you, I address the entire Church, your silence is perilous . . . A solemn, public condemnation is called for."[27]

William settled down to a minute study of Abelard's "heresies," linking them with those of Arnold of Brescia, a militant, reformationist critic of Church abuses who anticipated Wycliffe and Martin Luther. The Church, he proclaimed, should emulate Christ and give up its great properties. William's coupling the names of Abelard and Abelard's former pupil Arnold may have been decisive in the calling of the Synod of Sens.

Together, Bernard of Clairvaux and William of St. Thierry drew up a list of damning particulars, Bernard contributing his "Treatise Concerning the Errors of Peter Abelard." The Sens council promised to be one of the century's most prestigious: young King Louis VII let it be known that he himself would preside. Bishops, abbots, and an archbishop of France would sit in judgment. Abelard indicated he welcomed a debate with Bernard before such a distinguished panel. Bernard, however, met with its Church members beforehand. They agreed upon nineteen articles specifying the heresies Abelard was invited publicly to refute. Instead of the debate he had solicited with Bernard, he was to be put on trial. Bernard had refused the confrontation, he would explain, because Abelard was a "Goliath of the dialectic,"[28] whereas he was a simple man armed only with faith (a sling, it would seem, in which he showed insufficient faith).

Whether from illness or failure of heart for such a trial, Abelard chose silence. The assembled prelates reached their judgment, sending a letter to Pope Innocent II in Rome that advised the condemnation and excommunication of Abelard for heresy. (Arnold of Brescia was similarly condemned, ultimately to be hanged in Rome for revolutionary activities.) Only to Heloise would Abelard profess the faith and beliefs sustaining him, which neither Bernard nor the Council of Sens could wring from him.

"Heloise, my sister," he wrote,

> once dear to me in the world, now still more dear in Jesus Christ, logic has made me hated by men. The perverted—whose aim is to pervert and for whom wisdom is perdition—say I am a supreme logician but lacking in understanding of St. Paul. They proclaim the brilliance of my mind but doubt the purity of my Christian faith; and here, it seems to me, they are more influenced by public opinion than by the evidence.
>
> I do not wish to be a philosopher, if it means rebelling against St. Paul. I do not wish to be an Aristotle, if it means separating myself from Christ, for there is no other name under heaven whereby I can be saved. I adore Christ, Who reigns at the right hand of the Father. I embrace Him with the arms of faith whose

> divine power performed glorious works in the virginal flesh born from the Paraclete. And so, to banish all anxiety and uncertainties from the heart that beats in your breast, I want you to have this reassurance from me: I have founded my conscience on that rock upon which Christ built His Church. Here, briefly, is what is written upon it: I believe in the Father, the Son, and the Holy Ghost, the true God in one nature, in whom the Trinity of Persons is so comprised as to preserve the Unity in substance.

This was the faith by which he lived, the faith from which he derived his strength. He confessed no wrong, for he recognized no error. So Abelard closed his profession of faith to Heloise.

Ailing, broken, old at sixty, Abelard set off for Rome to contest the council's judgment with Pope Innocent II himself. The route was long; he stopped at monasteries along the way; his reception remains uncertain, save for the last stop—at Cluny, where he was warmly welcomed by Peter the Venerable: Cluny's abbot had had his own doctrinal conflict with Bernard of Clairvaux. Perhaps the period's most benevolent figure, Peter the Venerable ruled over a vast community and more than 1,600 subordinate Cluniac monasteries. Wisely he advised Abelard to tarry and rest; prudently Peter counseled his making peace, as had he, with Bernard, and so Abelard did. The reconciliation now strikes one as a kind of death of the Abelard we have hitherto known, for it meant renunciation. At the same time he heard of his formal condemnation by the pope to "perpetual silence" and the burning of his books on the piazza of St. Peter's Cathedral. His health further declined; Cluny's abbot sent him to St. Marcel for its milder climate. There, in April 1142, the second, final death of Abelard soon followed.

Peter the Venerable's long letter to "the abbess Heloise" is touching, delicate, and revealing. Peter knew their story well. Indeed he had known of Heloise, he wrote, "by name and reputation" when he himself was a youth, "not yet for your religious life, but for your noble and praiseworthy studies. Men spoke of this wonder, a woman, still belonging to the world, who gave herself entirely to the study of literature and philosophy, permitting nothing, neither the pleasures of the world, nor its vanities and delights, to distract her from the worthy ambition to study the liberal arts." She had surpassed "all women . . . and almost all men." Then, as did Abelard, she "left logic for the Gospel, Plato for Christ, the academy for the cloister."

He did not write this in the way of flattery, Peter quickly adds. Heloise was not only a "burning coal" (witness her ardent story) but also a "glowing lamp" (of intelligence) illuminating the path for others to follow, comparable to Penthesilea, queen of the Amazons, and Deborah the prophetess. He would dearly love to speak to her at length about all this in person, "because your renowned erudition and even more your piety, which many have praised, attracts me greatly to you. If only our Cluny possessed you"—it would have riches beyond the treasures of kings.

But if not Heloise, Cluny has at least possessed Abelard, "your man, the servant and true philosopher of Christ, whose name will ever be honored, Master Peter, whom Divine Providence had sent to Cluny in his closing years, enriching it with a gift more precious than gold or topaz." The saintliness, humility, and devoted piety of his life among them "cannot be briefly told." He had dressed poorly, lived frugally, and walked humbly. "His reading was perpetual, his prayer devoted, his silence unceasing."

The delicacy of Cluny's venerable abbot remains intact and impeccable: "Thus Master Peter brought his days to an end." He who had been the great worldly teacher had become the disciple of the gentle, humble Son of Man.

> Venerable Sister, he to whom you were first joined in the flesh, then by the better and therefore stronger bond of Divine love, with whom and under whom you have served God, is now sheltered in the bosom of Christ. In your stead, indeed, as a second you, Christ now protects him and will restore him to you on the day of the Lord's coming, to the sound of the Archangel's voice and the Divine trumpet.

In the first days of her widowhood Heloise's concern was for the body of Abelard. He had requested that it be buried at the Paraclete. Secretly Peter the Venerable had the body removed from the cemetery of St. Marcel and brought it himself for interment in the chapel of the Paraclete. He celebrated Mass with Heloise and her sisters, and talked with her for the first time (as impressed by her as had been Bernard of Clairvaux shortly before).

Heloise had not yet finished: she asked Peter the Venerable for a trental of Masses to be said for her soul's repose after her own death; she requested—and received—a sealed letter of absolution for all Abelard's sins (which she would suspend above his tomb) and another confirming the gift of his body (so there would be no taint on that score); lastly she asked Cluny's abbot for some prebend for her son Astrolabe (he would do his best, Peter promised, though bishops were being difficult).

Now presumably Heloise could rest, and ordinarily *her* story is brought to an end at this point, as if her death followed with inevitable swiftness upon his, her life having been defined by his. However, it would hardly be doing justice to one whose death came twenty or twenty-one years later and whose direction of the Paraclete has caused her to be called "one of the Church's great abbesses."[29] During those years the Paraclete expanded its influence and grandeur to become one of the most distinguished religious establishments of France. Half a dozen daughter houses were required for the growing number of applicants; twenty-nine documents record the special privileges and generous donations received, many of them from the popes, the latter including farms, mills, woods, tithes, and wealth.[30]

Legend does not dwell on this. Rather, it has Heloise watching over Abelard's tomb until she joined him there in 1163 or 1164, dying, as he, at the age of sixty-three. Their bones were several times removed, until finally, perhaps permanently, they have come to rest in Paris's Père Lachaise cemetery, where other lovers also lie.

According to a thirteenth-century account, when the legend of Heloise had its beginning, at the moment when Heloise's body was borne, as she had willed, into Abelard's tomb, his arms were seen to open—"to embrace her." More likely, as has also been said, it was Heloise's arms that opened to embrace Abelard.

2

THE LADY AND THE KNIGHT: COURTLY LOVE

> By nothing is man made so worthy as by love and the courting of women.
> —Bernard of Ventadour (twelfth century)

NOW, Lancelot du Lac is undoubtedly the most alluring and splendid of the knights of King Arthur's Round Table. Yet he fell in love with King Arthur's wife, and Queen Guinevere with him. Nor did it require a magical philter to bring them, unlike Tristan and Iseult, to an adulterous bed. Love unaided led them to it. And so, in about 1177, when Marie, Countess of Champagne—daughter of Eleanor, herself queen of two kings, whose traits may be found in Queen Guinevere—commissioned a poet of her court, Chrétien de Troyes, to write the love story of Lancelot and the queen, one can understand his quandary. His epics had celebrated a purer courtly love. Yet, in obedience to *his* sovereign's lady—who gave him "the material and the treatment of it," he says in his opening verses[1]—Chrétien wrote down the initiatory adventures of Lancelot, *The Knight of the Cart,* which others have since followed. And although he seems not to have had the heart to bring it to its close (he dictated the ending to a colleague), Sir Lancelot remains "an incarnation of the ideal for manhood that exists . . . in the hopes and fancies of the feminine imagination."[2]

As an infant, one recalls, Lancelot had been carried away and reared by the Lady of the Lake, who had given King Arthur his magical sword, Excalibur, and Lancelot his name. Lancelot's own invincible sword, which he alone had been able to draw from its sheath, had been won at the Round Table, where he had speedily become supreme among the knights. Chrétien assumes all this to be common knowledge, as was Lancelot's devotion to King Arthur's queen, when his eloquent, rhymed chronicle—the earliest written record of their love story—begins.

To Arthur's court at Camelot—when France was half British and Britain could have become French—came riding an unknown knight in full armor, who declared that he held many of the king's subjects captive. However, he would surrender the captives, he said, were there a single champion to whom the king would entrust the queen, that he might escort her to a rendezvous in the nearby woods and successfully bring down the challenger and so bring her back again. It was agreed. Unfortunately, first to ask for and to receive permission to be the court's champion was the conceited seneschal Sir Kay, who was quickly unhorsed by the unknown challenger, who then swiftly rode off with the queen. Fortunately Sir Gawain, the king's nephew and second only to Lancelot among the knights, had followed Sir Kay at a distance, but unfortunately at too great a distance, for he arrived too late. The queen and the stranger had already disappeared. However, as Sir Gawain pursued them, leading two horses he had brought for the queen and Sir Kay, he encountered a weary knight whom he did not recognize, astride a more weary horse. The knight besought one of the horses from Sir Gawain, received it graciously, and rode immediately in the direction of the abducted queen. The knight was Sir Lancelot. But his name will not be revealed by the poet until he meets up with the queen. The courtly lover must above all be modest, to the point of being nameless.

When next Sir Gawain came upon the knight, he found the borrowed horse dead from exhaustion, the ground trampled as in a great battle, and further along the knight himself, hesitating before a cart driven by a dwarf. The knight—Lancelot—had asked the dwarf for news of the queen, but the miserable, lowborn dwarf had replied, "If thou wilt get up into the cart I am driving, thou shalt hear tomorrow what has happened to the queen."[3] Thus was Sir Lancelot faced with his first test in the trial of his love for the queen. "For in those days," the poet Chrétien tells us, "such a cart served the same purpose as does a pillory now. Whoever was convicted of any crime was placed upon the cart and dragged through the streets and was never afterward heard, honored or welcomed in any court." Therefore Lancelot hesitated—but only for two steps—before he climbed into the cart. "Yet, it was unlucky for him," says Chrétien, "that he shrank from the disgrace and did not jump in at once, for he will rue his delay." The courtly lover must shrink from no humiliation in the service of his lady.

Other adventures follow in the series of tests of Lancelot's fitness for the queen's rescue. On one night he braved a flaming lance dropped from the rafters as he lay in bed; one day he crossed a sword bridge, sharp as a razor's edge, with his hands bared and his knees and feet unarmored, so that he might not slip. But the "test in the Castle of Lust"[4]—during the night before the bridge crossing—may be most worthy here of the retelling.

A damsel fair and charming, well attired and richly dressed, offered Sir Lancelot shelter, but on one condition—"that you will lie with me," she said. "Not a few there are who would have thanked her five hundred times for such a gift," interrupted the poet. But his hero was much displeased and made a very different answer. " 'Damsel,' said Lancelot, 'I thank you for the offer of your house and esteem it very highly; but if you please, I should be very sorry to lie with you.' 'By my eyes,' said the damsel, 'then I retract my offer.' " Thus Lancelot, "since it is unavoidable," lets her have her way, though his heart grieves to give consent; and the winsome damsel, too, who leads him to her domicile, "will pass through sorrow and heaviness. For it is possible that she will love him so that she will not wish to part with him."

In the damsel's castle they wash their hands and sit down to eat. Afterward, hand in hand, the damsel leads Lancelot to the great hall, in the midst of which a bed has been set for them. The damsel lies down first, then Lancelot, duty bound by his promise, though he has a terrible time removing his hose and untying the knots. He takes care not to touch the damsel, and when in bed, turns away from her as far as possible and speaks no word to her, "like a monk to whom speech is forbidden." She is certainly very fair and winsome, but "the knight has only one heart and this one is really no longer his, but has been entrusted to someone else . . . Love, which holds all hearts beneath its sway, requires it to be lodged in a single place."

So the damsel says to Lancelot, "My lord, I will leave and return to bed in my room. Now take your rest all night, for you have so well kept your promise that I have no right to make further request of you." Lancelot rather gladly lets her go, like one who is the devoted lover of someone else, and at daybreak rises to continue his quest of the queen. Battles and other trials confront him, including "the stony passage," which one might call "the rocky road to sexual maturity," before Lancelot finally rescues Queen Guinevere and King Arthur's captive subjects from the wicked knight, Prince Meleagant. And it is in the "Castle of Death" of King Bademagu, father of the prince, that Lancelot is led to the queen whom he has just rescued, only to hear her say to the good king, so unlike his son, "I care nothing about seeing him." "You are too scornful toward a man who has served you so faithfully," says the king. "Sire," replies the queen, "truly he has made poor use of his time." Now, Lancelot, upon hearing this, is dumbfounded, but he replies very humbly, "like a polished lover," expressing his grief but not daring to ask the reason for the queen's reproach.

Desolate, Lancelot thinks to kill himself, and word even reaches Queen Guinevere that he has done so; and so sorely does the queen grieve, that she, too, thinks to kill herself, sighing, "Alas! how much better I should feel and how much comfort I should take, if only once before he died I had held him in my arms! What? Yes, certainly, quite unclad, in order the better to enjoy him." For two days the queen thus mourns, and Lancelot hears of *her* death and sorely grieves until he hears otherwise, and then he rejoices. Again the good King Bademagu brings them together, and at last Lancelot hears from the lips of the queen why she had refused to greet him. "Did you not hesitate for shame to mount the cart?" says the queen. "You showed you were loath to get in when you hesitated for two whole steps. That is the reason why I would neither address nor look at you." "May God save me from such a crime again," replies Lancelot, "and may God show me no mercy, if you were not quite right!" He begs forgiveness. "Friend," says the queen, "you are quite forgiven." She then indicates the window of her bedroom that gives onto the garden, where they might talk at more leisure come nightfall. "I shall be inside and you outside," she says. "I shall be able to touch you only with my lips or hand, but if you please, I will stay there until morning for love of you. Our bodies cannot be joined, for close beside me in my room lies Kay the seneschal, who is still suffering from his wounds."

Eagerly Lancelot waited for nightfall, then stole softly through the garden to the queen's bedroom window, where she awaited him. He honored her with a gentle salute; promptly she returned his greeting, "for he was desirous of her and she of him." They talked not "of vulgar, tiresome affairs" but rather of noble things and drew close to each other, cursing the bars that came between them.

Then Lancelot asserts that the bars could not keep him from joining her, if she but consents. "Certainly," says the queen, "I consent." But she bids him to wait until she has withdrawn, and to remove the bars so quietly that the seneschal should not awake. He will indeed, says Lancelot, and so he does with uncommon strength, climbing through the window.

> First he finds Kay asleep in his bed, then he comes to the bed of the queen, whom he adores and before whom he kneels, *holding her more dear than the relic of any saint.*

> And the queen extends her arms to him and, embracing him, presses him tightly against her bosom, drawing him into the bed beside her and showing him every possible satisfaction . . . It is love that prompts her to treat him so; and if she feels great love for him, he feels a hundred thousand times as much for her . . .
>
> Now Lancelot possesses all he wants, when the queen *voluntarily* seeks his company and love, and when he holds her in his arms, and she holds him in hers. Their sport is so agreeable and sweet, as they kiss and fondle each other, that in truth such a marvellous joy comes over them as was never heard or known (emphasis mine).

"But their joy will not be revealed by me," says the poet, "for the most choice and delightful satisfaction was precisely that of which our story must not speak."

Lancelot's heart is heavy when daylight appears, for he must leave his mistress's side. Regretfully he departs by the window through which he had entered so happily, and as he leaves the queen's bedroom, "he bows and acts precisely as if he were before a shrine."

Such was the bold story that Marie, Countess of Champagne, had Chrétien de Troyes set down after giving him the content and the treatment—a portrayal of courtly love not only adulterous but *"idolatrous,"* despite Chrétien's qualms. For so scholars have since described Lancelot's love, and his *conduct*—as being exemplary of the courtly lover, who "accepts the total superiority of his mistress and humbly attempts to render himself worthy of her by performing whatever daring or ignominious feats she may command."[5]

How did this come about in a time—the Middle Ages—so profoundly misogynist? The answer may suggest the period's finest paradox: *by imposing her social superiority, the lady of the couple achieved sexual equality.* For her lover did not put her on a pedestal. She was already upon it. Witness Eleanor of Aquitaine, twice queen, and her daughter Marie, wife of the sovereign of the great duchy of Champagne (to both of whom we shall return). The key to courtly love, born in southern French courts and usually treated as a curious literary amalgam of neo-Platonism, Albigensianism, and Moorish poetry, is in this power relationship.

The châtelaine, or lady of the manor, is the capital figure. Her château, or castle, was in fact a fortified community, a walled oasis in a "barbarous countryside."[6] She and her damsels reigned in the great hall, or *court,* of the castle. They formed the budding core of French civilization, its future salons, civility, and discourse. Superficial, perhaps, but in France the superficial runs very deep. Its culture is the product of eight centuries of polishing, which began in these feudal courts.

The women of the castle were comparatively few, the men numerous—literally a small army of squires, pages, second sons of neighboring or distant lords; bachelor, aspiring knights, some of whom the lady has known from adolescence and who now regard her with as much filial love as feudal respect and allegiance, which they easily transfer from the lord of the castle to his lady. Frequently among them is the second son of the lord's brother (as Sir Gawain, who was King Arthur's nephew), adding a kind of vicarious touch of the incestuous, for the aunt was both mother and mistress (Sir Gawain's adoration for Queen Guinevere rivaled Sir Lancelot's). *Mistress,* then, of course, had its full sovereign meaning.[7] Wherever courtly love prevailed and the troubadours or minnesingers appeared, in southern Germany, as in southern France, the records testify to the marked scarcity of women relative to men.[8] At the least, this contributed to their privileged position.

Psychologically—it is another medieval paradox—the noblewoman was *not* prepared for marriage. As a youth she was taught to ride, to hunt, to train and fly falcons, to receive guests in her father's place. Youth was a joyous time brought to an end by marriage to a man she may never have seen and to whom she represented little more than another estate.[9] As her husband he had full power over her and their lands, but fortunately for her he had other preoccupations: war, hunting, jousts, and adventures—not without the profit of pillage. They took him from the castle. He was frequently away, sometimes for years, as during the crusades, particularly when he was taken prisoner by the Saracens and held for ransom. In his absence, his lady was sovereign—by his choice. He could trust her to safeguard his interests as a kinsman might not. Prince John, for one, Eleanor's English offspring, usurped the crown of brother Richard the Lion-Hearted when the latter was captured by the Austrians on returning from a crusade. In short,

> When the feudal seigneur left castle and fief, he left behind his wife—in quite a different situation than women had hitherto known. She was left as mistress—the châtelaine representing her husband, charged in his absence with the honor and defense of the fief. That elevated and virtually sovereign position at the very center of the domestic life gave women of the feudal period a dignity, a courage, an éclat which they had never before displayed.[10]

They not only governed the fief, they organized expeditions, levied armies, and took command, going to the aid of their husbands when they were taken prisoner or otherwise in trouble. Thus Mathilda ruled Normandy when her husband, William the Conqueror, left on the conquest of England. So Ermengarde ruled Brittany when her ducal husband went off for six years on the First Crusade. Another Ermengarde, who had inherited and kept her father's power, governed the county of Narbonne for more than half a century, despite two, possibly three, husbands. It was she who paid homage to the king and dealt out justice, conducted troops, and concluded alliances. More generally, wives achieved power as widows, ruling in the names of their minor sons until they came of age. Thus Blanche ruled over Champagne, Alix de Vergi over Burgundy, Marguerite over Flanders. It was an extraordinary period when the most powerful piece on the chessboard, known as the *prime minister,* was renamed the *queen.*

Perhaps rightly the most famous woman who ever ruled a great fief was Eleanor of Aquitaine (ca. 1122–1204). Though queen of two kings, as we have said, the first French (Louis VII), the second English (Henry II) and eleven years younger—"Queen of England by the wrath of God," she once wrote—her fame properly resides in that rule and in the courts she created. Here a confrerie of poets, clerks, scholars, and troubadours found their congenial atmosphere and matronage. And from French court to English court came troubadour Bernard of Ventadour, to pay his lady tribute, if not court; and courtly love itself reached an apogee matched only at the court of Eleanor's daughter in Champagne.

Was Bernard indeed the queen's lover? His poetry is often ambiguous and his language *may* be literary convention, but in the last song he composed, Bernard plainly enough says, "She may deny me her love, if she wishes, but I can always flatter myself that she once proved it to me."[11]

It would not suffice, however, to establish Bernard of Ventadour as Eleanor's lover. The question to answer is, what kind of a lover? What kind of a lover was a courtly lover of the twelfth century? To reply schematically, if not wholly satisfactorily: he could be platonic—in the Christianized sense of the word—and therefore "pure"; or his could be a sexual or "mixed" love; but it had always to be a *refined* sexuality, a *merited* love, rigorously tested.

Suitors were almost universally social inferiors striving upward, with no taint of shame attached to their ambition; indeed, quite the contrary. Bernard, for instance, was the son of an archer and a kitchen servant, both of whom belonged to the castle and fief of Ventadour. His earliest lyrics were addressed to the mistress of Ventadour with sufficient ardor for him to be sent away by the viscount. But his reputation was made, and he betook himself to Eleanor's court at Aquitaine, joining his fortune to hers—and subjecting himself to the suspicions of the first royal husband, as he would to those of the second.[12]

Bernard's is a more extreme case of the lower-class troubadour. Courtly lovers generally were elected from a class of knights, itself recruited by a nobility in need of mounted warriors and loyal vassals. The loyalty was normally won by grants of land, or portions of it, won by the knights themselves, who became lesser nobles in the process, retaining a sense of servility toward their superior. Typically, even as they climbed upward, they closed their ranks to newcomers, forging a code of chivalry armored against them and a concept of honor based initially on achievement and only later, ironically, on birth. The courts to which they belonged were smaller than the king's and comparatively freer, with a flair, character, and individuality of their own. But they were all cast in the mold characteristic of feudalism—vassal service. The *minnedienst,* literally love service, rendered the lady of the castle is now easily recognizable as the feudalization of love, emerging, as it did, virtually fully formed from its ready-made mold.[13]

Medieval marriage what it was, the nobleman's wife sought love outside the domestic limits. In that cluster of twelfth- and thirteenth-century attitudes called courtly love, no theme appears more frequently.[14] As Simone de Beauvoir has expressed it with characteristic bluntness: "The feudal husband was guardian and tyrant, and the wife sought an extramarital lover: knightly love was a compensation for the barbarism of official mores."[15] She appends a quotation from Engels's *Origin of the Family:* "The point where antiquity stopped in its search for sexual love is where the Middle Ages started—adultery." Engels continued: "A new moral standard arose for judging sexual intercourse. The question asked was not only whether such intercourse was legitimate or illicit, but also whether it arose from mutual love or not."[16]

Mutual love was not part of the feudal marriage contract. Conjugal duties applied singularly to the wife. She belonged to her lord and master, as a medieval document testifies: "A husband has the right to beat his wife, if she refuses to obey him, speaks badly to him, or disagrees with him, so long as he does it moderately and death does not ensue."[17]

The aristocratic husband who loved his wife and permitted it to be known was a rare—and remarked-upon—bird. Marveling at the fact, chronicler Gislebert de Mous records that Marie de Champagne's son-in-law, Baldwin of Hainaut, loved his wife and no other woman, "though it is rarely found in any man that he should cleave so much to one woman and be content with her alone."[18]

Marriages of nobles were matches of interest, aimed at joining powers, properties, fiefs, and great estates. Marriage contracts were drawn by parents with the care shown commercial or diplomatic treaties. When interests changed or were unreconciled, marriages were dissolved and wives dismissed, "repudiated," as occurred royally to Eleanor of Aquitaine twice. Local lords and seigneurs behaved as regally.

With regal casualness as well, they kept concubines close by, sometimes in the castle, and counted upon their wives to bring up the illegitimate children along with the legitimate. The chastity expected was very much on the distaff—that is, the flax spinner's—side. The wife's adultery could, at the election of the husband, be severely punished, but not the husband's. That was expected of the manly man. Powerful noblemen openly seduced lesser men's wives. Eleanor's grandfather, William IX of Aquitaine, boasted in song of having bedded the wives of lords Guarin and Bernart 188 times within a week.[19] The only accounting to which he seems to have been held was the accuracy of his account. William IX may well have been the first recorded troubadour, but he was not a courtly lover. He violated the "code" that would later be established in twofold measure: by his promiscuity and by his boasting of it.

The secrecy adjured of the courtly lover is completely understandable. A wife's adultery was classified in the early feudal age as a capital crime, together with homicide, bloodshed, theft, and rape. In 857, for instance, Pope Nicolas I confirmed the husband's right to kill his erring spouse. A century and a half later, a chronicler tells us, "Count Fulk Nerra of Anjou burned his adulterous wife." The second, or Gothic, feudal age, which witnessed the birth of courtly love, also saw a tempering of the terrible penalty. It now meant in most cases the wife's repudiation and confinement for life in a convent. However, even this was considered insufficiently severe if a husband discovered his wife in bed with her lover, who had been previously warned away: he still had the right to kill them both, provided he did it on the spot in hot blood. "In fact," a poet of Countess Marie's court informs us, though repentant and permitted to live, the erring woman "would be better off in the grave."[20] Nor were women of royalty necessarily spared. Early in the fourteenth century Marguerite of Burgundy, accused of adultery by her father-in-law, King Philip the Fair, was arrested, had her head shaven, and was shut up in a castle, there to die, most likely poisoned. Her lover was castrated before being skinned alive.

Such were the *possible* consequences of a woman's conducting herself with a fraction of her husband's freedom. It unquestionably made her subject a suitor to the sternest of tests beforehand. Could he be discreet? He had to prove it before he became her lover. At the same time there is parallel evidence of considerable agreeableness on the part of many husbands. How many and how often cannot be ascertained, but the attitude, despite its seeming contradiction with prevailing values, can be explained.

The feudal lord who chose to turn a blind eye and complaisant cheek, if not simply uncaring, sought only to avoid exposure. It was *his* honor, not his wife's, except as her dishonor meant his own, which was his supreme concern. Punishing her could mean pointing a finger at himself as a jealous, cuckolded husband—the never-failing figure for ridicule in France since the Gothic age. It is one of the enduring legacies of courtly love, which had permeated the upper class by the end of the thirteenth century and filtered down, adulterated and trivialized, to the bourgeoisie.

Nor had it left the clergy untouched. "In the best tradition of the troubadours," Le Roy Ladurie concludes in his meticulous study of the Albigensian village of Montaillou, 1294–1324, "the young and beautiful lady of Montaillou took a lover"—the first of several during and between periods of marriage. Among them was the priest of Montaillou, Pierre Clergue, who had "carnally known" a dozen of the women of the heretical southern French village—according to their own testimony to a member of the Inquisition.[21]

For Ladurie, courtly love has been proved to have existed. But was its practice in Montaillou, as he asserts, "in the best tradition of the troubadours"—that is, before courtly love became a parade of poses, a parody of itself? Scarcely. And the astonishing thing remains *not* that reciprocal respect and love between man and woman came into being at last, but that it lasted as long as it did as a social ideal, if not a social reality—three generations or more. The problem of that mutual respect and love is hardly unique to the feudal couple. It continues to be posed. But the difference between then and now is that more women then seem to have been in a position to do something about it. *They* imposed the conditions.

A la Lancelot, the courtly lover had to prove that he could master *himself* before he was permitted even to serve his mistress, demonstrate his capacity for selfless friendship before he was allowed to display that of a lover. The tables of male law were turned upside down.

> Courtly love service by its very nature was meant to mortify male pride. In this voluntary submission of the friend to the loved one, there was a profound verity: since it was the deeply ingrained misogyny of the male which, until then, had reined in the impulse toward mutual love, it was important that such love now have as its point of departure the symbolic humiliation of male power.[22]

The qualities required of the prospective lover make interesting reading. He had to be gentle, loyal, humble, nimble-witted, good-humored, sincere, courteous (to all women), and discreet. Having passed these public tests, he had to spend a night of trial *(l'asag)* with his lady, managed somehow without, of course, the husband's knowing. The night of trial both lay naked together, but it was the lady who took all initiative. In this regard the lines of Countess of Die, a Provençal poetess, addressed to her cavalier, are vastly instructive:

> Dear friend, sweet and gentle,
> If ever I had you in my power
> To lie with, of an evening,
> And kiss you with the kiss of love,
> Know that I would take great pleasure
> To press you in my arms in place of my husband,
> So long as I have your promise
> To do naught but what I desire.[23]

In response all was permitted the tested cavalier on the night of the trial but "the act"—that of penetration, possibly because it implied possession, as assured the husband at his will and as his right by the marriage contract. To the contrary—and as a result, surely—the courtly lover had to win that privilege by proving his respect, his consideration, his *friendship* first. Then, on another night, he might or might not, the lady willing, become the complete lover. If not, more than one troubadour declared it unessential—so many, in fact, that courtly love is still mistakenly equated with pure, idealized love and the lady of the poetry assumed to be in reality the Holy Virgin. Typical of the poetry of these unrequited but uncomplaining—and perhaps not unhappy—troubadours is this line from Arnaud de Mareuil to his mistress: "I prefer desiring you without having you to having another without loving her."[24] The point, once again, seems to be that the true lover can love without possessing.

In his famous twelfth-century treatise on love, *De Arte Honesti Amandi,* clerk Andreas Capellanus (Andrew the Chaplain) carefully denotes that this attitude and behavior constitute "pure love," "the kind consisting of the contemplation of the mind and the affection of the heart, going as far as the kiss and the embrace and the modest contact with the naked lover, but omitting the final solace."[25] Andreas, however, continues: "There is also mixed love, which gets its effect from every delight of the flesh and culminates in the final act of Venus." He does not condemn this kind of love; on the contrary:

> Mixed love, too, is real love, and it is praiseworthy, and we say that it is the source of all good things. . . . When two people have been united by pure love and afterward desire to practice mixed love, the substance of the love remains the same in them, although the manner and form and the way of practicing it are different.

Andreas adds that "all men ought to choose pure love rather than a mixed or common one,"

> but even if the lovers have made an agreement that neither may ask for anything more unless both are agreed to it, still it is not right for a woman to refuse to give in to her lover's desire on this point, if she sees that he persists in it. For all lovers are bound, when practicing love's solaces, to be mutually obedient to each other's desires.

Andreas Capellanus was an ordained priest and possibly at one time chaplain of Countess Marie's court of Champagne. He wrote his treatise, which has been translated as *The Art of Courtly Love,* at her request, between 1186 and 1196. It is impossible to be more precise; however, it should be noted that Countess Marie ruled the fief of Champagne from the death of her husband, in 1181 (when she was thirty-six), until the coming of age of her eldest son, in 1187.[26]

If a code of courtly love can be said to have existed, it is contained in Andreas's *De Arte Honesti Amandi.* Written in the conventional form of a letter to a young friend seeking advice on love, the text is largely a series of fictional dialogues between men and women of the middle and upper classes, although one *plebeius* demonstrates how a man of *his* lower order might make a successful pitch to a noblewoman.

The aim of love, Andreas's manual begins, is, by common desire, "to carry out all of love's precepts in the other's embrace." The path of love is suffering, for the man of the couple—upon whom Andreas's accent unsurprisingly falls—"burns with love from the sight of and excessive meditation upon the opposite sex." To be granted love in return, he must prove himself Christian, truthful, modest, courageous, and, on all occasions to all ladies, courteous. "Oh what a wonderful thing is love, which makes a man shine with so many virtues and teaches everyone, no matter who he is, so many good traits of character!" Yet "an excess of passion is a bar to love," for a man who is its slave cannot be *bound* by love: he lusts after every woman "like a shameless dog"—unthinking, ungrateful, no better than an animal.

To women belongs the freedom of choice, and the wise woman will choose her lover with care. A noblewoman should preferably elect a nobleman, but "she should not reject a commoner" after he has proved his worth: "character alone is worthy of love." Character alone truly ennobles, and "the most noble among men," says Andreas the clerk, ending his introduction, "is the clerk!"

The fictional dialogues follow:

A man of the middle class, for instance, addresses a noblewoman. He "reminds" her that originally "nobility derived only from good character, manly worth and courtesy"—wherefore his suitability as a suitor. "As for your objection that it is a disgrace for me to engage in business," he continues, "if I did not concern myself with honest and legitimate gains, I would fall into obscure poverty and so I could not do noble deeds"—and thus deserve his lady's love. "May God give you the reward suited to your effort," responds his lady, encouragingly. Another man of the bourgeoisie begs a noblewoman to teach him "those things that are specially demanded in love, those which make a man most worthy of being loved," so that he might merit *her* love. She proceeds to do so.

Andreas repeatedly drums upon the incompatibility of love and marriage. "I admit it is true that your husband is a very worthy man," says a nobleman to a woman of nobility, "but I am greatly surprised that you wish to misapply the term 'love' to that marital affection which husband and wife are expected to feel for each other after marriage, since everybody knows that love can have no place between husband and wife"—nor can marital affection be *friendship.* He appeals to the authority of "Andreas the Lover, chaplain of the royal court," whereupon the noblewoman replies that he must submit his case for judgment.

The Nobleman: I give you full power to appoint the arbiter in this dispute. However, I want to be judged by a woman, not by a man.

The Noblewoman: If it suits you, it seems to me that the Countess of Champagne ought to be honored in this affair and should settle the disagreement.

Accordingly a letter setting forth the matter was sent to the Countess of Champagne. She replied:

> To the prudent and noblewoman A. and the illustrious and famous Count G., Marie, Countess of Champagne, sends greeting:
>
> Since we are bound to hear the just petitions of everybody, and since it is not seemly to deny our help to those who ask what is proper, especially when those who go wrong on questions of love ask to be set right by our decision—which is what the tenor of your letter indicates—we have tried diligently and carefully to carry this out without any extended delay . . .
>
> We declare and we hold as firmly established that love cannot exert its powers between two people who are married to each other. For lovers give each other everything freely, under no compulsion of necessity, but married people are in duty bound to give in to each other's desires and deny themselves to each other in nothing . . . A precept of love tells us that no woman, even if she is married, can be crowned with the reward of the King of Love unless she is seen enlisted in the service of Love himself outside the bonds of wedlock. But another rule of Love teaches that no one can be in love with two men. Rightly, therefore, Love cannot acknowledge any rights of his between husband and wife . . .
>
> Therefore let this be our verdict, pronounced with great moderation and supported by the opinion of a great many ladies.

The "Courts of Love" of these great ladies have aroused a good deal of scholarly controversy. Did they really exist? They may well have been playful sessions conducted half in jest at Poitiers and Troyes, the capitals of Aquitaine and Champagne. Their verdicts and rulings may have had no more—*and no less*— social force than later books of etiquette, but as the latter they inform us about the morals and behavior expected at the upper levels.

There should be no illusion about the élitism involved. "It is not expedient that peasants should be instructed in the theory of love," Andreas warns, "lest while they are devoting themselves to conduct which is not natural to them, their kindly farms may through lack of cultivation prove useless to us." And should a gentleman be foolish enough to fall in love with a peasant woman, he should not hesitate, says the good chaplain, to take what he seeks "by force."

The peasant woman dispatched, Andreas returns to his proper subject: how may love won according to the rules be safeguarded? Through secrecy and discretion. A lover should even be sparing of praise for his lady when in the company of others. "Lovers should not even nod to each other, unless they are sure no one is watching them."

Gentlemanly behavior is codified, perhaps for the first time, as *courteoisie.* The courtly gentling of the knight, whose noble profession it was to kill and maim, was the necessary initial step in the long process of civilizing France—and it was the work of its women.

> A lover [Andreas states] should always offer his services and obedience freely to every lady, and he ought to root out all his pride and be very humble. Then, too, he must keep in mind the general rule that lovers must not neglect anything that good manners demand or good breeding suggests, but they should be very careful to do everything of this sort. Love may also be retained by indulging in the sweet and delightful solaces of the flesh, but only in such manner and in such number that they may never seem wearisome to the loved one. Let the lover strive to practice gracefully and manfully any act or mannerism which he has noticed is pleasing to his beloved . . . And what we have said you should understand as referring to a lover of either sex.

Love diminishes or comes to an end with a lover's indiscretion, but not necessarily with a passing infidelity, should chance present *him* with "an unknown woman in a convenient place" or "with a little strumpet or somebody's servant girl." Just for this, the lover is not to be considered unworthy. A lady, to be sure, is expected to be more of a lady—faithful.

Similarly, for Andreas, sexual freedom for a chaplain does not imply the same freedom for the nun. He renders a "comic" account of one of his own dallyings with a *religieuse.* Though courtly love came relatively close, it cannot be said to have eradicated the double standard.

The famous "rules of love," according to Andreas's construction, were given to a British knight after he had undergone a long, adventurous quest by the King of Love himself—King Arthur. Spread the message abroad, the knight was told, make the "rules" known to all lovers for the "salvation" of the ladies. Among the thirty-one rules or commandments were these:

> Marriage is no real excuse for not loving.
>
> He who is not jealous cannot love.
>
> No one can be bound by two loves.
>
> It is not proper to love any woman one would be ashamed to marry.
>
> The easy attainment of love makes it of little value; difficulty of attainment makes it prized.

Good character alone makes any man worthy of love.

A true lover considers nothing but what will please his beloved.

A man who is troubled by too much passion generally does not love.

Nothing forbids one woman being loved by two men or one man by two women, but they cannot simultaneously return both loves.

Andreas records cases brought before the Courts of Love of Eleanor of Aquitaine and Marie of Champagne, the Countess of Flanders and the Viscountess of Narbonne. "Which of two men, equal in everything but wealth, is preferable as a lover?" The question addressed to Countess Marie received this answer: "A handsome poor man may well be preferred to a vulgar rich man. It is more worthy for a woman blessed with an abundance of property to accept a needy lover than one who has great wealth. Nothing is so praiseworthy in a lover of either sex as to relieve the necessities of the loved one." But if both are poor, "their love will be of short duration. Poverty puts love to flight."

Has a lady, who had a lover and was afterward, through no fault of her own, married to an honorable man, the right to refuse herself to her former lover? Viscountess Ermengarde of Narbonne rendered the verdict of her court: "The intrusion of marriage does not exclude an earlier love, unless the lady has renounced love for ever." Asked whether a married couple, once separated, could resume as lovers, Viscountess Ermengarde responded: "If any two people have been married and afterwards separate, we deem love between them wholly wicked."

In another affair, the Countess of Flanders attracted much attention by her declaration that no woman should be misjudged for having given her love to an unworthy man, "since any woman who wants to be considered worthy must indulge in love, and it is not easy to search out the innermost secrets of a man's heart and intentions." The countess also declared: "We believe that a woman has a just and reasonable claim upon a man whom, through great effort, she has made worthy and set upon the path of good manners."

The go-between of a knight betrayed his mission by seducing the lady sought. The betrayed knight brought the matter before the Countess of Champagne.

> She summoned sixty ladies to her assistance and settled the affair with this decision: "Let that crafty go-between enjoy his evilly acquired love with a woman of his kind, and let that woman enjoy

the kind of lover she deserves. But let both be forever banned from the gatherings of ladies and the courts of knights."

A second knight had sought the love of a lady who already had a lover. She had promised the knight to grant him her favors if ever she lost her lover. She then married her lover and claimed that he was still her lover though now her husband. Eleanor of Aquitaine, queen at the time, passed judgment when appealed to. "We do not dare," she said, "oppose the opinion of the Countess of Champagne, who has already ruled that love cannot exist between husband and wife. We therefore recommend that the lady grant the love she has promised."

Often it was the noblewoman who granted gifts as well as took initiatives, particularly when she was "blessed with greater abundance." But courtly love scorned venality on the part of either lover. Andreas tells of the nobleman who had showered handsome presents on a lady who had provocatively accepted them, but who had offered in return a flat refusal of love. Here Queen Eleanor ruled with equal flatness: "Let a woman either decline presents or pay for them with her love, or let her suffer being classed with prostitutes."

The case which most aroused "all those serving in the camp of Love," as one would suspect, was that of "a certain knight who had shamefully divulged the intimacies and secrets of his love." A court of ladies, assembled in Gascony, unanimously decided that he should be excommunicated from civilized gatherings, lest his example encourage other male indiscretions, thus ending the reign of Love and women's right to have a lover.

That "right," like a delicate plant, was always threatened by intemperate exposure. The Church had not relaxed its opposition to courtly love, and husbands could at any time reaffirm *their* absolute rights. Undoubtedly the attitude of the Church explains in part the sudden about-face of Andreas (who was, after all, an ordained priest) in the concluding section of his treatise. Entitled *De Reprobatione,* it is usually translated as *The Rejection of Love.* Previous touches of cynicism scarcely prepare one for the volte-face. The first two sections of his manual, Andreas abruptly informs "friend Walter," to whom it was addressed, were designed simply to instruct him, at his urgent request, in the theory and art of love. "We believe, however," Andreas continues,

> that any man who devotes his efforts to love loses all his usefulness. Read this little book, then, not as one seeking to take up the life of a lover, but that, invigorated by the theory and trained to excite the minds of women to love, you may, by refraining from so doing,

win an eternal recompense and thereby deserve a greater reward from God. For God is more pleased with a man who is able to sin and does not, than with a man who has no opportunity to sin . . . [Moreover] no man, so long as he devotes himself to the service of love, can please God by any other works, even if they are good ones.

Adieu the conception of courtly love as ennobling. Love lowers a man, says Andreas contritely, and renders him useless. God, moreover, hates and punishes those who love "outside the bonds of wedlock." From love stem homicide, adultery, perjury, theft, false witness, incest, and idolatry. "By it one friend is estranged from another," and nothing is finer or greater than the friendship between men, "as Cicero has said." The familiar diatribe against the daughters of Eve follows: women are venal, miserly, envious, drunken *(sic),* deceitful, loud-mouthed, and fickle; in short, marked by Eve's original sin—"disobedience."

The precipitous reversal on the part of Andreas is still a subject of controversy. Had he, in Books One and Two, merely complied with Countess Marie's known opinions and then, in Book Three, returned to those of his Church? Chrétien de Troyes had similarly responded to the countess's request with his poem on Lancelot, which he never completed, because—it is presumed—he wished to show his disapproval for Lancelot's behavior. (That Countess Marie could summon even that much compliance from both men is quite as impressive.).

Another reading of the first two books of Andreas's treatise by some historians (the same as before) has him writing them with irony and Ovidian humor, not seriousness. If so, the irony was as lost on his contemporaries as on later generations. His manual was so widely read and influential that on March 7, 1277—almost a century after it had been written—it was formally banned by the Bishop of Paris as dangerous to faith and morals.

The banning, however, put an end neither to the influence of Andreas's work nor to courtly love. The treatise continued to be translated and read throughout Europe until the eighteenth century, its sentiments reappearing in nineteenth-century Romanticism and *its* perennial revivals. In the fourteenth century, *De Arte Honesti Amandi* was adapted as a textbook by the Spanish courts of love, but so modified that one rule states: "No gentleman should pay court to a lady without first having the permission of her husband."[27]

As for the existence—and persistence—of courts of love, "there is no doubt," says one of the more skeptical historians, "that in 1400 (French monarch) Charles VI founded a court of love, a serious literary and courtly assembly"—in which burghers and clergymen participated alongside princes and prelates.[28] Debates were ceremonially organized in the form of amorous lawsuits, and ladies of the court awarded the prizes. Among the seven hundred known members of the "club," however, was a goodly number of the period's most notorious rakes.

Courtly love, as it waned, institutionalized and codified, inevitably turned out feudal Casanovas—"false men swearing false oaths to women (for) they would have their sport where they could." So the fourteenth-century knight La Tour Laundry recounts, telling of his adventures in the countryside in the company of his friends. The full title of his work—*The Book of the Knight La Tour Laundry for the Instruction of his Daughters*—indicates that professionals of seduction were roistering about and a father who knew them well was offering his daughters fair warning.[29]

In historic fact, the degradation of courtly love accompanied the decline in social position and power of the châtelaine. By the fourteenth century the crusades had come to an end, bringing many of the masters back to the castles and fiefs their wives had ruled in their absences. It was but one of the factors, and a lesser one. The prevailing combination of forces was a church reasserting its antifeminism, a monarchy concentrating its own power at the expense of local fiefdoms, and a bourgeoisie dominating the new urban scene and much of the countryside with its philosophy of the domesticated housewife.

The signal and most effective demonstration of the French monarchy's bias and influence was its invoking the so-called Salic Law in 1316 and 1322 in order to deprive the daughters of Louis X and Philip VI from succeeding to the throne. Since then no woman has sat upon it. An entire aristocracy was affected by the royal action: succession to titles, offices, and lands of noble families was forbidden to women and to those descended in the female line.

As for the bourgeoisie, the denigrating note of its hostility to women—greater even than the clergy's—was first clearly heard in the famous rhymed stories known as *fabliaux,* whose antifeminine satire was particularly crude and often cruel.[30] Indisputably, however, antifeminism found its completest expression in *Roman de la Rose,* the most popular work of the Middle Ages.

Similar to Andreas's treatise, this extraordinary epic of 20,000 verses by two poets combines thesis with antithesis, courtly love with its repudiation—but the latter with far more devastating effect. Begun about 1220 by Guillaume de Lorris, *Roman de la Rose* was completed forty-five years later by Jean de Meun. Its popularity was immediate and widespread, reaching to England, where the first part was translated by Chaucer. That first part, however, need not hold our attention: Lorris is the lesser poet; his contribution is charming but conventional. Jean de Meun is another matter.

Roman de la Rose is an allegory. Its young hero meets la Rose at the castle of Love and is promptly smitten. Frankness, Pity, and Bel-Accueil urge la Rose to return the knight's love, but Danger, Shame, and Jealousy conspire to keep them apart. Reason descends from his tower, and Venus appears on the scene to join him in a debate about the destiny of the pair. So ends Lorris's contribution. The allegory is quite clear: the young knight enters adulthood through the discovery of sexuality and love (the rose) and seeks integration in noble society (the castle). Indeed it is a familiar feudal tale.

Jean de Meun picks up the narrative where Lorris had left it, adding more verses than he found. Where Lorris had been content to follow, in a fairly straight line, the traditional idyll of the knight and the damsel, Jean de Meun divagates and dwells on psychological and social speculations as cynical as any contemporary Frenchman's. By origin a bourgeois of Paris, Meun believes in neither the fidelity nor the chastity of women. He denigrates not only marriage but also the couple. Each, he insists, tries to dominate the other, the man the woman, the woman the man, but the woman is the more wily, the more deadly of the pair. He puts in the mouth of Genius the hoary litany of women's faults—leachery, treachery, and so on and so forth. Finally he brings *Roman de la Rose* to an end: the besieged castle is set aflame and taken by storm, and the lover plucks the Freudian rose. The original tale of courtly love has become that of allegorical rape.[31]

The "multitude of fervent admirers of Jean de Meun"[32] was met by a few defenders of women, among them ladies of the royal court, who, it is said, undertook one day to "strip Jean de Meun of his clothes and whip him."[33] The most striking reply would come a century later, from the first professional woman writer recorded in history, Christine de Pisan (1364–1431). Hereafter, one feels, women will best speak for women, when they speak at all. The observation itself stems from the medieval poetess. Books about the infamy of women, she remarked with Jean de Meun firmly in mind, have been written by men, not by women. As Chaucer's formidable Wife of Bath unforgettably put it:

> Who peynted the leoun, tel me who?
> By god, if women hadde written stories
> As clerks han with-inne hir oratories,

They wolde han writen of men more wikkednesse
Than all the mark of Adam may redresse.

Christine de Pisan was born in pre-Renaissance Venice. Her father was Tomaso da Pizzano, scholar, astrologer, and official of the Venetian Republic. Invited to the French court by Charles V, he settled with his family in Paris. Here, from the age of four, Christine grew up. Hers, she would write, was a happy childhood. Her father had become reconciled to her being a girl after he had consulted the stars and they had told him that she, as he, would be inclined to studies, which consequently he favored her with. At fifteen Christine was married to a man she had a voice in choosing, thanks to her father, and in all her writings she would express love and respect for her young husband—for his gentleness, consideration, and like respect for her.[34] At twenty-one Christine lost her father, at twenty-five her husband. She was left with the charge of three children, two younger brothers, and her mother. She never remarried: she feared, she said, that she would never again find her husband's like. Rather, with the encouragement of her friends, she determined to support herself and her charges by turning a pastime into a profession—composing poems and ballads for those who would commission and could pay for them. She chose, she would explain, as so many women writers since, "voluntary solitude;" that is, "a life of writing, of solitude behind closed doors"—a room of her own—"with all my senses awakened to what I had found in the wondrous world of books."[35] Four centuries before George Sand, she also chose "the behavior of a man," so that she might have some measure of a man's independence and freedom to express himself. "Chance taught me to be a man," she would write in *La Mutacion de Fortune,* a book-length poem of 25,000 verses. "A man I now am and a man I shall remain [though] it would please me more to be a woman again."

In *Le Livre du Duc des Vrais Amans,* Christine de Pisan writes as if she were the duke himself, reciting his story. More often, however, she writes as herself, speaking for women, springing boldly to their defense, as in her reply to Mathéolus's *Lamentations,* in which the author indulged in the usual dreary description of wives as the trial and burden of men. "Descriptions of married life," she struck back in *La Cité des Femmes,* "have not yet been written by women . . . How many have wasted their lives in marriage to hard men . . . How many have been cruelly beaten by their husbands. How many insults, injuries, servitudes and humiliations they have suffered." Instruct young women in law, she urged; they will need it.

From her earliest writing Christine de Pisan had vigorously disputed

Jean de Meun's exalted position. If women were as weak and debauched as he had portrayed, she wrote, why mount so heavy an assault? Why should men seek or need advice on how to subjugate them from Ovid or from Jean de Meun? The most celebrated literary quarrel of the century was launched, since several poets and philosophers took her side; notably Jean Gerson, Chancellor of the University of Paris and a favorite of the French court. To be more accurate, Gerson defended the *family* against Meun's cynical attacks. Christine de Pisan went beyond him to put the case for the entire feminine sex—and with sparkle and wit. A woman, she wrote, was the equal of a man by her very origin, since she had been fashioned from flesh, not, as he, from mud. Moreover, created from a man's rib, she should be at his side, not at his feet. In any event and in the worst case, women were no worse than men, even if they should submit to them for the sake of family peace—but certainly not in the name of justice.

The quarrel rose in violence, and then fell, to rise again after Christine de Pisan's death in 1431—the same year that Joan of Arc was burned to death at the stake as a "witch." Just two years before, Christine de Pisan had hailed the Maid of Orleans in a poem for having done "what no man had dared."

Thus ended the Middle Ages, in Huizinga's phrase, "in the mingled odor of blood and roses," as the Renaissance dawned.

3

RENAISSANCE TURNING POINTS: HENRY II AND DIANE DE POITIERS; MONSIEUR AND MADAME DE MONTAIGNE

DURING the prolonged sacramental crowning of twenty-nine-year-old Henry II, the golden, jewel-encrusted crown of his queen, also twenty-nine, weighed so heavily it was removed from her head and placed on a cushion—at the feet of the king's mistress, Diane de Poitiers, forty-nine. Yet not a bishop's miter quivered, nor a tonsured head shook.

Le couple at the crossroads of medieval and modern France, for all the world, was young Henry II and his mistress. They were the last of the courtly lovers—the last in time, the last, too, in the sense of the end of a series. To pair them, in turn, with Monsieur and Madame de Montaigne might seem as odd in their time as in ours, were not the Montaignes a prototypal couple of a new series, a bourgeois series, whose end, four centuries later, may—or may not—be in sight.

· I ·

DIANE de Poitiers (for a change, the story can begin chronologically with the woman of the couple) was born at the end of a century or the beginning of another, in 1499 or 1500, when Columbus was on his third trip to America—and would return from it in chains. Diane's mother died in her infancy. Her father, Jean de Poitiers, raised her as a boy, taking her hunting at the age of six. From childhood she acted out her name—Diane the Huntress, later Diane, Goddess of the Moon. She would ride for hours, training her lithe body for what since seems her life's destiny, hardening it with cold baths before dawn—and there are still women in France who follow that example, hoping for the same cold, lunar beauty.

As an aristocrat, Diane de Poitiers was taught to rule, though a woman, tutored for it by none other than Anne of France, elder daughter of Louis XI; and she was led to *expect* to rule, either at her future husband's side or in his stead. Three contemporary noblewomen, in fact, were quite literally France's strongmen during Diane's youth—Anne of France, Anne of Brittany, and especially Louise de Savoy, mother of Francis I and regent of France when, as so frequently, he was campaigning in Italy. (Eventually failing to make Italy French, he undertook to make France Italian.)

At fifteen, Diane de Poitiers was already a young belle at the court of Francis I—"a court without ladies," he liked to say, "is a springtime without roses."[1] Almost immediately she was married to Louis de Brézé, fifty-six, possibly a hunchback, but most definitely a grandson of Charles VII and Agnès Sorel—a figure of great wealth and power, the Grand Seneschal of Normandy. Diane never complained of her marriage and even seems to have felt a certain affection for her husband: she chided him when he failed to write during one of the Italian campaigns, celebrated the day of his return, and settled down serenely with him as *la Grande Sénéchale.* When Francis I visited Normandy for three weeks, she royally entertained him and his court of 1,500 followers, no small task for one of sixteen.

No scandal marked that occasion. Rather, it occurred five years later, when her father was accused of treason and imprisoned in the Loches château. She went to the king, implored that the wrong be righted, and failed. Her far more influential husband succeeded in obtaining a last-minute reprieve: Jean de Poitiers was on the scaffold, baring his neck to the axman, when the king's pardon arrived. However, another story made the rounds, retailed by a chronicler of the time known only as a *bourgeois de Paris:*

> It was rumored that the said Lord of Saint Vallier (Jean de Poitiers) had threatened to kill the King because he had raped and deflowered one of his daughters, and that it was for this that he had been condemned, and that had it not been for his son-in-law, the Grand Seneschal of Normandy, he would have been decapitated.[2]

Despite the patent absurdity of the story for Diane or for either of her two sisters—the one also long married, the other scarcely ten at the time—it has persisted down through the centuries that she who would be the mistress of Henry II had been the mistress of his father, Francis I. When Henry was thirty-two and Diane fifty-two, for instance, Venetian Ambassador Lorenzo Contarini was reporting home: "Still young, widowed and beautiful, (Diane de Poitiers) was loved and relished by King Francis I and others, *according to what everybody says,* then fell into the hands of this king Henry II" (original emphasis).[3] Even at an early age, Henry must have heard whispers about his father's mistress, the fabulous Diane, resulting in his nursing a fantasy that he would realize: in the full maturity of manhood, he habitually drank from a goblet shaped on the model of Diane's breast. The Oedipal factor in courtly love—young knight, older mistress—may never have been so manifest.

They first met when Henry was not yet an adolescent.

Once again Francis I had crossed the Alps into Italy at the head of his troops, but this time he had been taken captive and sent to a prison in Spain. And once again his mother, Louise of Savoy, had acted as regent, arranging a peace treaty and the exchange of the king for his two sons, Francis, nine, and Henry, barely seven. Diane de Poitiers had gone down with Louise of Savoy and the court for the exchange at the border town of Bayonne. There, remarking the morose, neglected younger son—as dauphin and heir Francis was his father's favorite—Diane impulsively embraced Henry, kissing him on the forehead. Four years later, more morose than ever, Henry was released, together with his brother, at Bordeaux. Here he found his father, still visibly favoring Francis; but here, too, he rediscovered Diane, the maternal lady of his prison dreams. It was a feeling reinforced when his father presented him Eleanor of Austria as his stepmother; then Louis de Brézé died, leaving Diane widowed and free.

Freedom for women of the *ancien régime* came with widowhood, once they had mourned their late husbands appropriately, and given little cause for scandal. Black, to be sure, was *de rigueur,* but nothing suited Diane better: she would dress in black and white the rest of her life, the black smartly contrasting with the smooth white skin of her complexion and of her high, firm breasts. She was not alone in this among Renaissance widows. Indeed clergymen warned solemnly against the provocative use of mourning clothes so as to invite "lascivious and improper looks."[4]

In the great tourney of 1531, the first year of her widowhood, Diane shared the coveted beauty prize with the king's twenty-two-year-old mistress, Anne de Heilly. Mistresses, too, were *de rigueur.* "Francis I," Brantôme relates, "wanted all his gentlemen to acquire mistresses, and when they did not, he scorned them as stupid and without merit."[5] King, queen, and mistress sat together. But in the parade of young knights that followed the jousting, young Henry dipped his standard in homage neither to the queen nor to his father's mistress, but rather to Diane; and later, when the dauphin had pleased his father by taking a mistress, Francis I had turned to Diane in concern about his other son, Henry. "Trust me," she is said to have told the king, "he will be my *galant.*"

Before Henry became anyone's lover, however, he was married, at fourteen, to Catherine de Medici, fourteen as well—a typical affair of state, a forging of alliances between France and the papacy, with Pope Clement VII, Catherine's uncle, himself performing the ceremony. Tradition and the pope now demanded that the marriage be demonstrably consummated, else it risked annulment by one or the other of the contracting parties; there was also the matter of assuring a *legitimate* succession.

At dawn following the nuptial night, Pope Clement VII was at the bedside of the royal teenagers. Unconvinced of the consummation, he delayed his departure for three weeks, finally leaving, still unsatisfied, to die ten months afterward—thus rendering the marriage alliance meaningless and Catherine de Medici innocently ridiculous. For years the French court would scornfully refer to her as *la marchande,* the merchant—were not the Medicis a family of bankers and merchants?—who had been placed with duplicity dangerously close to the French crown. Soon eclipsed by Diane, already the mythical moon goddess, the young Florentine resigned herself to that fate, too—wisely, as it developed, since it would endure for almost three decades—the French *ménage à trois* of husband, mistress, and humiliated wife.

The Renaissance is romantic largely in retrospect. In fact it was a brutal, cynical period. Catholic Francis I supported the Protestants against the papacy, the Moslems against the army of fellow Christian Charles V, then participated in the slaughter of first the one, then the other, as suited his political purpose. Holy Roman Emperor Charles V, who ruled over Spain and Spanish America, Austria, Naples, Sicily, and the Netherlands, coldly massacred thirty thousand Moslems in 1535 and made slaves of twenty thousand more for distribution among Christian lands. The religious wars in France, lasting half of the sixteenth century, would ravage towns and villages and mutilate more churches and cathedrals, when Protestants smashed the "statues of popery," than the French Revolution. Diane, during Henry II's reign, athirst for respectability, was fiercely Catholic, the reactionary, "implacable enemy of the Protestants."[6] As mistress of the king, she would find them her greatest decriers, and she would dread their possible effect on the essentially pious Henry.

Returning to the younger Henry, the death of his brother Francis, although now making him heir to the crown, did not efface for Henry the impression of being the less-favored son. His marriage, moreover, continued to be childless. He was apparently afflicted by hypospadias (a congenital malformation of the urethra), rendering him psychologically impotent. Apparently, too, he was rescued from his impasse by Diane de Poitiers, who had the intelligence to transform her act into a perception on Henry's part of *his* having made a conquest. The evidence is in Diane's poem to Henry, written in her characteristically bold hand, the large, angular letters forming a field of lances on the paper. The tenderness remains in touching contrast.

> Verily, one beautiful morning Love
> Came to me, bearing a sweet little flower . . .
> For the flower, you see, was in reality
> A fresh, comely lad.
> Trembling, averting my eyes,
> "No," I said. "Do not be disappointed,"
> Replied Love, proffering a noble laurel.
> "Better I remained chaste," said I to him,
> "Than be queen." Thus shivering and trembling
> Did Diane surrender. Now please, Sir, recall
> The morning I am trying to recall for you.[7]

In letters half the size of Diane's, Henry II would pen his own courtly poems.

> Alas, dear God, how I regret
> The time wasted in youth;
> How often had I hoped
> To see Diane my mistress,
> But feared the goddess
> Would not condescend
> To him who had known
> Nor joy, nor pleasure, nor contentment
> 'Til the hour he determined
> To obey her ev'ry commandment.[8]

He pledged Diane his eternal love.

No vow was ever pledged a king
As eternal as my love for you,
My only queen,
Against all time and certain death.
No moat, no castle wall
Need protect my vow, nor fortress,
Whose lady, queen and mistress
You are, for 'tis for eternity.[9]

When he was off to a war or a tourney, Diane wrote him:

Adieu, my heart's delight!
Adieu, my master, my Lord,
Adieu, noble sword! . . .
Adieu, sweet, dove-like kisses!
Adieu, love's secret games!
Adieu, my heart's love!
Adieu, my sovereign joy![10]

Whether in battle or in joust, Henry wore Diane de Poitiers's black-and-white colors, adopting them as his own until his death. In public they were a decorous, dignified couple, sufficiently discreet for an Italian ambassador to report, ten years after they had become lovers, that their relationship was platonic. Decorum, however, did not interfere with Henry's expected behavior as a future king. (The Frenchman, Montesquieu has remarked, does not take pride in constancy.)

Scarcely dauphin, Henry had an affair with a young Italian beauty named Filippa Duc, begot a child by her, and gave it Diane's name. Filippa would not be Henry's only transient paramour, but each time he would be neatly recuperated by Diane. Meanwhile childless Queen Catherine de Medici consulted the stars, drank foul concoctions guaranteeing fertility, and avoided riding (sterile) mules. Diane was as concerned as she: if the queen were repudiated and another wife taken, the new wife might not be as nearly complaisant about Diane in Henry's life. Thus, frequently, from her own bed, Diane would send Henry to Catherine's. Finally, in 1544, Henry had the legitimate son he sought; eight more children followed within eleven years. And each child was formally presented to Diane, each put under her charge: she chose their nurses, doctors, tutors, or governesses. During this time, on March 31, 1547, Francis I died, and Henry succeeded him as king.

Though queen with a retinue of her own, Catherine de Medici remained in the shadow of the royal mistress. But she continued to bide her time and sagely intrigued with Diane de Poitiers to keep the king at least to the two of them, as courtiers seeking advancement pushed their wives toward the royal bed. Having recognized mistresses and favorites was nothing new for a king of France, but what was "striking and stunning" in the court of Henry II "was the regulation of this 'disorder' in the royal household, the long-bearing sufferance of the outraged wife, the bland acceptance of official adultery by courtiers and public alike."[11]

King, queen, and mistress lived and traveled together. The towns they visited would erect great triumphal arches, decorated with the interlaced letters *H* and *D,* through which the *three* would ceremoniously ride. If she could not be queen, Diane resolved to be the power behind the throne, guiding the king adroitly in the period's deadly game of politics. She was as noble in origin as Henry, she would remind him, eminently qualified to have been his legitimate wife, had fate arranged otherwise. Diane was de facto prime minister of the regime; she was accepted as such by members of the court, whether they were for or—more discreetly—against her.

A Renaissance fashion is particularly revealing. Aristocratic women shaved their upper foreheads to achieve "a much sought after philosophical"—commanding?—"air"[12]—and one thinks of the portraits of Diane de Poitiers or of Queen Elizabeth. Intelligence, *savoir-faire,* imperiousness, and a magisterial maternalism undoubtedly bound Henry II to a twenty-year-older Diane de Poitiers, and would hold him for twenty-five years. But it would be mistaken to say they were the sole qualities.

Presumably the queen, too, wondered what held Henry so tightly to an aging woman, since he held *her* at a distance. Accordingly, if one can credit a piquant scene described by Brantôme, Catherine de Medici had several holes pierced in the ceiling above Diane's bedroom and observed with a friend what took place below.

> They saw a very beautiful, white, delicate, and fresh woman, half naked, half clad in a chemise, caressing her lover with a panoply of delicious follies, which he reciprocated, until they rolled from the bed to the floor, still in their chemises, and pursued their love play on the thick carpet, thus avoiding the heat of the bed.

Seeing this, Catherine wept, complained, then consoled herself, transforming the spectacle into a joke "and perhaps something else."[13] What else, Brantôme sayeth not.

Diane de Poitiers's effigy stamped her age, its poetry, statuary, painting, even its architecture. Her slim, athletic figure, her smooth, masklike face are still the symbol of the French Renaissance. One feels her presence in the gallery of the château of Fontainebleau, in the stony supports of Chenonceaux that step archly across the river Cher, and everywhere in the period's masterpiece, the château of Anet. She could not have been as striking, as lissome, as Jean Goujon's marble Dianes, but she succeeded in wrapping her age—except for her rivals at court and the Protestants at large—in her myth (she herself looking on coldly) as securely as she did the king.

Immersed in medieval romances, Henry II fancied himself as one of their chivalric heroes, Amadis de Gaule, and Diane as his "far away princess," the beautiful lady of the idylls. Together they read the romances, repeatedly the popular novel *Amadis de Gaule,* whose last two volumes were dedicated to Diane. Together the pair established a style that still held the French imagination a century later, as evidenced in Madame de La Fayette's *La Princesse de Clèves:*

> Never had France known such magnificence and gallantry as in the last years of Henry II's reign. He himself was a gallant, well-made, princely lover. Though his passion for Diane de Poitiers was older than twenty years, it was no less intense or diminished in its signs. Excelling in all physical sports, he chose them as his favorite pastime. Each day witnessed hunting or tennis parties, ballets, horse races or like divertissements, and the colors and the monogram of Diane de Poitiers were each time flaunted. She herself appeared in garments only her grandchild could have worn.

The other side of the glittering coin was scathingly underlined, one day, by the neglected queen (whose remark still reverberates in France, stirring memories of powerful, backstage mistresses as recent as Premier Paul Reynaud's Madame de Portes, not necessarily the last of a line stemming from the Middle Ages). After a particularly trying setback due to Diane, Catherine de Medici had withdrawn to her apartments. Diane had come, perhaps to appease her, and found the queen plunged in the reading of a book.

"What are you reading, madame?" Diane de Poitiers asked.

"The history of this kingdom," said the queen, "and I find that from time to time, in every age, whores have directed the affairs of kings."[14]

The exchange signals the approaching end. The last years of Henry II's reign were increasingly troubled, though he retained his juvenile confidence in Diane. Until the end, too, he took refuge in her company, preferably at the château of Anet, with its splendid park, groves, pavilions, and romantic paths, its royal kennels and cages for hounds, falcons, and leopards. Anet was by choice their enchanted abode, with Diane ensuring the enchantment (boredom was ever the royal nemesis: a king's mistress was perforce the king's entertainer).

The end itself was so fitting it would be condemned in fiction as too contrived. In 1555, in a since-famous quatrain among other rhymed prophecies, Nostradamus foresaw "a young lion overcoming an older in a singular duel on a field of battle, putting out his eyes in a golden cage so that he dies a cruel death." Three years earlier the royal astrologer had warned the king to avoid all knightly combat, especially in his forty-first year. Striking the Amadis pose expected of him, if indeed it was a pose, Henry had replied that he *wanted* to die at the hand of "any brave and valiant man," so that his death would be a glorious one.[15]

On June 28, 1559, Henry II, age forty, would not be dissuaded from participating in a tourney held in the environs of Paris's Place des Vosges. Conspicuous among the combatants, the king, as always, wore the black-and-white colors of Diane de Poitiers. For two days he fought and triumphed, mounted—it defies credibility—on a stallion named *le Malheur* ("Misfortune"). Looking down on the same field where the young Henry had first dipped his standard to her twenty-nine years before, Diane sat alongside three queens—of France, Scotland, and Spain—high in the tribune erected for the tourney.

On June thirtieth the king successfully tilted his lance against the Duke of Savoy, then unhorsed the Duke of Guise. It was five o'clock in the afternoon. The heat was stifling. Henry was visibly tired. But he insisted on one more run against the captain of his Scotch Guard, Gabriel of Montmorency. The queen sent a message, imploring Henry not to undertake the combat "for love of her." The king replied that he would break a lance precisely "for love of her."

The trumpets sounded. The two knights charged toward each other, lowering their lances as they spurred their horses. Each broke a lance against the other's shield, but each kept his seat. The king was brought a new lance. Montmorency, for reason unknown, chose to retain the one he had just used. Once again the trumpets sounded; once again they raced toward each other and clashed. But this time Montmorency's splintered lance slipped under the king's carelessly closed visor, penetrating the king's eye with such force that it emerged at the temple.

"I am dead!" Henry cried as he slumped and fell.

In ten days he was indeed dead, but during those ten days Diane de

Poitiers was kept from his bedside. On the eighth day Catherine had sent for the crown jewels given Diane by the king. On the tenth day, all hope lost, Diane returned the jewels and asked the queen's pardon for any injury done her. Banished from court, Diane retired to her estates, grateful for having had her life spared.

Six months before she died, at the age of sixty-six, Brantôme had met her and marveled: Diane de Poitiers was still beautiful. Every morning, she told him, she drank a broth composed of melted gold and mysterious alchemists' drugs. "Had she lived to be a hundred," he wrote, "she would not have aged. What a pity that earth should be heaped over such beautiful bodies!"[16]

Dignity intact, Diane de Poitiers never complained, though her former friends had abandoned her. She administered her lands and remaining fortune as she had administered France—now ruled, strongly and well, by the widowed queen.

Diane's death came quite suddenly, quite inexplicably.

· II ·

FRANÇOISE de La Chassaigne was twenty, Michel de Montaigne thirty-two, when they were married, in the fall of 1565. She brought him the largest dowry (7,000 livres tournois) of any woman entering the Eyquem de Montaigne family. They had six children, all of them girls, all except one (Léonor) dying within months of their birth. They were married twenty-seven years.

After twenty years of wedlock, Montaigne wrote: "A good marriage consists of a blind wife and a deaf husband."[17] That is, she does not see what he does; he does not hear what she says—a zero sum of communication, unless conflict can be called a kind of dialogue. For Montaigne, to put it bleakly, marriage was a battlefield in the war between the sexes.[18] If his was not the first declaration of that war, it was nonetheless one of the first clear statements of it:

> Wives naturally have an inclination for disagreeing with their husbands. They seize with both hands every pretext to go counter to them. . . . No action of theirs seems to them to have sufficient dignity if it comes by way of their husband's concession. They have to usurp it either by cunning or by insolence and always injuriously, to give it grace and authority. . . . As Cato the Elder said in his time, so many valets, so many enemies . . . and we might say in ours, wife, son, and valet, enemies all.[19]

The enemies, however, were not all worthy; the combat was between unequals, the naturally superior and the naturally subordinate, whose revolt consequently is "insolence." In Montaigne, one of the most advanced humanists of the Renaissance, we find ourselves with disturbing regularity back in the Middle Ages. It is a paradox observed a century and a half before him by Christine de Pisan. Idly she had picked up a book as a relief from her studies and read the usual attack on women. She put it aside and wondered, she tells us, how the wisest and most educated of men could assert, with no more proof than their own general agreement, that women were not only inferior by nature to men, but naturally evil and a sore trial for them.[20] Two centuries later Marie de Gournay, Montaigne's adoptive daughter, would lament the persisting view that there was "not one human race but two."[21]

Montaigne was a revolutionary thinker who rethought the relationship of the individual—that is, man—to authority but defended the principle of absolute monarchy. By word and example he preached self-study, self-reliance (before Emerson), and the happy acceptance of one's self, yet embraced Church doctrine on faith. Extending skeptical inquiry and doubt to the point that his *Essays* would reinforce freethinkers and be placed on the Vatican's Index of Prohibited Books, he sounds again and again, on the subject of women, as if he were an early Church father.

Nevertheless it cannot be said that Montaigne has been all things to all men. The accent of posterity, including women readers from Marie de Gournay to George Sand and Virginia Woolf, has fallen steadily on the first part of the paradox. We now recognize a familiar gulf between what he had been socially and culturally prepared to reproduce and what he would intellectually project, a demonstration of the lingering past in an emerging future. But there is more to discover in his life and writings than Montaigne's cultural lag. There are also—there is no better expression—his personal hang-ups.

Had he had his own way, Montaigne says, he would have remained single: he would not have married "wisdom herself," if she had wanted him. He was borne to it, "ill-prepared and contrary," by a "third hand," his father's.[22] He was, moreover, still plunged in grief for his beloved friend, Étienne de La Boëtie, who had died two years before.

One marries, he felt, out of custom and to found a family. So it was, thus it should be, a tradition unchanged. Montaigne's own ancestors were bourgeois merchants. They established the fortune he would enjoy as lord of Montaigne, a château and estate thirty miles west of Bordeaux, bought with its noble title by his great-grandfather Raymond Eyquem. Michel de Montaigne would drop the name Eyquem, possibly as too middle class; and, possibly for the same hidden reason, he would overpraise aristocratic virtues: courage over culture, Sparta over Athens, and, unlike Abelard, horsemanship over and against logic. Abelard, in contrast to Montaigne, was secure in his nobility.

Montaigne's security, on the other hand, was in the palpable ease of unearned wealth, the product of his ancestors' shrewdness in an expanding Bordeaux trade of wine, salt fish, and woad. His father was the first of the Eyquem de Montaigne family to take up the nobleman's true profession of arms. He had, at the same time, a veritable reverence for men of learning, Montaigne says disapprovingly, and raised his son Michel accordingly.

Montaigne wrote often and warmly of his father; he mentioned his mother exactly twice. It may have been because she was still alive when he wrote his *Essays.* Another reason might be that she came originally from a family of converted Spanish Jews who had settled in Bordeaux. A third motive might be her disputing mastery of the household after the death of Montaigne's father, toward whom, in fact, she showed considerable coolness, asking in her will that she be buried elsewhere than beside him.

To the later friction with his mother must be added a more important fact—his mother meant little or nothing to Montaigne in his infancy and early childhood. During these formative years, when the mother is normally the first person loved and a model for later love relations, he did not experience the embrace and warmth of his mother's love. Significantly, in his mature fifties, Montaigne would express his *thankfulness* for it!

> If I had had male children, I would have wished them my good fortune. The worthy father God had given me . . . sent me from the cradle to be nursed in a poor village of his, and there kept me so long as I was nursing, and even longer than that.[23]

His later lack of warmth for wife, children, and women in general seems to have found at least a partial explanation: as a child he had known only his father's attention and concern.

Brought home, possibly at the age of four, Montaigne was raised "by reason" and by paternal decision spared the rod. Each morning he was awakened by music, since his father did not want him "rudely snatched from sleep." Latin was his mother tongue, shaping his future lapidary style. From infancy he was taught no other; at six he was taught French. His mother and the servants had to accommodate themselves to his father's wish and instructions, learning a rudimentary Latin in order to respond to the child's speech. When he went to school, it was with a retinue of tutor and valet, who carried his books and papers. Schooling was conventional; at the university it involved the study of law. When he was in his early twenties, he was bought the post of magistrate in the Bordeaux Parlement, a body whose role was judicial, not legislative.

Here, in his mid-twenties, Montaigne met a fellow official, Étienne de La Boëtie, forming the most enduring bond of his life, though his friend would die only four or five years after their meeting.[24] Until then, he had known passion only once, and for a woman, in his early youth. "That served me as a lesson. . . . It is madness to fix all thoughts upon it and to become involved in a furious and imprudent passion."[25] He vowed self-control thereafter. He would be master of himself in every sense, disparaging sexual relations as "nothing but the pleasure of emptying one's vessels."[26] Love was slavery to another. Friendship, which only men could experience, as he and La Boëtie, was something else. The first was a "reckless and unconstant fire of fever," the second a "quiet, constant warmth."[27] *Love is no longer ennobling, but, rather, diminishing.* Courtly love has been dealt a wounding, if not quite deadly, blow.

Physically Michel de Montaigne, when he met La Boëtie, was of sturdy build, full face, soft eyes, small ears and mouth, trim beard, and sensibly conscious of his shortness—wherefore his lifelong preference for riding horseback, which makes all men (almost) equal. Etienne de La Boëtie was older by two years and four months but from the beginning conducted himself vis-à-vis his new friend in a much older, fatherly manner. He was ugly in appearance; yet, though Montaigne highly prized beauty, he was already disposed in La Boëtie's favor:

> We sought each other before we saw each other, because of the reports we had heard of each other, which had more effect on our affection than such reports reasonably have; I think it was by some ordinance of heaven. We embraced each other by our names. And at our first meeting, which was by chance at a great festival and gathering of the city, we found ourselves so taken, so acquainted, so bound to each other, that nothing thereafter was so close to us as each other.[28]

Testifying to a similar sentiment, La Boëtie wrote to Montaigne that their names would be forever coupled by their descendants as among the world's famous friends.[29] They called each other "brother." Like Montaigne, La Boëtie was grateful for his upbringing, his liberal education—thanks, in his case, to his uncle, who replaced his dead father. He was a more settled man than Montaigne, having married a widow with two children several years before and seemingly content with the marriage. He had previously written conventional love poetry. His remarkable work as a writer dated from his youth, *Contr'Un ("Anti-One"),* so relevant to our own times that it was republished in America, during the Second World War, as *Anti-Dictator.*

Montaigne's admiration led him readily to accept La Boëtie's counsel of moderation and restraint of his still-youthful exuberance.[30] Perhaps more accurately, he permitted himself to be gently pushed in the direction toward which he was already inclined. The two became inseparable, indistinguishable, in Montaigne's words. At lyric length he describes in his essay "On Friendship" the one perfect relationship he had experienced in his life, of such rarity that it occurs at most once in three centuries. "In the friendship I speak of, our souls mingle and merge with each other so completely that the seam which joined them is effaced and can no longer be found."

Immediately added is the passage memorized by all French students: "If you press me to say why I loved him, I feel that this cannot be expressed, save by replying: Because it was he, because it was I *(Parce que c'était lui, parce que c'était moi).*"[31]

The intensity of the feeling is incontestable. As an *explanation* of their friendship the last phrase is meaningless, except, as André Gide has commented, "when it comes to [explaining] love."[32] Oddly for one so personally aware of it (or perhaps because of that), Gide does not otherwise touch on the possibility of homosexual love in the passionate friendship of Montaigne and La Boëtie, even if unconsciously suppressed. Since La Boëtie's death—Montaigne would mourn six years *after* his marriage to Françoise—life had lost all its savor; it was naught but a "dark and dreary night. . . . And the very pleasures that are offered to me, instead of consoling me, redouble my grief in having lost him. We were halves of everything. . . . I was so remade, so accustomed to being everywhere a second self, that only half of me now seems alive."[33]

No pleasure had had more savor for him than the communication, "complete and perfect," he had had with his beloved friend.[34] Its like he never hoped to find with any other person, for the like of La Boëtie would not occur again. It was his loss that set Montaigne to writing the essays in which he communes with himself, later acknowledging the irony of confiding in a book for the public much of what he could not communicate to anyone close to him, since his friend was dead. "Will enough ever be said of the pricelessness of friendship, how different a thing it is from marriage?" he asked rhetorically.[35] And although marriage should aspire to the condition of friendship, he also wrote, "immoderate friendship for one's wife is a danger," since it overburdens marriage, which should be based on "reason" and "moderation."[36]

As a "diversion" from his grief at La Boëtie's death, Montaigne tells us, he "contrived" a love affair.[37] Two years later, at the age of thirty-two, he resigned himself to an arranged marriage.

Twelve years younger, fresh, buxom, and lusty, Françoise de La Chassaigne, too, was a descendant of distinguished precursors; more so, indeed, than Montaigne—both her father and grandfather had been presidents of the Bordeaux Parlement. But, unlike Montaigne, she had typically *not* been educated to take their place. She had been trained for domesticity—to become Montaigne's, or a socially equivalent gentleman's, wife. (Montaigne: "The most useful and honorable science and occupation of a woman is the science of housekeeping."[38]) She had spent her youth—contrast it with Diane de Poitiers's—learning cookery and needlework. (Montaigne: "A woman knows enough if she knows the difference between her husband's shirt and his doublet."[39]) At twenty she could know little of life, and had been expressly raised to that end. Knowing more than needlework and experienced in life, she might become a "talkative," disputatious wife. Thus, by common consent, the preference of parents—as of Montaigne's father choosing his son's wife—fell on youth. "A girl would accept more willingly the instructions of her husband and . . . be more adaptable." As for communication—conversation and comradeship—with her future husband, for the Renaissance, as for the Middle Ages, the art of speech for a well-brought-up lady of the middle class was reduced to "one simple rule: Silence."[40]

Such were Montaigne's expectations. Other than social, what were Françoise's? More to the point, what did she find? Frustration.

Her husband's successor in the Bordeaux Parlement and one of his best friends, Florimond de Raemond, wrote the following in the margin of his copy of the *Essays,* opposite Montaigne's advice to husbands that they be "moderate" in their lovemaking:[41]

> Often have I heard the author say that although he was still full of love, ardor, and youth when he had married his very beautiful and lovable wife, yet he had never played with her except with respect for the honor that the marriage bed requires, without once having seen anything but her hands and face uncovered, and not even her breast, although with other women he was extremely

frisky and debauched. I refer the truth of what I say about this to his conscience.[42]

The astonishment of Montaigne's friend is evident: he swears to its truth. Clearly Montaigne's prudish behavior went even beyond what was expected of contemporary husbands, from whom little enough was expected. They were warned by Renaissance moralists "that the girl who came to the marriage bed a virgin in body and mind might become debauched by the excesses and lack of modesty of her own husband," that the husband "who inflames his wife is to blame if afterwards she admits a lover." Some moralists advised eliminating all pleasure from the marital act, going so far as "to recommend methods that insure the least possible satisfaction to the wife."[43]

Whether one should or should not expect the exceptional from exceptional men, such as Montaigne, we do. In this instance, moreover, we are more justified, not only by his friend Florimond de Raemond's reaction to his confidences, but by the writings of several contemporaries. "Such moral advisers as Vives, Tasso and Bouchet," continues Renaissance expert Ruth Kelso, "more humane in their attitude toward women, though advising restraint, left room for unhampered, mutual pleasure as one of the great arguments for married life."[44]

Sexual love in marriage, for Montaigne, was "a kind of incest." He prided himself on his self-control (we might speak of a possible low libido or repressed homosexuality): he could lie next to "a long desired mistress" and restrain himself "without great difficulty" to "kisses and simple touching." He liked to sleep alone *"sans femme"*—"without woman" (or "wife"). He condemned *"ces mouvements indiscrets et insolents"*—"those insolent, uninhibited movements"—"that women invent, reducing themselves to the example and practice of animals."[45] ("Ladies don't move," Lord Acton would remark four centuries later, at the trial of *Lady Chatterley's Lover.* Nor, until very recently, have the attitudes of a gentleman.)

"Let wives learn shamelessness from another hand," said Montaigne. "They are sufficiently aroused for our need. In this I have never observed anything but nature's simple instructions."[46] It was opposite these lines that Florimond de Raemond had penned his marginal note. It is doubtful that Françoise de Montaigne had read them in her husband's lifetime. Needless to say she had had a more direct experience of her husband's following "nature's simple instructions"—and may well have sought "another hand." "I know a hundred honest men who have been cuckolded," Montaigne would write. He deservedly may have been among them.[47]

A curious legal document, dated less than four years after Montaigne's marriage, states that he had found a gold chain in his wife's jewel box, left there by his late brother Arnaud. The chain was subsequently claimed by his mother and formally "returned" to her before other members of the Montaigne family, the act duly registered by "Dumas, royal notary," on May 23, 1569.[48] (The rights of Frenchwomen were won very tardily. Not until 1944 were they allowed to vote; not until 1965 were French wives authorized to open their own checking accounts without first having the permission of their husbands.)

Obviously Montaigne, with the implied right of a husband to do so, had searched for *something* in his wife's coffer, and that a jewel. Shortly before, his younger brother had been fatally struck in the temple by a hard tennis ball, dying at twenty-eight. Speculation begins from these two facts.[49] Besides being young, it goes, Arnaud was a handsome captain, who had made himself available to the "very beautiful and lovable" but frustrated bride of his sexually squeamish older brother. In fine Renaissance style, he frequently adorned himself with the gold chain that mysteriously disappeared at his death. As disposer of his younger brother's property, Montaigne looked for it, became suspicious, and confirmed his suspicions by finding the chain in his young wife's jewel box. Confronted, confused, Françoise went to her mother-in-law in search of feminine solidarity, despite their own disagreements about running the household, and found it. Madame de Montaigne came forward to claim ownership of the gold chain, telling Montaigne she had loaned it to his brother and confided it afterward to her daughter-in-law, and now wanted it restored. All parties then went to a notary to witness the transaction, thus saving three faces—Montaigne's, his lately departed brother's, and his young wife's.

What lesson Françoise might have drawn we do not know. Montaigne, for his part, would write:

> Curiosity is everywhere vicious, but it is pernicious here [in cases of suspected infidelity]. It is folly to look into a disease for which there is no medicine that does not aggravate it and make it worse, of which the shame grows still greater and more public, thanks principally to jealousy, and of which the revenge wounds our children more than it heals us.

It is here that Montaigne speaks of knowing "a hundred honest men who have been cuckolded, honorably and not very indecently," and adds: "Each of you has cuckolded someone . . . it has now passed into custom. . . . The bitters as well as the sweets of marriage are kept secret by the wise."[50]

In his thirty-eighth year Montaigne resigned from the Bordeaux Parlement, and soon retreated to a tower of his château to meditate and to write. It was a retreat from a crumbling feudal society, from the wretched religious wars pitting Protestants against Catholics in bloody defeat, but Montaigne understandably thought of it in more personal terms. The black mood following the loss of his beloved friend, "the grief of that solitude," first made him dream of writing.[51] But it accompanied an accelerated quest for privacy and the desired end of peace best found in self-sufficiency. "For good or ill we depend on ourselves alone."[52] "The greatest thing in the world is to know how to belong to oneself."[53]

This persistent theme has given Montaigne meaning beyond his own story and time, so long as there is the problem of the individual and society, the individual and the family; indeed, the individual and the couple. Montaigne himself, however, was not beyond his own story, his own privileged situation.

> One must, if one can [he wrote], have wives, children, possessions, and above all health, but not to be so attached to them that our happiness depends upon them. We must reserve a back shop that is all our own, completely free, in which we establish our true freedom, our principal retreat, and solitude. Here we must conduct the everyday dialogue of ourselves with ourselves, so private that no external contact or communication disturbs it. Here we must talk and laugh as if without wife, without children, without retinue and valets, so that when the time comes to lose them, it will not be new to us to do without them.[54]

Montaigne's "back shop" was a study lined with a thousand books in a tower of the château that looked out in three directions: "on my household . . . my garden, my barnyard, my courtyard, and into most parts of my house." On the first floor of the tower was "my chapel," on the second, a bedroom suite, "where I often sleep so I can be alone," on the third, the study.

> There in my library I spend most of the days of my life and most of the hours of the day. . . . There is my headquarters. I try to make my dominion over it absolute, and seclude this one corner from all society, conjugal, filial, and civil . . . Wretched the man, to my mind, who has not in his home a place of his own, to pay court to

> himself, to hide! . . . I find it appreciably more supportable to be always alone than never to be able to be alone.[55]

Housekeeping was a wife's concern. The "domestic thorns," the "trivial pinpricks" through which life leaked away, wore *him* down, said Montaigne. Unfortunately Madame de Montaigne, he complains, seems to have felt the same way: she was not the most devoted and economical of housekeepers. He could scarcely wait until he had a son-in-law "in whose hands I could place full sovereignty in the management and use of my possessions." That way he would have the means and feel freer to make long voyages, another form of escape from domesticity.

> We have not struck a bargain, in marrying, to keep constantly tied to each other by the tail, like some little animals we see, or like the bewitched characters of Karenty, in a doglike fashion. And a wife should not have her eyes fixed so gluttonously on the front of her husband that she cannot, if need be, see his back.[56]

Perhaps the trips were also a flight, judging from the language used, from what Montaigne considered his wife's excessive sexual demands.

Six children, as mentioned, were born to the Montaignes, only one girl surviving infancy. On this he has remarked curiously: "I cannot, without effort . . . make a child save before sleeping, or make one standing up."[57] And somewhat callously: "I have lost two or three while they were still nursing, if not without sadness [*regret*], then at least without grief."[58] Elsewhere he has written that he would rather have produced a perfect book "through intimacy with the muses" than a child "through intimacy with my wife."[59] We cannot know what his wife felt. The nineteen letters written in her seventies (she died at eighty-two) are the only direct communication she left, and they are properly decorous, devotional, and pious, as befits letters to one's spiritual adviser.

The surviving daughter, Léonor, was entrusted to her mother by Montaigne, but with misgivings. He believed that girls must be educated by their mothers, but at the same time considered women bad educators: their "animal" maternalism warped their judgment.[60] He detested infants and did not "willingly suffer" their being raised near him: why, he protested, were they not brought up "naturally," as himself?[61] He would have preferred a boy child, but he never thought that a man's being childless made him less complete or less contented. Nor a woman? Montaigne never considered that question. At most he regarded women, his wife and daughter, with "indulgent contempt."[62]

The response, one might say revolt, of Madame de Montaigne was expressed obliquely in bitterness and acridity, in sustaining an anger "unreasonably" beyond its immediate cause, one reads in and between Montaigne's lines of complaint. However, such is the saving grace of his intelligence that he is capable of almost surmounting his own condition—on the fairly rare occasions when he focuses on society rather than singularly on himself.

> Women [he once wrote] are not at all wrong when they refuse the rules of life imposed upon the world, particularly since they are made, without them, by men. There is naturally plotting and dispute between them and us. However tight the agreement we have with them, it is still a troubled and stormy one.

Further in the essay he continued with the same insight. From infancy women were trained for love: "their grace, their adornment, their knowledge, all their instruction concern only that goal"—a goal, we know, he disdained as degrading.[63] Had he lucidly drawn the conclusion that if men and women were to communicate as equals, as friends, they must be equally cultivated, equally exposed to the cultural conundrums of their time, he would have added the dimension lacking in his probing of the human condition. It was there all the time, but he missed it. He admired and praised *distant, noble* women—Catherine de Medici and Margaret of Valois, who read and responded to his *Essays;* Diane de Foix, the Countess of Gurson, to whom twenty poets had dedicated their work in the lingering courtly manner—but he did not see the essential difference between them and the women of his household, his wife and growing daughter. They had been schooled for the world, not trained for domestic service.

In fact, devoted to his own repose and peace of mind, Montaigne found this training "natural." Let women read poetry, if they insist—it's a harmless pleasure; let them dip into history—it has its uses; and let them learn just enough philosophy to endure "the roughness of a husband . . . and such things."[64] For men the Renaissance ideal was essentially pagan—self-development, expansion, and realization; for Montaigne Socrates was the greatest man who had ever lived. The ideal for women was essentially Christian—chastity, submission, and obedience; in a word, "housewifery." "No single condition set so clearly and inescapably the terms of woman's existence as the clamping down upon her of this single destiny."[65] The role of the bourgeois wife was sharply defined by Montaigne: she was the economizer of the household, thriftily managing and restricted to the interior space, while the husband ranged the rest of the world.

Too late for the one, too early for the other, Montaigne met Marie le Jars de Gournay four years before his death in 1592. He was fifty-five, and she was about twenty-two; she would be the outstanding feminist of the century that followed his. Marie de Gournay was one of the first rare Frenchwomen who became what they were so carefully trained not to be—intelligent, independent, controversial, the spiritual daughters of Christine de Pisan. Like her, Marie de Gournay would defy convention by remaining free of a man's support and pay her way by writing.

At the age of eighteen or nineteen Marie de Gournay had read Montaigne's early *Essays,* and in a sense she never recovered. She recognized her own self-examination and her search for herself, an elective affinity, a narcissism calling to narcissism. It would be all the more astonishing that she failed to remark the antifeminism, even in her young womanhood, were not Virginia Woolf to turn a similarly blind eye in her self-identity with Montaigne three and a half centuries later.

Her father had died when Marie was still a girl; her mother had instructed her in the approved domestic "arts." But Marie had dreamed of something else, taking as her models Marguerite of Navarre, Marguerite of Savoy, and Marie Stuart, who at the age of fourteen had recited a Latin prayer of her own composition before the entire French court. In stolen hours she taught herself Latin and later Greek, with some help, by comparing the original texts with their French translations. During the years at Gournay she fell upon the *Essays,* which thereafter became "her constant companion," and she now dreamed of meeting their author and becoming—dare she dream that?—*his* companion and friend, even replacing the mourned La Boëtie.[66]

Marie de Gournay returned to Paris, where she had been born, with her mother. There, in 1588, she heard that Montaigne had arrived in the capital on a mission to the French court—as well as to supervise a new edition of his writings. Just previously, in Gournay, Marie had been told that Montaigne had been killed on his way northward to Paris. Impulsively she sent him an impassioned letter, telling him of her admiration for his work, begging him for a meeting. "The very next day," she tells us, he came to thank her for her letter. Surely she was an uncommon young woman; witness her adulation of him.

Montaigne saw before him an intense intellectual of twenty-two, possibly as small as himself, probably to his relief; nicely built but not beautiful, eyes spaced widely apart above a pursed, wistful mouth. Their friendship, Marie felt, had been decreed by fate: they resembled each other as a daughter her father. Certainly the sympathy was instantaneous. Did Marie de Gournay, as they talked together, as the days and months of conversation passed, make Montaigne review his received ideas about women? One might speculate that, after meeting her, he added to Book 3 of his essays such second thoughts as, "Men and women are cast in the same mold: except for education and custom, the difference is not great"—and cited Plato as advocating that both men and women participate "in all studies, occupations, functions, and vocations, both warlike and peaceful, in his Republic."[67] The discovery was tardy; Montaigne made no radical changes in the passages to the contrary. One can assume he remained committed to them.

Upon learning that she had lost her father at the age of twelve, Montaigne offered Marie de Gournay the title of spiritual kinship, *fille d'alliance,* or adoptive daughter. Joyfully she accepted the appellation and used it all her life—Marie de Gournay, *fille d'alliance de Montaigne.* During Montaigne's nine months in Paris, the two saw each other frequently. When Marie and her mother returned to Gournay, in Picardy, Montaigne visited them there. They would walk and talk, and together they read Plutarch's *Accidents of Love.* Montaigne dictated passages of the later essays to Marie, and he made her his literary executor upon his death; she would dedicate her first published work to him. But a sudden tempestuous outburst on her part seems to have taken him by surprise. The frustration it demonstrates, however, should not surprise us.

"I have seen a girl," he marvels, "who, to prove the ardor of her promises and also her constancy, stabbed herself sharply four or five times with the pin she wore in her hair, so that she broke her skin and bled in earnest."[68] In her edition of the *Essays* after Montaigne's death, Marie de Gournay further identified, *pinpointed,* the girl in mind by adding the phrase, "in Picardy."

Montaigne, everything seems to indicate, simply could not have a physically satisfying relationship with a woman, no more at thirty-five than at the age of fifty-five—which was *not* that of an old man in the Renaissance. He liked, he even respected, Marie de Gournay, but he could not love her. Nonetheless he wrote a carefully wrought appreciation of her and pasted it in a margin of his copy of the *Essays:*

> I have taken pleasure in publicizing in several places the hope I have in Marie de Gournay le Jars, my *fille d'alliance,* whom I truly love as a daughter. If youth can give promise, this soul will someday be capable of the finest things. The judgment she made of the first *Essays,* she a woman, living in these times, and so young and

> alone in her corner of the world, and the goodwill she devoted to me, because of the esteem she held for me before ever she saw me, is a happening very worthy of consideration.[69]

After having met Marie de Gournay, after having called her his spiritual daughter and having made her his literary executor, Montaigne wrote *this* of his beloved La Boëtie: "I well know that I will not leave behind any sponsor remotely as affectionate and understanding of me as I of him. There is no one to whom I would willingly entrust myself completely for a portrait; he alone possessed my true image, and he took it with him."[70]

Hardly more than Madame de Montaigne did Marie de Gournay, despite her passionate desire, replace La Boëtie in the mind—heart or desire—of Montaigne.

4

JEALOUSY: MOLIERE AND ARMANDE

MOLIÈRE, who is the essence of the French comic spirit, wrote *Le Misanthrope*—a conundrum still waiting a solution. How comic can a playwright be who is accused by some contemporaries of having married his own daughter, or, at the least, the daughter of his mistress? Whether or not true in either case, is there not something ineluctably incestuous in the consciousness of a much older man, as in the much younger woman, when they bed? ("All love is incestuous," said Chateaubriand.) And was Molière the more noble, or the less jealous, for being aware of his growing jealousy, or simply more melancholic?

How serious is the business of comedy, and how monarchistic can a bourgeois's son be as the entertainer of the Sun King in an age when actors were excommunicated and had to repent and renounce their profession in order to be buried by the Church? Which of his almost three hundred fifty personages was the playwright, who, as an actor in his own company, performed twenty-four of the roles—fifteen as a bourgeois, seven as a valet—almost always as a cuckold?

So many questions, so many answers.

Molière was a complicity of contradictions, and there was nowhere better for him to confront, if not resolve, them than on the stage, where contradictions are characters who rub against one another at least until the evening's conclusion.

We participate in the paradoxes. We derive pleasure from tragedy, and not only from the tragicomic, which no one has satisfactorily explained, not even Aristotle or Sade. Our pleasure stems from the playwright's despair as the comedies of his life darken into tragedies and life itself draws to a close.

Molière might have chosen differently. He was born, in 1622, Jean-Baptiste Poquelin, child of a respectable, moderately well-off family of upholsterers and decorators. When Jean-Baptiste was nine, his father was appointed royal upholsterer of the king's chamber, a post with the title of squire, which he could leave to his son. The office had its privileges and emoluments: it offered status and few pains. As *valet de chambre tapissier ordinaire du roi,* one arranged the royal furniture with another royal official while living for three months of the year in the royal household and receiving 337 livres for the year. (One could buy a house with a large room and a loft, two doors, two windows, and a fireplace for about 20 livres, or francs.)

Jean-Baptiste was sent to the Jesuit *collège* of Clermont. For five years he studied Latin and philosophy, and took part in school ballets and theatricals, before going on to law studies. Somewhere along the line, he lost his religious faith. At twenty he seems to have traveled with the court of Louis XIII in his ailing father's stead as *tapissier ordinaire du roi.* He may have rejoined the red-haired, twenty-four-year-old actress Madeleine Béjart, whom he had met shortly before in Paris, where they almost certainly had become lovers. Simultaneously Jean-Baptiste had been infatuated with the theater and with its star performer; but she, with insignificant lapses, would remain the faithful one.

Madeleine Béjart was beautiful, as all who saw her on the stage have testified. More important, she was strong and intelligent, as her life proved. Oldest of a large family, she was an actress and independent at eighteen—as independent, that is, as a young actress of the time could be. She had bought a small house in the elegant Marais quarter of Paris for 4,000 livres, half of the sum her own, the other half borrowed—and guaranteed by her known protector, Esprit de Rémond, Comte de Modène. His story, too, reflects the period. He was then thirty, his wife was twenty years older, and they were both immensely rich. The count, when in Paris, lived in the splendid town house of the rakish Duke de Guise; the countess, generally alone, in a distant château, untroubled and untroubling. At twenty, Madeleine bore the count a child, which he acknowledged as his own. At the christening he presented his legitimate son, age seven, as godfather of the child; Madeleine's mother, Marie Hervé Béjart, acted as godmother. Such were the times.

Involved in a court plot that was discovered, the Count of Modène was obliged to leave Paris and Madeleine for the provinces. This may have been the moment when Molière, still law student Jean-Baptiste Poquelin and stagestruck, first met Madeleine Béjart, he an impressionable eighteen, she a mature twenty-two. He may have performed with her, but two years later she left for a troupe in the provinces, presumably to be closer to the count, though she was still intimate with Molière. Perhaps, too, Molière persuaded his father in 1642 to replace him in

Louis XIII's suite during the royal trip to the south, so that he might see Madeleine.

Thus, it is possible that in June 1642 Madeleine had been separately with her two lovers. The precision has importance: nine months later, in February 1643—though the month and even the year are controversial—Armande Béjart, Molière's future wife, was born.

The year given for Armande's birth varies from 1641 to 1643; one recent French biography blandly offers all three on three different pages.[1] No birth certificate has ever been found. An official document dated March 10, 1643, mentions "a small unbaptized child," who is assumed to be Armande, as one of the "minor children" of Marie Hervé Béjart—whose husband, Joseph, is recorded elsewhere as having died the previous September 1642.[2] In all succeeding documents, Armande is specified as Marie Hervé's daughter, never as Madeleine's, and so she was presented to society.

Oddly, Madeleine Béjart is also listed among the *enfants mineurs,* in the March 1643 factum, though she was then twenty-five years old, the age of one's majority. Moreover, on the death of her father, Joseph, she had capably taken over the Béjart household, which consisted of her widowed mother, Marie Hervé, her brothers, Joseph and Louis, several sisters, and now the infant Armande—all living together.

Together with Jean-Baptiste, who was ostensibly lodged elsewhere. Inseparable from the Béjarts, he was henceforth committed to the theater for the remainder of his life. Within months of Armande's birth he signed away his right as royal *tapissier* in favor of his brother, with his father's permission, and received 630 livres. He then formed the Illustre Théâtre with Madeleine, Joseph, and Geneviève Béjart. Madeleine, who was effectively joint director, alone had the prerogative of choosing her own role in any production. The Illustre Théâtre opened its doors; Jean-Baptiste Poquelin was forever more Molière (the choice of name is a mystery).

Twice the theater company failed; twice Molière was imprisoned for debt. Finally freed with his father's aid, he reorganized the Illustre Théâtre with the help of Madeleine, and for a dozen years would tour the provinces.

The provincial years are the vague, uncertain ones, as if written in the dust and on audience's faces. The first year, one notes, the Duke of Epernon, taken with Madeleine's acting and her charm, lent the troupe his patronage and protection. But the patronage was insufficient. It had to be supplemented by tours of Brittany, Gascony, and Languedoc. Actors joined and left the company, though more joined than left. Among the newcomers were Louis Béjart, Madeleine's youngest brother; Catherine Du Rosé, the future Mlle. de Brie, and her husband; Thérèse de Gorla, the future, more famous Mlle. Du Parc (she would be the mistress of Molière, Corneille, and Racine), and *her* husband. (*Madame* was reserved for royalty and noblewomen). There were twenty to twenty-five performers in the traveling Illustre Théâtre; almost all will be met again in Paris, on Molière's return to the capital.

They lived and voyaged together with the intimacy of a small circus. By horse, mule, and cart they made their way to Bordeaux, Toulouse, Narbonne, Lyons. At each stop they would transform a covered tennis court or fairground into a theater, and with each performance, as Shakespeare did, Molière learned the tricks and art of holding a rough audience without losing himself. He acted, directed, mimed, managed, and buffooned; comparatively late—at thirty-three—he wrote his first complete farce, *L'Etourdi (The Scatterbrain,* which need not detain us). In Languedoc the Prince of Conti, persuaded by his secretary, who fancied Mlle. Du Parc, undertook to support the troupe with his money and his name. But in a few brief years the prince was seized by a *crise de conscience* and withdrew his support; ten years later he would accuse Molière of leading a new school of atheism. Princeless now, Molière and company resumed touring the provinces.

These, too, were the years of Armande's growing up from childhood to disturbing adolescence, from Molière's lap to her appearance on the stage as Mlle. Menou, age twelve or thirteen, her breasts budding and promising, her eyes already cat-slanted and clever. Surely she was semiconsciously rivaling Madeleine, Du Parc, and de Brie for Molière's attention. As surely his interest had formed with her breasts; no man normally can be unaware of the first blossoming of an adolescent girl—one more forward, moreover, than most. Had she not grown up in the intimacy—let others say promiscuity or loose morality—of a traveling theater group, witnessing the casual communal life, the changing of bed companions, accepting—rather, experiencing—it all as natural? To see Molière in her childhood as surrogate father, then as older brother, and, irrepressibly, possible lover, the line is not impossible, or unreasonable, to draw. And the *galants,* the provincial rakes and aristocrats who came to the makeshift dressing rooms to ogle and pay court, not always unsuccessfully. Were not actresses the fairest of game? And were they not beholden to a Duke of Epernon or a Prince of Conti for the protection and patronage that spelled bread as well as jewels and even the right to perform? This was still the *ancien régime,* when the lord had the feudal right (however rarely exercised) of the first night with the newlywed peasant girl of his estate. Such was the atmosphere in which Armande grew up and matured.

Withal it was an exhilarating and happy time, if one accepts what a footloose freeloader by the name of Charles Coypeau d'Assoucy tells us. He had attached himself to Molière's company in the fall of 1655, when it was playing Lyons. He had accompanied the troupe to Avignon, then to Pézenas and Narbonne, and then no more. But he left an account in his *Mémoires:*

> As a man is never poor who has friends, so having Molière's esteem and the friendship of the Béjarts, I have never been richer or more content. For these generous people did not stop at helping me as a friend, they treated me like a relative . . . I cannot begin to tell of all that I received from everyone of the household . . . More generous than any brothers one might hope to have, they did not tire of me at their table all winter long.

D'Assoucy ate and drank and caroused with the "jolly company," and reminisces. "No matter what I did, I was one of them—at home. I never saw such bounty, such openness, such goodness as among these people. They were truly the princes they played daily on the stage."[3]

The Illustre Théâtre prospered as it gained in experience. In his mid-thirties, after twelve years of trouping in the provinces, Molière was ready to try Paris again—and never again would he appear on a provincial stage. From Rouen he discreetly prepared his return. After several prudent inquiries in the capital, he secured the patronage of Monsieur, the king's only brother. On July 12, 1658, Madeleine Béjart, temporarily staying with Molière's father, signed the lease for a Paris tennis court, intending it as a theater. But the presentation of the troupe by Monsieur to the king took place elsewhere—in the guardroom of the Louvre palace. It was here that Molière, thirty-six, met Louis XIV, twenty, for the first, fateful time; and it began as a failure.

Aspiring to tragedy, considered then, as now, the nobler form, Molière attempted Corneille's *Nicomède.* At its close, sensing the royal coolness, he stepped forward and asked permission, which was granted, to put on a little *divertissement* he had tried out in the provinces—a slight and eminently forgettable farce of his own, *Le Docteur amoureux.* Success! The following day young Louis XIV, future Sun King, had Molière's company installed in the Salle du Petit Bourbon, adjoining the Louvre.

Was anatomy Molière's destiny? It is not one of the least of the ironies. His genius and talent coincided with his appearance: it was not made for tragedy. He had a broad face with a broadly flaring nose, a widespread mouth, with more widely spaced eyes (is the touch of melancholy our own addition?), and heavy, "elevatable" eyebrows. Moreover, Voltaire tells us, he had a "kind of hiccup that unfitted him for serious roles," but which made "his comedy the more enjoyable."

The first hit at the Petit Bourbon was *L'Etourdi.* But the first play to suggest Molière's satiric depth was *Les Précieuses ridicules (The Ridiculous Exquisites),* perhaps the first comedy of manners. Until then the influential *précieuses* were held in respect and in some terror. Afterward, such was the play's devastating success, they were, and still are, viewed as reflected in Molière's distorting glass.

The two *précieuses* of Molière's satire, fresh from the country, protest being rushed into marriage before they are even courted. "Matrimony," says Madelon, performed by Madeleine Béjart, "should never be brought about until after other adventures. A lover, to be agreeable, must understand how to utter fine sentiments, to express the gentle, the tender, the passionate, and all according to the rules." Irreproachable, it would seem. But the rules of the game for Molière's *précieuses* include the parody of the courtly code, pushed to absurdity in Mlle. de Scudéry's popular romances, then further pushed to the extreme in Molière's play by Cathos, the second provincial *précieuse.* "For myself," she says, "marriage is a shocking thing! How can one endure even the thought of lying next to a man who is . . . who is . . . naked!"[4]

One can hear the surefire laughter. One joins it. Then one pauses, and reflects. What if Cathos were played by a child of twelve who had been raised in a convent and suddenly thrust upon the world and into an arranged marriage with a strange man four times her age? The *précieuses* had arisen in just this world, where such a child was commonly forced into a nightmarish wedlock with a man of fifty; and they revolted, in their fashion, with the only weapons they had—elegant, *distancing* language and elaborate obstacle courses for would-be lovers.

Henry IV's prime minister, the Duke of Sully, had married off his daughter Marguerite at the age of ten to the Duke of Rohan; she was a mother at eleven. Foremost of the *précieuses,* Catherine de Vivonne had been married at twelve; her daughters would avoid that fate strenuously, four of the five retreating to a convent, the fifth marrying at thirty-eight. Early in the seventeenth century, as the young Marquise de Rambouillet, Catherine had established her famous salon and *chambre bleue,* where she received and refined her notable guests, setting the civilized tone of half the century. By the 1650s not only the habitués of the blue room were *précieux* and *précieuses,* but "virtually every literate woman in France . . . princesses, duchesses, bourgeoises, provincial and Parisian women, prudes and coquettes . . . [sharing] a heroic restlessness."[5] They were the first collectively conscious feminists, advocating divorce, trial marriage finalized at the birth of the first child, contraception, even free love. By the end of the decade the movement declined; the roots were too shallow in the essentially hostile male ground. The original drive became a mannered gesture, flowery, frivolous—in a word, *too* precious; only the urge for equal education endured. Then, in 1659, Molière's *Précieuses ridicules* was performed.

Leaving the theater, one male frequenter of the Marquise de Rambouillet's blue room was heard to say: "Yesterday we admired all the absurdities that have been so delicately [!] and sensibly criticized; we must now burn what we have adored, and adore what we have burned."[6] Exquisitely the marquise, seventy-one, responded to Molière's play by inviting him to put it on for the special benefit of her blue room. She is said to have been amused. Mlle. de Scudéry was among Molière's admirers. Gallantly he made amends in a later preface by declaring that the mirror he had held up reflected their provincial imitators, not their friends. Between 1661 and 1666 he rarely performed the play; and thereafter, until his death, not at all. "*Les Précieuses,* in truth, despite its comic force, was already overtaken by the change in ideas and attitudes upon which it was based."[7] The most serious of the *précieuses* would reappear as the *femmes savantes,* and as subject of another Molière satire.

Meantime, the Petit Bourbon having been demolished to make room for an expanding Louvre, Molière and company performed at the Palais Royal. Again he tried tragedy, playing the jealous prince of his own *Don Garcie de Navarre.* (The theme of jealousy recurs as often as that of love in all his work.) And again he failed. *L'Ecole des Maris (School for Husbands),* or how to train young women to be the faithful wives of older men, quickly followed, with predictable success. It was the ideal public spectacle, but it was also, as so often, despite Molière's disclaimers, a private journal.

The personal is immediately apparent in the timing and circumstance. Two months before *School for Husbands* opened on June 24, 1661, Molière had requested an additional share of the company's receipts, "for himself and for his wife, should he marry."[8] It was gladly granted. Eight months later Armande became Mlle. Molière. The interim play is Molière as suitor and prospective husband, with all the promises that implies.

The play's Léonor and Isabelle are two orphaned sisters raised from childhood by their guardians, Ariste and Sganarelle, to be their respective wives. Sganarelle keeps a tight, jealous rein on Isabelle; Ariste a lighter, wiser one on Léonor. With characteristic irony and double play, Molière sets up a dialogue between himself as the "bad" Sganarelle, whom he enacts, and himself as the "good" Ariste, though performed by another actor of the company. He has *School for Husbands* end happily. Léonor, eighteen, almost the age of Armande, marries the gentle Ariste, her sixty-year-old guardian (did that make Molière feel twenty years younger rather than twenty years older?), and will presumably remain faithful and loving forever after.

Life for Molière will not be a comedy. . . . But now he is in the very springtime of love returned. Armande has indicated she might marry him; wherefore the request for the second share. His new play would be the occasion for not only recovering from the fiasco of *Don Garcie,* but impressing Armande with its wit as well as with its success, and would publicly reavow his promise to be a tolerant and understanding husband.

Early in the play, Léonor's maid, Lisette, sets the scene with a remark to Sganarelle: "Are we among Turks, that women be locked up?" She continues: "The safest thing for men is to trust us." If a husband treated *her* with distrust, she says, she'd "give him grounds for his suspicions!"

SGANARELLE (*to Ariste*): You see the results of *your* education!

ARISTE: Locks and bars do not make a woman virtuous. It is her heart you must win. We must cheerfully educate the young, as I have Léonor, giving her freedom, and the things she likes, jolly companions, *divertissements, bals, comédies,* ribbons, and lace. Though her father commanded her to marry me, I would not force her, and though our years are not evenly matched, perhaps great tenderness and consideration will compensate for it.

SGANARELLE: How will you prepare her for the change in her life when you marry her?

ARISTE: Why should it change?

SGANARELLE: What, after you marry, she'll be as free as before?

ARISTE: Why not?

SGANARELLE: Ribbons and lace?

ARISTE: Undoubtedly.

SGANARELLE: Balls and parties?

ARISTE: Most certainly.

SGANARELLE: Young men in the house?

ARISTE: So . . . ?

SGANARELLE: Who will revel and feast at your expense?

ARISTE: Why not?

SGANARELLE: And pay your wife compliments?

ARISTE: Good!

SGANARELLE: And you will turn a blind eye . . .

ARISTE: That is understood.

SGANARELLE: Be off! You are an old fool. *(To Isabelle)* And you be off too! I want you to hear no more of this.

ARISTE: I prefer trusting my wife and living as I have always lived.

SGANARELLE: And *I* will live to see you cuckolded!

ARISTE: I do not know my fate, but I do know *yours,* if you persist in your tyranny.

By the play's end, Sganarelle has lost Isabelle to a young man. "A woman locked up," he has learned, "is already half lost." Léonor and Ariste, on the other hand, are to marry on the morrow.[9]

And, on January 23, 1662, Molière and Armande Béjart signed their contract of marriage before Marie Hervé Béjart and two of her children, Madeleine and Louis, as witnesses. Armande brought a dowry of 10,000 livres, a tidy fortune, officially given her by her mother, Marie Hervé, but most likely the gift of her "sister" Madeleine. On February 20 the pair was married in the church of Saint-Germain l'Auxerrois facing the Louvre palace.

Armande was now Mademoiselle Molière. We would say Madame, but the "mademoiselle" of the period, applied to a married commoner and single woman alike, has since taken on an ironic, stinging twist. Was Armande always Mademoiselle, or Miss, Molière; that is, the daughter of Madeleine Béjart and her lover Molière? Of all the Molière mysteries, this is not the least.

Almost unanimously Molière's contemporaries thought Armande to be Madeleine's daughter; several, and not the most inconsequential, thought Molière to be Armande's father and their marriage, therefore, incestuous. What is there to any part of it?

The year following the marriage, Montfleury, leader of the rival theater at the Hôtel de Bourgogne, formally "prepared a brief against Molière and presented it to the king himself. He accuses him," Racine continues in his letter to Abbé Le Vasseur, at the end of November 1663, "of having married the daughter after having slept with the mother. But Montfleury has no audience at Court."[10]

There was no formal response from Louis XIV; nor was there a formal defense or suit by Molière.

In 1670, Le Boulanger de Chalussay, a self-declared enemy of Molière, was explicit where Montfleury was darkly insinuating. In his satirical pamphlet, titled *L'Elomire hypocondre,* which everyone rightly read as the anagram for *Molière, Hypochondriac,* Chalussay has his Molière remark that to ensure a faithful wife, it is not enough to raise her from childhood, but rather "to have formed her before birth, as [I have] done." In 1676, three years after Molière's death, in the course of a lawsuit between a courtier and composer Lully, the latter cited Molière's widow (Armande) as a witness in his behalf. The courtier promptly impeached Armande's credibility in a factum made public during the trial:

> Everyone knows that the birth of *la Molière* was obscure and indecent, that her mother is very uncertain, her father all too certain; that she is the daughter of her husband, wife of her father, and her marriage incestuous . . . in a word, the orphan of her husband, the widow of her father.[11]

Boileau, an unimpeachable friend of Molière, believed Armande to be Madeleine's daughter and knew that Madeleine had been Molière's mistress. Though not the last word in accuracy by any means, Grimarest, who was Molière's first biographer (1705) and one of whose sources was Michel Baron, an actor in Molière's company, steadily refers to Armande as Madeleine's daughter and strongly implies that common opinion of Molière's own time held him to be her father. Many historians since, including Michelet, continue to repeat him.

Should we?

The question of Molière's fatherhood of his own wife can only be answered by other questions; no unassailable evidence has been found to refute it.

Would Madeleine and her mother have condoned the marriage of Armande and Molière if he, and not Joseph Béjart or the Count of Modène, were the father? Not very likely. Would Louis XIV have agreed to act as godfather of Molière and Armande's firstborn child, christened Louis, if he had suspected Molière to be the father of the mother of the child? Scarcely possible. But he might well have consented if he had cause to believe Armande the daughter of Molière's former mistress, but with another as her father, such as the Count of Modène (who would himself marry the daughter of a former mistress and be godfather of the Molières' second child, a common custom for a grandparent). The king had his police; they had their sources. He was amoral, but he was not irreligious: incest, the most mortal of sins, was punishable by burning at the stake.

Finally, would Molière have married his own daughter and fathered her children? We cannot know. We know only that the stories taunted and perhaps haunted him with their insistence on incest. Although this theme never crept into his plays (as it does constantly, for instance, in Racine's contemporary plays), it could never have been far from his mind. One still says of a much older man and his bride, "He could be her *father!*" (of a woman, "She could be his *mother!*"). In Molière's case the accusation was direct.

The newlyweds installed themselves in a ménage of their own, separate from the Béjarts, but not far from them or the theater. How long did the honeymoon last? A few days, a few nights, according to Grimarest: "No sooner was [Armande] Mademoiselle de Molière than she thought she was a duchess."[12] The animosity shown is almost universal: Armande has no friends among the chroniclers (and she nowhere speaks for herself). That she should take normal pride at twenty in being the wife not simply of the *patron,* but of Molière, the brilliant actor-director of an ascending company of players, the favorite *comédien* and comic playwright of the king; in having won him away from the day's most celebrated actresses, de Brie, Du Parc, and Madeleine herself, seems insufficient—too dull. Armande must be made suddenly arrogant, and unfaithful. It may be accurate, but it is suspect. Much of it stems from a skimming of Molière's *Ecole des femmes (School for Wives),* which was performed ten months after the marriage—as if disenchantment and jealousy on Molière's part, if not love itself, had all occurred for the first time within those first months.

In fact, three years before, when Armande was no more than seventeen, Molière had talked to a friend and former schoolmate, Claude Chapelle, of his love for Armande and his ambitious plans for her future. Chapelle testifies to this in a letter written in the spring of 1659. He regrets, Chapelle writes, that he cannot join Molière in Paris, but he wishes him well, and inserts a poem to a young and tender "willow," Armande, whom Molière has promised to "raise to his own summit." He adds: "Show these lines to [Armande] only. They are the image of her and you." But Molière should certainly not show them to his "other women . . . your three great actresses"—Madeleine, de Brie, and Du Parc.[13]

However long Molière had loved Armande before their marriage, he had not been long in recognizing it, nor long thereafter in knowing jealousy. Armande as an adolescent was undoubtedly a coquette. Any nubile adolescent, given the circumstances and surroundings of a traveling troupe of players, with their hangers-on and admirers, would be. As for Molière, he repeatedly asserts that a man cannot love passionately without being jealous, though one can be nobly jealous, as Don Garcie is, rather than ignobly, like Sganarelle. "Not to be jealous," says Climène in *Les Fâcheux,* a play written less than a year before his marriage, "is to love coldly." To Orante, who pleads the case of an unjealous lover, Climène replies—and one can hear Molière:

If, to please you, a man should never be jealous,
Then I know several men ideal for you,
Men, who in love are so indulgent,
They feel no pain in seeing you in the arms
of a dozen others.[14]

I will be understanding, Molière is saying to Armande, ingénue of the play, but I cannot promise to be unsuffering.

In *School for Wives* he enacted Arnolphe with his usual grimaces for comic effect, but it is a role since performed as that of a *bouffon tragique.* Arnolphe, a *"barbon,"* or "old man," of forty-two, has deliberately raised Agnès, seventeen, from the age of four in complete ignorance to assure himself an innocent wife. He states it flatly in the opening scene:

In a small convent, removed from the world,
I had her raised as I wished;
That is, instructing the ways and means to be employed
To render her *idiote* to the greatest extent possible.
The Lord be thanked, success followed my expressed intent,
Now grown, she is the perfection of ignorance . . .
And will make me a perfect wife.

Arnolphe installs Agnès in a country house and sets a loutish pair to oversee her conduct and keep her from a corrupting world—that is, young men—while he arranges for their marriage.

The play is a comedy of character with a simple plot, background for Molière's musing about the infidelity of young, courted women and the jealousy of confused, older men who would marry them. For despite Arnolphe's precautions, Agnès meets and falls in love with young, handsome Horace, and they plan to run off together. Alerted, Arnolphe intervenes. Furious, he lifts his hand to strike his ward, then stops and reflects, appalled at what he feels: "How strange to be in love! That men should be subject to such weakness for such traitresses! . . . Their mind is wicked, their spirit is weak. Nothing is more feeble, more imbecilic, more unfaithful. And yet, for all that, we do everything for these animals in this world." At this point Agnès's long-lost father appears and exercises his paternal right: he gives her in marriage to the man of her choice, the *"beau blondin"* Horace—Molière's dénouements are not his most brilliant devices. A friend, Chrysalde, consoles Arnolphe by saying that in this way he can be really sure of not becoming what he fears most, a cuckolded husband.

Armande is clearly not the convent-bred Agnès, any more than Arnolphe is Molière. It is not to the situation, but rather in and between the lines, that one must look. Chrysalde's is the expression of the eminent common sense that is the mark of Molière. How, he asks Arnolphe, can a young woman know right from wrong, good from bad conduct, if she is raised in ignorance? Arnolphe's platitudes in response are designed for ridicule. If the sexes are two halves of society, he says, then "the one half is supreme and the other subordinate, completely submissive to the commanding half . . . Obedience, humility, docility, and profound respect are what a wife owes to her husband, her chief, her lord, and her master." A man is no less worthy, replies Chrysalde in a later scene, for being deceived by his wife; it is a roll of the dice, the chance one takes when one takes a wife. How much worse to be tied to a "dragon of virtue," a harridan of honesty! All in all, cuckoldry is what one makes of it.[15]

The play was an instant popular success, but the ribald double-ententdres and rough dialogue of *School for Wives* proved too much for many of the court and most of the Church. The Prince of Conti stormed against it; Bossuet condemned it from the royal pulpit; the Hôtel de Bourgogne troupe mocked its "vulgarities." Molière riposted with a stinging skit, *The Critique of the School for Wives,* in which he satirized his critics, especially posturing marquesses and countesses of the Court. Louis XIV, in the process of domesticating the aristocracy, showed his own appreciation by commanding a new play for performance at Versailles.

There Molière and his companions put on *L'Impromptu de Versailles,* wittily, mercilessly parodying the actors of the Hôtel de Bourgogne, Molière himself cuttingly mimicking the portly Montfleury. As part of the performance, there is a mock rehearsal with playful exchanges between Molière and a six-months-pregnant Armande, who are acting themselves. Molière feigns dissatisfaction with her performance.

MLLE. MOLIÈRE: You should write a comedy in which you are the only performer, then you would be content.

MOLIÈRE: Quiet, wife, you're being silly!

MLLE. MOLIÈRE: A thousand thanks, monsieur my husband. That is the way it is! Marriage certainly changes people. You would never have said that eighteen months ago . . . Upon my word, if *I* were to write a comedy, it would be to justify women for the things they are accused of, and I would make husbands tremble by contrasting their crudeness with the civilities of *les galants.*

The last is a remarkably *précieux* remark given Armande by Molière, and one might add another, delivered by Mlle. Du Parc to Molière's wife: "Good God, you are a strange person! You furiously want what you want!"

But perhaps what most touches one today is *L'Impromptu*'s *tristesse,* the sadness of the actor's and playwright's lot—to make jaded courtiers laugh, "who laugh only when they deign to," as Molière said from the Versailles stage; to write plays that must please the king, for whom "it is wiser to write badly, but in time, than too late; and if one is ashamed for having failed, one can always have the glory of having quickly met the royal command." Molière's response to personal attacks is especially moving, as he reacted to several playwrights who had put his private life on the stage, calling him the true-life model for the jealous cuckolds he portrayed. He stepped forward, in *L'Impromptu,* dropped his clowning posture, and replied:

> Let them take from my plays what they will . . . I gladly give them my work, my face, my gestures, my words, my tone of voice, my way of speaking, to do with what they will, if it profits them. I am not opposed to any of that and will be delighted if what they use makes people happy. But while giving them all this, I should like them to have the graciousness of leaving me the rest and not touch on such things as they do when, I am told, they attack me in their plays . . . and *that* is the only response they will have from me.[16]

The king's response was to grant Molière, in the midst of the row over *School for Wives,* an annual allowance of 1,000 livres. The following January, he danced, dressed as an Egyptian, in Molière's *Le Mariage forcé,* to music by Lully. And in February he godfathered the child of Molière and Armande, who would die before December. Intervening, however, was the famous seven-day fête at Versailles in 1664—*Les Plaisirs de l'Ile enchantée.*

Three years previously, twenty-two-year-old Louis XIV had been struck by the splendor of the new palace and park of his own Superintendant of Finances Nicolas Fouquet—whose magnificence would cost the brash official his post and almost his head. The young monarch determined on the spot to create his own dream castle and gardens at Versailles. Only a month before, Louise de La Baume Le Blanc, Demoiselle de La Vallière, seventeen, a silvery blonde with a low, sweet voice and a slight, appealing limp, had become the royal mistress. Versailles, Louis decreed, would be their setting. In May 1664, the spectacular gardens of Le Nôtre, but not yet the palace of Le Vau, were ready for the week-long festivities the king gave for Louise, though they were ostensibly for the queen and the queen mother. Molière was entrusted with organizing the theatricals.

On opening day, Louis XIV himself, dressed in Greek armor as the hero of Ariosto's epic *Orlando Furioso,* led on horseback a mounted procession of knights around the grand rondeau basin as the court and six hundred guests looked down from a specially constructed amphitheater. An afternoon's tilting at a ring at full gallop down the allée royale followed, initiated by a fine, admired run by Louis.

At nightfall a myriad of tree-hung chandeliers, each with twenty-four candles, and two hundred tapers, held by an equal number of men in masks, lighted the grand rondeau. Lully's violins played as the Seasons entered: Spring on a great Spanish stallion, Summer on an elephant, Autumn on a camel, Winter on a bear. Pan and Diana (Molière and young Armande) then appeared, reciting verses to the two queens, as their attendants offered meats and the court sat down to supper.

On the second night, Molière and his companions performed his festival play, *La Princesse d'Elide,* in an open-air bosky theater. Hurriedly written, the play would be easily forgotten were it not for Armande, the evening's princess. She appeared onstage for the first time since her pregnancy, revealing her available charms to the *galants* of the court. Their applause, her success, the soft spring nights, the royal example of the king and his mistress, the heady sensuality of the fête, the handy groves of Versailles—Armande was vulnerable and Molière was betrayed.

So critics and chroniclers of Molière's time have written.[17] What truth is there to it? *La Fameuse Comédienne,* an anonymous and infamous portrait of Armande, is most specific, citing the names of the supposed lovers during the Versailles celebration—Abbé de Richelieu (no less), the Count of Guiche, and the Count of Lauzun. In fact, the abbé was off to the war against the Turks in Hungary at the time of the fête; the Count of Guiche was then in exile in Poland; and the Count of Lauzun, a notable figure, is not listed among the guests. Written after Molière's death, *La Fameuse Comédienne* (1688) is at best history in anecdotal hindsight, with a filling in of fictional happenings. Yet . . . Grimarest, in his apparently sincere defense of Armande, oddly lends substance to her accusers' fantasies:

> It is indeed difficult for a beautiful, soignée actress to be so careful of her conduct that it is beyond criticism. Let an actress but accord what is due to a grand seigneur and there is no mercy: he is called her lover. Molière believed that the entire court, all Paris, yearned

> after his wife. She failed to disabuse him of it. To the contrary, the extraordinary pains she took to be attractive to everyone *but him,* as it seemed to Molière, since he asked for so little in that fashion, did naught but increase his jealousy. In vain he told his wife in what manner she should conduct herself so that they might live happily together. She paid no heed to his instructions, since she thought them too severe for a young person such as herself, who, moreover, had done nothing for which she might be reproached. And so Molière did his utmost, after suffering domestic chillinesses and quarrels, to shut himself in his work and the company of friends and not to concern himself overly with the conduct of his wife.[18]

Essentially posterity reproaches Armande for not giving Molière the peace and repose he presumably needed. The assumption, of course, is that such is the mission and destiny of all wives of genius. Perhaps, however, like the proverbial grain of sand and the pearl, Armande served Molière's genius, as well as herself, by being precisely herself; a wife as domestic servant and sexual tranquilizer may well have served both of them least. Peace and repose and emotional nirvana are not necessarily the goal of marriage for anyone for whom marriage is not the goal. May not Armande have been a stimulus needed though not always sought? Molière's most trying time with Armande, and the king and the Church, was the astonishing period of his masterpieces, *Tartuffe, Don Juan,* and *Le Misanthrope,* produced in three successive years.

Molière loved Armande, and wrote about the irrationality of love. The resignation masking as wisdom, the jealousy he recognized as ignoble and impossible to control in his private life, he put masterfully into his plays. "How could a man such as he," Chapelle is reported to have said to him, "who knows so well how to depict the weaknesses of others, himself succumb to a situation he mocks daily? And his friend made him see that the most ridiculous of all was to love someone who did not respond with the same tender affection he showed to her."[19] Ridiculous but inescapable.

Unlike Molière, Armande has no spokesman, no defender, unless it is Molière. A long conversation reproduced (from hearsay) by Grimarest suggests Molière's appreciation of their drama—that of an aging, ailing playwright with a young and attractive actress-wife who very understandably is not attracted by domestic "peace and repose." Molière is addressing his close friends Dr. Rohault and painter Mignard:

> "Yes," said Molière, "I am the most miserable of men, and I have only what I deserve. I did not think I was too austere for domesticity, and I thought my wife would subordinate her behavior to her virtue and my designs. In view of her situation, I feel now that she would be even more unhappy than I, if she had done so. She has vivacity, spirit, she is sensitive to the pleasure of making the most of them. Yet, despite myself, this offends me. I find fault, I complain. This woman, a hundred times more reasonable than I, wants to enjoy her life. She goes her way and, assured of her innocence, she does not listen to my precautions. I regard her negligence as disdain. I would like the outward show of consideration, so that I might believe in it, and that she would want to be more careful in her conduct, so that I might be more peaceful in my mind. But my wife, always so free and at ease with her own ways—which would be above suspicion for any man less uneasy than I—leaves me without a thought to my pains; and preoccupied only with the desire to please everyone, as all women, without any particular design on anyone, laughs at my weakness . . ." Monsieur Rohault offered all the homilies of a healthy philosophy to persuade him not to give way to such distress. "Well," replied Molière, "I cannot be philosophical with a wife as lovesome as mine, and perhaps in my place you would suffer even more than I."[20]

The portrait of Molière at home filters through the lines, but without sufficient clarity. One must picture a man increasingly consumptive, taciturn in company, difficult to live with, moody, and quick to anger—in fact, the very picture of a man whose profession it is to make people laugh. Not very gay for a young wife. Grimarest on the later years: "He had become a very sick man, reduced to living on milk. A cough he had neglected had given him congestion of the lungs; he spat blood, which greatly inconvenienced him, so that he had to drink milk in order to continue working."[21] In 1660 it was already said that "he walked heavily," that "he laughed little." Lagrange and Vivot, members of his troupe who knew and loved him well:

> Though extremely agreeable in conversation when people pleased him, he hardly spoke in company unless there were people he particularly esteemed. That made those who did not know him say he was moody and melancholy. But if he talked little, he talked well. Moreover he was an observer of the manners and ways of everybody and made admirable use of his observations in his plays.[22]

A connoisseur of himself—he too, despite his disavowal, is in his plays—and keenly aware of his jealousy, Molière compensated in part with generosity. Armande could not live without "gambling, having visitors, meeting people, receiving gifts, in short, the pleasures of life."[23] He had promised them to her as a suitor; he did not withdraw them from her as a husband. But he did not participate in them. To the extent that consciousness of his jealousy and recognition of its injustice alleviated its impact, Molière was not a bad husband, but it did not make him a good companion. Nonetheless Molière, who was now a man of wealth, with an income of 30,000 livres a year, deprived Armande of nothing money could give her. But he gave her something greater—freedom of conduct and the permission, which was legally his to grant, to go on with her stage career.

He might conceivably have done otherwise. Indeed Chapelle, noting his sadness with concern, suggested to Molière that he have Armande shut up in a convent, as did other husbands with unfaithful wives, "and so secure peace of mind." To this Molière replied at length:

> I can see that you have never loved. . . . I was born excessively affectionate, and since my struggle to overcome this natural penchant was ineffective, I sought a happiness compatible with my sensitivity. . . . Thus I took my wife, so to speak, from the cradle. I raised her with care—and you no doubt heard the rumors *that* provoked. I persisted in thinking that I could form feelings in her through habit that time could not destroy, and I spared nothing in the effort. As she was still very young when I married her, I did not take note of contrary tendencies, and I considered myself less unfortunate than most men in my situation. . . . But I discovered so much indifference that I began to feel all my precautions had been futile. . . .
>
> On first discovering infidelity, I did everything to control myself, since I could not change her. . . . I took the decision then to live with her as an honest man whose wife is a coquette and who is persuaded that no matter what might be said, his name does not depend on the conduct of his wife. . . . But my indulgence did not alter her, so I decided to live with her as if she were not my wife. But if you knew how much I suffered, you would pity me. My feeling reached such a height that I began to sympathize with *her;* and when I think how difficult it is for me to overcome my passion for her, I tell myself that perhaps she has the same difficulty in vanquishing her penchant for being a coquette, and I find myself in a position of pitying her more than I blame her.

> You will tell me I must be crazy to love like this, but I believe there is only one kind of love, and that those who do not feel the same have never really loved. Everything is linked to her in my heart, so strongly that when she is absent, I can think of nothing else, and when she is present, I am carried away by such emotion that I cannot think or put it into words, I can only feel. I can no longer see her faults; I see only that I love her. Is that not the last stage of madness? And do you not admire the fact that my famous common sense serves only to make me recognize my frailty without helping me rise above it?[24]

The irony of the last did not escape Chapelle, no more than Molière's profound melancholy. He took leave, saying as he departed that he hoped time would bring a cure, if not some measure of happiness.

The reported conversation in *La Fameuse Comédienne* is apocryphal. The dialogue in *Le Misanthrope* is not. The harmony of mood and expression gives the conversation an authentic ring. It concords with the year of crisis before the play's creation.

In August 1665 a second child had been born. She was christened Esprit-Madeleine, in honor of her godparents, Count Esprit of Modène and Madeleine Béjart. Not long afterward Molière was stricken extremely ill and put on his diet of milk. For two months he did not perform. Relations with Armande were strained to the breaking point. It seems they separated, Molière often withdrawing to a house he had rented in Auteuil, a village adjoining western Paris. Chapelle and Boileau pressed him to give up acting entirely and devote himself to playwriting, so as to conserve his diminishing strength. He had refused; he would play Alceste, *le misanthrope,* and cast Armande as Célimène, cause of Alceste's despair.

Austere, morally demanding, Alceste reproaches Célimène, whom he loves, with her coquetry, her emboldened suitors. "Can I help it," she says provocatively, "if people find me so lovable?" She might, he replies sternly, be less impressed by their absurd suits and silly language. Philinte, philosopher and friend, counsels Alceste to compromise with the ways of the world. "I take people as they are," he says, "with great calm. I train myself to endure what they do. At court, as in the world outside it, I believe, my phlegm is as good a philosopher as your bile." Alceste, however, uncompromisingly renounces court and society and retires to solitude—to Auteuil.

Hardly the stuff of comedy. Molière's customary grimaces could not have masked the bitterness; it is congealed in the words. Does love blind you? Philinte asks at one point. No, replies Alceste, I love Célimène with my eyes open to her faults. "My reason tells me every day not to, but it is not reason that dictates to love." You are jealous of everyone in the universe, Célimène tells him. Because everyone in the universe finds welcome in your sight, replies Alceste. You should be happier than they, knowing you are loved, says Célimène. How can I know that you do not say the same thing to them? replies Alceste. Because I say it to you, answers Célimène.

Célimène has her own *modern* complexity and reasoning, for she asserts her own code of conduct—and Célimène, too, as much as Alceste, is Molière's creation. To an older, prudish friend, who has recounted gossip about her, "for her own good," she coolly replies that everyone is right, according to his or her years or inclination. "There is a season for gallantry and another for prudery. . . . I do not say I may not follow in your footsteps in time, since time brings everything, but the time to be a prude, madame, is not when one is twenty."

ALCESTE: If you will force yourself to a pretense of fidelity, I will force myself to believe it.

CÉLIMÈNE: Nothing and no one can make me stoop to the baseness of pretending. Why, if my heart tells me, should I not proclaim it directly?

ALCESTE: Ah, traitress!

CÉLIMÈNE: You do not love me as one should love.[25]

When, in a last appeal, Alceste suggests her joining him in his desert retreat, Célimène exclaims: "I? Renounce the world and bury myself in your desert while I am still young?" Never!

Theirs was a strange separation, if separation there had been. Alceste and Molière met almost daily at the theater. He chose her roles, wrote her words, directed her. They performed together on the stage. In truth, Molière never ceased to love and Armande never really left him, separated or not.

Into this setting the year of *Le Misanthrope,* Michel Baron, age thirteen, first entered their lives. The orphaned son of comédiens, the youth had already appeared on the stage with a troupe of strolling players. He presented himself to Molière. Touched, as ever generous, Molière took him on with a kind of paternal concern. Touched in turn, but with jealousy mixed with possible sadness for the son Molière and she had lost, Armande reacted differently. She was furious, and such was the attachment of Molière to his protégé that there were those at court who murmured of pederasty, *"le vice italien."* One day during a rehearsal, young Baron was slapped by Armande for not showing the proper deference. He quit the troupe on the spot for another. Molière sank into a profounder illness.

An exceptionally unproductive year separated *Le Sicilien* and *Amphitryon.* The first is the slightest of plays; the second was the most detested by Boileau, perhaps because of its cynicism. Jupiter, lusting for a mortal, Alcmène, who loves her husband, Amphitryon, takes the form of Amphitryon and nightly makes love to Alcmène. Jupiter to Amphitryon: "To share with Jupiter is not at all dishonorable." Molière, acting the part of Sosie, declares: "Of such *affaires* it is always best to maintain one's silence." It is the play's closing line.[26]

Sadder, more down to earth, *George Dandin,* the tale of a deceived husband's torments, was performed the same year. The ironies and paradoxes of Molière's private and professional lives seem to merge, despite himself. *Dandin* was put on as part of the entertainment of another famous Versailles fête, in 1668. Molière's closing line this time, as George Dandin, whose wife, Angélique, is played by Armande, is far less stoical. "When a man has married a wicked woman, as I have," he says, "the very best thing he can do is to go off and drown himself."[27] Cruel comedy indeed, but Lully's sumptuous ballets between the acts and the *bacchanale* that immediately followed made the program a prodigious success. It was performed later without the ballets in Paris, and has been so performed ever since. The success is of another sort. The ambiguities and nuances of the human comedy emerge: the young wife is not wicked; the middle-aged husband is a tragic figure, though a buffoon. I was not consulted, says the wife; I was given in marriage. "I am too young to be buried alive"—a line echoing Célimène's.[28]

Molière's lucidity is a continuing astonishment. He even tells us how he saw Armande in the special light of unexplainable love. The play is *Le Bourgeois Gentilhomme,* two years after *Dandin.* Armande is twenty-eight. She has the role of Lucille, daughter of the bourgeois who would be a gentleman, enacted by Molière. (Three times Armande played onstage daughter to Molière's father.) Cléonte is in love with Lucille, who, he fears, prefers another. He asks his valet to talk him out of love with Lucille.

VALET (playing the game): Her eyes are too small.

CLÉONTE-MOLIÈRE: True, she has small eyes, but they are full of fire, the most brilliant, the most piercing, the most moving eyes you will ever see.

VALET: She has a large mouth.

CLÉONTE-MOLIÈRE: Yes, but it has a grace like no other, inspiring desire and more appealing and sensual than any other in the world.

VALET: She is not tall, and her figure is not much.

C-M: No, but it is comfortable and elegant.

VALET: She pretends nonchalance in her speech and her walk.

C-M: True, but with grace, and her ways are engaging. They have I know not what charm to insinuate themselves into your heart.[29]

VALET: As for her intelligence . . .

C-M: . . . the finest, the subtlest!

VALET: Her conversation . . .

C-M: . . . charming!

VALET: She is too serious.

C-M: Would you prefer her flighty . . . like most women?

VALET: Since that's the way it is, I can see you will go on loving her.[30]

A new trial came with the return of Michel Baron, now a handsome young man of eighteen, to the troupe as a full-fledged member of the company. He was given the lead male role of Amour in *Psyche,* playing opposite Armande, and he made a stunning god of love, simultaneously sweeping Psyché (Armande) and the public off their feet. The two had a passionate affair, offstage—for two months. Perhaps Molière looked upon it paternally, with all the ambivalence that suggests. It is certain he regarded it with some tolerance and a good deal of patience, for at the end of the affair, Armande returned to him for a life together—and Baron would remain with the troupe and be at Molière's bedside during the last illness.

There were many Barons, but there was only one Molière, Armande seems finally to have realized with the passage of time, which is the passing of youth. And for Molière there was only one Madeleine in another sense of the passing of time, a lifetime of comradeship early achieved through love and enduring beyond it, if love can ever be said to have been left completely behind. When Madeleine Béjart died a year thereafter, it is trite to say that a part of Molière also died. But it is no less true, and not simply because he died exactly a year later to the day. On her deathbed, Madeleine dictated her will, making Armande her principal beneficiary—and reinforcing the probability of her motherhood. Dying, too, she signed the usual renunciation of her profession so that she might receive the last rites and be buried by the

Church. On the day of her death, February 17, 1672, Molière was at Saint-Germain with his company, entertaining the court. Hearing that Madeleine was dying, he hurried back. It is not certain he returned in time, but he was present at her burial.

The strong women of Molière's life reappear in his plays with an individuality and complexity of character that burst through the comic stereotypes he may initially have intended. The tension created is the heart of the drama, which is also Molière's dilemma. He too is inconclusively suspended between conventional attitudes and his own experience, between the easy laugh of traditional farce and the infinitely more difficult comedy of women's tragedy—to be given in marriage without a voice, to live in submission to and ignorance with an unloved and frequently enough inferior man.

Less than a month after Madeleine's burial, Molière put on *Les Femmes savantes,* his next-to-last play. He had worked on it for at least four years. ("I have never really been content with what I have done," Molière once remarked to Boileau, underlining the unresolved drama within the drama of his plays.[31]) Learned women, pedantic women, women who pursued knowledge as if they were men, *femmes savantes* were summarily dismissed by Montaigne and seemingly not better dealt with by Molière. The differences, however, are more significant: that of a century of time, that of an essayist and a dramatist, who must enter the skin of his personnages to bring them alive, and that of the two men—Molière's comrades and companions included women; Montaigne's were exclusively men (too late the *précieuse* and *savante* Marie de Gournay).

Philaminte, her daughter Armande, and a half-mad maiden aunt, Bélise, are the would-be *femmes savantes* of a bourgeois family whose putative head is the well-meaning but weak-willed Chrysale. Their younger daughter is the sage, too *sage,* Henriette, who loves Clitandre, who formerly loved and was rebuffed by the chilly, "philosophical" Armande. The role of Chrysale was performed by Molière, Armande's by Mlle. de Brie, and Henriette's, to add to the confusion, by Armande.

The Armande *of the play,* supported by her father, soon reclaims Clitandre, who, scornful of "pedants," now loves Henriette. He seeks the spinsterish aunt Bélise for help in his suit; she mistakes his confidences for a veiled declaration of love. Clitandre then seeks the aid of Chrysale's common-sense brother. Meantime Philaminte has chosen the pretentious rhymester Trissotin as the husband for Henriette, a decision Chrysale fears to oppose. Encouraged by his brother, however, he resorts to trickery. He pretends sudden bankruptcy, which drives off Trissotin at the moment of marriage, leaving Clitandre to take his place at Henriette's side—and Armande to be consoled by "philosophy."

The plot, of course, is but the pretext for the exchanges, each character dialectically propelled to the extreme expression of a point of view. It begins in the opening scene.

ARMANDE (*to Henriette*): So you are thinking of marriage? What put that vulgar idea into your head?

HENRIETTE: Marriage, for me, means a husband, children, a home. I do not see why that idea makes you shudder.

ARMANDE: How can you sink so low as to make an idol of a husband and call brats children? Let such things for lesser women than you. Devote yourself to nobler pleasures, to things of the mind. Marry philosophy, my sister. *(Then, struck by the sudden thought)* It cannot be Clitandre whom you intend to marry!

HENRIETTE: It is.

ARMANDE: But he is mine![32]

And Armande thereafter is torn between her feminism and her "femininity," which, for Molière, is her true nature, erroneously disdained.

Offended when Clitandre informs her that he wants Henriette as his wife, Armande replies sharply, "That is for our parents to decide." And she leaves him.[33]

HENRIETTE (*to Clitandre*): It is Mother who counts; it is she you must win, by flattering her opinions.

CLITANDRE: I could not flatter them in your sister, I cannot in your mother. Frankly, I do not like learned women.
[Whereupon he delivers the famous verse lines.]
I consent that a woman have some knowledge of everything,
But I would not want her to have that shocking passion
Of being learned for the sake of being learned.
I would like her, when questions are put to her,
To know how to plead ignorant of what she knows.
I would want her to conceal her studies
And know things without wanting me to know it.

Elsewhere Chrysale seems to echo Montaigne when he says of women, "they are *savantes* enough when they know the difference between breeches and a doublet."[34]

If Clitandre may be taken as Molière's spokesman and, in this instance Chrysale, who, then, if not also Molière, speaks through Philaminte, mother *savante?*

She studies the great globe in the living room and looks at the stars through a glass; she reads and attempts to instruct herself; she supports what passes for science and scientists—but also such pretentious fools as Trissotin. She is preposterous *and* dignified in the lines Molière gives her:

> I profoundly resent the wrongs done to women regarding their
> mind,
> And I want to avenge us—all of us—just as we are,
> For that abject class to which men would reduce us,
> Confining our talents to the frivolous
> And closing the door to sublime knowledge on us.

She would "discover nature through a thousand experiments and to all questions raised invite every point of view without espousing any one of them." Who could fault that? But Molière does not have Philaminte stop there. He has her speak of joining "elegant language to high science" and later say to the absurd Trissotin that she had "clearly seen men on the moon" through her glass, and that the "most beautiful project of our academy . . . would be to remove ugly syllables from the most beautiful words."[35] The public is reassured in its laughter.

Once again Molière is attacking the *précieuses,* whose affected refinement now encompasses pedantry. But he is hardest of all upon the Trissotins. "A learned fool," says Clitandre, "is more fool than an ignorant fool." And to Philaminte, he adds: "I hate only that science and thinking that spoil a person. They are good things in themselves, and becoming, but I would rather be ignorant than *savant,* as some pretentious people."[36]

Philaminte nonetheless has the last *noble* speech. Accepting her husband's "bankruptcy" with stoical calm, she scolds him for his show of catastrophe and counsels a "less common air."[37] Her constant strength and serenity throughout led to a writer's mid-twentieth-century suggestion that Molière "in the secret of his heart preferred the *femmes savantes* to their despiser."[38] A similar insight inspired a recent production of the play at the Comédie Française (born of Molière's troupe) with Philaminte and Armande as tragic figures. The audience was confused, uncomfortable. One could hear the laughter become uneasy, hesitant, then die. The ambiguity defeated both comic and tragic intent, the fault Molière's. In striking at pedantry, male and female, he had hit at women who almost pathetically were trying to instruct themselves, a defiant effort he had himself applauded in *School for Husbands* ten years before and had not necessarily since deplored.

The laughter was dying in Molière as well. The reconciliation with Armande was complete with another pregnancy, which should have been a new spurt of life, but the child born in September was buried in October. Professionally, too, there was death in the air. Lully had supplanted Molière as the king's prime entertainer, and Lully was an immoderately ambitious man. By early 1672 he had achieved a monopoly on music and dance in all France by threatening to return to Italy if he did not receive it. Louis XIV confessed to Colbert that he could not do without him for the royal *divertissements.*

Lully's ascendance caused Molière's decline. The gratitude of kings, he knew better than anyone, lasted the season of a rose. When Lully had Louis forbid any theater employing more than six singers and a dozen musicians, the decree aimed directly at Molière's productions, which incorporated music and ballet. That same winter Molière challenged the decree by performing *Psyche* with the original number of singers, dancers, and instrumentalists and with Lully's own score. But it was an inconclusive clash. Molière's heart was no longer in it. His last child had just been buried and his cough racked him mercilessly.

On February 17, 1673, deadly ill, Molière insisted on performing, as usual, in his latest—and last—play, *Le Malade imaginaire.* Armande and Baron begged him to remain home this one time for his health's sake. "What would you want me to do?" he replied. "There are fifty poor workmen who have only their day's wages to live on. What will they do if there is no performance? I would reproach myself for having failed to give them one day's bread, if I possibly could."[39]

Rising from his bed, Molière went to the theater and prepared for the four-o'clock curtain. He had the title role: he was the imaginary invalid. He went on stage. Shaken throughout by convulsive coughs, he converted them, to the audience's delight, into his customary comical hiccups and managed to finish before he collapsed. He was carried home and cared for by two nuns. He asked for a priest, but none came from the parish. Night fell; he coughed more violently, burst a blood vessel, choked on the blood, and died. The abbé who arrived came too late.

Since there had been no last rites, no dying renunciation, the Archbishop of Paris refused him a religious burial. The widowed Armande went to the king at Versailles and threw herself at his feet. "If my husband was a criminal," she cried, "it was Your Majesty himself who approved his crimes!"[40] The king paused, then continued down the

Hall of Mirrors, his courtiers glacially following. Quietly the next day, however, he arranged with the archbishop for a discreet burial. There would be no Church ceremony, and burial would have to be after sunset, so that it would be little remarked, but it would be religious and in Church grounds. A great crowd nonetheless followed Molière's coffin to the cemetery in the light of torches.

THREE days later Molière's troupe performed *Le Misanthrope,* with Michel Baron in Molière's role and Armande again as Célimène; a week later *Le Malade imaginaire* was put on, with Armande resuming the role of Angélique, the "invalid's" daughter. So recently widowed, she was harshly criticized—by those ignorant of stage tradition. For Armande, however, it was Molière's company that had to go on, and she became its director in Molière's place. Perhaps for this, Michel Baron and three others left to join the Hôtel de Bourgogne troupe. They were missed. Worse was loss of the theater itself to Lully, who took it by authority of the king for his Académie de Musique.

Armande could have comfortably retired, and remarried with the considerable wealth left her by Molière, but she chose otherwise. Together with La Grange, she managed to keep the company together, find a new theater on rue Guénegaud, and advance 14,000 livres of her own for the lease. Somehow, too, Louis XIV was persuaded to order that the Marais troupe join Armande's, which, thus reinforced, reopened with *Tartuffe.*

For twenty-one years after Molière's death Armande held the stage and during most of them managed the company. Once, when she was ill, the public demonstrated its concern and hastened back to the theater when it heard she had returned. She sang French and Italian songs with a pretty, touching voice, and was known for her meticulous professionalism. "Without being beautiful," said a critic at the end of her career, "she was *piquante* and capable of inspiring great passion."[41]

In May 1677, at the age of thirty-six, Armande remarried. Her husband was actor Guérin d'Estriché, a member of the company since 1674. It was a satisfactory, even a happy, marriage of love and convenience.

Rumors of Armande's coquettish, immoral conduct had long since ceased; so suddenly upon Molière's death, in fact, that one wonders about their truth during his lifetime.

5

THE POET AND THE SCIENTIST: VOLTAIRE AND THE MARQUISE DU CHATELET

GABRIELLE-EMILIE du Châtelet was all passion, all mind. Voltaire considered her a genius and compared her to Newton. Until her death, they were lovers and intellectual companions, living together in a union blessed by Emilie's gentle warrior husband, the Marquis du Châtelet.

Mme. du Châtelet had chosen her father well (as well as the husband he would choose for her), Baron Louis Nicolas Le Tonnelier de Breteuil, *Introducteur des Ambassadeurs* of Louis XIV. He was cultivated, rich, and charming. He early recognized the exceptional quality of his daughter Emilie (as Voltaire would call her) and raised her accordingly almost from her birth, December 17, 1706. In fact the quality cannot be that easily separated from the upbringing.

It may have helped that when Emilie was six, her father was sixty-four: there is rarely a bad grandparent. Emilie's first known passion was study, not simply reading. To increasingly fluent Latin, which would be her second language, she added, largely thanks to her father, Italian and the beginnings of English. She was less interested in Spanish, since she suspected that the one book for which it was famous was too frivolous. Barely adolescent, she translated the *Aeneid.* Then, quite literally, she fixed upon the stars and studied physics and astronomy, laboriously acquiring the geometry and algebra, and later calculus, they required.

Her parents' town house faced the royal Tuileries gardens; it had three rooms devoted to books, and she had the run of them, equally with her brothers. The children, moreover, had an entire floor to themselves. Soon Emilie would discover a passion for the theater, especially the opera, singing, and ballet, and for pompons and dresses. Scarcely wedded, she would discover gambling, and never recover.

Florent-Claude, the Marquis du Châtelet, was thirty, and Emilie eighteen, when they were married. He was a regimental colonel and head of a Lorraine family that extended back to Charlemagne and the crusaders. His country house was the neglected Château of Cirey, his estates earned little, but his bride had brought a handsome dowry and her own income—as good a basis for marital freedom and equality as has yet been found. It mattered, since the colonel was either off to the wars or away on garrison duty much of the time. His forbears had all been soldiers, his father a Marshal of France, but he, fortunately for his young, ardent wife, was the least aggressive of men. Jealousy, moreover, was simply regarded as socially bad manners. He was, in summary, a modest, honest man; proud of his wife's intelligence—indeed, of her intellectuality—leaving her to her interests as she to his, though not so exclusively as to eliminate children. A girl was born to them in the first year of marriage, a son in the second. There would be none other for six years, since the separations, though extremely amiable, lengthened, the colonel with his regiment at Semur, the marquise in residence in Paris.

With one instructor following the other, Mme. du Châtelet pursued her study of physics and mathematics; she also gambled at the card table, frequented the opera, and had her first love affair, as was expected of her. Unfortunately she never did anything casually.

Ladies took lovers—the active voice is of more than passing interest. The nobleman's wife of the prerevolutionary order was a remarkably liberated woman. Contrasting monarchy and republic, Montesquieu put it succinctly in his *Esprit des lois:* "In a republic, women are free according to the law and slaves according to custom"—in a monarchy it is vice versa. And it was particularly true of the aristocratic class in the Age of the Enlightenment, the age of Voltaire, Diderot, Helvétius, *les lumières.* There were constraints, of course, and a wayward undercurrent of a husband's permissiveness, as summed up in an eighteenth-century gentleman's remark: "I permit my wife anything but a footman."[1]

Conventionally, each member of a newly married noble couple would establish—or continue, in the case of the husband—a separate circle of friends and activities, with a polished regard for the proprieties, especially on the part of the wife. The husband, too—if young, he also had had little to say in his marriage—wanted freedom to find love outside the usually loveless wedlock; nor did he seek the tyranny of a loving, and thus possibly jealous, wife.

After only three months of marriage, Mme. d'Epinay had been severely scolded by her mother for complaining to her husband of his spending nights with his mistress. "My mother called me a child," she records in her memoirs. "She said I had conducted myself indecently

. . . that my husband was quite properly offended . . . and I myself felt like a child."[2]

Possibly the young Mme. du Châtelet was not unlike the young Mme. d'Epinay. A proto-romantic—this is also the age of Rousseau—throughout her life she would give herself intensely, and ask for reciprocity. M. du Châtelet may have held her at the conventional distance. Her temperament lends credence to the story always told of her "first declared love affair," though it is based on an account first rendered by Maurepas, a lifelong enemy of Voltaire, and consequently not inclined to tenderness toward Voltaire's future companion. It has since been embroidered with emotional dialogues, a "final interview," and a "cup of poisoned soup."[3]

> The Marquise du Châtelet [recounts Maurepas] . . . in despair at seeing herself abandoned by the Marquis de Guébriant, whom she idolized, wrote him a letter of eternal adieus, telling him she wanted to die, since he no longer lived for her. Guébriant, who knew that she was subject to such transports, ran to her house. The porter refusing him entrance, he forced his way in, flew to her room and found her in bed, sleeping from the effects of an almost fatal dose of opium. He sent for help and saved her life, and she, not being able to bind him to her, even after this proof of her love, consoled herself with others.[4]

Others? There was another at least, it is fairly certain: the Duke de Richelieu, grandnephew of the Cardinal, thirty-three, in some ways the Don Juan of his time, though warmer of heart and capable of friendship with women he had loved or had been loved by. His liaison with the young Mme. du Châtelet gives the lie to a celebrated portrait of her, penned by the bored, bitter Mme. du Deffand. He truly had a pick of the period's beautiful women; and if Emilie was not among the most beautiful, his choice and the several paintings of her indicate a handsome, winsome woman, totally unlike the harridan described by Mme. du Deffand: "big, dried-up . . . with an apoplectic complexion, sharp face, and pointed nose." Such, she added, "is the face of *la belle Emilie.*"[5] Since Mme. du Châtelet was indeed known as "the lovely Emilie," the intended irony is somewhat lost—and blown away by the observation of Voltaire's jealous niece, Mme. Denis, that, alas, she was "very beautiful."

At twenty-one Voltaire became society's darling, the age's greatest entertainer. He had a dancing wit, and frequently dined out on it. He was a slim, elegant snob, and remained one, but he had an unbridled tongue, pen, and sense of the absurd, and they saved him, if not from himself, at least for us. At twenty-two he was sent to the Bastille for a satirical lampoon in Latin on the Regency, which briefly succeeded the Sun King's reign. He emerged from "prison" (where, as one of the privileged, he had had his own books, furniture, and linen) with the name he had finally chosen for himself, Voltaire, and a finished play, *Oedipus,* begun when he was eighteen or nineteen. Daringly the title itself suggested the incest charged against Regent Philippe of Orléans. Performed at the Comédie Française, it had the most successful first run of the century. The remarkably indulgent regent rewarded Voltaire with an allowance of 1,200 livres (well over $2,000 today). In a fashion that would be his trademark, Voltaire thanked the regent "for continuing to supply [his] board, but would wish His Royal Highness would no longer supply [his] lodging."[6]

When Louis XV displaced the regent several years later, Voltaire produced the long historical poem *Henriade.* It lifted him to the first rank of writers. Disapproved officially, it was "secretly" printed in Rouen, circulated from hand to hand in the salons and at Court, and translated into seven languages. The very young Crown Prince Frederick of Prussia told his cronies he preferred it to the *Odyssey.* The disapproval was that of the Church. Voltaire's epic poem recounted religious crimes through the ages, with the Massacre of St. Bartholomew as its springboard. But he triumphed at Court, was presented a purse of 1,500 livres by the Queen, and became the intimate of courtiers—so long as he held his tongue.

There was a series of liaisons, more or less serious, with the Marquise de Bernières, wife of the Rouen parlement's president, and Adrienne Lecouvreur, the day's most famous actress. The latter would lead to the brink of a duel with her official lover, the Chevalier de Rohan-Chabot, a second stay in the Bastille to prevent it, and a release on the promise to leave France for England (lack of freedom, even in luxury, remained a horror for Voltaire).

Everywhere in England (or so he would always recall) Voltaire encountered a generosity of spirit, a tolerance for eccentricity and freethinking, that would make it the land of his reference thereafter. For almost three years he resided across the Channel, schooling himself to the extent of his capacity in the physics of Newton (arriving in time for the funeral) and the empiricism of Locke; meeting Pope, Gay, Swift, and Congreve; and missing Paris, French social life, and the Court. He found English manners impeccable, the climate execrable, and the food inedible. He would forever needle the French with remarks about the freer state of England, but when he was finally permitted to return to

France, he was never to go back to England. Life across the Channel had been not only a kind of finishing school, but also the basis of a lifelong independence financially. An English edition of the *Henriade* brought a handsome total of 150,000 francs, which he judiciously invested on the Continent. Voltaire firmly believed that a man should make money in order to write, not write in order to make money. Eventually he would acquire a fortune thanks to his investments and shrewd real-estate ventures—he would cross France to snap up a bargain—as well as to the Pâris banker brothers and their war-profiteering contracts, and to the death of his father and the legacy he left to Voltaire.

And he accrued fame and its concomitants—enemies, particularly among the powerful clergy. Periodically in trouble with the Church, he sheltered in the châteaus of his "adorable dukes," Sully or Richelieu, and prepared his next literary missiles against the enemy. The plays he wrote, so unperformable today, established his reputation; his letters, books, and pamphlets, the satirical verses that brought on all his troubles, have won him his immortality. The *Lettres philosophiques,* written in London and sent to Thieriot, a friend in France, later "secretly" published in Rouen, are among the finest provocative examples. The attack on Pascal, equated with blasphemy, was "somehow" appended to a pirated edition of the *Lettres.* The root cause of man's unhappiness, Pascal had remarked in an oft-quoted passage, was "his not knowing how to remain quietly at peace in his bedroom." To this the humanist Voltaire replied, anticipating existentialism and revealing the explosive energy that would propel him throughout life: "Man is born for action as fire tends upward and the stone downward. Not to be occupied and not to exist are one and the same thing for man."

Voltaire's *Lettres* were among the first salvos of the Enlightenment against Church and Crown. (Reading them, Lafayette would remark, had made him a republican before the age of ten.) On war, for instance, with the monarchy clearly the target: "Our Lord, who bade us to love our enemies . . . surely does not want us to cross the sea to cut our brothers' throats, merely because murderers dressed in red, with hats two feet high, recruit citizens while making a noise with two [drum]-sticks on the stretched skin of an ass." On religious beliefs: "An Englishman, like a free man, goes to heaven by whatever route he chooses," with the right to "profess, unmolested, whatever religion he prefers." In other letters, Voltaire defyingly proposed Newton in the place of Descartes and, with Locke, elevated human experience above divine revelation as the source of possible knowledge.

There were few in France with whom Voltaire could even hold a conversation at this high level. Scientists and philosophers were rigidly Cartesian and starchly suspicious of the new English thought.[7] Meeting Madame du Châtelet at this time was like falling upon an oasis in an uncharted desert. Still young, still ardent, though almost twenty-seven and the mother of three (who mentions the fact that Voltaire was crowding forty?), the marquise struck him with her unexpected perceptions, the uncommon approach of a methodological mind appealing only to the rational, the scientifically observable. Not only could she understand what he was talking about; she could take him a step forward, helping him with the physics and calculations of the Newtonian principles he rather more intuitively professed. Each, in fact, was as eager as the other to learn; each, therefore, as eager to be taught in as nonsexist a pairing as we have yet come upon.

Mme. du Châtelet was tall and commanding, which seems to have suited Voltaire, and when she talked Newton and Locke, calculus and Latin poetry, he decided he loved her. "How fortunate," he would exclaim, "that I can admire her whom I adore!"

It was not a chaste love, though Voltaire never matched Emilie in ardor; his chronic intestinal troubles did not help. At the age of twenty-four, he had written to his somewhat puzzled mistress, Marquise de Mimeure: "You make me feel that friendship is worth a thousand times more than love. It even seems to me that I am not at all made for the passions. There is something in me which finds it ridiculous to love and even more so in those who love me. Well, that is that. I renounce it forever."[8] Voltaire may have been preparing his lady for his leaving her, but there were other ways of doing it.

In the spring of 1733, when he was presented to Mme. du Châtelet at the Opéra, Voltaire was in a particularly dolorous state. Several weeks before, he had written friends that he was almost too ill to write how ill he was. "I am in the horrors of moving," he informed Emilie on May 6, "the pains of *colique,* but tomorrow I will send you what you want. I have more desire to see you than you can have to console me."[9] There is more intimacy than indelicacy in this declaration of diarrhea. But throughout the summer, there was also between them a courtly dance, a minuet of verse, love, and decorum, for theirs was a very small, gossipy world. It was already rumored that the marquise had flung herself at Voltaire in the spring at the Opéra, brazenly kissing him on the mouth. He went to her defense, speaking everywhere of *la divine* Emilie, for whom he was sighing. That was in July, when they were already lovers; for in August, it is Voltaire who complains that Mme. du Châtelet is too much the philosopher! The delightful quatrain is in a letter to Abbé Jacques-François de Sade (uncle of the future, more celebrated marquis):

> J'avouerai qu'elle est tyrannique.
> Il faut pour lui faire sa cour
> Lui parler de métaphysique
> Quand on voudrait parler d'amour.[10]

("I confess that she is tyrannical. To pay her court you must talk metaphysics, when you would like to talk love.")

He also complained, more prosaically, of her mundanity and the precious time wasted in card playing—she the beautiful Emilie of the "lively and sublime mind . . . of a genius worthy of Horace and Newton."[11]

They loved, but their separate lives continued with the possibility that they might veer apart. Mme. du Châtelet's meeting of Pierre-Louis de Maupertuis, a seductive thirty-five-year-old scientist who was a superb mathematician, offered one possibility. He was introduced to her by Voltaire, who admired his work and arranged for all three to meet at the Opéra, but for Maupertuis to drop by Mme. du Châtelet's place first. If he were not so ill, Voltaire wrote him, "I would seek you everywhere to learn how to think, and to enjoy the charm of your conversation. You are the only mathematician who . . . has imagination. You unite a salutary metaphysics to mathematics and above all you have health. Oh, extraordinary, happy man!"[12]

Along with lessons in algebra that winter—while Voltaire was preoccupied with illness, rehearsals of a play, an opera for Rameau, and writing a new tragedy—the attractions of the extraordinary, healthy, and happy Maupertuis were strongly felt by the healthy and not quite happy, and certainly unfulfilled, Mme. du Châtelet. Maupertuis encouraged her falling in love, then characteristically withdrew when it happened. Emilie's fervent letters to Maupertuis have been preserved, and those to Voltaire have not, though it is likely she was writing to both men. As to her loving two men simultaneously, one might say, to begin with, that she did not yet feel committed to either; and, to end with, why not? Her infatuation with the one was no secret to the other; and Maupertuis, everyone was aware, had other fish frying as well.

"My soul has need of you," Emilie wrote Maupertuis at six o'clock one January morning, "as much as my body needs repose. Come at any time, alone or with someone." The letters follow almost daily: "I have worked a great deal and I hope you will be less discontented with me than the last time." "Please come, I am sick, I have a thousand things to tell you." "It is not surprising that leaving you one thinks only of the pleasure of seeing you again." "I am not going out. Come and see if you can teach me how to elevate an infinite nominal to a given power." Desperately: "I sent for you at the Academy and at your place to tell you I would be at home yesterday evening. I spent it with binomials and trinomials. I have no more work unless you set me a task; I desire one extremely."[13]

Maupertuis was not forthcoming. Voltaire had anticipated it in verses to Emilie. He is a true scientist, he told her, whom "I cherish. He will unveil the stars and the secrets of mysterious nature. But if not the secret of happiness, what then will he have taught you?"[14] If there can be a touch of wisdom in a touch of jealousy, then they are both there.

In April 1734 Emilie and Voltaire left for the wedding of the Duke de Richelieu in Burgundy. Voltaire had arranged the match and, moreover, took it upon himself to advise the newlyweds not to love each other too much; in that way, the love would last. "Better to be friends for life," he said, "than lovers for a few days."[15] It reflected the growing emotion for Emilie in the intimacy of the countryside, in the long hours spent together, talking and discovering their similar goals, principles, ambitions. With the departure of the duke to the battlefield, where he rejoined the Marquis du Châtelet, they were left even more to themselves. Maupertuis, if not entirely put out of Emilie's mind, was thrust into a remoter corner of it. At the end of April she wrote the scientist that she hoped he would stop at the Monjeu château on his way to Switzerland and give her a few badly needed lessons. Blithely: "I am here in the most beautiful spot of the world . . . Voltaire, who knows I am writing to you, asks me to send his regards." Then, abruptly: "He is worried, and rightly, about the reaction to his *Lettres.*"[16]

There is the perfect mixture of Emilie: Maupertuis held in reserve (once having loved someone, she never ceased loving him somewhat), further mathematical studies (not to be separated from the emotion Maupertuis inspired in her), and Voltaire. The order is that of the letter. Increasingly, concern for Voltaire would outweigh, without canceling, everything else.

Jore, who had printed the *Lettres philosophiques,* had just been sent to the Bastille because of them, and Voltaire's Paris residence had been searched. Imprisonment threatened, a *lettre de cachet* to that effect was on its way to Monjeu. Voltaire sped off; rumors were put out that he had left France. Even Mme. du Châtelet may not have known where he was hiding. Anxiously she asked for Maupertuis's influence, as an important Academician at Court. An appeal to Count d'Argental was more efficacious. From his "desert" hiding place, Voltaire wrote him in appreciation: "You know how much I owe to the generous friendship of Mme. du Châtelet . . . It is to you and her that I shall owe my freedom." He also begged the count "to close the mouths of those he hears calumniating so true, so uncommon a friendship as hers."[17]

Tongues were indeed wagging. Anything that touched Voltaire, and now the marquise, was of lively interest. Mme. du Châtelet ordinarily was reckless of appearances, but this time she reserved her confidences to a few, such as d'Argental, Richelieu, and Abbé de Sade. On May 12 she wrote the latter a deeply revealing letter:

> I do not have the strength to see my best friend, with the terrible health he suffers, in prison . . . He has bound himself to me more tightly than ever. I did not think that friendship could cause such sharp pain . . . I spent ten days here [since the duke left] between him and Mme. de Richelieu; I have never spent happier ones. And now I have lost him just when I felt the happiest to be with him . . . Flirtations, annoyance, anything can console us for the loss of a lover, but time, which heals all wounds, is only worsening mine.

Emilie partly discloses a still-secret plan: "I shall be going soon to my château [at Cirey]. People have become insupportable; they are so false, so unjust, so full of prejudices, so interfering. It is better to be alone or living with those who think as we do." But . . . "Alas, we spend our lives making plans we never execute."[18]

For once Emilie was too pessimistic, though there was cause for it. The public executioner was ordered to burn Voltaire's *Lettres philosophiques* in a public square. He himself was not yet freed from a threat of imprisonment. However, the refuge of the Cirey château was not far in the offing.

First Voltaire visited his dear friend Richelieu, wounded at the siege of Philippsburg—in a duel with a fellow officer! He was nobly entertained by the king's men and enjoyed himself hugely, until he heard that the king's police were still looking for him, and he took off for Cirey. Meanwhile Mme. du Châtelet was . . . Mme. du Châtelet, true to her several selves. After returning to Paris, she remained there while Voltaire undertook the immense alterations and furnishings required to make the empty shell of the Cirey château livable for the two of them. She resumed her social life, her gambling, her lessons with Maupertuis, and acquired another mathematics tutor, Claude Clairaut.

To be fair, one should mention that Mme. du Châtelet also lost her third child in August, born the year before, after several weeks of illness. It contributed to her delay in joining Voltaire. She was more moved by it than she had thought possible, but it did not prevent her writing to Maupertuis on the night of her child's death that his coming would console her, since she was alone (and one should note M. du Châtelet's own absence from his child's deathbed). Not before October, and after Maupertuis had departed for Basel, did Emilie arrive at Cirey.

But Voltaire, too, had not pined in the interim.

Cirey, to commence with, was situated on a hillock in the country woods of Champagne, ideally close to the Lorraine frontier. Thus Voltaire could easily slip across at the first report that the police were coming. The neighboring village had a cluster of about twenty houses; but there was also a local aristocracy, which meant he had little trouble forming the society he needed, the audience for his wit, preferably of women—they were far more amiable than men, he said. Two ladies embraced the opportunity of adding a Voltaire to their provincial lives, the young Countess de la Neuville and the older, plumper, but more jolly Mme. de Champbonin, who chanced to be a former schoolmate of Mme. du Châtelet. Voltaire courted both, frequently staying with the countess, the other joining them (the count is unmentioned), whenever the noise of the masons at work drove him out of Cirey. And when he was at Cirey, they would come to him, bringing gifts of fruit and game.

Such was the scene when Emilie descended in October. "She has arrived!" Voltaire announced happily to Mme. de Champbonin, who had become his devoted slave. "She arrived just when I received a letter from her saying she would not be coming very soon!" With Emilie arrived hundreds of parcels and no end of disorder. "We now have beds without curtains, rooms without windows, china closets but no chairs, charming phaetons but no horses to draw them."[19] But in all the disorder and confusion was a laughing, joking Emilie. What if she did take charge on the spot and change all his plans, putting windows where he had ordered doors, stairs where he had indicated fireplaces, and fireplaces where he had intended stairs! Voltaire was enchanted.

As for the husband in all this household arrangement, Monsieur du Châtelet was *proud* of his wife's having elected, and been chosen by, so eminent an intellectual companion as Voltaire, who, moreover, was bringing the family château and estate brilliantly back to life (on the basis of a long-term, low-interest loan, which Voltaire in due time would reclaim!). Of such, too, is *la civilisation française.*

Voltaire, furthermore, invited his two lady friends to join them at

Cirey. "When all three of you are here together, it will be an earthly paradise."[20] What if there was no bed as yet for Mme. de Champbonin, who received the first invitation ("Why, oh why," Nancy Mitford sensibly protests, "must three people have three beds?"[21]). A carriage would be sent to her, so that she could spend the day. The remarkably unjealous, or simply generous, Voltaire had even invited Maupertuis, before the two ladies, to stay with them on his way back from Basel: "The most beautiful person in the world spends her life writing you in algebra, I write in prose to say I am your admirer, your friend, etc."[22]

Maupertuis, however, did not stop off at Cirey. It was Mme. du Châtelet who joined *him,* or sought to, with varying success, that winter before Christmas. Still threatened by imprisonment, Voltaire had stayed behind, working on *Alzire* (a play), the house, and a new, long poem on Jeanne d'Arc, *La Pucelle,* which would invite more thunder from the Church authorities. Indirectly he heard of Emilie's *"extrême dissipation"*—it may have meant gambling—while he resumed his courtship of the provincial ladies. Nonetheless, it was thanks to the unflagging efforts of Mme. du Châtelet, aided by Richelieu and every powerful friend she had at Court, that Voltaire, after first disavowing his *Lettres* and especially the anti-Pascalian thrusts, was permitted to return to Paris and public life by the end of March 1735. Along with the permission, the King's Police Chief sent him the fatherly advice that he "act his age," now that he was no longer young.[23]

Paris was disappointing. There were too many petty distractions, preventing him from working. Possibly, too, Mme. du Châtelet spoke too much of Maupertuis, who was being lionized by a society so taken with the new "science" as expounded by the *grand homme* that it had no time for theater or poetry. But Voltaire had something of his own in verse, *La Pucelle,* which would stun Paris with its irreverent blasts at religious belief, patriotism, and military courage once it was published (so, please, he would urge those to whom he was reciting it verse by written verse, not a word! and the word, of course, spread, and its author was once again threatened with the Bastille).

Something more profoundly personal led to Voltaire's abrupt departure from Paris for Lunéville, where, a day's journey from Cirey, Stanislas Leczinski, former king of Poland and father-in-law of Louis XV, had established a skeleton court in the Duchy of Lorraine. This was the couple's situation, which reached a precarious turning point as the spring of 1735 came to an end.[24]

Were Emilie and he finally to live together at Cirey, as they had talked about doing, or he alone and she occasionally? It was *not* jealousy of Maupertuis, but a certain pride, a sense of precious time lost. They would separate for a few weeks of reflection: "it would be for Emilie to decide—Voltaire and her studies, or Maupertuis and 'dissipation.' "[25]

Impulsively Mme. du Châtelet made up her mind, but not without a certain difficulty; less than all would never fully satisfy her. Yet her sincerity is beyond question. To Richelieu, stationed at Strasbourg with his regiment, she wrote on May 21: "All that is truly dear to me is at Lunéville and Strasbourg. I am losing my life away from what I love, here in this great city which, in twenty-four hours, has become a desert." What might be lacking in her happiness at Cirey would be Richelieu from time to time! "Friendship, for me, is not an insipid, tranquil feeling. The ultimate happiness of spending my life with someone I adore does not keep me from my feeling for you. It is a sentiment which I will never hide from him, and which he assuredly shares with me."[26]

The flow of long, reflective letters to Richelieu courses on throughout the month of May and part of June. His undoubted friendship for Voltaire reinforced her own for him; Maupertuis, catch-as-catch-can lover, was not the same friend. "You know how to love your friends," she told Richelieu, "not only with all their faults, but when they are unhappy." The more she thought about her situation with Voltaire, the more certain she was that they should live in the country, away from Paris, "where, sooner or later, I would lose him." As for herself, "I love him enough, I avow to you, to sacrifice the pleasures of Paris for the happiness of living with him where he is safe from danger, from his own rashness and destiny."[27]

Though her decision has been taken, Mme. du Châtelet does not cease her self-examination or the probing of her lovers. On June 15 she wrote Richelieu that she was leaving for Cirey in four days. That should prove to a questioning Voltaire the solidity of her love. The answer to his jealousy or to his fear of not being sufficiently loved—the first far easier to dispel—will be "to be happy at Cirey. That is the veritable metaphysics of love." As for Maupertuis, he was planning an expedition to the North Pole, no less. (Actually, he would go to Lapland.)[28] "He has a disquiet of mind which renders him unhappy, proving it is the heart, more than the mind, which must be occupied. Unfortunately for him, he is more at ease in algebraic calculations than in loving. I mean, loving as I do."[29]

So much for Maupertuis? So much *more* for Voltaire.

Mme. du Châtelet spoke of spending "three months" at Cirey, most likely out of concern for her husband's feelings, or, more precisely, though amounting to the same thing, his uneasy family's. Announcing a trip of three months would cause less talk. The concern is in every letter, and the plea to Richelieu to help her through his friendship and prestige with her husband. May 22: "If you see M. du Châtelet, as no doubt you will, speak of me with friendship and esteem. Above all, praise my trip to him, my courage and the good effect on society. Speak simply to him of Voltaire, but with interest on your part and friendship." May 30: "The only thing that disturbs me and I must manage is the presence of M. du Châtelet. Here I count a great deal on you, what you will say to him. Peace [therefore his prolonged stay at Cirey] would destroy all our hopes." June 15:

> There is much I have never told to you or anyone, not even to V. But there is some heroism, perhaps madness, on my part in closing myself up, the three of us, in Cirey. Never matter, I have made up my mind . . . . At least I can hope that love will thicken the veil over my husband's eyes, for the sake of his happiness and ours . . . Don't forget your eloquence with him . . . I leave in four days.

By the end of June, Mme. du Châtelet and Voltaire were at Cirey, and it was not, each knew, for the summer but rather, each felt, for a lifetime, no matter what they were saying to others. It was momentous for both of them. It constitutes the very beginning of Voltaire's memoirs (1759):

> I was weary of the idle and turbulent life of Paris, of the crowd of fops, of the bad books printed with official approval and royal privilege, of literary cabals, of the meanness and rascality of the wretches who dishonored literature: I found in 1733 a young lady who felt more or less as I did, and who resolved to spend several years in the country to cultivate her mind, far from the tumult of the world. It was the Marquise du Châtelet, the woman who in all France had the greatest disposition for all the sciences. . . .
>
> Seldom has so fine a mind and so much taste been united with so much ardor for learning; but she also loved the world and all the amusements of her age and sex. Nevertheless she left all this to go and bury herself in a dilapidated house on the frontiers of Champagne and Lorraine, where the land was very infertile and very ugly. She beautified the house, to which she added pleasant gardens. I built a gallery, in which I created a very fine collection of scientific instruments. We had a large library.[30]

If, for Voltaire, theirs was fundamentally an intellectual relationship, to call it *merely* that would be grossly to underestimate what intellectuality, and intelligence, meant to both. They were primary, the sine qua non, the without which, nothing. The memoirs were written twenty-four years later, but the appreciation was almost immediate. After six weeks of Cirey with Emilie, Voltaire enthusiastically communicated it to everyone. Not only had Mme. du Châtelet assured his refuge and safety; she had challenged public opinion in doing so and was paying for it by what people were ignobly saying. But the miracle of miracles, what bound him to her and made it possible to forget the whole world, was that each day at her side meant a new discovery, a new enlightenment.

Life at Cirey was organized around their work—their studies and their writing. Even the furnishing and decorating of the château, the refashioning of the gardens and terrace, in which they took so much delight and showed so much taste, held second place. Voltaire's *Century of Louis XIV* steadily advanced, though he would spend twenty years upon it. Emilie made rapid progress in calculus, geometry, and physics, approaching each matter with an exactitude that led Voltaire to remark that both he and her son's tutor (whom she taught Latin so that he might teach her son) were learning "how to think, the two of them, from her."[31]

In second place, too, must be put the five-day interval that September when Mme. du Châtelet hastened to her ill mother near Paris and from there wrote to Maupertuis, who had not yet departed for the "Pole": "If you still love me a bit, come and see me. You know my mother well enough for that. But if you wish, she need not know that you are here."[32] His not responding is not important, no more than if he had. On returning to Cirey, Emilie could honestly write to Richelieu, "I have left everything to live with the only person who has ever been able to fill my heart and my mind. . . . I have never had a real passion for anyone as for the one who is now the enchantment and torment of my life."[33]

The torment was the recurrent warnings from Versailles. But another problem had also occurred—the return of M. du Châtelet following the Peace of Nijmegen. "I count on you," Emilie had written her dear duke the very day the peace was signed (September 22), "to come here before him."[34] The duke did come, and then left, but the problem was not insuperable: there was a suite of rooms for each of them—the marquis, the marquise, and Voltaire, who was in the midst of arranging an entire wing for himself and Emilie. When the marquis was in residence, which was less often than his wife had feared, he would take his meals with his son and the tutor ("the coachmen's dinner," it was unkindly called by Emilie and Voltaire, who, depending on their work, snacked at irregular moments) and retire early. He never imposed. In fact there was a fondness among the three. The problem was essentially the families, the Breteuils and the du Châtelets, as they affected Emilie's husband.

One of the pair's earliest visitors, when the marquis *may* have been away with his regiment, was the Chevalier de Villefort. His account is legendary—"pure fairy tale," Emilie said dismissingly. He had arrived, he said, to find the house shuttered against the daylight. He rang. No answer. He rang again. Finally a *femme de chambre* opened the door to him and led him by lantern light through long corridors and dark, deserted rooms. They stopped. The maid went ahead to ask the marquise if she would see him. She would. The long, lantern-lighted walk continued through more deserted rooms. He was led to a door that opened onto a resplendent salon. The Divinity of the house, sparkling with diamonds like an operatic Venus, sat at her desk, which was covered with books and instruments, scribbling *x* and *y* on scraps of paper. The visitor asked to see Voltaire. He was led up a secret staircase to the Magician's rooms. They knocked at his door. No reply immediately. The hour for conversation had not yet been rung. Nevertheless, in the chevalier's honor, Voltaire joined them, and they supped at the sound of a bell. The dining room had two wall openings for plates: one for incoming, the other for outgoing. No servants. The supper was long, the food and wine superb. A second bell announced the hour for moral and philosophical readings. A third bell: time to retire. At four in the morning a fourth bell rang, waking M. de Villefort. He didn't stir. A servant came. Would monsieur care to partake in a poetry reading in Voltaire's gallery? He would, reluctantly. The picnic the next day was more fun, Voltaire and Mme. du Châtelet riding in a carriage, the visitor on horseback, a second carriage for servants, a third carriage for books.

The fairy-tale atmosphere has a substratum of fact: Emilie's display of jewelry, the minute scheduling of work time, the separateness, when they worked, in their togetherness. Voltaire was then engrossed in *Alzire,* a play set in Peru, dealing with colonial occupiers and subjected people. It expressed his horror at injustice and oppression, which alone, he felt, might preserve his writings "from the obscurity in which their faults might otherwise bury them." A dedicatory *Epistle to Madame la Marquise du Châtelet,* added to the printed play, is remarkable for its statement on learned women and Voltaire's personal tribute to Emilie, as close to a public love letter as he dared to come (and which had the repercussions Voltaire might have expected).

First, an apology for dedicating a piece of transient verse to one who reads geometry books as others read novels; who, born for the social amenities, prefers the search for truth as a *femme savante.* As for those who satirized *les femmes savantes,* such as Molière and Despréaux, who mocked their efforts to study the stars, they would have done better to look through a telescope themselves. Women study what they *like* to study, Voltaire continues; men choose what can bring them fame or fortune. He had always cultivated literature and the arts for their own sakes, "but now, Madame, I cultivate them for you, to merit, if at all possible, to spend the rest of my life at your side, in the heart of refuge, peace, and perhaps truth." Regarding the play he was dedicating to Mme. du Châtelet, all he could add was that "I composed it in your house and under your eyes . . . You corrected its faults."

The last was not a gesture of conventional politeness; no creator really spurns aid, criticism untainted by competitiveness. Each day, or night, Voltaire would read to Mme du Châtelet what he had just written. He valued her more precise mind as he ventured more profoundly into critical deism, cultural and philosophical history, and Newtonian physics. If a play was in process, such as *Alzire,* it would be tried out in the tiny theater Voltaire had fashioned, and which still exists in a loft of the château. Besides Mme. du Châtelet, who sang and acted exceptionally well, everyone available was recruited for a performance: her husband, who did less well but did it amiably; their little girl, who boarded at a local convent; the servants; guests and their servants; and the neighbors. Voltaire, perhaps because of his astonishing productivity, was unusually open to suggestions. So, too, was Mme. du Châtelet. In person or by letter she constantly sought verification of her mathematical calculations involving, particularly, the law of gravity and its applications in the fields of motion and energy (and here her correspondence is undecipherable for one unversed in algebra, conic sections, and physics).

Almost daily after lunch, Emilie and Voltaire read a chapter of the Bible analytically and critically, leading to her work on Genesis and the New Testament (in manuscript at the Troyes Library). During the first year at Cirey, Emilie was also deeply involved in a translation, complete with commentaries, of Mandeville's *Fable of the Bees.* As she progressed, she discussed it with Voltaire, who had originally brought the book to her attention. Subsequently, often word for word, her additions and comments would appear in Voltaire's *Treatise on Metaphysics* of the following year.[35] They both found in Mandeville's work the rational explanation of social behavior, based on the study of natural phenomena and free of religious apriorities, that they were reaching for in their own work and studies. Emilie called Mandeville an "English Montaigne but with more method and a sounder idea of things than Montaigne."[36]

Early in her preface to Mandeville's work, Mme. du Châtelet explains her own philosophy and conduct—what impels her. "The mind rusts," she says, "more easily than iron." Just as the Indian fakirs lose the usage of the muscles of their immobile arms, so one loses the capacity to think "if one neglects to cultivate it." To nourish thought, it is best to fix a goal in one's studies, as in life—"to know who one wants to be." Irresolution is fatal. After indirectly addressing the women of her class in this manner, Mme. du Châtelet turns directly to men and speaks to them of women, especially herself:

> I feel the full weight of the prejudice excluding us universally from the sciences. It is one of the contradictions of the world which has always astonished me, since there are a few great nations whose laws permit us a say in our destiny, but none where we are educated to think.

In the course of his long lifetime, Voltaire wavered and hesitated and contradicted himself about the capacity of women as compared to men. The period in which he lived inculcated a conventional attitude despite himself; his experience with Mme. du Châtelet, quite another. During the second year at Cirey, he wrote to a Monsieur Berger (October 18, 1736): "Women are capable of doing everything we do . . . The only difference between us is that they are more likable."[37] Voltaire was not only a witness to it, but a partner in Emilie's characteristic probing of the matter, still striking in its currency.

> One should reflect [she continues in her preface] on why, over the centuries, women have never produced a first-rate tragedy, poem[?], history, painting [?] or book on physics . . . If I were King, I confess, I would order this scientific experiment: I would eliminate an abuse which cuts off half the human race. I would have women participate in all the rights of man and particularly those of the mind. Now, it would seem, they are born to deceive and one leaves them scarcely any other exercise. In any event, the new education would benefit all humanity . . . I am convinced that many a woman is unaware of her talents because of her noneducation, or buries them under prejudice or through lack of intellectual courage. My own experience confirms me in this opinion.[38]

There was division as well as sharing in the activities at Cirey. Emilie clearly took the lead in science, and held it, guiding Voltaire in his studies of Newton and later of Leibniz. She was indispensable for the grasp of physics that resulted in his *Eléments de la philosophie de Newton,* which stunned and literally turned around the largely Cartesian world of scientists.[39] She induced him, while making her own inventory of metaphysics, to consider it seriously. Throughout the decade and a half of his Cirey period, the Mme. du Châtelet years, Voltaire's work would acquire a new density, a new critical depth, a new philosophical daring, the whole "characterized by growth, evolution, expansion, but especially by broadened intellectual interests and feverish intellectual activity."[40] Emilie's contribution is visible in every phrase. And Voltaire's to Mme. du Châtelet? Granting that thinking is essentially dialectical, the question offers no difficulty. In Voltaire Mme. du Châtelet found, and possessed, the age's most fertile and stimulating mind. Its daily friction would prevent any rusting.

ALZIRE proved a great success. Voltaire was allowed to enjoy it personally in Paris. All seemed well. Then, irrepressibly, he permitted a new poem, *Le Mondain (The Worldly One),* to circulate in manuscript. It was a light-hearted defense of luxury as the nourisher of the arts, with a few provocative suggestions, such as that the Garden of Eden was not exactly an aesthetic paradise. But that was enough for the Church to react and sanctions to be brandished once again. "In what century are we living," exclaimed Voltaire, "to declare a man a criminal for having said that Adam had long nails and to treat it seriously as heresy!"[41] As always, Mme. du Châtelet and a few friends at Court, such as d'Argental, pulled all the strings they could in his support; and the storm might have passed and peace returned to their life at Cirey, had not something occurred just then that presented the most dangerous threat yet to the Cirey pair.

It arrived in bad-to-mediocre French in about mid-August 1736: the first letter to Voltaire from a twenty-four-year-old German admirer, the crown prince of Prussia, the future Frederick II (the Great). After pages of praise, which Voltaire drank in with immense and uncritical pleasure, Frederick posed *the* problem of the couple for the next twelve years: who would possess Voltaire, the prince and future king of one of Europe's most powerful states—who could offer him refuge in luxury, freedom in writing, and an endless bath in royal adulation—or Mme. du Châtelet? "If I am not destined to possess you," Frederick ends his lengthy letter,

> at least I can hope one day to see the man whom I have so long admired from a distance, and to assure you face to face that I am, with all the esteem and respect due to those who, guided by the torch of truth, devote their labors to the public good, Monsieur, your very affectionate friend, Fédérick [sic], Crown Prince of Prussia.[42]

Voltaire responded in kind and at length, beginning an exchange of almost a thousand letters between them during his lifetime. Frederick was kept informed by his agents about life at Cirey, Voltaire's troubles, and the importance of Mme. du Châtelet to him, and cleverly acted accordingly. He wanted Voltaire without Emilie, but he never completely exposed his hand; rather, he concealed, or tried to conceal, it with flattery. "Please tell Mme. la Marquise du Châtelet," he would write Voltaire, "that she is the only one to whom I could concede M. de Voltaire and be reconciled, for she is the only one worthy of possessing you."[43]

When Frederick sent gifts via an ambassador, he also addressed a letter to his messenger, intended in reality for Emilie's reading: "Remember, you are going to the earthly paradise, to a place a thousand times more delicious than the isle of Calypso, where the goddess of the region yields nothing in beauty to the enchantress of Telemachus and in whom you will find a beauty of mind beyond that of the body . . ."[44] In return Voltaire sent back an enchanted ambassador and the beginning of his *Century of Louis XIV.* Frederick had asked for *La Pucelle.* He was told, to his extreme displeasure, that it was in the safekeeping of Mme. du Châtelet, who now regarded him quite rightly as the enemy.

In the meantime the present danger was still possible imprisonment because of *Le Mondain.* Advance warning came one day in December 1736. Despite the snow and freezing cold Voltaire and Mme. du Châtelet left that night for an inn at Vassy. Voltaire was then to go on alone to Holland and from there, the couple gave out, to Prussia. Voltaire wrote letters all through the night at Vassy, the most moving to d'Argental, before departing at four in the morning. He was glad, he said, to be going at last to a free country,

> but as I see the moment approaching when I must part forever from one who has given up for me Paris, her friends, everything that renders life agreeable, one whom I adore and should adore, you will understand what I am feeling. The situation is horrible

> . . . Your friend is before me in tears. My heart is pierced. Must she return alone to a château she has built for me, must I be deprived of my life's consolation, because I have enemies in Paris?[45]

At the Belgian border, Voltaire wrote to Emilie of his safe arrival and melancholic state of mind. She could see, Emilie informed d'Argental, by the sadness of his letters that he would do anything to be with her. "I made him understand the necessity of behaving cautiously and lying low if he really wished it." But what Emilie dreaded most was Frederick's siren call to his "land of freedom." Was not the mad king, his father, capable of doing harm to his son's "dangerous" friend, as he had to others? D'Argental must help dissuade Voltaire from going. "No Prussia! I beg you on bended knees!"[46]

Voltaire, in effect, never went farther than Amsterdam. Frederick was not yet king; Voltaire could wait. In the meantime he busied himself with his publishing affairs, wrote to his Prussian prince ("greater already than Socrates"), and, French authorities permitting it, returned to Cirey at the end of winter. Life and work resumed for both as before, with the addition of a newly equipped laboratory, where they conducted experiments in physics. Each, unknown to the other, was preparing a paper on fire for submission in a competition organized by the Academy of Sciences. Neither would win, but both would be honorably mentioned—and theirs would be the only studies based on experimental results!

During this time Voltaire was also taken up by the care of two orphaned nieces, daughters of the beloved sister who had died long since, her death now followed by her husband's. Marie-Louise, who was the older (born in 1712), is the only one who need concern us. Voltaire arranged for her marriage to a son of Mme. de Champbonin and offered a dowry of 30,000 francs. Marie-Louise refused. She had fallen in love with Nicolas-Charles Denis, a notary, and proceeded to marry him. Voltaire remained as generous as before, simply remarking: "I want her to be happy in her way, not in mine."[47]

Mme. Denis, twenty-six, and her husband spent part of their honeymoon at Cirey in April 1738. Everyone had a pleasant time, according to Voltaire. Mme. du Châtelet probably felt the same way; they both became fond of M. Denis—and she had no crystal ball among her instruments. Mme. Denis's surprisingly blunt account to Thieriot afterward, May 10, reveals *her* point of view. She was writing from Landau, where there was a military garrison with which M. Denis had dealings and where they had just settled. Her uncle had been ill all the time of their stay at Cirey. Mme. du Châtelet had become rather stout, but was very pretty and lively. However, Mme. Denis feared that her uncle was lost to his friends, "bound in such a fashion that it seems impossible he will ever be able to break his chains." They both lived in a terrifying solitude, leagues from any human settlement, surrounded by mountains and moors [!] and hardly ever seeing anyone from Paris. "Such is the life of the greatest genius of our century!" But her uncle was more bewitched than ever by Mme. du Châtelet, "who employs all the arts imaginable to captivate him."

Mme. Denis closed with a brief description of her own situation at Landau, which may be the most revealing of all: "I believe I shall accommodate myself to life here easily enough. I have a pretty house and there are four hundred officers at my disposal, from whom I will pick a dozen or so for my suppers."[48]

Both parts of the letter announced a difficult time for Mme. du Châtelet, though she could not know it. The marriage would be a happy one, but short, and she would have the niece, as well as the prince, maneuvering to "break the chains" shackling Voltaire to her.

Nine months later a more grateful guest was sheltered at Cirey, an unmoneyed lady of forty-three, Voltaire's age, whom they had met at the Court of Lorraine. Separated from a mad husband, who had beaten her and was now shut away, Mme. de Graffigny lived on such invitations to country châteaus, where a new face was almost invariably welcome—for a reasonable time. Since, at Cirey, she was generally left to her own devices by her busy hosts, Mme. de Graffigny wrote letters to Lunéville, where they were eagerly awaited. Allowing for the fact that she observed the dictum that one must never bore, and therefore one must embellish, the virtually daily letters to a M. Devaux ("Pan-Pan"), depicting the celebrated lovers of Cirey at home, are a literary windfall.[49] (She would go on to write a successful novel and play.)

December 4, 1738. Here she is at Cirey, just imagine! She had arrived two hours after dark and after a few misadventures. The Nymph of the château herself led her graciously to her luxurious bedroom. And here was the Idol, holding a little candlestick and robed like a monk, who gave her a thousand caresses and kissed her hand ten times. They left her to dress for supper. Mme. du Châtelet wears a printed calico dress and a huge black apron, her long black hair is swept up to the top of her head and falls in curls, like a little girl's, very becomingly. She talks "like an angel!" Soon supper will be rung. Good night, dear Pan-Pan.

Midnight, next day. Supper had been in Voltaire's quarters. On silver plates! He was dressed and powdered as if for Paris, and several lackeys attended to him. What conversation! Poetry, science, art, and such witty stories! On her left sat her host, M. du Châtelet, who said little and left early. He is supposed to be leaving for Brussels, which no one will regret. Then Voltaire rose, signaling bedtime or time to return to the writing table, she was not sure. She slept until noon today. A fat little lady (Mme. de Champbonin) who is also visiting and adores Voltaire came by to chat. She has exhausted all the books they have pressed on her at Cirey and keeps mostly to her room. Mme. de Graffigny herself was given Voltaire's manuscript of *Newton* the night before, which she *must* read! He rescued her from M. du Châtelet—what a bore!—and took her to his wing. What taste, what cleanliness! The bedroom is small, with a tapestry, but there is gilded paneling everywhere, with magnificent paintings fitted into it, and lacquered cupboards and silvered mirrors. The long gallery leading from the room is filled with statues, books, and scientific instruments, and there's a heavenly stove giving off a springtime warmth.

But this is nothing compared to the lady's rooms, which Mme. de Graffigny saw on the morrow. Her bedroom is paneled in yellow and pale blue, the alcove is lined with India paper, the bed covered in blue moiré. Everything matches, even the dog's basket. The small boudoir is so pretty, one could fall to one's knees in adoration. Each panel has a painting by Watteau; the ceiling is being done by a pupil of Martin who has been at Cirey *for three years!* Such jewels and snuffboxes, fifteen or twenty of them in gold and lacquer and precious stones, she who didn't even have one in tortoiseshell when Mme. de Graffigny first met her! (They were among the gifts from Voltaire, who thus assured Emilie's having things of value should he die.) And then there was the bathroom. Sheer enchantment! All tiled except for the marble floor and porcelain baths, the little *cabinet de toilette* paneled in celadon green—gay, gilded, and divinely carved—with a sofa and chairs in the same carved, gilded wood. (Mme. du Châtelet's daily bathing was legendary at the notoriously negligent Court of Versailles.)

Pan-Pan has asked about the daily schedule at Cirey? Now, that is something to marvel about—and adjust to! Since the lady often works through the night and goes to bed at the cock's crow, the morning coffee is not served before eleven, and then in Voltaire's gallery, accompanied by heated discussions and arguments about philosophy and physics. The noon meal is strictly for the "coachmen"—M. du Châtelet, Mme. de Champbonin, and the son. Voltaire and the lady may look in, but usually they go to their rooms until four, when they may or may not have a bite. Then back to their rooms, supper at nine, conversation, theatricals, and readings until midnight. One day in February, they all performed over twenty acts of different Voltaire plays as well as two and a half operas—between noon and seven the next morning. The lady had sung an entire opera by herself. As for Voltaire, he did not always know his parts, but he improvised quickly and wittily on the spot. One evening he put on a magic-lantern show and had them in stitches with his stories—but he finished by setting the magic lantern on fire!

Mme. de Graffigny was particularly struck by Mme. du Châtelet's capacity, writing speed—the preface to a translation in scarcely half of an hour—and stylistic clarity. She had read both essays on fire and preferred the lady's by far! "Our sex should raise an altar to her." Since Mme. du Châtelet had written it in secret, she had worked by night, sleeping no more than an hour, dipping her hands in ice water to keep awake, and so for a week.

Of course the lovers had their little quarrels, also, as when Voltaire was scolded for drinking a glass too much of Rhine wine for his health, or one night when they were sitting in Mme. du Châtelet's bedroom, chatting. Mme. du Châtelet thought Voltaire's coat not quite appropriate—despite its beautiful lace—and told him to change it for another. He refused, because of the cold. She insisted. He replied sharply in English, and left for his room. After a long moment, she sent for him. He wouldn't return. Finally he did. They talked back and forth in English until all was well again.

Pan-Pan should be very careful about repeating what Mme. de Graffigny was writing to him. It seems her letters to him were being opened, because "somehow" the last stanza of *La Pucelle,* which she had only *mentioned,* was being misquoted by everybody at Lunéville and causing a great deal of mischief. There has been a terrible scene with her hostess and Voltaire, but they have since apologized for their suspicions. Voltaire generously and sincerely, Mme. du Châtelet unconvincingly. Unknown to Mme. de Graffigny, the Cirey pair was in a state not only because of the pirated stanza, but on account of a violent attack on Voltaire that had just been published, *Voltairomanie,* by a persistent enemy, Abbé Desfontaines. Despite Mme. du Châtelet's attempted restraints, Voltaire invariably spent himself refuting Desfontaines or bringing him to trial. Soon, however, Mme. de Graffigny would leave to become another lady's houseguest, the Abbé would be obliged to denounce what he had written, and the pair could relax.

The relaxation took the form of trips away from Cirey. Voltaire needed a change, Emilie decided, perhaps because *she* felt the need. Four years of honeymoon, however successful, is a fairly long time. Voltaire was normally restless; she was intensely social. She was always intense. That had put off her previous lovers, and it must have meant a strain for Voltaire. On one of their journeys to Paris, Voltaire wrote to Mme. de Champbonin, saying he was going there to follow Mme. du Châtelet, but why she was going there was a mystery to him. The initiative seems always to have been Emilie's, whether they went to Brussels because the du Châtelets had a long-pending law suit there; or to Holland, with Emilie taking along a protégé of Maupertuis to give her lessons in algebra as they traveled. The trips do not put into question their togetherness, since they took them together. They did not have to; they were not locked in marriage. The chains were of their own forging. It may well have been more difficult for M. du Châtelet, from the viewpoint of appearances, when they journeyed together than when they resided at Cirey, since everywhere they went they were received and fêted as a couple.

And as always each worked wherever they paused, Voltaire on his play *Mahomet,* Emilie on her *Institutions de physique,* which would be the first lucid introduction of Leibniz to the French. Published, it had considerable success. Voltaire shared the general admiration, but not Mme. du Châtelet's for Leibniz, whose metaphysical "monads" exasperated him. He regretted the diversion of Venus-Newton, but it would be temporary. Of more permanent interest is Mme. du Châtelet's preface, dedicated to her son. It reiterates her attitude toward the self-sufficiency, the "consolations," of study, best undertaken when one is young and the mind is open. She counseled her thirteen-year-old son to begin with geometry first, then go on to physics, "the key to all discoveries."[50]

At about this time Voltaire was writing (in English) to his old friend Sir Everard Fawkener, British ambassador to Turkey: "I would pass some months at Constantinople with you, if I could live without that lady whom I look upon as a great man and as a most solid and respectable friend. She understands Newton; she despises superstition, in short she makes me happy."[51] Almost daily Voltaire wrote in this fashion about Mme. du Châtelet during their decade and a half together—in letters, poems, epistles, and dedications. So he continued to write to Frederick, who ardently wanted Voltaire with him, but without his lady, whereas Voltaire seemed as determined as ever not to be without her.

Finally, on the death of his father, May 31, 1740, the crown prince became king. On June 6 he wrote anew, pressing an invitation upon Voltaire, *alone.* In July he sent verses of remarkably reckless passion. When Voltaire ultimately comes to him, Frederick writes, at last he will look upon "those clear piercing eyes" from which nature could not hide its secrets, and "kiss a thousand times that eloquent mouth . . . *toujours également enchanteresse et charmante.*"[52]

Voltaire dallied. Mme. du Châtelet, like the Queen of Sheba, he replied to the last invitation, would also like to see Solomon-Frederick II. Alas, no, returned Frederick, two divinities would be too blinding. Meanwhile, he would greatly appreciate Voltaire's dashing off to The Hague and stopping the printing of his *Anti-Machiavel,* written in his youth. Now that the prince was king, he had second thoughts. Voltaire departed for Holland without Emilie, who was rightly suspicious of a maneuver, but he soon returned to her in Brussels. Traveling in Prussia not far from the Belgian border, Frederick invited *both* to meet him in Antwerp. Then he fell ill, he wrote, and invited Voltaire alone, since he was too sick, he said, to see a woman. Again Emilie was deeply suspicious, but somewhat more resigned. She would "lend" Voltaire to the Prussian king for a few days, she wrote to Maupertuis, who was with Frederick as future head of the Berlin Academy of Science (thanks to Voltaire).

The Frederick whom Voltaire found in September 1740 was indeed ill, shaking with fever, a little man in a large blue dressing gown. But he rose, and they dined together with Maupertuis and others. Voltaire read from *Mahomet.* Frederick was less charmed by Emilie's new book, which Voltaire had also brought, though he praised it to him (and derided it in private). Three days passed, and Frederick had to return to Berlin, but he obliged Voltaire to go to Holland on the *Anti-Machiavel* affair, rather than to Brussels, where Emilie was impatiently awaiting him. The king was more determined than ever to possess Voltaire—"every drop of ink is a flash of wit sparkling from his pen . . . He transported us"[53]—and he seemed to have won the first trick.

Mme. du Châtelet, however, was not without resources. In Paris because of her mother's death, she went down to Fontainebleau, where Louis XV had brought his suite. She would finesse the king by having Voltaire reinstated in Louis XV's eyes and installed at the French Court, which was far more inviting than the beckoning Prussian's imitation. She appealed to Prime Minister Fleury. She even enlisted the support of Frederick, who could not openly refuse. Voltaire cooperated with delight. He wrote Fleury, saying he would be staying with the Prussian king again. Could he on that occasion bring a personal message from the prime minister? By coincidence and fortunately for all conspirators, Europe was in a state of confusion following the successive deaths of the Prussian, Russian, and Austrian rulers within several weeks. What did the new Prussian king have in mind? France wanted to know, wrote Fleury to Voltaire in return. Could he find out from his friend the Prussian king? Beside himself, Voltaire left directly for Berlin, though he had not seen Emilie for some time.

In Berlin, Frederick II played with the amateur emissary—having caught on to it quickly—and revealed nothing he was not saying to the French ambassador or writing to Fleury himself. In the meantime they visited and chatted and exchanged verses somewhat beyond the most precious literary conventions, calling each other *coquette* and *mistress;* and Frederick did not dissimulate his homosexuality or that of his entourage. It was, rather, dissimulation of his military intentions that disillusioned Voltaire, who was essentially a pacifist. The day after the king gave a masked ball, his troops invaded Silesia (December 13). Voltaire had departed shortly before, after a fortnight in Berlin; decidedly, the conqueror-king was not the philosopher-prince. There was a personal distaste as well, as Voltaire's note disclosed to Maupertuis before leaving. "I must embrace my philosopher," he wrote, "before saying farewell to the worthy, singular whore [Frederick] who arrives."[54] But to Frederick he was writing almost simultaneously that his heart was torn at leaving:

> For four years you have been my mistress,
> To which a love of ten years should be preferred,
> So I leave to fulfill a sacred duty.[55]

The Prussian king would continue to beckon and offer the attractions of power, and Voltaire would respond, but the spell had been broken.

In the meanwhile the seven- (not ten-) year-old relationship of love between the Cirey pair had not fundamentally altered. Mme. du Châtelet had been faithful in both their fashions, for each was still first in the other's affections and would still sacrifice any other when the choice was to be made. While Voltaire was coquetting in Berlin, Emilie was at Fontainebleau, staying, as usual, with the Duke de Richelieu, whose wife had, sadly, died that summer. Once again the love that never completely went cold flared anew. It was a physical feeling on the part of a sensual Emilie, as well as a passionate friendship ancillary to her love for Voltaire. It had occurred five years earlier, Richelieu had said no, and she had written to him: "I should never have avowed what I just have. . . . and I never would console myself for it if I were not sure that despite your resolutions you cannot prevent your heart's friendship for me."[56]

In the fall of 1740, for the second time, Richelieu had said no, and Emilie again felt compelled to explain herself:

> I do not know why I avowed what I did in Fontainebleau . . . I said it because it is the truth and because I believe I owe you an accounting of everything I feel. No thought went into my confession; indeed, had I reflected, I should never have made it . . . Undoubtedly my feeling for you would be incomprehensible to any other person, but it does not diminish my intense passion [for Voltaire] which now causes my unhappiness [that is, his extended stay in Berlin].[57]

If one has ever loved, Emilie seems to be repeating, as she and the duke once loved, which feelings have since been transmuted into a strong friendship, then it is natural and not wrong that they love in passing without betraying either themselves or anyone else. From Paris, on her way to Brussels, where she hoped to meet Voltaire on his return from Berlin, Emilie had already written Richelieu of her greatest fear—that the separation from Voltaire might last for years and become permanent: "I am burning inside . . . seized by a terrible fever, and I hope to end soon like poor Madame de Richelieu"—but more quickly, by suicide.[58]

At last, after a slow, cold journey from Berlin, Voltaire reached Brussels and rejoined Emilie, and their reunion was very moving. "Never," he exclaimed, "has Mme. du Châtelet seemed so far above the King!"[59] As for Mme. du Châtelet, she wrote d'Argental the next day (January 7, 1741): "I defy the Prussian King to hate me more than I have hated him . . . He can take as many provinces as he wants so long as he does not take that which is the charm of my life."[60]

Voltaire and Mme. du Châtelet remained in Brussels for several months; the lawsuit was dragging on interminably. Meantime Voltaire reworked his play *Mahomet* and wrote at considerable length, with Emilie's indispensable aid, on kinetic energy. But he was becoming bored with the methodical process of finding truth through physics, those "barren shades." He was Voltaire, not Newton; he would "return" to verse and philosophical history, in reality never abandoned.[61] In April the two went to Lille for the first-night performance of *Mahomet* and dropped in on Voltaire's niece and her husband, then stationed there. They also spent time in Paris, never quite seeming to settle down again in Cirey, except briefly, as if between travels elsewhere. Yet a study of the time passed would show a greater share spent in their Champagne refuge. Perhaps one records the trips because tranquility is less notable, as are the peaceful years in history books.

Perhaps, too, the verses of Voltaire to Emilie when he came back from Berlin should not be taken for a turning point. He had never been an ardent lover, a *pistolet,* as the French say. Nonetheless, arriving in Brussels, Voltaire had announced to Mme. du Châtelet that he was now "too old [at forty-six] to make love! 'The heart does not age, but this immortal is condemned to live in a ruin.' "[62] Was it too soon after the stay with Frederick? In any event, these verses follow:

Si vous voulez que j'aime encore,
Rendez-moi l'âge des amours;
Au crépuscule de mes jours
Rejoignez, s'il se peut, l'aurore.

On meurt deux fois, je le vois bien.
Cesser d'aimer et d'être aimable
C'est une mort insupportable;
Cesser de vivre ce n'est rien.

Du ciel alors daignant descendre
L'amitié vint à mon secours;
Elle est plus égale, aussi tendre
Et moins vive que les amours.

Touché de sa beauté nouvelle
Et de sa lumière éclairée,
Je la suivis mais je pleurais
De ne plus pouvoir suivre qu'elle.[63]

("If you want me to continue loving, give me back the age of love; to the twilight of my days join, if you can, the dawn. One dies twice, I see it well. To cease loving and being loved is an insupportable death. To cease living is nothing. Deigning to descend from the sky, friendship has come to my aid. It is more moderate, as tender as, and less alive than love. Touched by its new beauty and its clear light, I follow it but weep, for I can follow nothing else.")

And so the next few years passed, with gossip about Mme. du Châtelet's passing fancies and Voltaire's efforts to get into the French Academy and Frederick's to extend his conquests, Voltaire among them. Intermittently Frederick did succeed in getting Voltaire to Berlin. Emilie found the fourth trip, during the summer and fall of 1743, the most trying. Once again Voltaire was on a "secret" mission for Versailles; once again Frederick perceived it and mocked him unmercifully. He even tried to damage Voltaire's relations with the French Court so irreparably that only the Prussian Court would remain for him. Voltaire discovered this and foiled Frederick, losing that much more of his trust in the Prussian king. Before returning to France and Emilie, however, he made a side trip to Bayreuth. There he enjoyed himself hugely with Frederick's sister and the ladies of her small court, and negligently wrote long letters to Emilie concerning it, after an unusually long silence. And once again in Brussels, awaiting him, Mme. du Châtelet suffered and was ill, but not in silence.

What was Voltaire doing in Bayreuth without the king? she asked d'Argental rhetorically. Would he ever return? He sounds "absolutely drunk" in his letters, and now he is on his way to Brunswick to see another sister of the king's. He's mad about those silly little German courts *(courettes).* She was counting the days and weeks. It would be five months (which should have been five weeks) before Voltaire finally rejoined Mme. du Châtelet in Brussels. On the way, he, too, had written d'Argental, defending himself against Emilie's complaints about her ill health and his behavior. On his arrival he added a Voltairean postscript: "I am very happy to see that your friend is in better health than I!"[64] She probably was. She had tangible proof that Voltaire still preferred her to the Prussian king and all the *courettes* and courtesans of Germany. And she exulted to their mutual confidant, d'Argental: "Because I love him and you know that, there are no wrongs which that does not erase." But . . . "tell him that people should never separate when they love. There is always something lost in love in an absence of five months. The heart loses the habit of loving."[65]

Before returning to Cirey, Voltaire and Emilie stayed in Paris, but before going there, they stopped off at Lille to see Mme. Denis and her husband. This time nothing else had drawn them there.

In Paris, while Voltaire worked, Mme. du Châtelet played cards, and steadily lost, obliging her to ask him for the loan of fifty louis d'or. Gambling, for her, was one of the emotions that spelled happiness—if one gambled great sums. "The soul," she would soon write in an essay on happiness, "needs to be shaken up by hope or by fear. Only that which makes it feel its existence intensely makes it happy, such as gambling, which perpetually grips us with both passions."[66] Though in ill health that winter, Voltaire seems to have had an affair with an actress, about which Mme. du Châtelet appears to have been familiar. However, when M. du Châtelet wrote with some impatience from Cirey, asking for her return, and she appealed to Voltaire to return with her, he agreed: Mme. du Châtelet, as always, came first. Voltaire had, moreover, an opera to write for Rameau. It had been pressed upon him by Richelieu, now charged with festivals and entertainment at Versailles, no mean charge, in view of an easily bored king. Rameau, Voltaire knew from experience, was difficult. Cirey provided the ideal solitude. They arrived there in April 1744. Within a few days they had news of M. Denis's illness, several days later of his death. Voltaire invited his niece to spend a month with them at Cirey: "I speak to you of spending a month at your side, my dear niece, when I would like to spend my life with you."[67] *Without* Mme. du Châtelet? It is unlikely, but it is also unlikely she saw this letter. At the same time Voltaire was writing of his happiness with Emilie and inscribing it over the door of his gallery. (One is always mistaken to arrive at simple conclusions about complex, or perhaps even "simple," people: "Uncle and niece had already made love," says Theodore Besterman rather flatly, and Voltaire, "in all probability," had used the actress in Paris and discussions of "stage business" with her, "as a cover for his encounters with Mme. Denis."[68])

The summer at Cirey was one of Voltaire and Emilie's happiest. If he was having problems with his opera vis-à-vis Rameau, it mattered less, he said, because he had Mme. du Châtelet by his side; her presence was a comfort, her judgment infallible. In July they received Charles Hénault, president of the Parlement of Paris. To his *surprise,* Cirey was a delight whose like he had never seen. "They are there, the two of them, alone," he wrote to Count d'Argenson,

> living a most agreeable life. One makes verses, the other, triangles. The architecture of the house is romantic and surprisingly magnificent. Voltaire has an apartment ending in a gallery which looks like [Raphael's] *The School of Athens,* where there are assembled instruments of all kinds, mathematical, physical, chemical, astronomical, mechanical, and so on, all this surrounded by ancient lacquer, mirrors, paintings, Dresden porcelain. I tell you, one thinks one is dreaming.

Voltaire had read to him from his opera. Hénault was astonished to hear that Rameau had turned literary critic and was rewriting Voltaire's verses![69] He reverted to the Cirey couple in his memoirs, still fascinated by what he had witnessed. Theirs was a delicious, peaceful retreat and refuge, he wrote, a serene communion of souls, of talents, of mutual admiration, of philosophy allied to poetry.

In the fall Voltaire and Mme. du Châtelet went up to Paris, where Mme. Denis had already installed her new household. From this point on, there is no longer any room for uncertainty. The love letters between Voltaire and his niece, discovered in our own century, leave no doubt: his strong family feeling had turned to passionate love. His erotic letters, generally in Italian, are explicit (one can only regret that those surely written to Emilie, at least during the first years, were destroyed on her death). *"Baccio il vostro gentil culo et tutta la vostra vezzoza persona"* ("I kiss your lovely ass and all your adorable body"). But his passion, as always, had his bad health to contend with—it was ever *"una gran nemica del piacere"* ("a great enemy of pleasure").

Voltaire was obviously not a young woman's ideal lover, but he was rich and famous and generous, and Mme. Denis, everything indicates, was shrewdly self-interested. She would find supplemental lovers (Voltaire's protégés), avoid remarriage, and wait. Meanwhile, Voltaire would be grateful: Mme. Denis gave him an erection, when, apparently, Mme. du Châtelet no longer did—and perhaps one day Mme. Denis no longer would. July 27, 1748: *"Io figo mile baccii alle tondo poppe, alle transportatrici natiche, a tutta la vostra persona che m'ha fatto tante volte rizzare e m'ha annegato in un fiume di delizie"* ("I press a thousand kisses on your round breasts, on your ravishing bottom, on all your person which has made me stiffen so often and plunged me in a flood of delight").[70]

Passionate as it was, Voltaire's liaison with his niece remained *secondary* to his alliance with Mme. du Châtelet, as if that were sacred and untouchable, and he always kept his meetings with Mme. Denis in the tightest secrecy *from everyone.* But the liaison was there, constantly in the background of the closing years.

Voltaire's opera was a success, and he was made Historian to the King and given a small room (number 144) at Versailles for his use. With the utmost care, he invited Mme. Denis to his room (March 1745), warning her that it was "near the foulest-smelling latrine [*piu puzzolente cacatoia*] of the palace." But there was never a parting from Emilie: they went and were received everywhere together ("as man and wife," Frederick remarked sardonically but accurately). When, in April 1745, they traveled to Châlons to see Mme. du Châtelet's sick son, Mme. Denis was duly reminded of the "duties of friendship." When, in February 1748, they had left Cirey for Lunéville, Mme. Denis was told her uncle-lover infinitely preferred "your boudoir to any Court!"[71] But he *had* gone to Lunéville rather than to Paris.

The years of complete clandestinity are almost incredible, though manifest in the dates. Mme. du Châtelet simply did not know. She and Voltaire continued their life and their work together; he was in and out of trouble with the authorities, as usual, and she went on gambling. One evening at the queen's table, she lost the equivalent of a hundred thousand dollars. Voltaire, who was standing by, could not restrain himself. "You are playing with cheats!" he cried to her in English. Almost immediately realizing he had been understood, they packed and left Fontainebleau that night. Their carriage broke down, they had to borrow money from a passing acquaintance, and finally they sheltered in the château of the Duchesse du Maine, a power in herself as the widow of Louis XIV's favorite bastard son. Even after the storm had blown over, Voltaire and Emilie spent much time with the duchess at either Sceaux or Anet, her country house in Normandy.

It was a critical period for Mme. du Châtelet. Her restlessness at Anet in August 1747 was observed by a lady-in-waiting of the duchess. Three times within as many months, this lady wrote to Mme. du Deffand, the Cirey lovers had changed residence, all because of Mme. du Châtelet. Their last home had been Paris, which they left because Madame had found it too noisy. "It upsets her thinking, and right now she is reviewing her principles," shutting herself off from others until nightfall.[72]

To the lady-in-waiting, Mme. du Châtelet was simply engaged in one of her "yearly exercises." In fact Emilie was deep in a momentous summing up, *meant for herself,* a review of her life up to this time, in writing, so that she might develop it systematically and logically, as with everything else she worked on seriously. The resultant *Essay on Happiness* was not published in her lifetime; nor was it meant to be, for family reasons, particularly on her son's account. It was too personal: exploring her life with Voltaire was one thing, proclaiming it was another (a woman could publish a book on Newton but not on herself).

Mme. du Châtelet reveals that if she was unaware of Voltaire's love for his niece and their passionate rendezvous, she was certainly not insensible to the change in him, despite the more than simply *loyal* affection he continued showing her. The remarkable Emilie reveals the change she sensed, and goes *beyond* it—and once again one understands Voltaire's admiration, his profound love for Mme. du Châtelet. The passage occurs in the middle of her journey into herself and the sources of happiness. It is best, she has just said, if one's happiness does not depend upon others. "For this reason of independence, the love of study is, of all the passions, the one that contributes most to our happiness." However, she now continues, posing the inevitable paradox, obviously the passion that gives one the most pleasure, renders one happiest, and makes one yearn to live is love, which is dependent entirely upon another. The mating of twin souls is everything; "all they need is health." But a soul, a heart, such as hers, tender, constant, unrestrained in its passion, loving even if unreciprocated, is born once in a century. For two to occur at the same time is a miracle. It had happened to her:

> For ten years I was happy with one who had subjugated my soul, and for those ten years I was with him, side by side, without a moment of distaste or of dragging time. When age, sickness, perhaps also, somewhat, the easiness of satisfaction diminished his desire, I went for a long time without perceiving it. I loved for two.

She had been happy; the change had come; she had cried. Chains such as those that bound them could only be broken at the price of violent upheavals. She had been wounded; she had forgiven. Her kind of constancy was rare. Had age and illness not extinguished Voltaire's desires, they would have been, she was sure, directed toward her. Incapable of her passionate love, as he was now, he still devoted his tender friendship, his whole life, to her; and slowly, insensibly, she, too, had been led to the tranquil sentiment of friendship, which, together with her passion for study, made her reasonably happy.

But Mme. du Châtelet relentlessly asked herself, "Can a heart as affectionate as mine be satisfied with such a tame, tranquil sentiment as friendship?" It should, she replied to her tearing question, it *had* to at her age (forty!). "Passions, once you are past thirty, no longer sweep you away with the same impetuosity. There is no passion you cannot overcome, once you are convinced it can bring you only unhappiness." Thus Emilie attempted to explain the resignation she was now calling wisdom.

The drama, the poignancy, of Mme. du Châtelet's search for the principles of happiness was this tension between rationality, to which she gave her whole allegiance, and passion, to which she gave her person, her "heart." The very phrase describing her priority among the sources of happiness, the *passion* of study, is an essay at reconciling them: passion does flood the mind, whether with love or the elegance of an algebraic equation.

Freedom of the mind (she continued) and freedom to love are equally to be cherished. To be happy you must be free from prejudices (generally religious), enjoy good health, strong tastes, and, of course, passions. And what if, finally, passion brings unhappiness? "Only the unhappy are interesting"; to them alone are great tragedies devoted. Above all, you should decide what you want in life. (Compare Goethe: "One must be careful about what one wants in life, because the chances are one will get it.") Otherwise one flounders in uncertainties, undoing in the morning what has been done in the night. Repentance is one of the most useless and disagreeable feelings to which we choose to subject ourselves. We must not look back. To dwell on past mistakes is as futile as to dwell on inevitable death. "We have nothing else to do in this world than to be happy."[73]

That summer at Anet, Mme. du Châtelet was also undertaking what she had been preparing for most of her life—the translation and annotation of, and commentary on, Newton's massive *Principia Mathematica,* the most difficult, the most important scientific work of several hundred years (his conception of the solar system is still essentially our own). Mme. du Châtelet's own great work on it, however, was interrupted and almost brought to a complete stop.

It was not because of the new quarrels with Voltaire (recounted by Longchamp in his memoirs). Even if true, they were trivial, as easily mended as Emilie's Dresden cup—supposedly broken by Voltaire in the heat of a *philosophical* argument, and replaced by him. Another of the valet's anecdotes is more significant. When, one cold winter night early in 1748, they were traveling from Paris to Cirey and their coach had turned over, they enjoyed it! While help was sought by the footmen, they simply sat on cushions laid on the snow and marveled at the brilliancy of the night's stars, regretting only their missing telescopes as they speculated on the course and destiny of the planets.

The fatal interruption, rather, was due to Mme. du Châtelet's falling in love at the Court of Lunéville with the Marquis de Saint-Lambert.

The marquis was about thirty-two; she was forty-one and a grandmother. The fatality was not in that difference. Neither the one nor the other was too young or too old. Jean-François Saint-Lambert was, in some ways, rather like the Duke de Richelieu, though, unlike him, unmarried; a handsome prize, judging from his success, in the carrousel of court love. He was a poet-officer, which means he had some *esprit* (which eventually took him to the French Academy). Most of all he was a courtier, which meant he had sufficient income as an absentee landowner to center his existence around the lives, loves, intrigues, and entertainment of a court, with an occasional sortie, as an officer, to some silly field of absurd combat. Actually Saint-Lambert was a cut above the other courtiers. He was intelligent and coolly aloof, which made him all the more attractive, and capable of constancy, despite the usual succession of mistresses, the last among them Mme. de Boufflers, the favorite of King Stanislas and a rather dear friend of Mme. du Châtelet.

The affair began as a flirtation on his part to make the inconstant Mme. de Boufflers jealous. With the force and rapidity of a forest fire out of control, it became passionate—on the part of Mme. du Châtelet. They made love in a secret little room, away from the palace, that had been arranged for Mme. de Boufflers, who knew about it and laughed lightly at it—she had previously given Mme. du Châtelet a key to the trysting place.

Voltaire knew of it, too, and did not laugh, though he may have experienced some relief. He was writing some of his most erotic letters, at this endearing distance, to Mme. Denis. Scarcely more than he, however, was Emilie putting into question their own enduring intimacy. In her frank, open fashion, she invited Saint-Lambert to join her, M. du Châtelet, and Voltaire at Cirey (April 1748), and enclosed directions.

He did not follow them; he did not come. Saint-Lambert, nevertheless, seems to have fallen in love, if one can love briefly and if the one letter we have from him can be taken literally. "My dear love," he addresses Emilie, and speaks of her, too, as "my dear heart." Only she can ever bring him happiness, he says. But there is a passage, almost immediately preceding, that casts a chilling light on the abysmal difference between their two temperaments. "Take care of your health," he advises; "cool yourself frequently. Remember the grand principle of Mme.———: everything that overheats, ages; everything that remains cool, remains young."

When Saint-Lambert failed to follow her to Cirey, Emilie was troubled at the thought of his being "alone" at Lunéville with Mme. de Boufflers. Emilie's letters become increasingly pressing, complaining; yet they have a terrible lucidity. She and Saint-Lambert had had a secret, lover's rendezvous in Nancy, before she went to Cirey with Voltaire and then on to Paris for rehearsals of his new play. In that short interval there has been a sharp change. What happened since Nancy? Emilie asks with anxiety; Saint-Lambert's letters are so curt, so noncommittal. "All my doubts about your character, all my resolutions against love have not guarded me against the love you have inspired in me . . . If you can love me only weakly, if your heart cannot give itself without reservations . . . what are you going to do with mine?"[74]

That will be the leitmotif as resolutions and rationality are torn to shreds. "One must have passions to be happy," Mme. du Châtelet had written, "but one must make them serve our happiness." Passion was in the saddle, riding her. She knew it, but she was also the passion, and knew that as well. She had even incorporated it into her philosophy of happiness: if a person had the good fortune to be susceptible to illusion, it was impossible for that person not to believe he or she was not more loved than was perhaps the case. "One should love so much, one loves for two."

She had even been sensible about the most likely result:

> The great secret of not being miserable in love is never to be mistaken about our lovers, never to show eagerness when he is cooling off, to be always one degree cooler than he. It will not bring him back, but nothing will bring him back. There is nothing to do but forget someone who ceases to love us.

"I know," Mme. du Châtelet had glumly added, "that this secret is not easy to practice." But "nothing degrades so much as efforts to regain a cold, inconstant heart."[75] A man's pursuit of a woman may be courtship; a woman's of a man is humiliation.

Knowing this, Emilie nonetheless hotly pursued the Marquis de Saint-Lambert, who, quite unfortunately, behaved so well that she would not be delivered of her passion before sixteen months had passed. "I will do anything," she wrote, "to see you, to live with you." "I have a fever, I have not eaten for five days." "Love me as much as you want and I will never be unhappy."[76] Incessantly she repeated in letter after letter, *"Je vous adore."* Passion had reduced her to the stutterer of that simple phrase, "I love you," so maddening, so vapid, so tedious, so repelling for one who no longer does. Mme. du Châtelet had written no less in her essay.

Desperately, for the first time in any contingent affair, so despairing was she this time, Mme. du Châtelet wrote of spending her life entirely with Saint-Lambert, at Lunéville or Cirey (!), and "forget[ting] the rest of the world" for him.[77] Ironically Voltaire would write the same to Mme. Denis in October 1748, when he and Mme. du Châtelet had *both* gone to Lorraine—although Voltaire was ill and had urgent matters in Paris as well as his niece—so that Mme. du Châtelet might be close to Saint-Lambert. "I spend my life," he wrote, "thinking about how I can spend the rest of my life with you."[78] In truth, they each talked of devoting themselves completely to each of their lovers, but in some undefined future.

Here Longchamp's story about one evening at Commercy, where the Court of Lorraine was spending a season, tells us much about three of the foursome and puts beyond doubt which of the two was the true couple. Voltaire had gone unannounced to Mme. du Châtelet's room before supper, directly to her boudoir, as always. He discovered Emilie and Saint-Lambert in apparent *flagrante delicto.* He flew into a rage and spoke to them harshly. Remarkably poised, Saint-Lambert coldly suggested to Voltaire that he leave and meet him elsewhere, with whatever weapon he chose. Ill, fifty-four, Voltaire preferred simply to leave, though still in a fury. He ordered Longchamp to find a carriage that night; they were departing for Paris. Instead, the valet went to Mme.

du Châtelet, who immediately sought Voltaire. Longchamp records the conversation that he says he heard through the thin wall separating his room from his master's.

Mme. du Châtelet began in English, possibly with "Dear lover," her pet name for Voltaire, and continued in French. She protested her innocence, despite the appearances. "What," said Voltaire, "you expect me to believe that after what I saw? I have sacrificed everything for you—my health, my fortune—and now you betray me!" "No," she replied,

> I still love you. But for a long time you have been complaining that you are no longer able to———. I am terribly sorry. I am the last one to want your death. Your health is very precious to me; no one is more concerned about it than I. And you have also shown great concern for mine . . . but now, you will agree, you can do nothing about it without sacrificing yours. Should you be so angry when it is one of your friends who can oblige?

"Ah, madame," cried Voltaire in admiration, "you are always right! But since that is the way it is, you should see to it that it does not occur before my very eyes."

They chatted amiably for about half an hour longer; then Mme. du Châtelet went to her room, leaving behind a pacified Voltaire. The next day she mollified Saint-Lambert and persuaded him to apologize to the older man—which he did. "No, my child," Voltaire responded, "I was in the wrong, and it is all forgotten. You are still in the happy age when one can love and be loved. Make the most of it. An old, ill man like myself is no longer up to these pleasures."[79]

All three dined with Mme. de Boufflers the next day, all three settled down to semitranquility. Voltaire and Saint-Lambert exchanged verses and compliments, Mme. du Châtelet resumed (as Saint-Lambert sagely counseled) her translation of Newton.

But it could not, and did not, endure. Early in January 1749 at Cirey, Voltaire remarked that Emilie was unusually listless and perturbed. He inquired about it. She explained: she was pregnant. Saint-Lambert was the father; there could be no one else. (Among the major inventions of the century, Voltaire listed that of the Chevalier de Condom. It was not, however, commonly used. The most practiced form of contraception was male withdrawal—it is still. For women there were also crude germicides and the douche.)

Sent for, Saint-Lambert came on horseback within hours. All three consulted; then peals of laughter were heard by Longchamp and the other servants. Perhaps at that point the three had arrived at their strategy: M. du Châtelet would be led to believe the child was his. But how, since the married pair had not shared the same bed for so many years?

On the pretext that a lawsuit was threatening, the Marquis du Châtelet was sent for. Mme. du Châtelet closed her letter with an exceptionally warm greeting to him. The good man came almost immediately. He was wined and dined and listened to as never before at Cirey. At supper the next night Emilie sat next to him in a low-cut gown and all her diamonds, Voltaire told erotic stories, and everyone drank a great deal. M. and Mme. du Châtelet went to bed together, and for three weeks behaved like newlyweds. At the end of the three weeks Mme. du Châtelet announced the happy news to M. du Châtelet that he would again be a father, and they all celebrated, then separated—except for Voltaire and Emilie, who left together for Paris.

In Paris Voltaire found his niece and his usual frenetic life; Mme. du Châtelet flung herself into her work. They lived, as usual, in their house on rue Traversière. Emilie's letters to Saint-Lambert are as ardent as ever, and even more reproachful: he has resumed his liaison with Mme. de Boufflers and is trying for an army post away from Lorraine, which Emilie takes as an effort to get farther away from herself. But the letters, long as they are, fill the interims in the work on physics, the mathematics of physics, and *Principia.* Claude Clairaut is often with her, double-checking the calculations, the conclusions, the exact phrasing in French of Newtonian physics written in Latin. The young scientist is so frequently with Emilie that Voltaire has spurts of jealousy.

Mme. du Châtelet, however, was more concerned, as her time approached, about where she might have her child. She decided upon Lunéville, where she would be close to Saint-Lambert and away from the gossips of the French Court. She even addressed a letter to Mme. de Boufflers, soliciting her help with King Stanislas, so that she might be invited there and have the queen's own small apartment for the lying-in. Emilie added that M. du Châtelet, who was now Grand Maréchal at the Court of Lorraine, "also strongly desires it."[80] Five days afterward she wrote to Saint-Lambert: she was terribly anxious; she had heard *he* was ill! Then two weeks later (April 21) she informed him that she had arranged for money to pay the debts that made him feel he must leave Lorraine. Some of the money might come from King Stanislas, who was visiting Versailles, she said. Moreover, the King had just told her he would be happy to have her at Lunéville! "Yes, I adore you! Good God, I am happy!"[81]

Saint-Lambert considerately suggested that Emilie come well ahead of time to Lunéville. She could not, she wrote in reply; she had this damn work to complete. Suppose she should die in childbirth? "Don't reproach me my *Newton,* I am being punished enough by it. I have never made a greater sacrifice than to stay here and finish it. It's a terrible task and I need an iron head and health to do it."[82] All this time Voltaire was with her steadily, reading her preface, finding it remarkable, a masterpiece, as he told d'Argental and Hénault.

In early June Mme. de Boufflers arrived in Paris and went directly to her friend Mme. du Châtelet. A few weeks before, Emilie had heard from her husband, who had "naively" disclosed that Mme. de B. and Saint-Lambert were quite openly lovers. Yet even this, or, rather, this too—in addition to Emilie's advanced pregnancy—seems to have brought the two women together in the friendship, the understanding between them, that overarches their relationship. For eight hours they talked. "All the time, *almost* all the time," wrote an enraptured Emilie to Saint-Lambert, "we talked of you . . . She says you love me passionately and that you tell her that constantly . . . I feel that no matter what you do, the two of you, I will love you both forever."[83] She would have liked to leave for Lunéville on the twenty-third, she added, but her work with Clairaut did not permit it. One more week! she implored, and wrote in the seventh month of her pregnancy:

> I rise at nine in the morning, sometimes at eight. I work until three, when I have coffee. I return to my work at four and leave it at ten to have something to eat. I chat with M. de Voltaire, who sups with me, until midnight, when I resume working until five.

The effort was killing her, but the drive to finish could not be arrested. Perhaps if she and Saint-Lambert were together . . . "I can no longer like anything I cannot share with you, for I do not *love* Newton. I am finishing him because it is reasonable and honorable to do so, but I love *you.*"[84]

It was Voltaire, of course, who accompanied Mme. du Châtelet to Lunéville, going by way of Cirey, where Saint-Lambert was to have met them but did not. Yet he was attentive and gentle at Lunéville, for the most part. Then he left for Haroué for several days; the tension was too much for him. "My belly has fallen horribly," Emilie wrote to Saint-Lambert, "my kidneys are giving me intense pain, and I am so sad this evening." If only he were with her![85] The next day Mme. du Châtelet transmitted a voluminous manuscript to the Royal Library of Paris (now the Bibliothèque Nationale) for registry. It was her *Commentary on the Mathematical Principles of Newton,* which terminates her great work. The letter of transmittal is the last letter from her hand.

Two days later she gave birth to a baby girl. It was an easy delivery —to everyone's surprise. Meantime Saint-Lambert had returned to Lunéville, and all seemed well for several days. Then Emilie had a fever. She asked for an iced drink and was given it, drank a considerable quantity and had convulsions, lived one more day—and died.

Everyone wept; then there was a terrible silence. M. du Châtelet was led away, and one by one the others retired, leaving only Voltaire and his valet and Saint-Lambert. Voltaire, grief-stricken, staggered outside to the terrace, fell, and struck his head. The other two hurried to help him to his feet. Seeing Saint-Lambert through his tears, he sobbed, and in a pathetic voice said, "Ah, my friend, it is you who have killed her." Then, suddenly furious, he cried out, "My God, sir, whatever got into you to give her a child?" Saint-Lambert left without uttering a word.[86]

To their friends Voltaire wrote of his great grief—and we believe him. To Frederick the Great's hypocritical consolations he was exceptionally cool. Mme. du Châtelet had shared and sustained his life; he had shared her dying. Cirey was no more. He would pack his things there and forward them to Paris. But before going to Cirey with M. du Châtelet, who had requested it, and his son, Voltaire wrote Mme. Denis the day of Mme. du Châtelet's death:

> My dear child, I have just lost a friend of twenty years. For a long time now, as you know, I have not looked upon Madame du Châtelet as a woman, and I am sure you join me in my cruel grief. To have seen her die, and in such circumstances and for such a reason! It is horrible. I am not abandoning M. du Châtelet in our mutual sadness. I must go to Cirey; there are important papers. From Cirey I shall come to Paris to embrace you and find in you my one consolation, the only hope of my life.[87]

From Cirey, Voltaire wrote: "Regret me, one day, as I regret Madame du Châtelet."[88]

He did not hurry back to Paris. It was a month before he arrived, "sick, sad, and lost." He did not want to see anyone. He hardly left his house. He could not console himself for the death of Mme. du Châtelet. "During the night he rose in agitation, and in his disturbed mind he thought he saw her, and he cried out and dragged himself from room to room, looking for her."[89]

6

PAIN AND PLEASURE: THE MARQUIS AND THE MARQUISE DE SADE

DONATIEN-Alphonse-Francois de Sade, from whose noble name the word *sadism* has been derived, was considered an exceptionally fine catch for Renée-Pélagie de Montreuil, whom Sade admirers have since described as the ideal, devoted wife, a veritable "saint of married life."[1] Sade's family was related to the Royal House; Renée-Pélagie's was immensely rich. His title of nobility—marquis in his youth, count upon his father's death—dated from the early twelfth century; the wife of his forebear, Hugues de Sade, was the beautiful, haunting Laura of Petrarch's sonnets.

Donatien de Sade was born on June 2, 1740, in the absence of his father and almost, had it been possible, that of his mother. His father was always absent in temperament, cold, withdrawn, the grand seigneur; and more literally as Louis XV's ambassador, then to Cologne, later to London. Almost invariably he was accompanied by the countess, Sade's mother (until *she,* one day not long afterward, suddenly withdrew to a convent). Sade was not even born "at home," but rather in the Paris palace of the Prince de Condé. His playmate was the young heir to the family puissance, Louis-Joseph de Bourbon—until they fell out.

Sade's account of the early years—as Valcour, in his novel *Aline et Valcour*—is clearly autobiographical, if less typically self-deprecating:

> Allied by my mother to the grandest of the land; by my father to all that was most distinguished in Languedoc [Provence]; born in Paris in the heart of luxury and abundance, I believed, as soon as I could reason, that nature and fortune had joined forces to shower me with their gifts; I believed this because people had been foolish enough to say it to me, and this absurd bent made me haughty, despotic, and quick to anger; it seemed to me that all

should give way to me and the whole world yield to my caprices, and that I had but to form them for them to be satisfied; I will offer you but one instance from my childhood to convince you of the dangerous principles that were so stupidly permitted to flower in me.

Born and brought up in the palace of the illustrious prince (a relative of my mother), who was almost my age, I was urged to stay close to him so that, knowing him thus intimately from childhood, I would have his support the remainder of my life; but my vanity at that time, which did not yet understand such calculations, took offense one day in our childish games that he wished to take something from me, and more especially that he thought his rank, with great reason, entitled him to do so; I revenged myself by repeated blows, without any consideration's stopping me, and only force and violence could part me from my adversary.

It was about this time that my father was engaged in diplomatic negotiations; my mother had gone with him, and I was sent to my grandmother in Languedoc, whose too-blind gentleness nourished in me all the faults I have mentioned.[2]

Little blond Donatien was too much for his grandmother. Age five, he was turned over to his uncle, Abbé François de Sade, friend of Voltaire and Emilie, biographer of Petrarch, and as dissolute an ecclesiastic as many of his time. It was scarcely a secret that he kept several women, among them a mother and daughter, for his dalliance at the Saumane château, not far from his brother's—Donatien's father's—castle of La Coste. (Later in life, the Abbé would spend a few hours in prison for excessive demands upon local prostitutes, then go free, unrepentant and unchanged.) Other than his uncle's example and whippings at his uncle's hands, little is known of these four years at Saumane during Sade's youth before he was sent, age ten, to the Jesuit *collège* Louis-le-Grand.

"I returned to Paris," Valcour tells us, "to go to school under the tutelage of a firm and intelligent man"—the good Abbé Amblet—"without doubt most suited to form my youth, but with whom unfortunately I did not stay very long." Nor is there a record of Sade's having received any prize for brilliance during his years at Louis-le-Grand. There is simply a note that, barely fourteen, he was removed from school and sent to a regiment, with which he served as a second lieutenant after some months of training. ("My father," says Valcour, "in a hurry for me to serve, did not finish my education.") Sade's father, having mismanaged his estates, was pressed for money.

In 1756 the Seven Years' War began. Sade performed well on the battlefield as a captain and off it as a teenage libertine. His father, not mentioning the former, reproached him for the latter. He replied at length. He wanted to live well and amuse himself.

> *Voilà toute ma confession.* I am opening my heart to you, not as a father one often fears without loving, but to the sincerest, tenderest friend I believe I have in the world. Cease having reasons to feign hating me, give me your tenderness forever . . . Send me news of yourself as soon as you can, I beg you; you cannot know the pleasure I take in your letters when I receive them. But do not send me the four words you ordinarily write.[3]

Sincere, hypocritical? Revealing, in any case.

In 1763 the war was over. Sade returned to Paris and his family, its fortune and revenues more reduced than before (though adequate, most likely, for all but the most privileged of the *ancien régime).* He found his father and mother now living separately, but without rancour, the count as a solitary misanthrope, the countess in a Carmelite convent, but without having taken the veil. The count probably exaggerates in his letter to his brother the Abbé, when he says he will surely die in poverty and is already depriving himself of "even the barest necessities." As for his son Donatien-Alphonse-François, he adds, he considers him "a gambler, prodigal, and debauched," a devotee of actresses and prostitutes, whose debts would pursue his father even if, as he was sorely tempted, he would leave Paris to get away from the son.[4]

The solution, however, was the classical one: to find the prodigal son a wealthy wife. The count shrewdly settled on Mademoiselle Renée-Pélagie de Montreuil, elder daughter of the Seigneur de Launay, who was president of the Cour des Aides; in other words, a high-court justice and an extremely rich man, thanks to his enterprising father and just as much to his clever wife, Marie-Madeleine de Plissay, whom all referred to as la présidente.

Sade, in the meantime, had fallen in and out of love with several young women (if love is *le mot juste*), whose families neither wanted nor needed any part of him. Two weeks before the day fixed for his marriage to Renée-Pélagie de Montreuil, he was still in Avignon "courting" Mademoiselle Laure de Lauris, whose lineage was almost as illustrious as his own. Laure, however, was no more a lady than he a gentleman. Not because they had slept together, as emerges from his letter to her at this time, but because she had "given" him gonorrhea, as leaps from the same furious epistle, dated April 6, 1763.

"Perjurer! Ungrateful wretch!" Sade unceremoniously begins. "What ever happened to those sentiments of lifelong love?" Speaking in her name, Laure's father had just broken off their engagement. "Who obliges you to break the bonds that were to unite us forever?" He himself had obtained his father's consent for their marriage, he says, though actually it was for his descent to Avignon, despite the wedding date set with the Montreuils. "What am I in your eyes? A thing of horror? Of love? Tell me!" She had promised to enter a convent rather than to marry another man. "Beware of inconstancy; I do not deserve it. I vow to you I will be furious, and there will be no horror I will not commit. The little affair of the c[lap] should make you be more considerate of me. I confess I shall not hide it from my rival, nor that it will be the only secret I shall confide to him."

The letter is long, blowing hot and freezing cold, and it ends: "I adore you and love you a thousand times more than my life . . . I swear to you that we shall never be anything but one for the other."[5] Whereupon Sade returned to Paris for the wedding, though the marriage, to anticipate very slightly, would not necessarily end their love affair, if Laure would or could have it so, and Sade would make at least one more try.

As for the marriage, Marie-Madeleine de Montreuil, la présidente, was the dominating figure, her husband characteristically a figurehead, and Sade's father simply the man who gave the bridegroom away. She was clever and charming—Sade would say her charm came from Satan—and extremely influential in Court circles. Her ambitions were high but limited to the family, whose affairs she managed with great energy and few scruples. Focused as she was on securing the future of her elder, twenty-one-year-old, unprepossessing Renée-Pélagie by marrying her to the twenty-two-year-old Marquis de Sade, la présidente had, astonishingly for her, allowed herself to be fooled about the character of her future son-in-law. In a letter to his sister, the Abbess of Saint-Laurent, Sade's father confesses to the deliberate deception by concealing from Madame de Montreuil what he knew of his son. It was not merely a matter of Sade's having sown a few wild oats (la présidente was even aware of his descent to Avignon). That was typical of the period and generally expected, as were mistresses after a man's marriage. It was something more troubling, which Sade himself alone could, and would, reveal too late to her.

The marquis had made no objections, strenuous or otherwise, to the marriage. Whatever he had said to Laure in Avignon, it was really a matter of indifference to him; his father's wish sufficed. Possibly the rather tall, plain, and spinsterish Renée de Montreuil, dark-eyed and dark-haired, had a certain appeal for the small (five-foot, two-inch) fair-haired Marquis de Sade (beauty in a woman is banal, he would write; the repugnant and ugly are more exciting). At the same time he took note of the younger, prettier sister, Anne-Prospère, la présidente's favorite. Sade himself was a dandy, inclined to plumpness. He had a small oval face, a small undistinguished nose, and a roundish chin; his eyes were a pale blue, his hair blond and thin, promising early baldness, his forehead high and slightly bulbous. But he was fluent and could be seductive. No marquis with royal connections, moreover, was ever without charm for the ambitious mother of an unmarried daughter.

The wedding of the pair, as if an affair of state, received the prior blessing of the king and the queen and various dukes, princes, and princesses of the blood—royal blood, that is. The wedding contract was signed in the Paris mansion of the president, after intricate negotiations; the Montreuils were shocked by the refusal of Countess de Sade to give her diamonds to her son's bride for the wedding, as was the custom. "She is a terrible woman," wrote the count to his brother the Abbé; "her son will be like her."[6] The contract itself covered eleven pages, its codicils another dozen, taking into account possible contingencies and above all aiming, on the Montreuil side, at protecting their daughter and limiting Sade to the interest on her dowry and other substance, leaving the capital intact. Meanwhile the Montreuils were generously to pay the way of the young couple during the first five years of their wedlock. On the Sade side, the count ceded his lieutenant-generalship of several provinces to his son, each with a revenue, as well as the châteaus and part of the revenues of La Coste, Saumane, Mazan, and other southern estates.

Devoted as was the young Sade to the aristocratic principle of pleasure, these considerable sums flowing in yearly were the sine qua non of a life particularly his own. Declaring the right not only to his body's pleasure, but to that of others, he pushed to the furthest extreme yet an aristocratic way of life inevitably leading to the great Revolution—toward which French nobility was rumbling like a runaway golden coach.

Heedless, and dazzled by the wedding's brilliance, Madame la présidente de Montreuil sent a euphoric note to the Abbé:

> Monsieur your nephew could not be more amiable and desirable as a son-in-law, with his air of reasonableness, gentleness, and good upbringing that your care seems to have fostered in him. My daughter, too, is deeply appreciative of your generous attentions to her.[7]

The count and the marquis were soon quarreling about the revenues due to the latter, the count insisting on deducting previous years' support. Madame de Montreuil powerfully backed her son-in-law. "La présidente," complained the count to the Abbé, "is mad about the marquis." Possibly, but she was more likely blinding herself because of the auspicious beginning of her daughter's marriage. Sade was behaving himself; he may even have been intrigued with his new acquisition and her initiation into his rites. For Renée-Pélagie, as for any virginal bride, her husband was her first lover, in Sade's case a man without inhibitions, awakening in her a sexuality that she could not but identify him with thereafter. La présidente was soon writing the Abbé, *confidant* of all parties, that the marquis "loves [her daughter] greatly and could not treat her better." But, she added, the bride's "heart is heavy," for the marquis had departed for the Court at Fontainebleau, and from there was going on to Dijon.[8]

Had Sade left for Fontainebleau, however? Within weeks of his wedding he had rented a "little house" in the suburbs of Paris, where he engaged in a private *"débauche outrée,"* in his father's phrase. In truth, Sade was already bored. He was restless with Renée-Pélagie, he would later explain in a letter to the Abbé. Despite a certain respect for his wife, he frankly found her "too cold, too pious."[9] But the prostitutes he took to the "little house" found *his* demands so outrageous, they brought charges against him, and the affair came before the king. Sade's arrest was ordered, and he was incarcerated in the fortress dungeon of Vincennes, on the eastern edge of Paris, on October twenty-ninth of the year of his marriage.

"Contritely," Sade requested the police authority to inform his poor, "worried" wife of his whereabouts. As for himself, "I merited God's vengeance." He had sinned, he wrote; he wished to repent. Send him a priest, he begged. In the meantime, might he not have his valet de chambre to serve him in prison? One thing more: "I also hope, monsieur, that you will not tell my family the true reason for my detention."[10]

After two weeks, Sade was released from the prison of Vincennes and restricted to residence in the Montreuil château of Echauffour in Normandy. Two months later, with full knowledge of why he had been imprisoned, Madame de Montreuil wrote his uncle the Abbé to say her son-in-law was again behaving himself, but "time alone will reassure me." Wellborn and bred as was the marquis, he could not but change his ways with greater maturity. Was it not the way of all men? "As for my daughter, you can understand what must have been her pain. She has taken the attitude of a virtuous wife . . . To my count, she is three months pregnant."[11]

Renée-Pélagie either miscarried or the child died shortly after birth. The following spring Sade was authorized a visit to Paris to deal with his estates' affairs. On July 15 he met Mlle. Colet, an actress. On July 16 he wrote her *two* declarations of love. She became his mistress, and he shared her with another marquis; each was aware of the other. Though Sade's restriction to Normandy was formally lifted by the king, close surveillance of his activities was continued by Police Inspector Marais, whose detailed reports constitute fascinating documentation of the period. In December, for instance, the inspector reported Sade's frequentation of a bordello run by a Mme. Brissault. She was one of the inspector's underworld contacts. "I strongly recommended to her," Marais writes, "not to furnish [the marquis] with girls for his little houses."[12] In February 1765 Sade declared his love for a demoiselle met at a ball, again boldly in writing, saying he would have married her had they met when he was single. In April, Inspector Marais notes that the marquis is one of the lovers of another young woman, La Beauvoisin, whom he takes with him for two months at the La Coste château, now his, where he presents her as his wife. (The marquise had not yet been to La Coste.) *Scandale* when it became known, but la présidente concealed it from Renée-Pélagie. Instead, she asked the Abbé to break Sade's liaison with La Beauvoisin, as *she* had done, she says, in the case of Mlle. Colet. But even if the Abbé succeeded, la présidente preferred Sade's staying in Provence, rather than returning to Paris. In the city he would simply find another mistress, tire of her, and take another, thus piling up even more debts. "I would rather he took a mistress in Provence," she wrote. Ideally it would be some married woman, since "they are always less dangerous than a kept woman."[13]

In August, however, Sade returned to Paris, accompanied by La Beauvoisin, leaving behind a debt of 4,500 livres. Ten days passed before he informed his mother-in-law and wife of his arrival. So la présidente reports to the Abbé. Sade's father has faded from the scene, his mother is unheard from, his wife still kept in the dark—though she seems at last to suspect *something,* at least, her mother tells Sade's uncle. After La Beauvoisin, Sade dallied with others, generally actresses or dancers, though he took an occasional trip to La Coste with Renée-Pélagie. "Let him sow his wild oats," the Abbé counseled la présidente; "he is still in his passionate youth." It would pass, as she herself had stated. "I have spoken to him a good deal about his wife," the Abbé continued, "as you can well imagine . . . He told me that his wife was ignorant of his follies and he would be in despair if she knew of them. That, at least, is something."[14]

In January 1767 Sade's father, the count, died. In April, Sade resumed his liaison with La Beauvoisin. In August, Renée-Pélagie gave birth to the Sades' first child, Louis-Marie. In October, Inspector Marais was reporting: "It won't be long before one hears of the horrors of monsieur le Comte de Sade," and he speaks of a new "little house" in Arcueil, which Sade had rented the previous year in the suburbs of Paris.[15]

The following April, at nine o'clock, Easter morning, dressed in a gray redingote and wearing a hunting knife, the Marquis de Sade observed a woman begging alms in Paris's Place des Victoires. He beckoned to her. Rose Keller, thirty-six, widowed wife of a pastry cook, approached. He offered her a gold coin if she would come with him. She protested that she was an honest woman, not a prostitute. The marquis reassured her: the coin was for a bit of housekeeping in Arcueil. She accepted. He had her wait in a nearby room before they went on to Arcueil in a carriage; presumably his valet was arranging for other women in the meantime.

In the little house at Arcueil, Sade had Rose Keller wait once more, in an upstairs bedroom, whose door he double-locked. He then took her to a ground-floor bedroom and told her to undress. She refused. He threatened her with his hunting knife. She undressed slowly; Sade stripped her of her shirt. He himself was wearing a vest over a nude torso and had a kerchief tied around his head. He flung Rose Keller onto a divan, face down, and bound her, spread-eagled on her stomach. He flogged her hard with a whip. She screamed. He thrust his knife at her; she choked back her screams. He flogged her again with a whip of corded knots, sometimes using the handle. He stopped to annoint the wounds, then recommenced the whipping. She begged him not to kill her before she had made her Easter confession. *He* would confess her, Sade replied. The blows fell harder and faster, rising to a crescendo as Sade uttered high, piercing cries and "had his orgasm."[16]

Sade unbound his victim, had her dress and wash the bloodstains from her undergarments. He gave her a burning unguent for her whiplashed body, returned her to the upstairs bedroom, and locked her inside. Desperately Rose Keller tore two blankets into strips, which she tied together to lower herself to the ground. She climbed over a garden wall and reached the street. Sade's valet chased her, caught up with her, and offered money for her silence. She refused the money and went on, meeting several women of the village, to whom she told her story. They took her into a courtyard, lifted her torn skirt, and verified the wounds, then led her to the home of Mme. Jouette, wife of a local official. Again Rose Keller told her story. The lady fainted, recovered, and heard the account in full the following day. She encouraged Rose Keller to bring charges against the marquis, who had departed in the meantime for Paris.

In Paris, Sade acquainted Renée-Pélagie with enough of the story to cause her to send for Sade's old tutor, Abbé Amblet, and a lawyer, arranging for them to meet with Madame de Montreuil. La presidente promptly took charge, dispatching the two men to Arcueil with instructions to buy off Rose Keller at any cost. There Rose Keller demanded a thousand écus to withdraw her charges—and settled for half. But the case against the marquis was not dropped.

Though whips were at hand in most bordellos for their fanciers, and flagellation occurred frequently enough, Sade had gone beyond the bounds and outside the permitted space. Magistrates of the Paris Parlement, moreover, were already stirring in revolt against aristocratic excesses, such as Sade's. (Only in Paris and London, Sade would complain in *Aline et Valcour,* could a man be punished for whipping prostitutes, whereas in more civilized Italy and Poland he was punished only if he had not paid for it.) The Paris magistrates pressed the charges despite Rose Keller's withdrawal. Sade was put under arrest by order of the king and held in a château prison near Lyons, where Renée-Pélagie rented rooms to be near him. Acting swiftly, the Montreuils brought their considerable influence to bear, meanwhile, persuading Louis XV to grant Sade a *lettre d'abolition,* which amnestied anyone of noble birth for crimes ordinarily punishable by death. In June the king's *lettre* was registered by the Paris Parlement, since there was no alternative except outright defiance, and Sade's case was dropped. He was not released from prison, however, before November, and then with an accompanying royal order—that he retire to his estate at La Coste and conduct himself properly.

Renée-Pélagie planned to join him there. "She has done too much not to complete her work by showing him her utter attachment," Madame de Montreuil informed the Abbé. Nonetheless la présidente asked Sade's uncle to keep a neighborly eye on his nephew when he arrived in Provence.[17] Advanced in pregnancy, the marquise did not immediately join her husband. She returned to Paris from Lyons as Sade left prison for La Coste. Nor was she idle in the capital: she attempted to tidy up their finances, selling some of her jewels to pay off the debts for the "little houses." In contrast, at La Coste, the marquis was carrying on as before, adding masked balls, dances, and other fetes to his usual entertainment, which drove la présidente into a fury. Fortunately, she wrote the Abbé, her daughter was with her in Paris rather than "shut up in that château with such a man."[18]

With a sudden manifestation of family concern, in the meantime, Sade's widowed mother had petitioned the king to lift his restriction on Sade's staying at La Coste. The request was granted in April 1769; "for his health's sake," Sade was permitted a stay in the environs of Paris.[19] In May a second son, Donatien-Claude—probably conceived during a visit of Renée-Pélagie to the imprisoned marquis—was born to the couple. Sade played the attentive husband, father, and possibly lover. Restlessly, a year later, he tried to join a cavalry regiment in Burgundy, but its deputy commander would have none of him. In April 1771 a third and last child was born to the Sades, Madeleine-Laure. In September, such was the pace of his agitated life, Sade spent eight days in prison for unpaid debts. Upon his release he returned immediately to La Coste, where he found the patient Renée-Pélagie and the attractive Anne-Prospère, her sister, now a canoness on leave from her convent. Within two months, Renée-Pélagie was writing a none-too-mysterious note to herself: "a bad project—horrible, horrible."[20] But to what extent was she not already the willing victim, even the accomplice, of a triangular situation arranged by her most special spouse?

Their mother fumed that winter when she heard that Sade had hired an acting couple to perform his plays at La Coste and had brazenly impressed both daughters, as well, to perform before a local public. "It is an indignity to which I shall put an end," she vowed, indignant too at the high costs of Sade's self-indulgences.[21] But la présidente could not have known the true drama at La Coste. Sade had installed two bedrooms for himself in the forty-two-room castle, one adjacent to his wife's suite, the second in a wing of its own, invariably locked in his absence. The tall, slim, sensually inquisitive Anne-Prospère had become his paramour. The libertine had appealed to the canoness, the canoness to the atheist, and incest, for so love between in-laws was viewed, to both. Together with matricide, incest would be the supreme sin and pleasure in Sade's world of fiction. To be noted with irony, at the same time, is the fact that even as he was bedding with his wife's sister, he was forbidding the performance of a play not his own in the village of La Coste, as was his seigneurial right, on the grounds of its "immorality."

Withal Sade was bored. Rather, he suffered the deadly ennui of insatiable desire. In June of 1772 he went down to the city of Marseilles, then, as now, the great port of purchasable varieties of pleasure and vice. He went on some trumped-up business affair with his valet

Latour, a tall, pockmarked man who was dressed in a blue-and-yellow-striped sailor's suit and who had packed a whip in his luggage. After checking into a hotel, Sade told Latour to make the arrangements for an orgy—the antiquated word is particularly apt. The detailed description that follows is gruesome but required reading, for the Marseilles *affaire* is one of two—the other, that of Rose Keller—that speak to us directly about Sade's sexual practices; the rest is surmise drawn from his novels, such as *Justine, Juliette, The 120 Days of Sodom,* which have been called a prisoner's fantasms.

Latour rounded up four prostitutes—Marianne Laverne, eighteen, Mariannette Laugier and Rose Coste, each twenty, and Mariette Borelly, twenty-three—on the morning of June 27. In an apartment reserved for the occasion, Sade had Marianne lie in bed alongside Latour, after having sent the others to another room. With one hand he whipped Marianne; with the second he stroked Latour, bringing him to an erection while calling him monsieur le marquis, as the valet addressed him as La Fleur ("Flower"). He then had Latour leave the room and gave Marianne sweets flavored with aniseed and saturated with cantharides—Spanish-fly extract. He told her to eat up, so that she would pass wind. She swallowed seven or eight candies and refused more, though pressed by Sade. She had the choice, she was told, of being sodomized by the valet or by his master. She replied, "By neither"—or so she would testify. Sade handed the young woman a whip of parchment, bloodstained and studded with nails, and ordered her to beat him with it. After three strokes, she stopped, having no further heart for it. Sade had her get a twig broom and use it upon him, but she became sick from the candy and had to leave the room.

It was Mariette's turn. Sade had her bend over the bed and flogged her with the broom while Latour looked on. Then he asked her to beat him and marked the strokes with his knife on the mantlepiece—215, 179, 225, 240, the police would note, several of the numbers possibly indicating the strokes *he* had given. Afterward, as Sade sodomized Mariette, Latour sodomized him. Mariette was followed by Rose Coste, who was fornicated by the valet, then whipped by the marquis, who simultaneously stroked Latour, who ended by sodomizing Rose, who was succeeded by Mariannette. The latter was stroked by Sade and stripped for a whipping, but took fright at the bloodstained whip lying on the bed. Marianne, though sick and vomiting in the kitchen, was recalled to the bedroom, the door relocked behind her. Sade offered the two women more sweets. Mariannette accepted them but did not eat; Marianne could no more. Mariannette was thrown on the bed and her skirt lifted. Sade thrust his nose at her behind, hoping for wind, then sodomized her as Latour sodomized him, and ordered Mariannette to break wind so that Latour might sniff it. She ran to the door, and Marianne began to cry. Sade threatened them, then finally let them depart after giving each an écu of six livres, promising ten more if they returned that night. So ended the morning of June 27, 1772 in Marseilles.

That evening, wishing to profit to the maximum of his stay in the port city, Sade spent the time with another prostitute, Marguerite Coste, brought him by Latour. She, too, was offered the tainted sweets, which she consumed, was proposed sodomy, which she scornfully refused (she would say), and was paid six francs. The following Sunday morning, the marquis left at dawn for La Coste, leaving behind two very sick young women, who went to the authorities in complaint. Within a week, the Royal Prosecutor of Marseilles decreed the arrest of Sade and his valet, charging them with poisoning and sodomy, each accusation punishable by death, even if death had not actually occurred from the poisoning.

Such is the picture of the mature Sade, a kind of chiaroscuro of classical sadism and masochism, of flogging and being flogged, of both inflicting and having inflicted pain for sexual pleasure. Put this way, however, the dichotomy masks the key to Sade's sexuality, attitude, and practices. Sex, he repeatedly insists, is power, the domination and humiliation of one's partner. There is less pleasure if the other is also enjoying it, since equality destroys the godlike sensation of despotism at the supreme moment. Pain is a more powerfully felt pleasure, which offers the piercing sensation of being utterly alive. To suffer pain, as in a flogging, and to inflict pain is *not* to be in self-contradiction, so long as one dominates and decides for the one or the other. Indeed, being ordered to whip another, since it is not freely done, is further humiliation, as Marianne Laverne's experience and reaction make clear. The one who commands the beating, whether of self or of another, has the power and the pleasure. Sadism and masochism are an inseparable sadomasochism, or algolagnia—the enjoyment of sexually related pain, whether inflicted or "suffered." Who commands, and who obeys? That is the key.

One might also ask: how did Sade arrive—or *remain*—at the stage of sadomasochism? Reference to his virtually motherless and fatherless infancy and youth is here inevitable, if facile. Matricide, as mentioned, would be a recurring theme in his novels. He is obviously "sadistically" taking his revenge and then, in the consequent feeling of guilt, "masochistically" exposing his fictional characters, men as well as women, to spanking and whipping and worse, with a sadism turned inward. For his admirers, however, the "divine marquis" has universality as well as specificity: he describes the sadomasochist buried in all human beings, most conspicuously in men (unlike Freud, who considered sadism essentially masculine, and masochism, because of its passivity, feminine; but who would also have it that cruelty, the exercise of power, is a component of "the instinct of mastery," here rejoining Sade.[22])

But if this is a somewhat simplistic tracking of Sade's sadomasochism, how does the marquise fit into that scheme, their situation? For Simone de Beauvoir, one reads with some astonishment, the marquis and the marquise, tyrant and victim, "form a genuine couple"; that is, a compatible, understandable, and perhaps justifiable, if not exactly ideal, pair.[23] There is, surprisingly, no expression of sympathy for the victim. For Beauvoir, no less than for Sade's male intellectual admirers, Sade's "greatness" as a pioneering writer, blasting "bourgeois morality," sanctions all, whether the whipping of prostitutes or the submission of his wife. For Freud, to be sure, that submissiveness is in the very nature of femininity; but certainly not for a Beauvoir in full possession of her feminism, as distinguished from the Beauvoir *béate* before male genius, whether Sade's, in her view, or Sartre's. More disturbing (to continue the digression) is the recent popularity among French women of *Histoire d'O,* an excessively masochistic account of a woman named O, who had chains linked to her labia from her neck. More than one who called herself *féministe* admitted her pleasure in reading the novel. One explained: "In the end O was liberated—of body, of will, of freedom. Of freedom! I confess it is a contradiction."

This, as prelude to the Marquise de Sade.

Informed of the charges brought against her husband, Renée-Pélagie unhesitatingly helped him get away before the police arrived from Marseilles. Moreover, she participated in arranging for her sister Anne-Prospère to leave with him for Savoy, then part of the Sardinian kingdom, together with Latour! A traveling couple would be less suspicious, but there was complicity as well in her giving a boost to Sade's love affair with her sister. Losing no time, Renée-Pélagie also went down to Marseilles to plead for her husband and to buy off the witnesses. She succeeded with the latter, but not with the prosecutors.

They pressed the case throughout August, and the king's own prosecutor brought sentence in September against the accused in their absence: guilty of poisoning and sodomy, the Marquis de Sade was to be beheaded and his domestic servant Latour hung and garroted after making public penance. Their bodies were to be burned and the ashes cast to the wind. And such was done in effigy on a public square of Aix-en-Provence, September twelfth.

During these months, in the meantime, Sade was traveling in Italy with Latour, a second valet called La Jeunesse, and sister-in-law Anne-Prospère, he as the Count de Mazan, and presenting her "everywhere as his wife, permitting himself all the privileges of that station."[24] Worse for Sade than the sentence hanging over him was the crime, for la présidente, of having run off with her preferred, younger daughter. With that act he had earned the literally undying enmity of the mother, and she vowed his destruction: Sade must be jailed for life for the sake of both daughters, particularly the yet-to-be-married Anne-Prospère.

That Sade had "kidnapped" Anne-Prospère, as he was accused, can be disproved by her brief return to La Coste in October to procure some money (from the marquise!) and her rejoining him in Nice (then Italian) three weeks later. By now newssheets and gazettes were full of their escapade, and it became a public scandal. Quickly and effectively la présidente went into action. Discovering their whereabouts through a careless letter from Sade (blandly requesting her aid in the Marseilles prosecution), she used her influence at the French Court and the Sardinian embassy to have Sade arrested in Chambéry, where he thought himself safe, and taken to the fortress prison of Miolans by order of the Sardinian king. It was December 1772. Anne-Prospère seems quietly to have returned to her convent, and the imprisoned Sade was soon promising in writing to break off all *"commerce"* with her and to return all compromising letters—as la présidente most urgently sought. He had already given his word of honor not to attempt to escape.

As for the marquise, she could not remotely have had the slightest semblance of innocence concerning the marquis, after the *affaires* of Arcueil and Marseilles and the Italian frolic with sister Anne-Prospère. If Sade is a parody of the pre-Revolutionary aristocrat as husband, raised from birth to believe himself above all laws and with a sovereign right to all pleasures, Renée-Pélagie had become the epitome of the "devoted wife," the willing victim, the moral masochist of her upbringing, conforming to the Biblical injunction, honoring and obeying her master. On March 6, 1773, after traveling for a week from Paris by post chaise, dressed in a man's apparel, the marquise arrived at Chambéry to see her husband and to help him escape from prison. Her companion and confidant was Alberet; they called themselves the brothers Dumont. She had Alberet deliver letters from her to the governor of Savoy and the commandant of Fort Miolans prison. They were addressed as if she were on the French side of the border. The first outrightly asked for Sade's release, the second for permission to see her husband. Each was refused, since both authorities had been alerted by her mother, strongly urging that neither release nor visit be granted, because "the results would be dreadful."[25] Only an unsealed letter to her husband was permitted the marquise, in which she acquainted him with her failure. This put him into such a fury that his jailers feared he would hurl himself from the prison parapets, and walks were forbidden him.

Discouraged, the marquise departed for La Coste via Lyons—and Sade took another tack. He became docile and all charm as he and Latour, who had joined him in prison, plotted his escape. Surveillance was slowly relaxed. One day in April, Sade requested that he be allowed to dine and sup in the canteen, since the food brought him was often cold, as it had to be carried so far from the kitchen. Permission was accorded him. Adjacent to the canteen, Sade had observed, were the toilets, with an unbarred window large enough for a man to squeeze through and drop to the ground, thirteen feet below, outside the fortress wall. On April 30, together with Latour and with the aid of an accomplice at the foot of the wall (arranged by the marquise?), Sade made his escape through the latrine window. He left behind a letter to the fort commandant, thanking him for his hospitality and assuring him that "my family, the only cause of my imprisonment, will see to it that you do not suffer [from the escape]." Do not attempt to follow, Sade warned, because "fifteen well-mounted and well-armed men await me outside the fort."[26] It was pure bluff. All that night Sade and Latour walked, until they reached the French frontier. They rested, and then went on to Grenoble, and eventually Bordeaux (to be close to Spain), and finally to La Coste in the fall.

The break between Renée-Pélagie and her mother deepened as la présidente now directed her formidable energy and influence toward Sade's incarceration in France. Not for an instant, however, did the marquise drop her guard as her mother redoubled her efforts. On instructions from Sade, still under sentence of death, Renée went to Paris to plead his case at Court and counter her mother's actions. La présidente proved the stronger. In December she obtained an order from the king to have Sade imprisoned. In January 1774 Police Inspector Goupil, with an escort of four archers and a troop of cavalry, descended on La Coste and burst into the castle. They found only Madame de Sade. Informed in time, the marquis had hidden out in the vicinity. His pursuers ransacked his rooms, especially his study, seized and burned his private papers, ever la présidente's first concern, and then left, threatening to return. In response, Renée-Pélagie filed a petition against her mother, which turned out to be as futile as it was fruitless. Mme. de Montreuil was adamant and untouchable. She was then negotiating with the Beaumont family about the marriage of a son to her daughter Anne-Prospère, and they had set as their condition that

Sade be locked away for the rest of his lifetime. (The marriage, in fact, would never take place.)

Returning from hiding after a few weeks of almost comic hide-and-seek, Sade set about resuming some control over his estates, although the marquise had been formally named by the magistrates as administrator of their properties and guardian of the children, in view of his condemnation. He replaced his intendant by Gaspard Gaufridy, a notary who would serve la présidente at the same time (although Sade did not know it), in an ambiguity and ambivalence of professional loyalties virtually impossible to explain. Conceivably, faced with contradictory demands, he did what he honestly thought best for both parties; or perhaps Gaufridy was simply multiplying his income by a factor of two. In the long run, and it would continue over two decades, he served Mme. de Montreuil's interests more consistently, possibly because she served them so supremely well herself.

Had the French police really determined to arrest Sade, they could have done it: they now knew where he was, and with a few precautions could easily have taken him. The Court, however, reluctant as ever to take public action against one of its own—a marquis with royal blood, however tainted—seems to have been inclined to hope for Sade's self-reform or at least a more discreet dissipation. There were the signs of some change as the marquis lived quietly and relatively inconspicuously at La Coste in the role of grand seigneur. In actuality he had never really swerved from the destiny of his desires, nor was he now, particularly since the death of Louis XV in 1774 canceled the *lettre de cachet* against him.

The complaint against her mother having gotten nowhere, Renée-Pélagie left Paris for La Coste. On the way back, by arrangement, she was met in Lyons by the marquis.

Here the complicity of the very special pair must be set in high relief. For here in Lyons they *both* recruited the "harem" of domestics for the orgies of the winter of 1774–75 at La Coste: Nanon and five younger girls, each fifteen years of age, as well as a boy of the same age, supposedly to serve as Sade's "secretary."

Precautions were taken to keep secret from the parents that the employer was the notorious nobleman of the Marseilles *affaire.* Direct contact with them in the recruiting was undertaken by Nanon and the marquise's maid Gothon. The final assemblage at La Coste, the collection of personnages, the plans for the winter, could fit with little change into Sade's orgiastic novel, *The 120 Days of Sodom.* The Marquise de Sade's participation is not the least intriguing part.

"Too pious and too cold" the marquis may once have found her, but she was no longer that bride. Renée-Pélagie had undergone a "progressive erotization,"[27] even if it had not radically uprooted all the piety or completely thawed all the coldness (to speak of her "essential frigidity," however, would be to speak out of the usual bias). Had she become the ideal wife for a husband such as Sade? Not quite, even were it possible, but she would do—if not admirably, then remarkably well. As for Sade, in his introduction to *The 120 Days,* he has one of his four libertines say:

> Do you think I seek a wife in order to have a mistress? I want a wife that my whims may be served, I want her to veil, to cover an infinite number of little secret debauches the cloak of marriage wonderfully conceals . . . We libertines wed women to hold slaves; as wives they are rendered more submissive than mistresses, and you know the value we set upon despotism in the joys we pursue.[28]

As for the marquise, Sade may be talking directly from his own experience in his characterization of Eugénie de Franval (Renée-Pélagie, in any event, springs instantly to mind):

> Honest, sensible, well-bred, lovingly anticipating the every desire of the only man in the world she cared about, Madame de Franval bore her chains during the early years without ever suspecting her enslavement. It was easy for her to see that she was merely gleaning meager scraps in the fields of Hymen, but, still too happy with what little he left her, she devoted her every attention and applied herself scrupulously to make certain that during those brief moments when Franval acknowledged her tenderness he would at least find everything that she believed her beloved husband required to make him happy.[29]

(The following spring, when the prior of Jumiège wrote the Abbé de Sade that his nephew should be shut up for the rest of his days, he would add: "The marquise is no more worthy than her husband." Members of the French Court would similarly say she was as "mad or guilty" as the marquis.[30])

That winter La Coste was transformed into a truly fortified castle, the high walls made higher, the drawbridge lowered for only a few hours at midday. Secret rooms and passages were created, for use should the police suddenly arrive to arrest the marquis. The windows were kept shuttered, day was turned into night, and supper was served at three in the afternoon. The rest of the time . . . Nanon became pregnant, attributing it to her husband, although Sade was certainly the father. Of his own admission, he "used" (and abused) the five young girls;[31] they were sodomized and whipped and would bear the marks, and the young secretary played the role usually alloted to Sade's valets. The marquise herself, the girls would testify, was "the first victim of a fury that one could only regard as madness."[32] The marquise would deny it loyally; to "victim" must be attached "willing."

The tawdry details emerged after the parents brought charges of kidnapping and child abuse and a Lyons court undertook a criminal investigation. There Renée-Pélagie hurried with her denial and did everything, as usual, to hush up the new *affaire* by buying off the parents and disposing of the witnesses. The "most damaged of the children" was taken secretly to Saumane and put under the care of the very embarrassed Abbé, convinced by the girl's state of his nephew's complete guilt.[33] Another of the girls was placed in a convent but would fly its walls and tell her story. Renée appealed to her mother for help, and la présidente obliged, impressing Gaufridy into service; she was still determined to save the Sade name for the family, and the family, as well, from Sade. Renée also appealed to the reluctant Abbé. Rather, she threatened him in a letter probably dictated by Sade: *his* recent and sordid past would be exposed if he did not continue to help his nephew by sequestering the whip-scarred girl. Renée's own uncomplaining devotion wrung a compliment from her mother: "She would sooner be hacked to pieces than admit to anything that might harm the marquis."[34]

On May 3, 1775 Nanon gave birth to a baby girl, who would die in July. On May 18 the Abbé wrote to the Minister of the King's Household, requesting that his nephew, currently at La Coste, be seized and incarcerated as a madman dangerous to society and his family. In mid-June Sade was complaining to Gaufridy of the general conspiracy against him, while "using" two or three young girls who had replaced the others at La Coste. In July, he was again in flight in Italy, accompanied by his valet La Jeunesse and leaving the marquise to cope with problems of money and all else pending and accumulating and piling up. Among Sade's letters to Renée is one reminding her to take care of his wardrobe, so as to assure that new shirts would have the right cut of collar. The following July (1776), bored by Italy, the marquis was back in France. That fall began a new but familiar *affaire* involving young women hired as domestics, but used, or at least approached (they would claim), for other purposes, and so on and so forth, denied routinely by Sade but most likely true. In late December, he was warned by Gaufridy of a police descent, and escaped in time, only to take a suicidal trip to Paris in February together with Renée.

The Dowager Countess de Sade had died in January at the convent on rue d'Enfer, but the marquis and the marquise did not learn of it before their arrival. Sade stayed with his old tutor, Abbé Amblet, who greeted him warmly. The marquise may have stayed with her mother, whom she foolishly told of Sade's arrival several days later. For on February 13, 1777, Police Inspector Marais, armed with a *lettre de cachet* procured by la présidente, arrested the marquis, conducted him to the Vincennes fortress, and at 9:30 that night officially registered him as a prisoner.

The date marks a new station of the cross, largely of the marquis's making but scarcely less carried by the marquise.

For months she did not know where Sade had been taken. She thought it was to the Bastille, and she prowled around its walls, trying to catch sight of him, but when she paused, she was told to move on. Even the drawbridges seemed raised against her. Nevertheless Renée-Pélagie had written almost immediately after his arrest to Sade (February 15), sending the letter blindly through the authorities. "How did you pass the night, *mon tendre ami?*" she anxiously inquired, using an accustomed *tu.* She tried to reassure him that she was seeing *everyone* about his case. "Count on me as your best friend, whom nothing can shake." In the margin of the letter, next to "your best friend," Sade would sardonically note: "a rotten plank."[35]

It may have been much later and in a black mood when Sade scrawled the marginal note, for his first letter to the marquise from captivity, at the end of February, is a *cri du coeur:* "I am overwhelmed by despair . . . My blood is too hot to bear such terrible confinement . . . If I am not out of here in four days, I shall crack my head against these walls."[36] His second letter, dated March 6, is a virtual declaration of desperate love, perhaps the first Renée-Pélagie had ever received from her husband:

> When will they let me out of here, *grand dieu,* this tomb in which I have been buried alive? . . . My only companions are my tears and my cries, but no one hears them . . . Where is the time when my dear friend shared them? . . . You are all that is left to me on earth: father, mother, sister, wife, friend, you are all of them. I have only you, do not abandon me.[37]

Renée would not abandon him, but Sade's pleas quickly became demands and accusations. The marquise, he cried, was in cahoots with "the Hyena" (her mother) to keep him in prison, "in a tower closed off by nineteen iron doors and with light reaching me through two small windows with a score of iron bars."[38] Constantly she sought to reassure him, only to be accused of lying. At last, in June, Renée learned his whereabouts, but was refused permission to visit him. Upon hearing this, she wrote Gaufridy that, should her husband be authorized to go to Aix on a new appeal to quash the death sentence of 1772, they must somehow manage his escape.

In the meantime, she worried about his health, his hemorrhoids, and arranged for a doctor and the proper ointment. Sade responded with silence: he had found a new form of torture. On August 12 Renée wrote: "I do not know what to make of your silence." September 9: "I cannot express to you how much your silence afflicts me." October 3: "My only consolation would be to receive word from you."[39] At long last Sade replied with a letter, saying he needed a new vest. The marquise hastened to fill the request, adding six pairs of stockings, a pair of gloves, a hair ribbon, eight pounds of candles, two pounds of cosmetic powder, a *pot* each of apricot marmelade, apple jelly, and fine cherries, six other vests, two night bonnets, three toothpicks (for his ears), a bottle of eau de cologne, and a half dozen of other items, including books and writing materials. Twice a month Renée-Pélagie would bring Sade packages—the maximum allowed—and leave them at the prison, since she was still not permitted to see him. She asked in return simply that he write, and she informed him of his sons, now in la présidente's care, and his daughter, boarding in a convent. (The three children had been told that their father was traveling.) Sade replied that each object he received confirmed his suspicions that he would not soon be released; as for the children, what she said proved that she was abandoning them.

On January 5, 1778, using his blood for ink, Sade wrote to la présidente, begging her to put an end to his imprisonment. She was not ready for that, but she did wish to clear his name. In May, the marquis was given the choice of pleading insanity, as la présidente advised, or appearing in person at Aix before the High Court of Provence. He chose to go down to Aix and personally appeal his death sentence. He left in June under the guard of Inspector Marais. Two hundred were crowded outside the courtroom, hoping to catch sight of the notorious marquis. In vain. He was taken in through a side door. Inside, he was rapidly freed from the conviction of poisoning, for lack of evidence, found guilty instead of "acts of debauchery and excessive libertinage," fined fifty livres, and forbidden to live in or visit Marseilles for three years.[40] Then he was turned back to the custody of Inspector Marais, for a return to the dungeon of Vincennes!

Sade was still under the *lettre de cachet* obtained against him by his mother-in-law in 1777, "that monstrous piece of tyranny, by which a person was kept in preventive imprisonment . . . made doubly intolerable by being granted to certain private persons for reasons of family interest or private revenge." In this manner, the marquis would be confined to prison for "all but ten of the thirty-seven years that remained"[41]—and the marquise would be his voluntary prisoner.

One brief interlude of freedom occurred between Aix-en-Provence and the prison of Vincennes. It lasted thirty-nine days.

The marquis and his police escort had stopped at Valence for the night. While three of the guards dined, he had gone to a toilet, slipped through the hands of a fourth guard, and made his escape down the stairs and into the fields. Then, as if bent on self-destruction, Sade had gone to La Coste, the first place he would be sought. Hardly arrived, he wrote to Gaufridy, asking for "lemons and all the keys"! He adds, explaining his insouciance, perhaps: "I believe you are right when you say, 'They will not pursue you.' I am not sure, but I do not think they have."[42] A second letter indicates, moreover, that Sade still held to hopes of appeasing la présidente, especially since he had been "exonerated" by the High Court at Aix.

Sade's guest and companion at La Coste was a sprightly lady met during his youth at Saumane, Mlle. Marie-Dorothée de Rousset, who served him in the absence of La Coste's housekeeper, Gothon. The marquise would be told of Mlle. Dorothée, and, typically, the two women would become friends. In the meantime, the marquise was quite literally held in Paris by her mother.

Not until late July had Renée-Pélagie been informed by Madame de Montreuil of Sade's descent to Aix-en-Provence, and of what had happened there. Upon hearing at the same time that her mother intended to maintain the *lettre de cachet* imprisoning Sade, she flew into a rage, and they had a "terrible row," in Renée's words.[43] Still ignorant of his escape, she told her mother that she was going down to meet Sade on his way back. Informed that he was actually at La Coste, she announced her intention to join him there immediately. "Spitting fire and flame" (Renée's words again), la présidente threatened to have *her* locked away, saying she refused to have her daughter "further debased and compromised." But what had piqued her mother most, Renée wrote Gaufridy, "was to see that my words and thoughts were my own and not M. de Sade's, whom she thinks prompts me as if I were a parrot."[44]

Early in August, Renée warned Sade that he was in danger, but, "like a child," he did not take it seriously.[45] On the nineteenth, however, apprised that there were suspicious characters in the vicinity, the marquis stayed away from La Coste for several days and nights, then carelessly returned, and was arrested at four in the morning of the twenty-sixth. On the seventh of September, he was back at Vincennes, locked into cell number 6, down in the dungeon.

"What a blow for me!" the marquise wrote to Mlle. de Rousset, whom she was awaiting in Paris. "What a miserable abyss I am in again! How to get out, whom to trust?"[46] When Dorothée de Rousset arrived to stay with the marquise, she found her frightfully thin and touchingly attentive. Together they went to see officials, trying vainly to see the marquis, and twice monthly filled a basket for the prisoner. He corresponded with each, particularly appreciative of Mlle.'s lively wit, he said, calling her *"sainte"* and bitterly reproaching Renée-Pélagie for her "treachery" and collusion with her mother. *"Exécrable!"* he cried.[47] To each accusation Renée attempted a reassuring reply, but one day she would register her own moving complaint, though still trying to reassure rather than wound:

> I fear you are confusing me with those who have done you wrong. I am keeping your letters preciously, so that I might show them to you when you get out and thus prove to you that your interpretation of what we are doing is false and how bizarre is your attitude. I can see you turning on your heels, but look! I prevent you from leaving, I close you in my bedroom and you will not leave it until you have read everything, confronted everything, and say to me, *"Ma petite femme,* I must do justice to you." And then you will not be able to say that I am wrong.[48]

Repeatedly, however, Sade would reproach Renée-Pélagie for holding out yet another promise of liberation, and would eventually accuse Mlle. de Rousset of the same behavior, because of her cheery optimism. He broke off their correspondence, though her efforts in his behalf loyally continued. He quarreled with everyone at Vincennes, from its governor to the guards and his fellow prisoners, not least among them Mirabeau, who called him a *"monstre."* Sade, in fact, was close to madness, as shown by his obsessive numerology. He was attributing "signals" to any number occurring in Renée-Pélagie's letters or to the quantity of candles or cakes she sent him in a parcel, often combining them with the day of the month, to arrive at the day of his release. Here, too, he attacked his wife, accusing her of being the tool of her mother, both deliberately deceiving him, as that day of release he had calculated came and went, and he was still in prison.

One night in February 1779, Sade had a dream of Petrarch's Laura coming to him and comforting him, but though he clung to her to prevent her leaving, crying, "Oh, my mother!" she left him. "Laura always affects me," he wrote Renée-Pélagie, "and I am always like a child." He closed *that* letter to his wife with, "I love you and embrace you with all my heart. Have a little more pity for me."[49] The marquise also appears in a recurrent dream Sade related to her two years later, and clearly as a mother figure. "There is not a month when I do not dream it," he wrote, "and most singularly it is always the same thing. I see you much older than when I last saw you, always with a secret for me that you refuse to tell me, and always unfaithful, *in every sense of the word,* and that at the instigations of your mother. I must have dreamed that dream five hundred times."[50]

The year ended with Sade coughing badly and Renée-Pélagie borrowing money to meet their debts. La présidente, as the price of her *lettre de cachet,* was required to pay for Sade's keep (roughly a marshal's salary), but his "extras" came very high, and these, among other charges, were Renée's to meet. Sade himself was suspicious and uncooperative, refusing to give her a *mandat* for the revenues of La Coste. The new year began with Mlle. de Rousset multiplying her efforts, to no avail. Even she was shocked when, together with the marquise, she was exposed to Sade's file at Versailles. "There are serious motives, very grave, which make me fear a long imprisonment," she wrote to Gaufridy in October. "M. [le ministre] and Mme. de Maurepas, two princesses, and several others who saw and read the motives said to me, 'Fortunately he is where he is. His wife is as mad or as guilty as he when she asks for his freedom.' "[51] As for herself, she added, she would be happy indeed to return to Provence, after the sad scene in Paris.

As 1780 ended, the marquis was again damning the marquise for her "abominable lies," and closed his letter written on the eve of the New Year (December 30, 1780):

> May you, you and your execrable family and their lowly valets, be put into a sack and hurled to the bottom of the water! Then let me be quickly told and I swear to Heaven that it will be the happiest day I have ever had. *Voilà,* madame, my season's wishes and greetings, in which your whore of a Rousset is included from head to foot."[52]

In the semiobscurity of his cell, Sade's eyes weakened and his erotic fantasy took flight. (Mirabeau, too, wrote pornography out of frustration.) The obscenities Sade crowded in the margins of Renée-Pélagie's letters became frequent. His own correspondence alternated abuse and provocative sensuality. How he would love to "measure" with the marquise as before, he writes, back and front! Before anything else, when he is finally free, he will kiss her eyes, her breasts, her behind, oh, that lovely white behind! But he broods, too, about the accusations dangling like a sword above him, condemning him to confinement. "Yes," he writes Renée, February 20, 1781, "I am a libertine, I confess it. I have conceived everything that can be conceived in this genre, but I have surely not done everything I have conceived and I surely never will. I am a libertine, but I am not a *criminal* or a *murderer*."[53] (emphasis Sade's)

Among the marquis's prison phantasms was onanistic sodomy, and his demands in this regard entailed a particular and acute embarrassment for the marquise. The practice of self-sodomy had begun several years earlier, and is first mentioned in a letter dated October 1778. It contains Renée-Pélagie's annotations as well as Sade's listing of the monthly totals of *"introductions"* of what he called *"prestiges,"* makeshift phalluses of carved wood, small boxes *(étuis),* and crystal flasks *(flacons).* He recorded 6,536 *"introductions"* between September 1778 and December 1, 1780. Sade's sexuality and character, as is by now more than obvious, were hugely and compulsively anal, or "sadistic-anal" in Freudian language—ordinarily a phase of childhood following the oral and normally evolving into a mature, genital phase, unless arrested by some infantile disturbance, such as, presumably, Sade's being deprived of his mother.

In a letter of June 1781 addressed to the marquise, Sade was most specific: he asked for a crystal flask, "16 cm in circumference and 24 or 25 cm in length." She might order two, Sade said, one for herself. In May 1783, Sade's order suggests racial phantasms: "A box of 24 cm in length, 21 cm in width, and 8 cm in depth, made of ebony or rosewood."[54] He apparently enclosed a paper cut to measure.

Dutifully and somewhat naively, Renée-Pélagie tried to follow Sade's instructions, but she had her problems, she wrote him on September 30. First of all, she was confused by some contradiction between his measurements and the model he had sent. As for the box itself, "I do not know where to go to order it, since the workers think I am crazy when I ask for a box of that shape. They laugh in my face and refuse to make it. Besides, they want money in advance, for fear of being left with the box."[55]

Sade insisted. He was not at all happy with what she had sent him previously. Renée-Pélagie's reply, November 23: "I assure you that I had all the difficulties in the world to have the one I sent you made, and which is too small. None of the workers want to make the boxes, and they all regard me as if I were a madwoman . . . Please give me the pleasure of asking someone else to get it for you."[56] A month later she was still begging to be relieved from such requests.

For four years and five months the marquise had not been permitted to see her husband at Vincennes. Then, on July 13, 1781, she had been allowed to visit him, but only in the presence of a witness. The date also marks a curious crisis of jealousy on the part of Sade, which endured most of the year.

The man the marquise discovered, after so many years of not having seen him, had lost his hair and grown fat, and his pockmarks were now accentuated by his prison pallor. As for the marquis, he undoubtedly had had a more maternal image in his mind (one thinks of his recurrent dream), and had been shocked by Renée-Pélagie's appearance and dress—"decked out like a whore," he wrote immediately after the visit, with her "white dress and the hair escaping its covering." If she were to appear like that again, he would refuse to see her. She must come dressed in black, with no curls showing and "the breasts completely covered, not indecently displayed, as the other day."[57]

Innocently, Renée-Pélagie had mentioned to Sade that a new friend, the Marquise de Villette, had invited her to stay, and that she had asked a certain Lefèvre, formerly a secretary-valet of Sade, to procure several of the books he had demanded—Buffon, Voltaire, Montaigne, and various esoterica. Sade became furious. How could the marquise enjoy herself in society—moreover, with a woman who was "somewhat lesbian"[58]—when her husband was suffering in prison? It was the mention of Lefèvre, however, that brought on Sade's *crise de jalousie.* Typically he combined his psychotic obsession with numbers and his suspicion of Lefèvre as the marquise's lover in an "analysis" of her last letter:

> Your odious enigma has been deciphered. The day of my liberation is for February 7, 1782 or '84 . . . the detestable and imbecilic play with words is in the name of the day's saint . . . Saint Amand, and since one finds Fèvre in *February* [février], you have linked the name of that scoundrel to the numbers 5 and 7 . . . The day of Saint Amand being February 7, Lefèvre, who is linked to 7 and 5, became that day your lover. . . . Oh, *mon Dieu,* how you make me suffer![59]

The true object of Sade's jealousy can be deciphered from notes he had made in the margin of Renée-Pélagie's letter, opposite its date, August 5: "*Voilà* the number of that fine gentleman! together with 7, apparently that is what he measures"—that is, 13.55 by 18.9 cm.[60] Sade envied his wife Lefèvre's penis. (One wonders how often this is the case with jealous husbands.)

With the solemnity the accusation demanded, Renée-Pélagie vowed that "from this moment on, that person shall never put a foot in my home." As for Madame de Villette, the vow was as formal that she would never stay with her. "I add to that promise," Renée wrote to Sade, "a further promise that I will immediately leave the place I now inhabit for a more austere convent, where I will see only those people who are useful to you, and this until you are free and I can join you forever."[61] Sade's letters nonetheless continued with such violence that they were frequently kept by his jailers from his wife, and in October, her visits were suspended, for fear of her being attacked by the mad marquis.

It was at this time that Renée-Pélagie, "the saint of marriage," resumed going to Mass and seeing a priest.

In January 1782 the marquise was again permitted visits to Sade, only to have them interrupted in September, because he had struck one of the guards in a new attack of violence. Meantime he had finished his *Dialogue between a Priest and a Dying Man* and had begun *The 120 Days of Sodom,* or *The School for Libertines,* most likely in August, when he had been forbidden all books, because they "overheated his brain" and induced him to write "improper things." The marquise had begged him to be more careful about what he wrote, since his writings were doing him harm, and to change his ways. "The beast is too old," Sade had replied.[62]

In 1783, Sade's sight further deteriorated—and his demands increased. So did the obscenities of his letters, which were once again withheld from the marquise. Knowing of her resumed churchgoing, he added blasphemy to the obscenity. On Easter Day it delighted him to write to her: "Good evening, go eat your good little God and assassinate your parents. As for me, I am going to shake my cock, and I will be convinced, I assure you, of having done less evil than you."[63] A week previous, Renée-Pélagie had sent her husband another demanded *étui* in unflagging obedience; and to his Easter Day letter, she replied simply: "I must repeat that what you write is doing you a terrible harm and that only a completely different conduct will advance you toward what you and I want most."[64] But it was that winter when she also wrote Sade of her intense personal embarrassment in procuring him his *étuis* and *flacons.*

In February 1784, while Sade was madly calculating from various "signals" that he was about to be made an ambassador (shades of his father) by Louis XVI, he was in reality transferred from the Vincennes dungeon to the Bastille. It was worse, he immediately wrote the marquise, than the prison at Vincennes. (It was not.) He had been transferred "naked," he said; would she bring him a complete wardrobe on her first visit—"two shirts, two kerchiefs, six napkins, three pairs of stockings," and so forth, "and several of the books on my last list"? In March he was brought what he had requested, as well as "six pounds of candles."[65] In April his effects were forwarded from Vincennes. They included two mattresses, several boxes and flasks, and 140 volumes of books. The marquise was now permitted, and faithfully made, twice-monthly visits.

In mid-1785 Renée-Pélagie was still writing Sade: "There is only one true happiness for me in this world, and that is to be reunited with you, and that you be content and happy." But a new qualification instantly follows: "You will always see me in accord with your wishes, so long as they cannot harm you. We will live and die together."[66] Is there a glimmering of a tangential development in the life of the marquise, despite her devotion to the marquis? Is it more than a revived religiosity, than the dampening of passion by middle age? Sade increasingly took his vocation as a writer seriously—currently filling, in fine, spidery script, both sides of a thirteen-yard roll of paper with the extravagant revels of *The 120 Days,* a scenic catalogue of all the forbidden fantasies and taboos from infanticide to matricide, incest and coprophilia. And in 1786 Renée-Pélagie increasingly occupied herself with her rather less dreamlike offspring, Louis-Marie, nineteen; Donatien-Claude, seventeen; and Madeleine-Laure, fifteen. The children were imperceptibly replacing their father in the marquise's attentions and affections. For years the myth had been maintained that he was away on a long voyage, "explaining" the delay in the letters they received from him. The discovery of the truth was inevitable and unpleasant, though Madame de Montreuil, who retained charge of them, was genuinely fond of her grandchildren. La présidente's control over them was a source of unending conflict between the marquis and the marquise.

Many times Sade bitterly referred to their children as *hers* and the Montreuils'. "I have no children," he once wrote Renée-Pélagie, adding an unconcealed threat, "but I am of an age still to have them"—with another.[67] He disputed their education, if only to assert his authority. As a writer he maintained the rights of adolescents, but in practice insensitively tried to dictate to his children, such as choosing the regiment and uniform of his eldest son, which he wished to be the same as that he had belonged to and worn. He was furious with their mother when he failed. (The complex of Abraham, to give it a name, is as much a reality as that of Oedipus.) Told by Mlle. de Rousset that his daughter, Madeleine-Laure, was not very pretty, he had answered rather harshly that she really meant "ugly."

Once again the visits of the marquise were suspended because of Sade's misconduct in prison. Once again she formally appealed for their restoration, but this time, and perhaps more and more over time, her heart seems to have been less in it. She was aging, ailing, and rheumatic. Perhaps, too, the sight of Sade had something to do with it. As gluttonous as his murderous predecessor Gilles de Rais, he had become so fat that he could not change his shirt without assistance. Governor de Launay, explaining his refusal of Renée-Pélagie's request to his superior, Police Lieutenant General de Crosne, tells us more about the Sade couple at this time (July 7, 1786):

> The prisoner, who is extremely difficult and violent, is constantly making scenes . . . The police offices have many of his letters, which are filled with horrors about his wife, his family, and us. On his walks, for no reason at all he would insult the sentinels. It is because of his wickedness, which seems to increase when he has the visits of his wife, that M. Le Noir [Crosne's predecessor] thought it advisable to forbid them, at least for a time. . . . Since he sees no one, he has become more behaved. The goodness and decency of Mme. la Marquise de Sade lead her to ask to see him, but almost every time she receives torrents of insults and stupidities. The truth is she is in fear for her life, should he find his freedom one day.[68]

The marquise, however, was writing quite differently to the marquis. It may have been playacting, the conventional comedy of conjugality for which she had been trained and that she had practiced for so many years, it had become mechanical. August 22, 1786: "All my sentiments are for you; all my wishes are that your liberation will soon reunite us. . . . I am building a thousand castles in Spain for the moment you are free, for our activities, for all that will contribute to your happiness."[69] The twice-monthly visits were reinstated and faithfully resumed; then there is a new tone in the marquise's letters, a new assertion of self. To a nasty letter from the marquis, she replied for the first time in kind, and used, as he, the cool, second-person plural form. Early in 1787 she dared to recommend the prison chaplain to Sade. "This priest," she wrote, risking the blast in return, "is a man of intelligence, not at all a religious hypocrite, with whom one can talk literature. He is someone with whom you can converse. I advise you to ask for him."[70] Sade's reply was elaborately and predictably blasphemous.[71]

Egocentric as ever, Sade had asked about Renée-Pélagie's sister Anne-Prospère. He had oddly heard nothing for years. The marquise's answer is dry and burning:

> The silence I imposed on myself never to speak to you of my sister, my dear friend, was reasonable, since to have broken the silence in order to satisfy you would only have led you to false conclusions and disquiet. This is the last time I will speak of her. Do you insist upon my answering your questions, vowing in turn never to ask me to open my mouth about it and to remain calm? Very well, it is to calm you that I am replying.
>
> What is the reason for her leaving my mother?
>
> Nothing that concerns you or dishonors her.
>
> Is she my enemy? No.
>
> What sort of place is she living in, without indicating the street or the quarter? Whatever it is, it can do you no harm. Even this reply is useless.

Anne-Prospère, in fact, had died on May 13, 1781. For six years the information had been kept from Sade.

The letter continues, responding now to Sade's mockery of religious holidays lately observed by the marquise:

> Keeping Lenten fast, far from damaging my health, is an occasion for sensible diet, and I am never ill at such a time. Believe me, my dear friend, I am sorry to see you thinking as you do. Your fate is certainly not indifferent to me, for I would give my blood to assure your happiness in this world and in the other.
>
> You fall into another error in thinking that devoutness is sad. True devoutness is never fierce, nor is it gloomy, as you will see. For I shall not leave off my religious duties when you get out, since one of the essential duties is to make our surroundings happy. So you see that my duty is allied to the inclination of my heart, and you have nothing to fear.

There is the small but unmistakable sound of a worm turning:

> I will not pester you to think as I do, though I do not and will not stop hoping for it, since neither forced homage nor accommodation can please the Lord.[72]

Sade replied that the marquise must be depriving herself of her usual bath, for nothing seemed to him "drier" than her last communication. There was more of the same cat-and-mouse playing through the years 1787 and 1788, but with less certainty as to who was which. In October 1787 he haughtily told the marquise to pick up the sixteen bottles of wine she had left for him, since the wine was "vinegar." He also "complimented" her on her adroitness in finding pretexts for entertaining herself in society, "while I lack for everything." But more plaintively, Sade protested an occasional new irregularity in her visits. "I have no other consolation," he complained, yet ended the year threatening to view her "as the greatest enemy I had during my detention," if she did not deliver his latest brief to the authorities.[73]

"I," replied the marquise, "refuse to see you, to listen to you?" As for the last, "You will certainly regret having suspected me to be among your enemies." To the governor of the Bastille she wrote that she had found the marquis *"triste, mélancholique,"* and feared for his life.[74] She succeeded in having Sade permitted magazines and newspapers, so that he might still have contact with the world outside. When she was authorized to visit her husband weekly instead of twice monthly, she came to see him twenty-three times in the first half of 1789, and could acquaint him personally with the new agitations in the streets of Paris. They were soon reaching the Bastille.

On July 2, 1789, stirred by the sight of the crowd, Sade tore a metal tube from his toilet and employed it as a loudspeaker. From his window he shouted that the prisoners inside—a total of seven—were being slaughtered, and the people should come to their rescue. Launay urgently wrote his superior: "He is a dangerous man to have here!"—and he importuned for Sade's transfer elsewhere.[75] On the fourth of July, as a result, the marquis was removed to the asylum for the insane at Charenton. At one in the morning, six armed men conducted him from his cell, allowing him to take nothing with him.

July fourteenth the Bastille fell to the crowds of Paris. Sade's cell was sacked; his furniture, suits, and linen, his library of six hundred volumes, and his manuscripts were "torn up, burned, pillaged."[76] Fortunately the manuscript roll of *The 120 Days* had been hidden in a cell wall. Sade, however, thought it lost, and bitterly berated the marquise for that, since she had fled the same day to the country (the manuscript would turn up after his death). On the nineteenth the marquise returned briefly to Paris and her Sainte-Aure convent. To prison officials, she disclaimed responsibility for Sade's belongings, but made an effort to have him removed from "the asylum of the insane among whom he found himself."[77] On October 5 Renée-Pélagie, her daughter, and a maid joined the aristocratic exodus from the capital, as the women of Paris marched in the rain to Versailles to fetch the royal family back to the capital. Her sons, she wrote to Gaufridy, were managing as best they could with their military units.

On March 13, 1790 the Constituent Assembly declared all *lettres de cachet* of the ancien régime invalid. On the eighteenth Sade's two sons, whom he had not seen for almost fifteen years, came to Charenton to inform him of the decree. On April 2 Sade was freed.

He went directly to the man who was in charge of his affairs in Paris, who provided him with a bed, a meal, and six louis. The following day Sade presented himself at the Sainte-Aure convent and asked for the marquise. *She refused to see him.*

She intended, Renée-Pélagie had Sade informed, to seek a separation. Sade, it seems, was not surprised—and one wonders not why it happened, but why the marquise had taken so long.

The rest, so far as the Sades as a couple are concerned, involves the usual dreary details of the allotment and management of revenues and estates; in a word, money.

· Epilogue ·

The marquise would live with her daughter, Madeleine-Laure, until her death in 1810; the marquis would die four years later, but most of the years between his liberation, in 1790, and his death, in 1814, were spent, it now seems needless to say, in prison. He was jailed by the Jacobins in 1793 for being too "moderate"—he had opposed the death penalty, declaring that one could kill but not judge. After the Terror had come to an end, he was again liberated, only to be imprisoned once more under Bonaparte in 1801—for being the author of "the infamous novel *Justine*" (which he promptly denied having written) and of "an even more horrible work titled *Juliette,*"[78] the story of a Sadeian superwoman who treats men as they treated Justine, which, consequently, is comparatively unknown. He went from prison to prison, until finally, at the request and the expense of his family, he was transferred to the asylum of Charenton, where he died and was buried.

7

ROMANTIC LOVE AND THE DAILY LIFE: MARIE D'AGOULT AND FRANZ LISZT

THE Franz Liszt–Marie d'Agoult love affair began to end, in prescribed Romantic fashion, at its very beginning, though the final parting occurred three children and six years later. In truth, *no* love affair could have fulfilled Romantic expectations. No mind, body, or heart has yet been made to sustain that all-consuming heat. Perhaps the burden imposed upon the couple by the Romantic conception of love as *la grande passion*—and still weighing upon it—was hardly less heavy than that of the loveless, arranged marriage of the previous century.

True love, the Romantics believed, came once in a lifetime, and had to be seized before it took flight. "Romanticism" itself is as untidy a term as one might wish, representing emotions and sentiments washing away the banks of reason and intellect that classically shore up the passions. Mario Praz renounced defining it in his *Romantic Agony,* and resigned himself to extensively quoting the Romantics. Their creed was the liberation of art, life, and *self* from the claims, morals, and conventions of society, a rebellion inviting, as it defied, punishment. Born philosophically with Rousseau, the movement and age triumphed in France in 1830, with Victor Hugo; to subside before the century was twenty years older, with Stendhal. And as Stendhal did, Marie d'Agoult, too, after embracing the Romantic creed, would reject it—too late, one might say, but for Liszt it would be much, much later.

As is fitting and proper, the "fatal" meeting with Franz Liszt, twenty-two, came as a love-at-first-sight thunderclap for Marie, Comtesse d'Agoult, twenty-eight, married and mother of two. Most likely she had seen him before as the Hungarian child prodigy at the keyboard, but "this time it was something else."[1] She had been invited to a salon performance in the Paris town house of the Marquise de Vayer, together with several younger musical ladies; the countess played the piano surpassingly well and sang with a small, pleasant voice. Franz was late, the marquise was explaining, when the door to the salon was opened and he appeared.

"A strange apparition struck my vision." It is Marie d'Agoult addressing us through her memoirs:

> I say *apparition,* for lack of another word to render the extraordinary sensation induced in me, to begin with, by the most extraordinary person I had ever seen. A tall figure, thin to excess, a pale face with large, sea-green eyes suddenly flaring like a wave catching the sunlight, a suffering, powerful face, an uncertain walk that seemed to glide over rather than to touch the ground, a distraught, unquiet air like that of a phantom about to be called back to the dead, and so I saw the young genius before me, whose seclusion was awaking a curiosity as lively as the envy provoked by his triumphs in the past.[2]

Formally presented to the countess, Franz took his place beside her with the experienced ease of the often-seduced—rather than seducing—beautiful young man of the remarkably experimental period. It was late 1832 or early 1833. He spoke freely, familiarly, wildly, and vehemently to the dazed Marie. Wild, impassioned theories and "bizarre judgments" poured into a startled but thirsting mind, "more accustomed to banal, received opinions."

Marie d'Agoult, still marveling: "His flashing look, his gestures, his smile, now profound and infinitely tender, now caustic as if he wished to provoke me into contradiction or into intimate assent." She scarcely responded, and was then "rescued" by the marquise, who asked Liszt to accompany the young ladies at the piano as they sang. Marie joined her "moved voice"—a light mezzo-soprano—to theirs. "The song ended, Franz . . . turned and saw me. A light crossed his face, then immediately darkened, and for the rest of the evening he did not come near me."

That night Marie d'Agoult had difficulty finding sleep. When finally it came, she was "visited by strange dreams."[3] Marie d'Agoult was neither in the mood nor of the mind, however, to leave it at that.

Born Marie de Flavigny, she was a descendant, on her father's side, of ancient French nobility, and on her mother's, of wealthy German bankers, the Bethmanns, most likely converted Jews. Marie never mentions the latter probability, though it was the common assumption in Frankfurt, where she was born, a midnight child, December 30–31, 1805.[4] In any event, Marie was brought up proud, rich, and aristocratic, initially in Frankfurt, but soon afterward in France, particularly after Napoleon's fall. Blond, blue-eyed, willowy, and tall, she felt both German and French—"six inches of snow on twenty feet of lava," she would often quote her friend Sainte-Beuve.[5] When still a child she had met Madame de Staël, French aristocrat, writer, and rebel, and the poet Goethe, who might jointly be considered the godmother and godfather of "her emancipated mind."[6] One might add, banal as it may be, that she adored her father, Count de Flavigny, and disliked her mother. The "all or nothing" of Rousseau, Marie herself would say, "the need for exclusive possession" of another, would be her demand of both love and friendship.[7]

At the age of twenty-one Marie married Count Charles d'Agoult, sixteen or seventeen years older, a colonel of the cavalry lamed in the Napoleonic wars. Marie admits she had the choice of accepting or rejecting him, but, not quite recovered from the death in her youth of her father ("all grace and beauty"), she had accepted the arranged marriage, bringing her husband a dowry of 300,000 francs and the expectation of a million more on the death of her mother.

The honeymoon of the couple along the English Channel was not a complete failure: the count was a decent, modest chap, and would remain so. He was attentive; he may even have been moderately in love. He put it more strongly in a letter from Dieppe to Marie's mother, July 10, 1827: "Believe me, my dear mother-in-law, day and night I shall see to it that my wife is well. I love her exceedingly. I want very much to keep her. She is now my whole existence."[8] Returned from his honeymoon, installed with his young wife in Paris's highly fashionable Faubourg Saint-Germain, the count—in the hindsight of his memoirs—"quickly" recognized their profound incompatibility:

> A few days of my new existence were sufficient for me to foresee that the tranquil intimacy rising from the same duties, interests, and home would never be true of my household. Mme d'Agoult, as I have said already, had great and charming qualities, but the words *duties, sacrifices, consideration, devotion* were as foreign to her education as to her dictionary [sic], though they do count in life. A cold character, rather elastic religious and moral principles, and a romantic imagination could indeed offer some danger in the future. Moreover, she was set some regrettable examples in her childhood, and childhood forgets nothing. She never really knew

> what she wanted. Her dreamy nature became attached to an aristocratic name and existence, then to triumphs in elegant society, the laurels of the writer and the artist, celebrity and applause, for she was writer and artist.

Count d'Agoult is leaping ahead in his backward look. However, even on their honeymoon, he adds here, the calèche taking them to Dieppe was loaded with her writings, paper, and books, which she never left behind. "She was always writing, either to her friends or to posterity."[9]

A bride's underemployed intellectuality is probably the greatest threat to a husband's domestic tranquility.

Countess Marie d'Agoult was duly presented to the Court. As important, if not more so, she established her own salon and had her own friends, in the interims giving birth to two daughters, Louise and Claire, two years apart. The count was more moved by the births than the countess. "Maternal love . . . ," Marie would write, "is not a sentiment of the mind but rather a blind instinct in which the lowest brute is superior to woman."[10] The countess was seen more often in the salons of Paris than by her children, though her case was far from unique. Romantic restlessness, the hunger to exercise wit, intelligence, talent, and coquetry drove the period's remarkable women—Mme. Récamier, Marie d'Agoult, George Sand—as it did its male poets and painters—Vigny, Musset, Hugo, Delacroix. Their terrain was the Paris salon, and their play, as in the past, strictly according to the rules, which were rigorous yet liberating. However, the greater freedom, as to be expected, fell "naturally" to the men. Both sexes were not simply content with the salon as the established locus for extramarital preludes; marriage being what it was among the upper classes, they had created it out of their mutual need. Marie d'Agoult testifies to this in her *Souvenirs,* as she explores the first years of her marriage to the count.

Habitually after the first year, Marie writes, and above all after the first child, the young wife "entered a state of perfect freedom, receiving, going, and coming at will without offending common practice." Here Marie may well be *asserting* her freedom rather than speaking for her husband (witness his memoirs). Yet she continues:

> In Paris's aristocratic society, the husband as such scarcely counted. After a very brief time, to take full charge of his wife would be thought a mistake. To find her lovable, to love her, would be considered ridiculous. To be seen assiduously at her side either at home or in other salons was to label oneself a fool or a nuisance . . . It was a pleasure to see how quickly he took the habit of going

elsewhere. Since men's clubs and circles had not yet been imported, every *galant homme* was obliged to find a salon of his own or have his evenings to himself. The idea of spending an evening at home together never occurred to Parisian couples; and to receive friends in common was not considered pleasant, or even possible. Moreover, hostesses did not at all like to receive husband and wife together; that, they said, chilled all talk. *Le bel esprit,* the desire to please, coquetry, verve, piquant remarks, everything that lent liveliness and grace to Paris conversations, were snuffed out in the insipid company of married couples; to revive them, each had to go to a different salon where nothing reminded either of duty's heavy chain. It was an arrangement, a convention, quickly and tacitly established among couples.[11]

Society gained, Marie adds, *not* the ménage or the family: they are the last consideration of a French marriage. There is no distribution of blame, other than to the period—its ennui, its spleen, so splendidly caught by Baudelaire. The first six years of her own marriage, Marie d'Agoult informs us, "to a man of heart and honor," soon formed a "terrible emptiness" inside her. "I tried to fill it with worldly pleasures"—salon, theater, music, flirtations—"and by the multiplicity of meaningless duties, but in vain." As for the two children, "between their father and myself, these laughing little creatures were more often the cause of trouble than not."[12]

In this spirit Countess Marie d'Agoult had gone to the salon of the Marquise de Vayer on the arm of her current *chevalier servant,* the dashing little dandy Eugène Sue, to listen to the private (though paid) performance of society's darling, Franz Liszt.

To be paid was not to young Liszt's particular discredit, only to be paid much less than the great Rossini, who also performed privately, entering by way of the servant's door, but for a considerable sum. To mention it, however, is to remind oneself of Liszt's status, however elevated, in Paris's *haute société,* that of a performer, albeit of genius, whom a lady of high birth openly takes as a lover by paying a high social price. Liszt was not of "one's kind"—nor, as important, was he as humble as his origin.

The father of Franz Liszt had been a steward in the household of a Prince Eszterhazy, his mother the daughter of an Austrian dealer in dry goods. Franz himself is recorded as Hungarian, though he learned and spoke little, if any, Hungarian. His meager education, save for piano lessons, was in the German language, and he is better thought of as Austro-Hungarian, like the empire under which he was born in October 1811—almost exactly six years after Marie d'Agoult. At the age of ten he was removed by his ambitious father to neighboring Vienna for advanced piano tutelage, and at twelve brought to Paris as a child prodigy. France became his home and French his language, though he would always speak it with an accent. He was quickly adopted by aristocratic circles and was soon receiving 2,000 francs for a salon performance. He was, in short, the exploited gifted child, and as he grew older, he seems to have realized it. "Spasms of self-contempt" were succeeded by "sulks and fits of religious mania." Sternly his concerned father told him: "You belong to music and not to the Church." Before dying (when Franz was not quite sixteen), his father is said to have warned his son of the *second* great allurement in his life. "I fear for you on account of women," he said. "They will trouble and dominate your life."[13]

The father had already witnessed the reaction of women to Liszt's beauty and the passionate style of his playing: their erotic pursuit and, despite his youth, their occasional success. Two women, at the least, are known to have entered and "troubled" his life before he met Countess Marie: young Caroline de Saint-Cricq, whose father, a royal minister, simply dismissed Liszt as his daughter's piano teacher; and, more recently, Adèle Laprunarède, who would soon abandon him for a duke. Of the two, Franz Liszt would not long be writing in forced explanation to a Marie d'Agoult jealous of the past: "I was only a child, almost an imbecile where it concerned Caroline, a coward and a miserable poltroon with Adèle."[14]

The third allurement should, in fact, be listed first: music, with an accent on the piano. Composing was still ancillary, and the incipient approaches were piano transcriptions of orchestral works, notably Berlioz's *Fantastic Symphony.* As for Liszt's theatrics at the piano, the devilish influence had been Paganini's virtuoso tricks with the violin in Paris in 1831. Joined to that impact and the exercises it demanded was Liszt's compulsion to devour, as if at one sitting, all the culture deprived him in his performing youth. "For two weeks," he wrote a pupil and friend,

> my mind and fingers are working like the damned; Homer, the Bible, Plato, Locke, Byron, Hugo, Lamartine, Chateaubriand, Beethoven, Bach, Hummel, Mozart, Weber are all about me. I study them, meditate on them, devour them with fury. Furthermore, I do four or five hours of exercises: thirds, sixths, octaves, tremolos, repeated notes, cadenzas, etc. Ah, if only I do not go mad, you will find an artist in me. Yes, an artist such as you

> demand, such as we need today. "And I too am a painter!" cried Correggio the first time he saw a masterpiece . . . Though small and poor, your friend never ceases repeating these words of the great man since Paganini's last concert . . . God, what suffering, misery, and torture in those four strings.[15]

Liszt wore black à la Dante, adding a white Byronic collar. Onstage he would strip his gloves, drop them dramatically to the floor, toss back his long hair, turn his Florentine profile to the public, and then—demolish the piano. In the salon he more seductively tempered his instrument to the space and the audience.

The effect upon Marie d'Agoult has been recorded: her difficulty finding sleep that night, her "strange dreams," her being haunted by what she had seen, and heard, and felt; haunted too, no doubt, by Liszt's abrupt withdrawal, the darkening of his face. *She* pursued *him.* Marie d'Agoult had "complete independence," she insists: "There was no obstacle of any kind to the frequent conversations we soon held, Franz and I." They talked of "the soul and of God . . . human destiny . . . future life." Marie was fascinated; a new world unfolded before her of art, daring, unrest. Franz was passionately republican—that is, revolutionary—for all Europe was monarchical. He had Saint-Simonist friends and probably took Marie to their utopian socialist meetings. Though "very Catholic," Marie marveled, "his unquiet spirit drove him to the edge of heresy." He despised mediocrity; "all the superb or desperate revolutionaries of Romantic poetry were the companions of his sleepless nights." He detested any aristocracy not based on genius or justice. "So many names, so many ideas, so many sentiments, so many revolts, almost completely unknown to me until he came!" Their roles were reversed: the younger man was the teacher, the older woman the pupil, and she adored it. "My mind was no less avid for knowledge than my heart for love," and she found both in Franz.[16]

They read together—Shakespeare, Dante, Goethe, in their original languages; together they visited a hospital for the insane—they were the new humanists; shared a visit with Chopin, Liszt's friend; and probably became lovers before the spring of 1833. Was their lovemaking (one searches for the lightest expression) as ethereal as Shelley's skylark? Even the way one makes love is socially conditioned by the sentiments of one's time, the attitudes, values, and class of the lovemakers as well as their particular relationship as equals, as dominant and subordinate, or whatever the combination. "Even when he [Liszt] was most passionate," Marie fondly remembers—or prefers putting it—in her otherwise-embittered memoirs, "most altered by desire, one felt nothing gross in these desires, and the most delicate pudency would not be offended by them."[17] Most likely Marie d'Agoult is romanticizing; ours is too gross, or simply too physical, a generation to believe otherwise. In any case, reality would enter their dream soon enough and disturb it, as would happen intermittently and increasingly over the years.

That spring Marie invited Franz to join her family at Croissy, a splendid château and estate near Paris that had once belonged to Colbert, which she had bought with *her* money from the Prince de La Trémoïlle. Entering the salon, for the first time Franz saw Marie with her two children, Claire and Louise, aged five and three (the count is unmentioned in Marie's memoirs). "What happened suddenly in his mind?" Marie asks. "What thought struck him like an arrow? I do not know." She did indeed. There was little room in Romantic love for children, one's own or another's. The sight of the newly beloved as the mother of two almost ended their idyll, and Marie could not be unaware of it: "His beautiful face altered; his features contracted. We could not speak for an instant. Franz stood at the door. Trembling, I took several steps toward him; we did not dare to speak."[18]

From that evening, says Marie sadly, their relations changed. With persistence, however, she continued to seek him even as he fled her. When they did meet, she found a different Franz, who spoke to her with a new cynicism in praise of worldliness and the free and easy life of the libertine. Surely she knew he was attempting to discourage her perseverance, although at the same time he may have been speaking half truths. He even "praised what he called my beautiful existence; he felicitated me on my grand position in the world; he admired, he said, my royal residence, the opulence and elegance of everything that surrounded me. Was it seriously?" When he played, the piano vibrated with "shrill, discordant sounds . . . Franz, to whom my presence no longer brought either peace or joy, seemed to nourish I know not what secret resentment against me. Once I even surprised in his regard a pale flash of hatred. What was it? I did not dare to ask him."

One is embarrassed as one reads, but one allows for the period, when lovers behaved as was expected of them. Had they not been reading Romantic literature—*Childe Harold, Manfred, Werther, Obermann*—would they have loved as they loved at all? Predictably, Franz Liszt is brought to his knees at Marie's feet:

> One day, under the blow of a cutting word whose wound I could not bear, a plaint escaped me. My long-restrained tears flowed. Franz looked at me in consternation. He remained silent; he

> seemed in struggle with himself, torn by conflicting emotions, which made his lips tremble. Suddenly, falling at my feet, embracing my knees, he entreated me in a voice that I still hear, with a profound and sorrowful look, to grant him pardon. This pardon, in the burning grasp of our hands, was the explosion of love, a mutual vow to love each other, to love each other undivided, without limit, without end, on the earth and as long as the heavens last! The hours, the days, the weeks, the months, that followed, were complete enchantment.[19]

They were not. Franz's letters to Marie, which she carefully preserved, indicate an indeterminate backing and filling on his part, but no appreciable halt in their lovemaking. Franz, that winter, had found a small apartment that he called a *Ratzenloch,* or rathole, for their meetings; his letters frequently end with endearing German phrases, specially *Nicht eines Engels, nicht Gottes, nur Dein* ("not an angel's, not God's, but thine"). Liszt to Marie d'Agoult, September 1833: "All my friends find me horribly changed; several ascribe it to a *grande passion;* others say it is the beginning of madness. You know that I am neither in love nor mad." November: "It was, perhaps, great madness to have loved as I did."[20]

If their lovemaking was lyrical and evanescent for Marie d'Agoult, for Liszt it was a form of worship, and Marie's body no less than a way opening to . . . "God!!!" Ecstatically one mid-1834 morning he wrote to her:

> Yesterday I had no need for *evening prayer* . . . Your breath was still on my lips, on my eyelids; the beat of your heart continued to resound in mine and extended to infinity that double, intense life you revealed to me, that we have revealed to each other . . . There was no longer space, nor time, nor words, but rather Infinity, Love, Forgetfulness, Sensuality, Charity!! God!!! God, such as my soul seeks; God, such as despair and excess sorrow sometimes present; God, all-loving and all-powerful.[21]

Yet it was rare for Marie d'Agoult to feel secure, she who sought unshared love, exclusive passion. Her reproaches to Liszt about his past reflect her concern about their future, whose lines she discerned in the inconstant present. "Never will the love of a woman suffice you," she said prophetically. [22] Much more is gathered from Franz's responses than from Marie's letters, since fewer of the latter have come down to us, thanks to Liszt's lesser interest in preserving them. He apologized, as we noted, for his affairs with Caroline de Saint-Cricq and Adèle Laprunarède, accusing himself of having been a "child," an "imbecile," a "poltroon." Marie, it seems, persisted, cuttingly (her wounding flaw). Franz explodes:

> A false and vulgar man, such as you suppose me to be, would never have told you, "I have no love save what you give me!" I do not *take back a single iota* of my past life, however shameful or bitter it may have been! Not an iota. I completely accept everything, and were I a hundred times more criminal, I would still accept everything, for I want the woman I love to be *happy* to pardon me. It is from her alone that I would *accept* forgiveness . . . All that is now in the past; let this be the last time, I entreat you, for both you and me.[23]

Countess Marie tried to draw Liszt across the social gulf between them, dreaming of their being together in *her* world. Liszt, angrily: "Do not speak to me of your dreams; *I could never* decide to take my place with you in such a society. . . . As for my *line of conduct* . . . I would prefer no longer hearing you even mention it. . . . For the hundredth time I repeat to you, it would be impossible for me to change my way."[24]

Liszt's unspeakable "line of conduct"? His next letter offers a clue: he is seeing a woman, possibly among others, out of his past:

> You want me to tell you again about Maria? So be it. I saw her again this morning; she was grief-stricken, her eyes flowing with tears, and I heard her cry out from her entrails: "Love me, save me!" As Adèle before her. I did not say a word. She seemed to understand my silence. "Then, your life," she said, after hesitating, "is devoted entirely to that woman? To that woman . . ." Yes, to her, to the grave, *à Dieu!*
>
> This, I swear to you, will be the last insignificant incident in our life, so overabundant with pure and noble things. *The future will be resplendent* with purity and dignity.[25]

Liszt probably meant it. He seems equally sincere in his infidelities, his remorse, and his promises of fidelity. But why, he must have asked himself, should he accept constraints on his freedom as never before; why limit himself to one woman, though he "loved" her, when there were so many asking to be loved, to be made happy, rendering him the same? Might it not be better for both if they parted, amicably, perhaps;

he to his free, artist's life, she to her life as a *femme du monde* ("a woman of the world")? The thought occurred to each; they discussed it, wrote about it, spoke of "separation." Franz Liszt to Marie d'Agoult:

> Society, the family, the world, have nothing to do with it. The matter is and remains religious, that is, between God and conscience. Sometimes, too, I feel sorrowfully that I have put a weight upon you that you will not know how to bear. . . . I know not what remorse is penetrating me and freezing me to the marrow of my bones . . . Oh, your letters kill me . . . Yes, there are words that are never pronounced in vain, at least at certain hours. That of *separation* has been said and resaid by me and by you. However miserable and cowardly the virtues of a *femme du monde* seem to me, they are the only ones that will suit you hereafter. Moreover, madame, you have two daughters and the future grows dark.[26]

The abiding rival for Liszt's allegiance, however, was not another woman but rather the cassock, his perdurable religious fervor, stirred at this time by the Abbé Félicité de Lamennais, an austere radical priest in his early fifties. The Abbé was vigorously enlisting followers for reform of the irredeemably royalist Church, incurring the wrath of the Vatican in the process. The Christian socialism of his most recent publication, *Paroles d'un croyant*—"a book small in size," said Pope Gregory in a damning encyclical, "but immense in its perversity"—had spread his name and influence throughout liberal Europe. His conception of the artist as "prophet of the new order"[27] particularly appealed to Liszt's groping sense of his own mission and destiny. ("Liszt," remarked his friend Heine, "likes to poke his nose in all the pots in which God is cooking the future of the world."[28]) Several times that year he made long pilgrimages to Lamennais in Brittany, alone, which did not endear the Abbé to the countess. That feeling was augmented by her own growing skepticism and loss of faith. When Franz sent her a copy of the Abbé's last work, with passages marked for her close reading, she replied with rational refutations and objections—and he was hurt.

A second rival, in Marie's eyes, was George Sand, the most famous —and the freest—woman of her time. Though less beautiful, she was equally striking and, to boot, a writer; therefore an "artist" with more likely appeal for a man such as Liszt. Marie was mistaken on several grounds. When Sand first met Liszt, it was during the most intense moment of her liaison with Musset—after the fiasco at Venice and their return. More to the point, Franz was not quite to her taste—she compared him to spinach, which she particularly disliked. "Monsieur [illegible] confided to her diary on November 19, 1834, "thinks only [illegible]nd the Holy Virgin, who does not in the least resemble me."[29] [illegible] he seemed disposed to fall in love had he been encouraged, [illegible]lso noted, she had been content simply to curl under his piano [illegible] he played; and that, then, was physical enough for George Sand. [illegible]ly, there would be her long, affectionate, and ambiguous relationship with the competitive, aristocratic Marie. Indeed, Sand's bold way of life was, in fact, a model for both Liszt and the countess as they considered their future and weighed its risks.

Franz himself had presented Marie to George Sand in George Sand's Paris apartment, where she appeared to the dazzled George Sand like "one of those marvelous princesses in the tales of Hoffmann . . . a golden-haired fairy in a long blue robe" who had descended from the heavens "to the garret of a poet."[30] Marie, on first seeing Sand, had asked herself: "Is she a man, a woman, an angel, a demon? Does she come, as her Lélia, from heaven or hell?"[31] Later Sand would write to Marie d'Agoult, "I believe I can say . . . that I love you, that I regard you as the only beautiful, estimable, and truly noble object of the patrician world. You had to be striking for me to forget you were a countess." She had also found Marie formidably intelligent. "You say you want to write? Write, then! . . . Write quickly, without reflecting too much," write out of the present, not out of memory. Write about women, Sand would add.[32]

In November 1834 Marie's younger child, Louise, became ill; in December she was dead. Marie despaired, felt at a loss and alone in her feeling, for she oddly recalls in her memoirs that Liszt was in Brittany with the Abbé, writing her cold letters, unresponsive to her sorrow. Actually he was in Paris at the time. "Be blessed," he wrote upon hearing of Louise's death, "oh my God, be blessed forever! You thought of me constantly at the bedside of your child . . . You tell me that you always thought of me at that cruel moment. Thank you and blessings on you forever, Marie!" He suffers along with her, Franz says, at the same time that he urges her to examine and probe her sorrow. The next phrase helps explain Marie's recollection of Liszt as absent, since it suggests he had been preparing her for a separation, distancing himself psychologically: "Perhaps you understand, too, why I have made such an effort to accustom and habituate your soul to unhappiness." To speak directly of their parting now seems too cruel, but it leaves Franz painfully confused. "I think I am going mad, but I love you so much, so greatly, so highly. Your maid told me . . . that you have spoken of drowning yourself, of never again seeing Claire, etc." It is too terrible, Franz writes. If only he actually were as egotistic and insensible as Marie says he is, but, alas, he is *not.* "Try to come here," Franz continues, "today or tomorrow, any hour you wish."

> The day when you can tell me with all your mind, all your heart, all your soul, "Franz, let us erase, forget, forgive forever whatever was incomplete, distressing, perhaps miserable in the past; let us be everything one to the other, because at this hour I understand and forgive you as much as I love you," that day—and may it be soon—we will flee far from society, we will live, we will love, and we will die alone together.[33]

It brought the *grand rapprochement.* In March 1835 Marie was pregnant, most likely by her choice. (Primitive but effective means of contraception were available; George Sand, who also had two children bearing her husband's name, would have no more, despite the many lovers.) That spring Marie d'Agoult additionally presented Franz Liszt with an article appearing in the *Gazette Musicale.* Written by her, it was signed by him, and it is difficult to decide which may have endeared, or entrapped, the twenty-three-year-old Liszt more effectively, the child he fathered, or the article he "authored." In either case, after first talking to Franz, Abbé de Lamennais came to Marie d'Agoult in May, and on "bended knee," according to the countess, pleaded with her not to go off with Liszt, abandoning husband and child. (Had Franz indicated his own hesitations to the Abbé?)

> Eloquently painting . . . the unhappiness of those led by the spirit of revolt, the blame put upon them by honest people . . . Abbé de Lamennais wrung a mute protest from me based on his own example. "He himself," I thought, "did exactly the same. Would the priest who broke with his Church . . . want to resume his chains? Is sincerity no longer the first virtue of noble souls in his eyes?"[34]

Marie proved unshakable.

The lovers left for Switzerland, Franz preceding Marie to Basel, where he awaited her. Before her own departure, accompanied by her unsuspecting mother and brother-in-law, Marie d'Agoult wrote a farewell letter to her husband, May 26, 1835:

> I do hope that instead of the happiness that is no longer possible for either you or me, you will at least find peace and repose. I do not conceal from myself my wrongs and I ask your forgiveness in the name of Louise, who is asking God for forgiveness and mercy

> for the two of us. I will never speak your name but with the respect and esteem that are due to your character; as for myself, all I ask for is silence on your part before a society that will shower insults upon me."[35]

When she arrived in Basel, Marie wrote to Franz from her hotel, Three Kings (Drei Könige):

> Let me know the name of your hotel and the number of your room as soon as possible. Don't go out. My mother is here; my brother-in-law has left. By the time you read this I will have spoken to her; until now I haven't dared say a word. It's a last great trial, but my love is my faith, and I thirst for martyrdom [!]. Wednesday. Drei Könige.
>
> Franz to Marie, in reply (in English):
>
> Here I am, since you sent for me. I shall not go out till I see you. My room is at the Hôtel de la Cigogne number twenty at the first étage—go to the right side. Yours.[36]

Almost a week passed before Marie moved into the Hôtel de la Cigogne. Was the problem with her mother or a reluctant Liszt? Perhaps both. Marie d'Agoult, it seems certain, suffered the mortification of the lady as pursuer and Franz Liszt the sensation of the pursued, the one speaking of "martyrdom," the other of being "sent for." The enthusiasm on both sides is remarkable for its absence. Thus the "years of pilgrimage," as Liszt would title the pieces he would then compose, were, inauspiciously, to begin. But . . . the very mention of Liszt as composer suggests immediately that it was not he who necessarily suffered the more or profited the less. His "passage to Switzerland opened a new era in Liszt's music," writes his biographer Eleanor Perényi, who spares little sympathy for Marie d'Agoult ("he was too young to be tied to a demanding older woman").[37] Yet it was the countess who would indefatigably press Franz Liszt to give up his career as a performer (she called it that of a *"bateleur,"* or buffoon) and devote himself to composition (by which, of course, Liszt is now judged and alone brought back to life).

For a month "the galley slaves of love" (Balzac's devastating description of the pair in *Béatrix)* made excursions into the mountains and countryside of Switzerland, recapturing some of the romance of their first days. Resolutely Marie writes of "granite ramparts, inaccessible mountain peaks . . . hidden valleys, black pines . . . murmuring lakes, distant rumblings of precipices . . . dear, dolorous ghosts of my youth."[38] Memory as literary phrases. Had the excursions endured, so might have their belated honeymoon, but too soon they settled in Calvinist Geneva, the last place for adulterous lovers, one of them four months pregnant.

Liszt found the apartment they would occupy, a grand affair covering an entire floor, with windows looking out on the Jura and the Rhone. Letters had awaited their arrival, two for Marie. Mother and brother each asked her to reconsider her delicate situation, and return. A separation would be arranged, they said diplomatically, and she could do as she wished, if only she would do it more discreetly. They would see to it that she lived independently and well. In a postscript, Claire embraced her mother and asked when she might be returning. Marie replied that the good Lord Himself had called upon her to sacrifice herself "to the grandeur, to the salvation, of this divine genius who has nothing in common with the rest of mankind and should not be subject to the common law."[39] She is less certain of Liszt's divinity in later memoirs, recalling the episode. She had wanted to tell him what her mother and brother had written, but refrained—Franz, she glumly notes, might have advised her to accept their generous offer!

Upon seeing her reading the two letters, Franz had asked, quite casually, whether the news from France was good. She had replied, as casually, *yes.* He had said nothing more, "as if he wished to know nothing more." That silence, she felt, marked "something . . . irrevocably changed . . . an empty space in which our thoughts no longer met."[40] It had never happened before, Marie remarks. In fact it had happened often.

Fairly quickly, Franz assembled former friends, and new ones, in Geneva, and Marie d'Agoult soon had her accustomed *chevaliers servants* about her, notably Louis de Ronchaud, a young poet who proved faithful all her life. She resumed her studies, profiting from a well-stocked municipal library; Franz set himself to composing as Marie sat by, book in hand. "Pretending to read," she writes, "I was profoundly moved to see him devoted to his true art, to that wonderful genius that shone from his eyes." And she would be Beatrice to his Dante! "Yet, strangely, it was not his musical genius that most interested me in Franz." Marie d'Agoult does not explain further *what* most interested her in Liszt. Romantic memoirs of women rarely, if ever, speak of sexuality (in contrast to those of a man such as Musset and his *Confession of a Child of His Time).* Liszt as lover was in the prime of his youth.

"Several months," says Marie, "passed in this fashion, peaceful and tender."[41]

In reality it was several weeks. Soon after the arrival in Geneva, Franz received a letter from a young pupil, Hermann Cohen, better known as Puzzi, who begged to join him. He immediately replied favorably, without consulting Marie beforehand. She who yearned to maintain their intimacy intact, their relative isolation undisturbed, was deeply hurt. Puzzi arrived on August 14. Meantime Pierre Wolff, another pupil and friend, who had persuaded Liszt to give lessons at the Conservatory of Geneva, had arranged, with Liszt's consent, for a public performance. Marie, this time, was furious: where indeed was the promised privacy, the exclusive devotion to composing Liszt had pledged? Once again he was reverting to "the depravity of one who entertained for money."[42]

Actually the concert was organized for the benefit of charity, but it was Liszt's performing that rankled Marie d'Agoult. Nevertheless, she attended the concert, as was expected of her, half hidden in a loge behind a screen. Her feelings when she heard the repeated applause, to which Liszt each time responded, are revealing of the unbridgeable gap between them, not only of social class: "It was Franz I saw, and it was not Franz. It was like someone impersonating him on the stage . . . His playing also disturbed me; it was indeed his prodigious, striking, incomparable virtuosity, yet it seemed foreign to him."

Was it not, rather, "foreign" to the countess? "Where was I? Where were we?" She had lost Franz to his public; he had lost *himself* to the public and was lost for Marie. Once again, "from that day there was a change in my existence."

Everyone now sought Liszt in Geneva, above all "the women, for his beauty, for his passionate air, for his mysterious, romantic life." Franz could not resist them. "Several of them discreetly expressed their sympathy to me," notes Marie, but she prefers accenting the fact that womanizing left him no time for his "great works." And now when he did compose, it was in response to music publishers asking for commercial pieces.[43]

As the coterie of admirers clustered around Liszt, the social isolation of Marie intensified, thrusting her into a kind of Calvinist purdah. Liszt was everywhere sought and accepted; she was not. One recalls Anna Karenina and Lieutenant Vronsky in Italy, society's solicitation of the one, its ruthless isolation of the other, driving her to suicide. Here Marie d'Agoult penetrates to the cause—the double standard called eternal, so long has it lasted:

> As usual, public opinion concerning our common act did not apply the same judgment. . . . It placed the full burden of its disapproval upon the one whom inexperience and complete sacrifice of self to the loved one can almost always excuse. Since these stiff Calvinists wished, without too much concern for principles, to enjoy the talent of Franz, they freely invented and recounted a thousand circumstances that exempted him from all blame . . . They bitterly blamed *me* for having abducted Franz and kept him from a brilliant career, from winning a fortune and honors, and for having chained him to my own fate. Several, on the other hand, affected to consider me but an episode in his life as an artist, and that for not very long.[44]

The journal of a Swiss society woman, Madame Boissier, colorfully supports Marie d'Agoult's memoirs. Mother of a former pupil of Liszt, she had known him since 1832 and now received him in Geneva. He was simply mad, she writes blithely, living with a woman "at least thirty years old, and a faded blonde!" who has abandoned "a living husband and five or six children." Granted the woman is Countess d'Agoult of the highest French society, she is clearly debauched and a cradle snatcher, says Mme. Boissier gaily. When she bends toward Liszt, in contrast, Mme. Boissier is most benevolent, one might say maternal, overflowing with forgiveness and understanding:

> He is a poor young man horribly spoiled by society and success . . . He had the misfortune of living in a literary world that nursed him with its dangerous doctrines, its false ideas, its disbelief . . . Liszt is immersed in a highly immoral system that is attached to the Saint-Simonians on the one hand and to Mme. Dudevant [George Sand] on the other. The benediction of marriage and other such bagatelles make him shrug his shoulders. He abandons himself to his passions with complete frankness and ease. If need be, he would present his countess to me without blushing. He had, he may still have, a noble soul, but he is mad.

After a third visit from Liszt—without "his countess"—Mme. Boissier further softens her view, finding him "full of verve, fire, wit, and genius," explaining his conquest of the young ladies of Geneva with approval. But her stories of his "mistress," Countess d'Agoult, are merciless, gossipy, and mistaken.[45]

The birth of Blandine shortly before Christmas did not ameliorate or in any way change Marie's situation vis-à-vis Geneva society or, for that matter, Franz Liszt's. He was no more fatherly than she motherly, and the child "was farmed out much of the time,"[46] so as not to disturb either parent. But the birth was first registered with Geneva officials:

> Blandine Rachel, natural daughter of François Liszt, professor of music aged twenty-four years, born at Raiding in Hungary, and of Catherine-Adélaide Méran, *rentière* aged twenty-four years, born in Paris, both unmarried and domiciled in Geneva. Liszt has freely and voluntarily acknowledged being father of the said child and has made the declaration in the presence of Pierre-Étienne Wolff, professor of music aged twenty-five years and J. James Fazy, aged twenty-six years, proprietor, both domiciled in Geneva.[47]

Marie d'Agoult is still criticized for having her age recorded as twenty-four—that is, the same as Liszt's—but the harsher criticism concerns her not having acknowledged parentage of her child, unlike Liszt. The latter attack is distinctly unfair, and based on an ignorance of the Code Napoléon, which dealt categorically with such family affairs. Children born in marriage were assumed to be legitimate, giving the husband a father's full rights, even if everything indicated he was not the father. Years later Countess d'Agoult was still trying to explain this. "My children," she wrote to a Dr. Guépin, ". . . could not be legally mine without their being Monsieur d'Agoult's. Regarding this, Liszt and I were of the same thought: to avoid such a monstrosity. Wherefore they were registered with a declared natural father and an unknown mother."[48]

It was a bad moment, though it is redundant to speak of it as exceptional. Understandably, Marie recalls in her memoirs that Franz, seeing her state, proposed their immediately leaving for a new life in Italy. "Italy!" Marie exults. "The magic word, like a bolt of lightning, split the cloud hanging over my thoughts . . . One more time youth and love swept me away."[49] It would be another year and a half, in fact, before they left for Italy, however urgently Marie felt about their departure from Geneva. But it would not be time wasted.

Franz gave lessons and performed at a few concerts, and Marie engaged in literary exercises, especially essays on music that were published as *Lettres d'un bachelier-ès-musique,* generally in the *Gazette Musicale* of Paris—and unabashedly signed by Franz Liszt. There would be a dozen *Lettres* over the years; occasionally Franz would suggest an outline or furnish a few draft paragraphs. Typically he wrote to Marie in February 1837, when on tour: "Here is somewhat of a sketch for the article, which should not be very long, unless you want to make it long.

It is a real service I am asking of you." The writing was swift, publication remarkably rapid. "Your *Lettre du Bachelier* was decidedly a very great success," Franz rejoiced. "I shall never dare write anything again!" March 1837: "Your two articles arrived at the same time. What zeal, what facility!"[50]

After Liszt had played to a half-empty hall in Geneva, there was personal satisfaction too for Marie in a *Lettre* attacking Swiss taste. Artists, wrote the countess, would do well to pack up and leave the citizens of Geneva to their favorite pleasures—financial speculation and other such puritanical diversions. Conscious rivalry with George Sand, whose *Lettres d'un voyageur* were immensely popular and served as a model, was not absent from Marie's ambitions. When Marie had remarked about it to Sand, saying it was a kind of standing joke with Liszt, Sand, as noted, had generously replied: "Write, then! Write about the state of women and about their rights."[51]

The rivalry involving Liszt was largely in Marie's mind, the product of insecurity and Liszt's infidelity. The relationship with Sand was more ambivalent and given to quasi-erotic byplay. In January 1836, for instance, George Sand had written lengthily to Marie d'Agoult of her envy of Marie's "beautiful blond hair and large blue eyes," and so on, but also of her own staunch advocacy of the oppressed against the oppressor, the slave versus the tyrant—this in reply to Marie's exhortation that Sand "soften" her "anathema against the aristocracy," of which Marie was so conspicuous a member. However serious her social attitude, Sand nonetheless was employing a teasing attack as a sort of preliminary play. "Leave your countess's crown with me," she continued, "and let me smash it. I will give you a handsomer one made of stars." People called her bold, she said; in fact

> my greatest torture is my timidity . . . If you want me to love you, you must begin by loving me; it is quite simple. . . . I will be insufferable until I am sure I cannot make you angry or disgusted with me. Oh, then, I will carry you on my back, I will cook for you, I will wash your dishes, anything you tell me will seem divine . . . Then you will know that no one on earth loves as I, because I love with cynical realism, that is, without blushing for the reason for my loving.[52]

That spring Liszt would be in Paris, writing to an absent Sand, who had left for the country: "Dear George, I came to Paris *to find you again;* imagine my disappointment to find you have flown. Can't we see each other again?"[53] Liszt had felt cramped in Geneva, and justly. Moreover, he had considerable need for the money that only concerts could bring him. His pride was offended that he could pay for necessities out of his Geneva lessons and appearances, but not for Marie's—and his—accustomed luxuries. Having a great deal of money of her own, however, Marie d'Agoult did not see the need, certainly if it meant diverting Franz from composing. As for his compulsion to perform, it was both incomprehensible and infuriating.

While en route to Paris, Franz had attempted to explain in a letter from Lyons. Piano playing, he wrote, "is my only fortune, my only title, my unique possession that I do not want *anyone* to touch."[54] Furthermore, during his long absence from Paris, the Austrian pianist Sigismund Thalberg had preempted Liszt's place in the public's eye, and Franz was returning, he felt, as if "from Elba," to reclaim it. Arriving in Lyons, he discovered that Thalberg had already departed, but he determined to go on with his plan to reconquer the French public.

In Paris, Liszt arranged for a small hall and a select audience, so that the musical world itself might see and hear his more mature playing. The virtuosity was now under better control, the extreme mannerism under tighter self-discipline, and he played Beethoven's *Hammerklavier* with a mastery that won Berlioz's praise. His mission accomplished, Liszt was expected back in Geneva as quickly as he had promised Marie he would be. Liszt tarried, however, offering a variety of pretexts—he hoped to see Abbé de Lamennais, he had to see his music publishers, and so on. He did not mention George Sand or his dalliance with Princess Cristina Belgiojoso, the Paris socialite who had her own scheme for Liszt's conquest.

George Sand was another matter. Firmly she replied from the country, reminding Franz of Marie, of her "dream" of being with them *both,*

> curled under the piano of Your Excellency, or perched on a Swiss rock. . . . I believe you have found a treasure in Marie. Guard her forever. God will demand of you an account in heaven, and if you have not used her well, you will be deprived of the sound of celestial harps for eternity.[55]

A month later, Liszt was back with Marie d'Agoult in Switzerland. She was overjoyed, if the word is not overcharged, although he would leave her on occasion to give a concert elsewhere. But he would write; and a letter from Dijon, dated July 23, 1836, penned at four in the morning, gave her particular pleasure (*"lettre adorable,"* reads her diary), as it revealed his remorse and told of his need for her:

Sorrow and ennui gnaw at my poor heart. Music exhausts me, humanity bores me, and nature without you is naught but incessant destruction and reproduction. In brief, there are no longer sun or stars in my firmament. I must see you and begin *for good* a new life at last. I would like repose, profound repose. I aspire to I don't know what strange yet simple existence, ordinary and mystical at the same time. A completely ideal existence, completely solitary, completely in you and in God, as I feel and adore Him. Oh, give me repose, give me *your peace,* as Christ gave His peace to His Apostles.

I feel an irresistible need for you. I love you profoundly, but I cannot say it to you as you wish. Why, too, do you ask me to translate and parcel my soul in pretty phrases? Do you think I can do that?

I am not yet completely cured of the past. My wounds hurt on certain days. So put your kind hand on my breast, and let me sleep on yours, there where I have hidden all that I have of sorrow, and of genius, and of *tendresse.* Oh, if only you knew what I have given you, time and time again; what infinite aspirations, what sublime sighings, what desires and dreams have become lost in you.[56]

Had Marie d'Agoult's reply been preserved, the exchange would have been a model of the Romantic mélange of God, sex, ennui, and spleen, with rather less of the first and more of the last on Marie's part. Franz probably wrote out of a midnight or dark early-morning mood of loneliness, at the same time recording his sense of the void growing between them—or if not growing, not narrowing—into which he sincerely believed he had poured heart, soul, *all,* in a lost effort to fill it. When Franz and Marie were together, the void was starker, not reduced; the physical contact was more like a spark than a bridge across the gap. They were not changing *toward* each other; the change they sought would have to be in the scenery. Romantic couples fare better in travel than in caecal intimacy.

In September George Sand, her two children, and a maid came to Switzerland for a long-promised visit. By the time they reached Geneva, however, they discovered that Franz and Marie d'Agoult had already departed for Chamonix, leaving behind a Genevese friend, Adolphe Pictet, savant, philologist, and artillery officer, to bring them to their new meeting point.[57] Here, at the Hôtel de l'Union of Chamonix, Sand opened the registry and found the entry of a "Mr. Fellows," who had replied to the requested information in a most Franz Lisztian fashion. *Occupation:* Musician-Philosopher. *Home:* Parnassus. *Arrived:* From Doubt. *Destination:* Truth.

In similar play, but with the disadvantage of all imitations, Sand registered her brood as the "Piffoël Family," the name deriving from the French slang word for a rather generous nose, *pif*—the mark of herself and son Maurice. She then added, *Home:* Nature. *Arrived:* From God. *Date of Passport:* Eternity. *Issued by:* Public Opinion.[58]

The Piffoëls dashed to the suite of the Fellowses, and when the chambermaid saw Mr. Fellows warmly embrace "Mr." Piffoël (Sand in trousers), she thought she had lost her senses. Then when "Puzzi" Cohen, who looked like a girl, revealed himself as a boy to Sand's daughter, Solange, who was dressed as a boy, and all whirled from embrace to embrace, even the elegant countess, screaming with delight, the chambermaid fled, spreading word through the hotel that number 13 was occupied by a weird tribe of men indistinguishable from women. Only the Swiss major kept his aplomb, and Marie shortly recovered hers.

In this wild fashion the tribe went on a week's excursion among the Alps, walking and talking, riding and talking, ever talking of Schelling, Hegel, and God. Or so Major Pictet, nicknamed "The Universal One" by the Genevese, carried on, trying to impress the famous lady novelist and his new, titled French friend, *la comtesse.* And as Marie d'Agoult, or "Princess Arabella," as Sand named her, "preserved her dignity with skirts and face-veils and parasols, riding sedately on her mule," Sand played the guttersnipe and gamin in counterpoint, smoking her perpetual cigar.[59] Philosophy in the open air was not her thing, and pedantry even less. Pictet's preoccupation with Schelling's phrase, "The absolute is identical only with itself"—"What can it mean?" he endlessly asked—provoked only a satiric sketch from Sand, which Pictet nonetheless reproduced in his little book on the Alpine excursion, *Une Course à Chamonix.* Once, standing before a mountain, the major extolled its magnificence, and Sand responded: "Can you conceive anything more stupid than a mountain?"[60]

When they reached Fribourg and its celebrated cathedral organ, Franz came into his own. Each had his or her turn. In Pictet's account Marie is all "grace," versus George Sand's "strength," "reflective intelligence" contrasted with the latter's "spontaneity and genius." Liszt was the "spirit of music" as he filled the cathedral with Mozart's *Dies Irae.*[61]

The final stop was Geneva, with a more stately round of theaters, concerts, and salons. One evening at home, Franz played a *Rondo Fantastique* dedicated to George Sand. That night, as the others slept, she wrote a counterpart in prose, and read it to the group the next day. Marie thought neither composition was up to the best work of its authors, she was pleased to observe. Long before, Liszt had teased her about her burgeoning sense of rivalry, saying the "laurels" of George Sand kept her "from sleeping." Marie, to her credit, had reported his remark to Sand.[62]

Before their mountain excursion, Marie had asked herself whether she would please or displease her Nohant friend. "That anxiety," she noted, "made me cold and awkward; her childish pranks put me off; I felt ill at ease and consequently was not very friendly; it made me sad, because I passionately desired her friendship."[63] The parting of the Piffoëls and the Fellowses was not quite as enthusiastic as their meeting, that mad day at the Hôtel de l'Union, but they promised to see one another very soon in France.

Sand's initial invitation was for Franz and Marie to stay with her at Nohant, but when Marie discovered that Liszt intended to remain in Paris while she went to Sand's country home, she refused. From Paris's Hôtel de France, where she and Liszt had taken over a suite of rooms, Marie wrote to George Sand, October 18, 1936, suggesting that Sand join *them.* "I feel I need it," Marie added. Sand accepted with joy. "Reserve me a room," she wrote back, "and we will make a single ménage as before and as afterward—*posteriori,* as Franz says, which means *Nohant* to me . . . Reserve me a room with a big bed for Solange and me, and a sofa or folding cot for Maurice."[64] (Blandine had been left behind in Switzerland by Franz and Marie.)

Two days later Sand and brood were installed on the floor below the Fellowses; together they shared the huge reception room of the upstairs suite. Marie was determined to defy Faubourg Saint-Germain's rejection of her by creating a brilliant salon of the capital's brightest lights. (In Geneva, she wrote Pictet, she had felt like "a fish on the grass."[65]) Soliciting George Sand to preside alongside her was part of the plan. They already enjoyed a number of notable friends in common—Meyerbeer, Lamennais, Heine, Sue, Leroux—and a faithful few of her former world followed Marie d'Agoult to her new salon, Countess Marliani eminent among them. Liszt, too, attracted his literary and musical circle, particularly the Polish expatriates—Count Albert Grzymala, poet Adam Mickiewicz, and the reclusive Frédéric Chopin.

In this way the Piffoëls and the Fellowses wintered in Paris, one memorable evening offering a joint concert by Berlioz and Liszt, who rendered the composer's exuberant *Grande Fantaisie Symphonique* on the piano, making it sound more orchestral than the orchestra and wringing the usual applause from the audience. Sharper critics, however, were still commenting on Liszt's extravagances, his *"grimaces"* and *"contorsions grotesques,"* and even his *"charlatanisme musical."* He had matured but insufficiently, and Liszt himself would admit in late life to having been too easily seduced by his audience in his performing years.[66] A *Lettre d'un bachelier-ès-musique,* written by Marie d'Agoult and signed (as always) by Liszt, appeared shortly after the Paris concert. Its sobriety, clarity, and elegance explain its success and the solidity (which Liszt lacked) that it lent its signer in critical musical circles. Meanwhile George Sand had left for Nohant, and with unexpected impatience Marie burned to join her.

"I yearn to see Nohant," Marie wrote, "to live your life, to make friends with your dogs, the benefactress of your chickens, to warm myself with your wood, to eat your partridges, and revive my poor machine in the air you breathe."[67] Going to Nohant meant leaving Liszt behind—to undertake the long-delayed duel with Thalberg—but somehow that seemed less significant to Marie d'Agoult. Did the intimacy of two women alone now appeal to her more? Certainly the public combat Liszt planned did not. Sand, in turn, was on tenterhooks. Marie always affected her that way. Perhaps it was Marie's acute sensibility or exigent eye, or simply her beauty. At the time, moreover, Sand was suffering the end of a frustrating affair with Michel de Bourges. And so she prepared her own bedroom for Marie's arrival, hanging it with new curtains and subjecting it to the test of Marie's portrait, as she wrote to Liszt, "to see whether the portrait yawned with boredom or caught a cold."[68]

Marie d'Agoult finally arrived, after a month's illness, and found the "forgetfulness and peace" she sought in the long rides on horseback she took with Sand along the banks of the Indre River and across "the flowering meadows of forget-me-nots."[69] When the going was rough, Sand would descend and lead Marie's horse by hand. There was kindness and coquettishness in the gesture. Franz, in the meantime, was pleading with Marie to rejoin him in Paris. On Sand's advice, she decided against it. She might keep him from working, Marie explained lamely.

Liszt came to Nohant instead on a quick visit, but the week of his stay he was nervous, preoccupied, and capricious, ostensibly brooding over his return to Paris to resume his piano duel with Thalberg. When Sand invited her Berrichon friends to hear him play, as he had promised he would, it was fairly certain he would not; and when it was announced he would *not* play, "he took it into his head to sit down and improvise."[70] One guest thought Liszt a poseur and described an evening at Nohant: Liszt sits at the piano, his flowing hair like a ruffled lion's mane;

he looks at the ceiling for inspiration, then drops his hands nonchalantly on the keys; discords precede a prelude that never follows; "suddenly he rises, closes the piano noisily, and declares, 'The bear will not dance this evening!' "[71]

After Liszt's departure, Marie wrote with forced gaiety to Ronchaud of his brief visit to Nohant. In a letter the following day (March 11, 1837), she was in full depression:

> I am mortally sad this morning. I have been crying bitterly. Yet the sun shines . . . Why does my heart overflow with sadness? Oh, my God, my God, could it be true that HE [Liszt] is condemned to an impossible task? Could my heart be a bottomless vessel into which he vainly pours all the treasures of his genius and his love? And that love and mine, is it anything but the sublime lie of two beings who wanted to give each the other a happiness neither any longer believed in for oneself? . . . Believe me, never throw yourself into the arms of a woman, asking her for anything you do not find in yourself. You will dream of heaven, as you lie next to her, and hear the angels . . . and then you will realize it is all an elusive, passing shadow, and you will be left alone to cry like a child, or blaspheme like an old man.[72]

Is there not a reversal of the truth; is it not, rather, Marie who is pouring her love into a bottomless vessel? The acerbity of the last, moving passage, which goes beyond Romantic hyperbole, suggests an awareness that has turned inward after the painful observance of Franz Liszt as intimate and lover. Yet, from Paris, Franz again urged Marie to rejoin him there, to play his Muse, as he played out his destiny as he conceived it. Marie went to him. The personal confrontation between Liszt and Thalberg occurred in the salon of Princess Belgiojoso, a competitive performance for the benefit of charity and *tout* Paris. Marie d'Agoult is silent about the spectacle. Fortunately Heine was there to describe Liszt at the piano: "The keys seemed to bleed. . . . Everywhere in the room were pale faces, palpitating breasts, and emotional breathing during the pauses. . . . The women are always intoxicated when Liszt plays."[73] Thalberg was more classically poised. Liszt won hands down in that audience, and Princess Belgiojoso's remark has become posterity's judgment: "Thalberg is the first pianist of the world; Liszt is the only one."[74]

At the end of April the Piffoëls and the Fellowses were again together at Nohant, only to separate at the end of July without too much regret. The three were too many, and to the three were added a few more: in her note of invitation Sand had said she must see Marie and Franz *and* their friends—Mickiewicz, Grzymala, and above all Chopin ("Tell him I idolize him"); Marie was expected to bring them all with her when she and Franz came to Nohant.[75] "Chopin," Marie had replied, "coughs with infinite grace," but he would come.[76] He would not; he would go instead to London. Other young men, however, would not be lacking at Sand's Nohant.

The George Sand Marie discovered, when she and Franz finally arrived, was at the low point of a woman spurned. The letters she was sending to Michel de Bourges were full of the humble, humiliating lines of one courting an unresponding man: she would be Michel's "devoted black," she was writing, his "faithful dog," if he demanded it.[77] Marie did not read the letters, but she observed and described Sand's state—and perhaps her own—in her diary: "Poor, great woman! . . . Charity, love, *volupté,* those three aspirations of the soul, heart, and senses, too ardent in that fatally privileged woman, have met doubt, disappointment, satiety, and—deeply suppressed within her—have made a martyr of her." A *man* of comparable genius, such as Goethe, Marie d'Agoult goes on, "embraces all in the immensity of his love," and she closes: "Oh my God, give George the serenity of Goethe!"[78] It was a good deal for Marie d'Agoult to ask, even of God, for a woman in the fire and prime of her life (George Sand was about thirty-three, Marie a year and a half younger); it would be many years before Nohant would become Sand's Weimar, and many more before Marie would find *her* serenity, if ever.

During the most harrowing weeks of June 1837, Marie's hostess was finding solace in Franz's music and the companionship of young, admiring men who came and went at will. From the bedroom on the ground floor, which she had redecorated for Marie and Franz, Sand, in her room directly above, daily heard his playing as she communed with the "Dr. Piffoël" of *her* diary. The notes silenced the "jealous" nightingales, she wrote, and set the linden leaves dancing. "When Franz plays the piano, I am comforted. All pain becomes poetry." As Sand herself was doing, Liszt was transcribing on paper with the artist's resource the finally captured phrase, containing, calming, resolving the interior storm.[79]

Sand noted Liszt's own "melancholy," his "secret wound," the artist's lot. In the case of Franz, a restless twenty-five, and Marie d'Agoult, in her thirty-first year and pregnant with their second child, the wound opening between them was personal as well. It was not the gap of age, though that played its part. It was more the demanding, increasingly critical turn of Marie's mind. She was conscious of it, and the self-awareness, as she had written Ronchaud, was like a "serpent's poisonous fang ever slumbering in my heart."[80] Realism was struggling to emerge from the Romantic murkiness, but there was a dry, bitter taste to it, a lack of generosity and warmth strikingly different from Sand's. Love was dead, or dying? "Then, long live love!" Sand cried. She was open to experience where Marie was self-enclosed. "Your penchant toward severity," Liszt would remark to Marie shortly before they parted, "grows by leaps and bounds."[81]

Scarcely a word from their hostess, however, revealed her awareness of *that* wound appearing in their relationship during the spring and summer of 1837. Rather, Sand scolded Liszt for his ingratitude: "Happy man to be loved by a beautiful, generous, intelligent, chaste woman. What more could you ask for, ungrateful wretch! Ah, if only I were loved!"[82] An evidence of George Sand's generosity was her calling Countess d'Agoult generous. Nevertheless, these were the soft, summery evenings at Nohant, warm with friendship and Sand's hospitality. Actor Pierre Bocage had arrived from Paris; another handsome man, Charles Didier, was expected. It was the eve of Sand's final farewell to Michel de Bourges, but her guests could not have suspected it from her manner. "That evening, while Franz was playing one of Schubert's most fairylike songs"—based on Goethe's haunting *Der Erlkönig*— Marie d'Agoult, still Sand's "princess," floated about the group on the terrace, dressed in a pale white gown, her head draped in a long white veil falling to her feet. She well knew the effect, and all eyes were upon her as the music swelled and the moon set, outlining the linden trees and Marie's slender figure. It was a stately dance to Schubert's music, ending on the hushed note of the child's death, and Marie, looking like a "medieval Lady," disappeared into the salon.

The flattering description is Sand's, yet the entente between Liszt and herself aroused Marie's resentment. Frequently when they were tête-à-tête, Marie would interrupt them with a cry to Liszt, "Time to work, lazy one!"[83] In fact, after the others had retired for the night, that is often what they did, facing each other across the same table. On one such night Sand finished a novel and immediately began another, an awesome performance. Meantime Franz was working on his piano transcriptions of Beethoven's symphonies.

But it was soon adieu to Sand from the Fellowses. The summer's flowers of friendship had faded, though the falling out of Sand and Marie d'Agoult was not to happen for another season. Their hostess made a jolly excursion of their departure, accompanying them on horseback with friends to nearby La Châtre, where Franz and Marie took the coach to Bourges on their way, at last, to Italy. In her diary

Marie reflects on her stay at Nohant, comparing herself with Sand. Not unexpectedly, she finds herself the rational, clearheaded one in the comparison, then concludes: "I finally realized how puerile it had been of me to believe (and the thought had often flooded me with sadness) that she alone could have given Franz's life its full development, that I had been an impediment between two destinies made to merge and complete each other."[84]

George Sand's own disenchanted view of Marie and especially the couple would manifest itself in the novel she inspired Balzac to write, *Béatrix (Beatrice).* Sand herself, Balzac explained to his beloved "Stranger," Madame Hanska, had felt that she was scarcely in the position to write it without causing personal offense. The title may be explained by Liszt's explosion one day, when Marie once too often referred to her playing Beatrice to his Dante: "Dante! Beatrice! It is the Dantes who create the Beatrices, and the real ones die at eighteen!"[85] Not quite as cruel is Balzac's portrayal of the pair as lovers dragging the ball and chain of their public affair, when pride alone holds them together (the original title was *Galley Slaves of Love*).

The summer in Italy, however, with a brief stopover in Switzerland for a passing look at Blandine, seems to have revived their love, or offered it respite, the effect of Italy so often on the Romantics. In view of their casualness regarding Blandine, it could hardly have been Marie d'Agoult's new pregnancy that brought them closer. Rather, it was the sun, the landscape, the excursion itself. In traveling there is the happy confusion of motion with action; in viewing masterpieces of building and painting, there *can* be the illusion of sharing the same vision and pleasure. But there is an astonishing statement of subordination, of traditional role playing, for so strong a woman, in Marie d'Agoult's notes. She may have defied society, but she has not yet found herself other than in relationship to *him,* her lover, albeit her chosen lover, Liszt.

"I feel," she writes, "as I travel lands with him, that he is my sole support, my sole recourse, my sole guide; that my destiny is in him alone, that I freely and willingly delivered it to him, that I have neither temple nor fatherland other than in his heart." Was it the Latin atmosphere as much as the Italian sun? A desperate roll of the dice—all or nothing? Marie d'Agoult even underlines the classic characterization of woman as man's mediator with the external world and the literal embodiment of the idea of beauty—then appropriately attributes it to Liszt: "Viewing splendid settings, imposing monuments, he told me he had need for beauty to be manifested through me; that I was for him what words are through which the beauty of things is revealed."[86]

Or was it "simply" advanced pregnancy? The most beautiful moment in Marie d'Agoult's memory was the stay at Bellagio, on Lake Como, *"in alta solitudine"* (her device and ideal), for here Liszt seemed to have settled down to compose, and Cosima was born on Christmas eve. "When you write the story of two happy lovers," Marie addressed Ronchaud in a *Lettre d'un bachelier,* "place them on the shores of Lake Como."[87]

But the second honeymoon proved as brief as the first. Marie's funds were vanishing at the considerable rate of five thousand francs a month, for neither Franz nor Marie, who could easily spend a thousand francs for a dress, refrained from any indulgence—carriages, livery, servants, or guests. The Count d'Agoult, fearing dilapidation of a fortune destined for Claire, began to arrange new difficulties by way of restraints on his wife's resources, particularly after hearing of the birth of the lovers' second child. "My husband . . . is no longer the *ideal husband,"* the countess deplored to Pictet, "he is the *real husband."* Her diary carries an earlier note: "Husbands die only in novels."[88]

Whether for reasons of money, career, or still-youthful restlessness, Liszt departed on lengthening concert tours, leaving Marie d'Agoult in Milan, where they had established their base after Bellagio. In her *Lettres,* Marie did not conceal her growing distaste for Italians, their culture, or "lack" of it, and even for La Scala, which scarcely won them new friends or preserved the few Marie might claim. Liszt, as "author," almost fought a duel as a result, but his tours took him elsewhere, exposing him to more customary affairs with women he met. To Marie's complaints he blandly replied, "It is my nature."[89] And to this, more than once, Marie remarked with bitterness that she would readily, gladly, be Liszt's mistress, but not *one* of his mistresses.

The move to Venice in March 1838 changed nothing but the drinking water: it sickened Marie. She who was already so thin that Balzac said she looked as though she had been squeezed between two doors, grew thinner. The other stresses continued. One evening, Marie records, she watched Franz play as a young woman of seventeen sat worshipfully beside him. Marie observed her fresh complexion; his pale, somewhat drawn, but still-youthful, face; and the habitual violence and passion with which he played (once, improvising at Rossini's place, he sprained a wrist), as if making love to his young listener. That night, says Marie,

> a forgotten bouquet on a table in my bedroom makes me ill. I fear sometimes that I am going mad, my brain is worn out; I have wept too much . . . Passion elevated me an instant, but I feel I have no

> will to live . . . I feel an obstacle in his life, I am not good for him. I throw sadness and discouragement over the days of his life.[90]

When the occasion for a long, needed separation finally came, it arrived as a flood. The Danube, swollen by heavy spring rains, had burst its banks, overflowing Pest and the farmlands of Hungary. Suddenly, opportunely, Liszt rediscovered a fatherland he had neither seen nor sought since childhood. The conscious hypocrisy was probably minimal; Romantic illusions are no less sincere for being self-deluding. The description of Liszt's reaction is Marie's, whose veracity at least applies to her own desperation. "One day," she writes, "Franz brusquely entered my bedroom . . ."

> He held a German newspaper in his hand. He had just read the story of the horrible Danube flood. . . . "It's dreadful," he said, "I would like to send everything I possess." Then, with a bitter smile: "But all I possess are my ten fingers and my name! What would you say if I went unexpectedly to Vienna? I would make a fantastic sum . . . It would take me a week, no more. What do you think?" "I think it is a good idea," I said, but I thought to myself, *Others could help those poor people, but what about me, alone and ill, who will come to my aid?*[91]

Franz departed; he would not return for almost two months. On leaving, he suggested to Marie that she put herself in the hands of a young Venetian admirer, Count Emilio Malazonni. She did.

In Vienna, as Liszt predicted, his reception was fabulous. "Not since Mozart and Beethoven," said the press unanimously, had the musical capital seen his equal. "In the memory of man, there has been no similar success in Vienna, not even Paganini." Liszt exultingly sent the clippings to Marie.[92] Flowers and gold coins were showered at his feet when he played; students carried him in triumph and dragged his carriage through the streets.

Liszt's letters to Marie became briefer and more rare. The names of several women appeared in them. One letter arrived with a woman's seal added to Liszt's. Marie d'Agoult angrily tore it to shreds, unopened. She was seen more frequently with the young Venetian count. He found her feverish one day, and wrote to Liszt of her illness "from anxiety," adding that only his return would cure her. Marie "fainted" when she read Liszt's reply to her friend. He could not possibly leave Vienna at this time, Liszt wrote; why did they not *both* come to him there? When Marie opened her eyes, her admirer flung himself at her feet, she recalls, imploring: " 'Oh, Marie!' (It was the first time he addressed me thus.) 'Poor woman! Oh, if only my life, my soul, my love could be something for you. Parents, friends, fortune, career [Liszt, take note], all would be abandoned, thrust aside.' "[93]

For a week Marie d'Agoult lay in bed "between life and death," then "feebly" wrote to Franz Liszt:

> You ask me to join you, though it is two hundred leagues from here to Vienna. I can scarcely go from my bed to my armchair, but you cannot come here. You leave my deplorable life to another's care. If I had died, you would have had to come, or would you indeed have left to others the care of closing my eyes? . . . Franz, Franz, is it you who abandon me thus?

Liszt returned, but not immediately. When Marie heard that he was back at their hotel, she "ran," she "flew," from the Piazza San Marco to be with him. "I threw myself into his arms." *Then* she told him: "Pray God that I still love you as I did." For two days Franz was contrite, saying he "was not worthy of me" and would quit the concert world. But he could not hold back talking of his Austrian triumphs for long,

> and the way he spoke of his stay in Vienna brought me back to earth. They had found a coat of arms for him—for *him,* a republican, living with a great lady [!] . . . Women had flung themselves at his head; he no longer was ashamed of his faults . . . He was right and I was wrong; he dressed elegantly and spoke only of princes. He was secretly pleased with his life.

Marie responded by telling him what she knew invariably cut him to the quick. She called him a *"Don Juan parvenu"*—an upstart Don Juan.[94]

The moment of unwanted truths seems now to have struck them both. Resolved, it might have brought them back together, but it effectively drove them further apart. Vienna had proved to him, Liszt flatly remarked, that he could make a fortune within two years, "not for himself," of course, "but for the child, Blandine" (Marie does not mention poor, plain Cosima). As for Marie, Franz continued, while he pursued career and fortune, she should return to France, her daughter, her family, and friends, reestablish her position in the world. "I was too subordinate, too dependent upon him. I had talent, genius, I must show it, crush my enemies, show them *who* I am." And he would return to *his* world . . .

Abruptly Liszt became menacing. "Don't play with me," he inexplicably warned, "because I will make you play for too high a stake." Marie was shocked by his sudden hardness, especially when "he coldly advised me to fall in love with the count." She replied with a plea: "Let us try again!" She entreated a change of air, a stay at the seaside. Liszt acquiesced. They settled in Genoa, where Franz had rented a handsome villa, carriage, and horses. Here, he said, Marie might stay while he undertook an engagement in Germany—or, instead, "go see your daughter, your family, your friends." Franz was her family, she replied. "He shed a tear." All she ever asked, Marie said, was one thing. "He pretended not to understand! Once he *did* understand. When he confessed his first infidelity, he had said to me . . . 'I was like a man who did not know wine could make him drunk, and he drank; now I will drink no more.' "

Below this entry in Marie's diary Liszt added his own caustic observation:

> You remember my words, but perhaps those you said to me in diverse circumstances have left no traces in your memory. As for me, I have not at all forgotten them, however I tried. When you can recall them, they will explain many things that seem unexplainable to you . . . down to today.[95]

From "a false and vulgar man" to "an upstart Don Juan," Marie's stinging phrases were never forgotten and never forgiven; Franz Liszt was too vulnerable.

The tour in Germany did not take place, perhaps as a gesture of conciliation to Marie d'Agoult. But shortly thereafter, still in Genoa, the countess found herself once again awaiting Liszt's return from yet another engagement, another passing affair. As provocative as it is painful is Marie's letter to Franz, June 25, 1838: "I think you can, and consequently should, love again . . . My love parches you. I think you could love her happily; me, you loved strongly . . . I shall no longer know how to love someone, but why should I deprive you of a love that could be a new source of life for you?"[96] Two months later Marie's diary signals the end of *that* affair. August 13: "The little sanctuary of poetry that Franz had built in his heart for E—— has collapsed. A gross, obvious and palpable platitude has brought it down." Madame E—— proved too common for Liszt. "In the evening he played his melodic Alpine flowers [pieces] for me."[97]

Liszt's pages in an album reveal his usual postcoital melancholy and remorse: "Why did I waste these precious gifts on petty women? . . . It would have been so easy for me to have put a crown of my innocence on Marie's head." The lines, he knew, would be read by Marie.[98]

Two weeks later, again on tour, Liszt was writing to Marie, September 1: "I cannot, I should not, live with anyone but you, my good Marie. All that is good, elevated, and vital in me perishes without you." She hectored him to compose rather than spend his talents in public concerts. She was right, Franz acknowledged—and continued performing. (No major composer wasted himself in performance so long as Liszt.) He confessed his failure to himself, his infidelity to Marie. The awareness led not to a change of conduct or direction, but to irritation turned outward. "Everything upsets me, annoys me, irritates me. I cannot even think of you unviolently . . . Marie, Marie, has the magical strength of your name been dissipated? Is it I who have broken our lives? Do not cry, my good sister." Franz will soon be telling "good sister" Marie he cannot *stand* her tears, but on September second he apologizes for the bleakness of the letter of the previous day, without withdrawing a single word of it.[99]

That fall, or late summer, the third unwanted child was conceived. Marie d'Agoult alternated between depression and unsustained hope; Franz Liszt remained true—to himself. Marie asked him to take back a ring he had given her, expecting, perhaps, protest and refusal. Quite the contrary. From a page of his album, November 14: "Somehow, putting the ring back on my finger, I seemed suddenly cured of a long illness, and I let myself go with all the confidence of my first youth when we met for the first time." The fidelity of love as a fatal illness . . . Liszt was the eternal adolescent. "Sometimes, in the morning, I willingly forget the ring. I feel a strange pleasure in haphazardly setting aside this sad and terrible sign of our union. Twenty times a day I think of putting it on and I do not. There are things violently and deeply felt that I do not at all want to write down."[100]

Had Marie d'Agoult read *these* lines then? In May 1839 Daniel was born to the pair. Of the three children, Cosima would forever feel unwanted, unloved, particularly by her mother; Daniel, during his brief lifetime, felt damned. As for Blandine, she was "the favorite," but one can immediately put *that* in its appropriate perspective. The revealing scene occurs in her mother's *Journal pédagogique*—and in mid-judgment, one must ask oneself whether the countess's way with her child was not more typical of her class than particular to herself.

Blandine is almost three. She is with her parents in Florence, an unusual circumstance.

> I establish her conveniently on cushions between her father and me [Marie d'Agoult writes] and say absolutely nothing. She cries tranquilly for an hour and then falls asleep. The rest of the day she is extremely serious or replies with a yes or no, but seems very aware of feeling progressively better and convinced of the uselessness of all resistance to me.

Blandine's mother also notes with satisfaction: "She seems to pay no attention to her father's music . . . she will not be a musician, and so much the better."[101]

The children bound neither parent to the other, though later in life the three would huddle together for solace and support against what they perceived as a hostile world. The hostility they sensed, in fact, was the clashing of their parents' worlds, of "two natures . . . diametrically opposed," in their mother's words: Liszt had need of *"les grands horizons,* the infinite, the unlimited, the unexpected, whereas I need rules, the well-filled frame, the feeling of duty accomplished, of an orderly pace."[102]

Again Marie and Franz spoke of separation, but quite calmly, since it was supposedly limited to a winter in Paris for Marie. They talked, that is, as "two civilized beings," to employ the current cliché that would cover over the desolation of collapsed love. A season's stay in Paris for Marie did not involve a new life, but that is what the former lovers were really talking about. Franz advised Marie to reestablish herself in the French capital, form a salon and "entourage of distinguished people . . . go everywhere one is expected to go."[103] But it was all supposed to be temporary. The full truth was too terrible, too devastating.

> In the evening on the terrace [Marie writes] . . . Franz is melancholy. "I am painfully aware that an epoch in my life is coming to an end," he says to me. ". . . I am of an age when nothing seems to suffice. I feel bitterly that I am not what I wanted to be. When one has smashed everything around oneself, one has also smashed oneself."

Marie, for her part, talks of the "atrophy" of her brain, of "anticipated old age" and "complete atony."

> I feel I cannot go on living like this, that I must soon die or fall into complete imbecility . . . How much I regret, at those moments when I feel these things (and they come almost incessantly), the blind and egotistical transport that made me bind myself to him![104]

The parting conceived at the birth of their love came in October 1839. They would meet again over the years, but increasingly rarely and rancorously. Liszt accompanied Marie d'Agoult to Livorno, where she would take a boat for France; he would go on soon afterward to Vienna. Marie had Blandine with her; Daniel was left with a nurse in Italy. All three children would eventually be under Liszt's charge and in the care of his mother; their charge and care would be a major source of the future rancor. Marie d'Agoult's boat docked briefly in Genoa, where she picked up Cosima and sent Liszt a farewell message. It is remarkably controlled and worldly, recounting the gossip and doings at Livorno (where she momentarily stayed after Liszt left), what she had heard from the French consul about Sand and Chopin, the status of the lacquered furniture she had ordered for her salon in Paris, and the like.

Then, literally shining through a self-conscious prose, is a glimpse of the future as Marie d'Agoult finally saw it:

> At the moment when I embarked at Livorno, the sun set in floods of gold and the moon rose melancholic among the pale clouds; little by little it emerged and lighted our crossing with a most magnificent light. I took this as a symbol of our beautiful, fugitive past, and of our future, which begins so sadly but which will be pure and serene.[105]

With this, Marie d'Agoult "turned her back on sentimental Romanticism," as Franz Liszt never would.[106] Most decidedly she was not Anna Karenina: she boarded the train instead of throwing herself under it, changed the direction of her life at thirty-five, and went on to write her own story.[107] She might have returned to her husband, who held the door ajar for her, but she did not. She established a notable circle in Paris, surrounded herself with painters, suitors, literary and political figures, and under the *nom de plume* of Daniel Stern wrote some of the most cerebral prose of her lingeringly Romantic period—*Essai sur la liberté, Esquisses morales,* and the monumental *Histoire de la révolution de 1848.*

Daniel Stern would not have fallen in love with Franz Liszt.

Or would she?

8

ONE PLUS ONE EQUALS THE TWENTIETH CENTURY: GERTRUDE STEIN AND ALICE B. TOKLAS

> It takes time to make queer people. . . . Brothers singular . . . we flee before the disapproval of our cousins, the courageous condescension of our friends . . . we fly to the kindly comfort of an older world accustomed to take all manner of strange forms into its bosom . . .
>
> —Gertrude Stein, *The Making of Americans* (1902–1908)

THE story of Gertrude Stein, I believe, and her meeting and mating Alice Toklas, who liberated her sexually and creatively, is one of the most satisfying chronicles of those that open our now-closing century. Unlike that of Radcliffe Hall or Virginia Woolf, for theirs is a chronicle of ultimate frustration and tragic incompletion, or even that of Natalie Barney, the adventuresome *amazone,* who never quite found or settled down with her equal, the account of Gertrude and Alice is one of fulfillment, even of happiness, until the end.

It is a story, too, of which I had a privileged glimpse as Gertrude's "adopted nephew" late in their lives. She had found a resemblance to her real nephew Allan, son of brother Michael, in the uniformed American she had met in Paris in the winter of 1944–45. As one, then, who has since survived alongside—and after—the survivor (Alice T.), I might offer an occasional observation.

No account, for instance, has failed to refer to Alice Toklas as the "lifelong companion" of Gertrude Stein, but with a faint tone of disparagement, as if it meant a lifelong echo. It is an odd concept of companionship.

Once, during a discussion of a dissolving marriage, Alice quoted a disturbing remark (of Henry James, she said; actually it was an observation of Oscar Wilde, whom she had—perhaps unconsciously—suppressed, in her proper Victorian manner, for his overt homosexuality), to the effect that a couple, whether friends, lovers, or husband and wife, can only live on the spiritual capital of the poorer one. Conversation —the essence of companionship (talk, said Nietzsche, takes up most of the time in marriage)—can only take place on the level of the lower common denominator.

Gertrude and Alice were equally, but differently, rich. The wealth, the experiences they shared, seemed doubled, not divided, by their sharing. They were as complete a couple as I have known—parents of their brainchildren, as well, if one insists on parentage as part of the complete couple. Their relationship was *emotional,* as when one falls in love; it was *sentimental,* which is a function of time, as when one has loved for almost forty years, as was their lot; it was *physical*—they slept in the same large bed, even in their old age, in a bedroom papered with pigeons on the grass; it was *intellectual,* which is most easily demonstrated; and it was *aesthetic*—to add the plastic, the compositional, the sense of style composing their couple.

But why were two Americans calling Paris their home early in the century?

Part of the reply is in a question Gertrude put to Picasso: "Why do we, who created the art of the twentieth century, prefer living in seventeenth-century apartments?" They agreed that true revolutionaries needed the springboard of tradition, a place to stand to lever the world. And why France? "I have lived half my life in Paris," Gertrude Stein would offer in explanation, "not the half that made me, but the half in which I made what I made." She observed further that creators had need of two civilizations, their own, and another in which to be free to create: "France was friendly and it let you alone . . . It is not what France gave you but what it did not take away from you that was important."[1]

So the "expatriates" of all nationalities headed for Paris and made it their home—Stein, Picasso, Joyce, Stravinsky, Chagall, Tzara, Dali, Modigliani; later, Man Ray, Hemingway, Buñuel, Beckett, Giacometti, Calder. They were as much part of the scene and the School of Paris as Proust and Cocteau, Matisse and Braque. They came in search of the freedom of which Gertrude Stein speaks. Rather, the freedoms: freedom to be their peculiar selves and think their peculiar thoughts (which flourish in tolerant, temperate climates); freedom to write and to publish what they had written; and for Americans fleeing Puritanism and prohibition, its latest manifestation, other freedoms, especially a place to live cheaply and well at half the cost of life in New York, Chicago, or San Francisco, thanks to the dropping franc and the rising dollar. If it transformed Paris of the mauve decade into a "great fair teeming with merrymakers,"[2] a great many, judging from their achievements, were hard-working merrymakers indeed.

The American half of her life that "made" her could well have been her unmaking. Gertrude Stein's very birth on February 3, 1874 (she was the last of five living children) would become, for her, more a matter of lottery than of inevitability. The total of five children had been set by her authoritarian father, Daniel Stein, affluent member of an influential merchant family whose origin was German and Jewish. "If two little ones had not died there would be no Gertrude Stein," Gertrude would write. "I would not have come nor my brother [Leo] just two years older and we never talked of this after we had heard of it . . . It made us feel funny."[3] She adds sadly in *The Making of Americans,* the *roman-fleuve* concerning the Steins, "A very little one, sometimes she [Gertrude] wanted not to be existing."[4]

Though Gertrude had a pampered childhood, that was not the child's impression. She disregarded her "not really very interesting" mother and half dreaded her quick-to-wrath father, though "mostly she was never important to him."[5] She was too sluggish, he thought, too slow, not Germanically thorough enough in her tutored studies. Leo was quicker, but suffered an even greater dread of his father—and would ascribe chronic stomach disorders to it. Their mother was sickly, their father unloving; Gertrude turned for affection to Leo, her governesses, and teachers. She was fourteen when her mother died, unmissed; seventeen on the death of her father. "Then," says Gertrude, "our life without a father began, a very pleasant one."[6]

"Between twelve and seventeen," however, she has reminisced, ". . . I went through the dark and dreadful days of adolescence"[7]—and it is doubtful that after seventeen, life was indeed "a very pleasant one," even without father. There are too many signs of restlessness, however sluggish, and of sexual uncertainty. For instance, "One little boy," Gertrude says of her early youth, "wanted her to do loving . . . but this was not very much of a success for [she] then had a nervous feeling and was not very daring."[8] (Quite normal, one might say, if "normality" had followed.) The restlessness derived, at least in part, from the family's rootlessness, its incessant displacements.

Gertrude was born in Allegheny, Pennsylvania, but spent most of her babyhood and early childhood in Vienna, where her father had moved because of business relations. Yet he was frequently away on trips, occasionally back to America. Gertrude was four when the family was removed to the comfortable Passy quarter of Paris. A year later the Steins returned to America to reside in Baltimore, Maryland, before going on a year after *that* to Oakland, California, where they changed residences three times.

However, Gertrude would always be happy to think of herself as Californian; it was more "pioneering," more American. Daily her father commuted across the bay to San Francisco, where he was now vice-president of a municipal streetcar system. Upon her father's death, Gertrude's oldest brother, Michael, left Johns Hopkins University in Baltimore to take his father's place as manager of the Omnibus Cable Company and as head of the family. Briefly they all settled in San Francisco, but soon Gertrude was sent to live with her mother's sister in Baltimore.

Michael Stein would be virtual patron saint of Leo and Gertrude, providing them with a small income most of their lives, though he himself would become bored with business, sell out at a profit, and retire permanently to Paris in 1903. Gertrude was forever grateful for Mike's gift of independence, but he remained a fairly distant father figure. She doted on Leo, and attached herself to him. Years later, after psychoanalysis, Leo would refer to their bond as "the family romance" almost always central in neuroses. "You used to get indigestion when we had a dispute," he wrote to Gertrude.[9] Whatever Leo did, she did; wherever Leo went, she went. In the fall of 1893, when Leo was attending Harvard University, Gertrude followed him by entering the Harvard Annex (for women), soon renamed Radcliffe College.[10]

"She was a blond good-looking young woman," Gertrude describes herself (as Martha Hersland) in her giant family novel, "full of moral purpose and educational desires. She had an eager, earnest intelligence, fixed convictions and principles by then, and restless energy."[11] She studied philosophy under Santayana and Royce, psychology under William James, and experimental psychology under Hugo Münsterberg. But it was James she would recall most warmly, and he would remember her as his favorite pupil. "Everything must come into your scheme," Stein said shortly before her death,

> otherwise you cannot achieve real simplicity. A great deal of this I owe to a great teacher, William James. He said, "Never reject anything. Nothing has been proved. If you reject anything, that is

the beginning of the end as an intellectual." He was my big influence when I was at college. He was a man who always said, "Complicate your life as much as you please, it has got to simplify."[12]

But first—the complication.

For those who knew Gertrude Stein during the last decades of her life, when she radiated serenity, the long years of sexual disorder and torment, extending well beyond her thirtieth year, still come as a discovery and a wonderment.

"Dirty" was the word for sexual relations, even for the adult Gertrude Stein. Although she would consciously delete it from her writing ("none of the later things have this"[13]), the taint stuck in her mind, emerging in her conversations. One wonders if she herself recognized the implications of one of her first memories of childhood. As a very little girl, she recalls in *The Making of Americans,* she was running in a muddy street, dragging someone else's umbrella. Her schoolmates raced ahead of her, and she cried out, "I will throw the umbrella in the mud!" When no one heeded, she did, bursting with desperate anger: "I have throwed the umbrella in the mud!" As a young woman, though not yet at the university, Stein also recalls, she had seen a man on the street hit a woman with an umbrella, "and the woman had a red face partly in anger and partly in asking and the man wanted the woman to know that he wanted her to leave him alone."[14] *Three Lives* (to which we shall return) is, similarly, the story of women who are more gentle, perhaps, but no less defeated, than the women of *The Making of Americans.* As everything that Stein has written—her Radcliffe short stories touch on incest—*Three Lives* is another item in the long account of herself, however obscured, but whose ending is not one of defeat, *as it might have been.*

In the fall of 1897 Gertrude Stein entered the medical school of Johns Hopkins University. Leo, of course, had preceded her to study biology at the university. For several years they shared a largish house in Baltimore until, bored with biology, Leo left Johns Hopkins to settle in Europe and study art. Gertrude moved desolately to a smaller house and, if a sister lodger is to be believed, she worried about her "blood" and weight and hired a professional fighter to box with her regularly. The house, the story goes, echoed with Gertrude's shouts of "Now give me one on the jaw! Now give me one in the kidney!"[15] So much for apocrypha, for the legendary image of a Gertrude Stein readying herself for a yet-to-appear disciple, Ernest Hemingway; or of the tough, imperturbable Stein met in the thirties, thus distorting the true image of the remarkably vulnerable young woman one sees in photographs at the turn of the century.

For two years Gertrude did well in her study of medicine. Her grades were equal to her Radcliffe reputation, but in her third and fourth years they fell off so badly that she failed to receive her medical degree. They declined even before Leo's departure, though his leaving Baltimore for Europe played a disruptive role. More wrenching was the agonizing love affair begun with May Bookstaver, a student at Johns Hopkins, during Leo's last year in Baltimore.

The story is told with remarkable frankness by Stein in her first completed novel, *Q.E.D.* Too frank for the time, the manuscript was put aside in 1903 and "forgotten" (says Stein); rediscovered in 1932, it caused Alice Toklas anger and great distress, and was finally published after Stein's death.[16]

As *Q.E.D.* opens, three young women in a passionate triangle are on shipboard, presumably sailing for Europe. All three are "college bred American women of the wealthier class." Adele, who is Gertrude Stein, suns herself on deck, adjusting "her large curves to the projecting boards." Mabel Neathe, who is actually Mabel Haynes, lies with her head in the lap of Helen Thomas (May Bookstaver), "the American version of the English handsome girl." Gertrude (Adele) is defending her middle-class "ideals" against May's teasing attacks. "You don't realize . . ." says Gertrude, "that virtue and vice have it in common that they are vulgar when not passionately given." Mabel, at this point, pretends boredom and tries to distract May from Gertrude. The chitchat between them brings a burst from Gertrude: "I always did thank God I wasn't born a woman," whereupon Mabel flounces away. Alone with May, Gertrude courts her in her rational fashion, continuing the explanation of herself. She hopes to achieve serenity, Gertrude says. How about passion? May objects. Oh, says Gertrude, of that "I have an almost puritanic horror." May: "That is what makes it possible for a face as thoughtful and strongly built as yours to be almost annoyingly unlived." Silence; then Gertrude replies: "I could undertake to be an efficient pupil if it were possible to find an efficient teacher."[17] They leave it at that.

"In reality," comments Leon Katz, after studying the Stein papers at Yale University, "when [Gertrude] asked for instruction, May burst out laughing. And Stein for a long time remembered her shock at being laughed at for her innocence. And she remembered it as the first significant step toward her genuine maturity."[18]

In the long, lazy days that followed on shipboard, affection slowly grew between the two young women, May efficiently taking the lead while Gertrude hesitated, undecided whether "she should yield or resist," then settled tiredly for the state of being "quite dulled." May accused her of possessing a nature incapable of much more than *"passionettes."* "You are so afraid of losing your moral sense," May said, "that you are not willing to take it through anything more dangerous than a mud-puddle [sic!]." Gertrude granted some truth in May's shrewd stroke, then essayed to explain herself again: "I never wanted to be a hero, but on the other hand I am not anxious to cultivate cowardice. I wonder."[19] And what Gertrude really wondered was what kind of woman *was* May. Someone who could love and be loved as deeply as Gertrude sought? How about *herself?* Gertrude wondered desperately. Intensely kissed by May, she had felt vaguely, apathetically "unresponsive." Haven't you ever stopped thinking long enough to feel strongly? May inquired. Gertrude shook her head. The ship landed. The young women parted.

All that summer of 1901 in the company of Leo (her "cousin" in the novel), Gertrude continued her self-examination as they slowly traveled through Tangiers and Granada before pausing in Paris. In the fall Gertrude returned to America and her torment, picking up the tangled relationship with May and Mabel, who had spent most of this time together.

Slow to draw conclusions (from which, however, she thereafter rarely withdrew), but with growing disquiet—indeed, disgust—Gertrude moodily studied the *power* relationship between the two women, one of whom she now knew she loved. Mabel Haynes was paying the way of the resilient, attractive, *willing* May Bookstaver. Hers was that power. In Mabel's attitude toward May, there was always "an implication of ownership that [Gertrude] found singularly irritating." Yet, again, May took the lead vis-à-vis Gertrude, literally seducing her in New York on the couch of a friend's borrowed apartment. For Gertrude, age twenty-seven, it was "the first time . . . something happened in which she had no consciousness of beginnings. [Suddenly] she found herself at the end of a passionate embrace." A sense of strain remained, however. May felt she was being dissected and exposed by Gertrude's probing questions and demanding ideals, though Gertrude clumsily reassured May that it was only her "cursed habit of being concerned only with [her] own thoughts," not at all intended to cause May suffering.[20]

The impossible situation was provisionally shelved by Mabel's reassertion of her "property" rights: she was taking May to Europe. That spring Gertrude rejoined Leo in Italy and spent the summer of 1902 pondering in England, mostly in the British Museum. Nothing seemed resolved, save one thing. She had neither "the inclination nor the power to take [Mabel's] place." She could offer May "nothing but an elevating influence," but "what is the use of an elevating influence if one hasn't bread and butter." May's want of butter, "if not bread," had to be kept in mind. So Gertrude wrote to May, who replied in protest that Gertrude was the "only thing in the world" for her.

In February 1903 Gertrude quit the "fog and smoke-laden air" of London for the "clean blue distance" of America, rejoicing in "clean and straight and meagre and hard and white and high" New York. And here very soon afterward Gertrude was greeted by May with a "kiss that seemed to scale the very walls of chastity"—but which filled her "with battle and revulsion"! Shocked silence on the part of May. Did Gertrude feel her old distrust again? she asked. Yes, said Gertrude shortly. Days later she tried to explain that her "puritan instincts" repeatedly made her say *no,* though she was learning to distrust her instincts. The two spent the night together in a kind of reconciliation. Mabel's proprietary claim on May, however, continued to nag at Gertrude. "She could not get rid of the feeling that she had stolen the property of another." Nor could Gertrude get over her "passionate tenderness" and yearning for May. All three meeting together in Italy proved their last gesture. "Mabel was insistently domineering, May subservient and Gertrude disgusted." On the night of their separation, Gertrude said to May, "Good-by. I do love you very much." "And I you," said May, who did not wish to say good-by, but rather wanted them to go on—as before. She wrote Gertrude to this effect. Impatiently Gertrude reacted, exclaiming to herself: "Can't she see things as they are and not as she would make them if she were strong enough as she plainly isn't."

"I am afraid it comes very near being a dead-lock," Gertrude groaned, dropping her head on her arms.[21]

Thus Stein closes *Q.E.D.,* a painful book to write, but one she had to in her "desperate attempt to understand and, by that means, to survive what had happened to her."[22]

This was the Gertrude Stein who would now settle in Paris at 27, rue de Fleurus with her brother Leo; who would exact from her experience with May "the hard knowledge of the part power plays in human relationships"[23]—not only for *Q.E.D.* but also for the masterful "Melanctha" of *Three Lives;* who would sit for her portrait by Picasso (age twenty-four), work steadily on her family novel, and wait without knowing it for the arrival of Alice Toklas.

"I led in my childhood and youth the gently bred existence of my class and kind," begins perhaps the most famous fictional autobiography—*The Autobiography of Alice B. Toklas,* by Gertrude Stein—since Daniel Defoe's first-person account of Robinson Crusoe.[24]

Alice was shocked when she first heard Gertrude tell of the "bad years" of her own adolescence. "I'd never heard of anything like that. I said so. I said, 'How horrible.' She said, 'Didn't you have that period too?' I said, 'Not I,' and she said, looking at me, 'Lucky you.' "[25]

In Alice Toklas's own autobiography, *What is Remembered,* which might more accurately be titled, *What I Care to Recall,* Alice rarely varies from the vicarious version of Stein's. She is quite content to repeat that she was "born [in 1877, three years after Gertrude] and raised in California, where my maternal grandfather had been a pioneer";[26] that he had possessed a gold mine before owning a ranch; that she had had piano lessons from her grandmother, who had been a pupil of Clara Schumann's father.

During her youth, Alice said, she had been taught to open a bottle of champagne by breaking it neatly at the neck, and to sweep up carefully the day after a party so as not to overlook any lost diamonds.

Alice was nine years old when a baby brother arrived, and too well established for him to take from her the center of the family stage. As did Gertrude, Alice spent part of her childhood in Europe, including a visit to Poland, the country of her father's origin. When she returned, she was enrolled in a school in San Francisco so snobbish, a little girl of her class immediately asked her if her father had a yacht. He did not. The little girl lost interest in Alice, Alice's mother in the school, and Alice was sent to another.

It may have been the same little girl, certainly one similar, who shook Alice one day and said, "You're a Jew! You're a Jew!" Alice ran home crying and asked her mother whether it was true. "Yes, of course you are," said her mother quietly, "now do your schoolwork." Alice's story, which she never wrote, often recurs to me when I read or think about her "reconversion" to Catholicism after Gertrude's death. Alice would claim she had been baptized as a very little girl, thanks to her mother, but no baptismal certificate has ever been found. (She was greatly reassured, she said, by her English confessor when he told her that she and Gertrude, an unconverted if unpracticing Jewess who vaguely described herself as "oriental" and firmly believed "dead is dead," would be reunited in Heaven, because "God can arrange anything.")

Alice attended a university conservatory to continue her study of the piano. Then her cancer-ridden mother had to renounce caring for the family, and Alice, at eighteen, was obliged to take her place. She learned quickly and acquired an efficiency that would prepare her for life with Gertrude, whose well-serviced childhood led her to always expect someone to look after her. When Alice was twenty, her mother died, and she had two households to manage—her father's and her grandfather's. Yet, she also managed to resume her piano lessons (with a student of Liszt's), and gave two concerts before her "musical career came to an end."[27] But meanwhile it permitted Alice to escape to the company of musicians and artists. (She arrived at one party costumed as Carmen, her glossy dark hair and glowing gray-green eyes—which later struck one as obsidian black, because of their unblinking intensity—immediately attracting the attention of a tableful of people.) Alice also escaped on occasional excursions and horseback canters in Monterey. When her grandfather died, her households were reduced and she had more time for herself. However, the years had passed; she was soon twenty-six, twenty-seven, a "spinster" of twenty-eight. Nevertheless, during the passage of time, she had found herself well before Gertrude had. Though she had flirted with the artists, "danced with the young men at the Mardi gras . . . kissed the boys good-by as they went off as soldiers to the Spanish-American war, her romantic attachments were with women: Nellie Joseph . . . and Lilyanna Hansen."[28] Harriet Levy may have been another. She had just returned with exciting tales of her trip to Europe, and now Alice's dream and goal were to go off to the Continent with Harriet, as soon as she could put aside the money for it.

Twelve days before Alice's twenty-ninth birthday, on April 18, 1906 San Francisco was shaken by a violent earthquake and swept with fire from broken gas mains. "Do get up," said Alice, rousing her father from sleep. "The city is on fire." "That," said he, with his usual calm, "will give us a black eye in the East." The story is Alice's.[29] Coolness was apparently a Toklas characteristic. Her father went off to see if his bank vaults were still holding. Alice packed the family silver and had her brother Clarence bury it in the garden; but first she had gone to see how her friend Annette Rosenshine had fared. After safeguarding the silver, she picnicked with Harriet and spent the night in Berkeley. Cleaning up at home, she found two forgotten tickets for *Phèdre,* went to the performance, and was impressed by Sarah Bernhardt's "golden voice" and famous smile, but typically noted "her visibly large teeth."[30] Few have had a drier way with an anecdote than Alice Toklas.

The earthquake brought Michael Stein and his wife, Sarah, hurrying back to San Francisco from Paris to inspect the damage to their properties. They came, as well, with the first paintings of Matisse to cross the

Atlantic. (It was Leo and Gertrude, however, who had bought the family's first Matisses, as they had the paintings of the young Picasso.) Harriet Levy had known Sarah Stein before her marriage and had visited both Steins on her last trip to Europe. When they spoke of their return to Paris, Harriet suggested joining them together with her friend Alice Toklas. Alice, however, was not keen on Sarah, though she immediately took to Mike. She persuaded them to take Annette Rosenshine instead, she and Harriet to follow in due time.

And in a year's time they did, sailing at the end of August 1907, when Alice was thirty years of age.

As soon as they arrived in Paris, found rooms, and unpacked, Harriet phoned the Michael Steins. Come at once, she was told, with Alice Toklas. They arrived in a fiacre and were received in an enormous salon. "In the room were Mr. and Mrs. Stein and Gertrude Stein," says Alice.

> It was Gertrude Stein who held my attention. . . . She was a golden brown presence, burned by the Tuscan sun [where she had summered with Leo] and with a golden glint in her warm brown hair. She was dressed in a warm brown corduroy suit. She wore a large round coral brooch and when she talked, very little, or laughed, a good deal, I thought her voice came from this brooch. It was unlike anyone else's voice—deep, full, velvety like a great contralto's, like two voices. She was large and heavy with delicate small hands and a beautifully modeled and unique head . . . often compared to a Roman emperor's.[31]

A bell had rung within Alice, she would say, a bell that would ring twice more when she met her two other geniuses, Pablo Picasso and philosopher Alfred North Whitehead.

And Gertrude's reaction on first seeing Alice?

Once when we walked through the Louvre museum, Gertrude paused before a Goya portrait of a young woman in a black mantilla. "There is something of Alice in that," she said softly. And there was. The same black hair, slight, sensual figure, distant yet enticing manner, half lady, half gypsy. All that seemed to lack was the hair on the upper lip, later quite marked, emboldening one to imagine the sensuous appeal and promise of a lightly moustached Carmen.

Gertrude was struck by Alice, and she resisted it. But after tea, she asked Alice to come the next afternoon to the rue de Fleurus, alone. They would go for a walk.

Alice arrived hours late; lunch with Harriet in the Bois de Boulogne had taken longer than she had anticipated. She knocked on the large studio door in the courtyard of the rue de Fleurus. It opened. She was confronted not by the "smiling countenance of the day before," but by a "vengeful goddess." Alice was at a loss. She had no idea what had happened, she says, then mysteriously adds, "Nor is it possible for me to tell about it now."[32]

Gertrude led Alice into the studio and wordlessly paced the length of the heavy Florentine table, then told Alice to look at the paintings while she changed for their walk. It was not *too* late. Alice was in no mood for the paintings, which were hung in tiers on the walls, although the rue de Fleurus studio was probably the only museum of modern art then to be seen: canvases of Cézanne, Picasso, Matisse, Renoir, Gauguin, Toulouse-Lautrec, a Valloton, a Maurice Denis, and older works —a Greco, a Daumier, a Delacroix, not to mention Leo's collection of Japanese prints, and more. Rather, Alice looked at the Renaissance furniture, the octagonal Tuscan table, with its hefty clawed legs; the double-decked Henry IV buffet with the carved eagles on the top; the terra-cotta figures, and other pieces of Italian pottery.

By this time Gertrude had returned, and they went for their walk in the neighboring Luxembourg gardens. Alice, said Gertrude, look at the autumn herbaceous border. "But I did not propose to reciprocate the familiarity." Miss Toklas would decide when first names were appropriate; she had not quite recovered from her reception.[33]

Nor had Gertrude Stein recuperated from the sharpness of her own reaction. Unknown to Alice, she had been reading her letters to Annette Rosenshine for a year and drawing *unfavorable* judgments, which she added to her other intricate character analyses of friends for her family novel. That night Gertrude was particularly harsh, noting Alice as "conscienceless," "sordid," "without ideals of any kind."[34]

During the winter of 1952–1953, Leon Katz interviewed Alice Toklas at length about certain details in the Stein notebooks that had been discovered among the papers she had left to Yale University. He had made a copy of the pertinent notebooks in connection with the doctoral thesis he was writing, "The First Making of *The Making of Americans.*" Carefully he had prepared Alice Toklas concerning some critical remarks Stein had jotted down about her. Finally they arranged a rendezvous for the following evening, so that Alice could look at them. At six o'clock the next morning Alice phoned Katz at his hotel. Could he not come earlier? He could. Eagerly she took his typescript when he arrived, and disappeared into the bedroom she had shared with Gertrude (its walls still papered with the pigeons-on-the-grass pattern). Alice emerged. "I am greatly relieved," she said. "Relieved?" said Katz, surprised. "But Gertrude called you 'immoral'!" "Immoral in manners," Alice replied, "as Henry James once said, but not in principles. I was afraid that Gertrude might have written that I was disloyal."[35]

Alice, in fact, was amoral, even if conventional, prudish but not puritanical, clearheaded, purposeful, and *largely* unprincipled (except in regard to loyalty to Gertrude). Much of this had been exposed to Gertrude in the letters of Alice to Annette and from what she had deduced concerning Alice's liaisons and conduct in response to her growing curiosity and interest. Wherefore the "conscienceless" and "sordid" Alice? As for her being "without ideals of any kind," Gertrude would discover to her gratification that devotion to her and to her writing would be "ideal" enough for the two. And as for the air of the "vengeful goddess" Gertrude had assumed for the tardy Alice, she already recognized in herself—and in her complex categorization of psychological types—an "independent dependent kind," for whom "attacking is their natural way of . . . winning in loving." Alice presumably was a "dependent independent kind," which had an "engulfing," "embracing," "resisting as their natural way of winning in loving." But Gertrude confesses that "often it is very confusing . . . There is in each kind a kind of sensitiveness . . . [and] yielding."[36]

The yielding was not immediate. The resisting endured for months. There was more steel in Alice than in Gertrude, and on occasion it flashed. ("Steel is beautiful"—Stein.[37]) The sensitiveness would last their lifetime.

Alice very shortly met Leo and all Gertrude's friends at the Saturday evenings of the rue de Fleurus—Picasso foremost and beforehand ("very dark with black hair, a lock hanging over one of his marvelous all-seeing brilliant black eyes"[38]); his intimate for the moment, Fernande, from whom Alice took French lessons; then, of course, Matisse, Braque, Apollinaire, Marie Laurencin, and others. Alice eased Harriet Levy onto Sarah Stein, who had a passion for guiding other people's lives.

The winter began "gaily," says Alice, but Gertrude ("attacking")[39] analyzed "me as an old maid mermaid which I resented."[40] Alice resented more being called a "mermaid" than an "old maid," for was there not something virginal and pure, after all, in being a "maid," and cold-blooded and fishy in being a "mermaid?" Gertrude's diagnosis, in any case, says Alice, wore thin and blew away. By the time buttercups were in bloom, Alice "had been gathering wild violets," if not yet sowing wild oats. Alice, as always, implies that their entente was instant and loving. However, she also blandly remarks that the corals she had bought for Gertrude were "inevitably" given to Harriet.[41] ("When as young," Stein would write of—and to—Alice, "you could get your way by being intriguing," as a child it had been by "being cuddling."[42]

Gertrude persisted in her fashion, arranging for all three women plus the complaisant Leo to meet in Fiesole the following summer. Leo and Gertrude arrived first. Alice and Harriet went down by train. The heat was so intense during the stretch between Milan and Florence, says Alice, that "I got rid of my cerise ribbon girdle in the dressing room of the train, throwing it out the window." When she returned to her seat, Harriet said, "What a strange coincidence, I just saw your cherry-colored corset pass by the window." In Fiesole, Gertrude and Alice went on their walks—"unforgettable," says Alice—without Harriet. One day, "the sun was giving a torrid heat"—again it is Alice talking—"so under some bushes I discarded my silk combination and stockings." Gertrude, another day, "took off her sandals." Provocative, at the least, but probably as important for Gertrude was Alice's excitement when she was shown the manuscript pages of *The Making of Americans.* This was particularly true after the return to Paris in the fall, at which time Alice *and* Harriet settled into an apartment not too far from the rue de Fleurus.[43]

Simultaneously Alice was settling more permanently into Gertrude's life. She acquired a Smith Premier so that she could learn to type Gertrude's manuscript. Indeed, she developed a "Gertrude Stein technique, like playing Bach [on the piano]." Evenings Gertrude would talk over her writing of the day, and the following morning Alice would type the results. In the meantime, at great effort, Alice had caught up with the hundreds of previous pages. She had the mornings to herself, since Gertrude rose very late, took long, meditative baths, and breakfasted at noon. And Harriet? Harriet was worrying, she said, about Alice's increasingly late returns at night to their apartment. A man might follow her! Alice paid no mind and made no change in her new habits—"it was a very happy time for me." Finally Harriet would be packed off to America, not to return.[44]

Leo posed another problem.

Gertrude's brother was less than responsive to her writing. He was too full of concern about his own blockages, his false starts and full stops, to have much sympathy for Gertrude's heroic grapplings with the new, the unborn, the yet to be conceived. It hurt Gertrude deeply. Early in *The Making of Americans* she indicated the depression into which it plunged her: "I am all unhappy in this writing." "I am really almost despairing." Then suddenly, halfway through the massive novel, Gertrude sings out: "Then some one says yes to it, to something you are liking, or doing or making and never again can you have completely such a feeling of being afraid and ashamed that you had then when you were writing or liking the thing and not any one had said yes about the thing."[45]

In other words, Gertrude had now met Alice. They were together; she had Alice's support. Alice's appreciation validated Gertrude's writing, until then so despairingly lonely and unlistened to.[46] While Gertrude was painfully giving sound to her own singular voice, her own "barbaric yawp," as in Whitman, Leo the beloved brother was "not loving," "not hearing." Now there was Alice—"she was the meaning which was the listening and she was the sympathizing which was the endowing." They loved each other. Of this, too, there was no longer any doubt. "Loving . . . and being loved," Gertrude at last felt that she was living, "and being living she was continuing and being continuing sound was coming out of her . . . She was succeeding. She was preparing." Leo was no longer "one of the two of them." Alice, who was the last, "was the first." Alice "was the one to have" for the one "intending to marry the one."[47]

The banns would seem to have been virtually posted by Alice's act of moving into a small room of the pavilion, adjacent to the studio, at the rue de Fleurus. Alice writes of the arrangement, however, as simply going "to stay with Gertrude and Leo." Leo himself seems to have welcomed the move for Gertrude's sake and distraction. He was entering on the courtship of an artist's model, Nina Auzias, who was already involved with three other lovers, each aware of the others, as was Leo. But he persevered, and eventually married Nina—in 1921. A new gaiety became apparent in Gertrude's writing; one might risk saying that even *The Making of Americans* was racing to a finish, thanks to Alice's liberation of Gertrude from the huge novel's intricacy and constraints. The significant change was signaled in the short portrait, *Ada,* written before the ending of the major novel and shortly before Alice's move to the rue de Fleurus. "A very good description of me," says Alice of *Ada,* which Gertrude titled *Alice* at one stage.[48]

One Sunday evening when Alice was substituting for the cook, preparing an American dish Gertrude prized, Gertrude excitedly stormed into the kitchen. Read this, she demanded, handing Alice a notebook. After dinner, said Alice. Now, said Gertrude. "Finally I read it all and was terribly pleased with it," says Alice, "and then we ate our supper."[49] The first literary love letter to her from Gertrude, in all likelihood, *Ada* traces their intimacy, as it were, from the time of Ada-Alice's birth and childhood. "The daughter was charming inside in her," exchanging "pretty stories" with her mother, and when her mother died, she "kept house for her father and took care of her brother."

Then she inherited money from her grandfather and "went away from them" to find someone else to tell her stories to, "someone who was loving" and "almost always listening." Soon the one and the other were both loving.

> Trembling was all living, living was all loving, some one was then the other one. Certainly this one was loving this Ada then. And certainly Ada all her living then was happier in living than any one else who ever could, who was, who is, who ever will be living.[50]

To love is to love forever; the beloved will be loved forever and forever be happy.

To love is also to be jealous, the first, fragile moments. In the summer of 1911 Gertrude and Alice went down to Florence to stay in the Villa Curonia of Mabel Dodge, whom Alice was meeting for the first time. The feeling of dislike was mutual and immediate between the latter two women, but contained during this visit. It would flare up the next time. Meanwhile, the following May, our two lovers journeyed to Spain on their first honeymoon, which had the unpredictable contretemps of a maiden voyage. Possibly reverberations of the Villa Curonia played a part, but paradoxically it was Alice's love of Spain, even before she ever saw it, that had the greater role. She was biased, she always said, because she was Californian. From Burgos to Valladolid to Avila, Alice's enchantment grew by leaps and bounds. At walled, medieval Avila it came to a climax.

Here Gertrude and Alice, after a rough trip, found themselves in a delightful inn, scrubbed clean and refreshingly neat. There was even a wedding party to greet them. But it was the beauty of the walled city and its surrounding farms and landscape that struck Alice and held her captive. Abruptly, she said to Gertrude, "I am not going to leave here. I am staying." "What do you mean?" asked Gertrude, astonished. "I am enraptured with Avila and I propose staying."

"Well," said Gertrude, "I will stay two weeks instead of two days, but I could not work here, you know that." This quieted her "temporarily," says Alice.[51] The implication of a continuing dispute is strong. But here, in the birthplace of St. Teresa, was reborn Gertrude's youthful fascination with the Spanish saint and the beginning of the identification of Alice with her. St. Teresa had been famously passionate in her devotion and faith; Alice would soon demonstrate her own passionate devotion to Gertrude and faith in her writing. Indeed, Alice's act of *leaving Avila* on Gertrude's insistence—if not pleading—that here she could not write, that living in Avila would mean the end of her writing, was first evidence of it. Alice's yielding would never be forgotten by either of the two (nor, perhaps, would Alice's hesitation).

The honeymoon resumed. The two went on to Madrid, where they watched gypsies dance and bullfighters perform ("Don't look," Gertrude advised Alice in good-husband fashion when a horse was gored; "Now you can look," she said as it was led away[52]); to Toledo; to Cuenca, Cordova, Seville, Gibraltar, Ronda, and Granada; then, by August, back to Paris. But by mid-September they were traveling again to Mabel Dodge's villa in Florence—for the second testing of (a "more secure"[53]) Alice.

Retrospectively Gertrude would write that Mabel had "very pretty eyes" but—was this for Alice's reassurance as she read and typed it?—"a very old fashioned coquetry," implying that Gertrude was beyond it. Mabel Dodge has testified differently. One afternoon during lunch, she wrote, she had felt Gertrude's aroused interest (Mabel thought of herself as bisexually irresistible). She had caught a glance from her that "seemed to cut across the air . . . in a band of electrified steel."[54] Alice, too, seems to have caught the look Gertrude directed at Mabel, for she instantly rose from the table and left the room. Gertrude hurried after her but returned alone, saying that Alice was suffering from the heat; she would lunch no more that day. That day also put an end to the Mabel-Gertrude friendship; Alice saw to that. Her love was devoted; it was also demanding. Gertrude's had been no less at Avila. The visit to Mabel sealed their union—or as Gertrude put it in her "Portrait of Mabel Dodge at the Villa Curonia": "An argument is clear . . . The present time is the best time to agree. . . . the union is won and the division is the explicit visit"[55]—that is, the separation of Gertrude from Mabel was the clear result of *that* visit.

The year 1912 was elsewise memorable. Gertrude had worked "terrifically" during the Spanish trip, says Alice; "I myself," says Gertrude, "was becoming livelier just then."[56] Her style gradually changed, "a long and tormenting process," as she tried to express "the rhythm of the visible world," to write down what she literally saw, concretely perceived but not *described.* "These were the days when she wrote 'Susie Asado' and 'Preciosilla' "[57] with such tantalizing lines as "Toasted susie is my ice-cream."[58] Possibly a line impossible to paraphrase, but what a toast to a café singer Gertrude and Alice had heard in Madrid! *Tender Buttons* followed, an arcane celebration of domesticity and sensuality with Alice—"objects," "food," and "rooms" (the title is sensuality itself)—but in which Stein tried to get as close to abstraction as words permit, in the spirit of Picasso's analytical cubist period. Words, however, as Stein would discover, are not pigment;

writers are not painters. It was impossible to put a word next to another word without sense, Stein concluded, "though I made innumerable efforts."[59]

The reception of Stein's new writing, so different from *Three Lives,* which is as readable as Flaubert's *Trois contes* (which inspired it), varied from misunderstanding to dismay to ridicule. "Damned nonsense . . . ," said Leo Stein of Gertrude's "Portrait of Mabel Dodge," "conveying absolutely nothing." He was convinced that Gertrude was "basically stupid," and frequently declared it,[60] and believed that her friends, particularly Alice, overpraised her writing, not for its own sake and merit, but out of misplaced friendship. "I knew it was not true," Gertrude would respond, "but it destroyed him for me."[61] Separation of brother and sister was now inevitable and necessary, and desired by both. In 1913 Leo wrote to mutual friend Mabel Weeks of the "definite 'disaggregation' of Gertrude and myself." "The presence of Alice," he continued, "was a godsend, as it enabled things to happen without any explosion." Both Gertrude and Picasso, he had now concluded, were "turning out the most Godalmighty rubbish that is to be found."[62]

Leo's attitude at least made it that much easier to divide the paintings when he and Gertrude separated, Leo to settle in Florence with Nina, and Gertrude to remain at the rue de Fleurus with Alice. The Picasso canvases went to Gertrude (there were twenty-two at the time of her death), the Renoirs to Leo, the Cézannes were equitably divided, and so on down the list according to choice or bargaining. With Leo gone, Gertrude simply tried to put him out of her mind, and largely succeeded. They did not meet again before 1931, when, Alice recalls, she saw Gertrude bowing to someone on the street whom Alice did not recognize. "Whom are you bowing to?" she asked. "Leo," replied Gertrude, and that evening, says Alice, "Gertrude wrote the so beautiful 'She Bowed To Her Brother.' In it she purged him and the whole miserable time he had given her . . . Goodness he made me suffer [too]."[63]

Without Leo to share living expenses, however, the income arranged by Michael became harder to manage upon; Alice's small income did not make up for it. Finding a publisher for Gertrude's mounting pile of manuscripts would be a solution. Until then, only one book of Gertrude's had been published, *Three Lives* (1909), and that had had a slight sale despite some favorable reviews. Advised to go to London to see personally about publication, to London the pair went (it was actually their second trip on the same mission). They were weekending with Dr. and Mrs. Alfred North Whitehead when World War I broke out. The weekend stretched into a stay of six weeks. The war news became so alarming, says Alice, "Gertrude refused to get up, preferring to stay in bed with her eyes closed but not asleep."[64] It was Alice, hurrying to Gertrude's room, who told her of the German defeat on the Marne. They then decided to return to France. In January 1915 they heard Paris's first air-raid alarm; in mid-March, as they were packing for Palma de Majorca, they experienced their first air-raid by German zeppelins. Their leaving Paris was not their bravest performance, but their year in Majorca was perhaps the happiest of their love time.

Happiness for the Romantics was a conjuration of place and climate, "sunny Italy" as its well-trodden example. "Sunny Majorca" came as a close second. Franz Liszt and Marie d'Agoult did *not* have too happy a time in Italy. George Sand and Chopin spent a miserable time in Majorca: it was winter and windy and Chopin's cough rapidly worsened. Gertrude and Alice were not Romantics, unless love itself is the essence of romanticism, and both knew George Sand's story well. Her ten-volume *Histoire de ma vie* was among the very few French books on Gertrude's shelves (Alice had bought the set on her arrival in Paris). Gertrude had even considered using "Jane Sands" and variants of it as her pseudonym for *Three Lives.*[65]

In Majorca, the summer heat and mosquitoes brought on discomfort and irritability on Alice's part, which risked extending the parallel with Chopin too far. (Gertrude was a glutton for heat.) However, the house the two rented just outside Palma and the relief of autumn turned the situation around. Or was it that love between the two reached its summit in the slightly cooler climate? Never had they been so isolated from others and so dependent upon each other. Alice was a discovery and rediscovery for Gertrude; Gertrude was lover and creator for the critical Alice. The reciprocity was exhilarating. Let none speak of the supremacy of young love à la Romeo and Juliet who have not known love in their maturity à la Antony and Cleopatra. Gertrude and Alice thought of themselves in these male-female terms. "Little Alice B. is the wife for me . . . she can be born along by a husband strong," Gertrude has written.[66] And nowhere in her work has Gertrude written so erotically as in the fifty-page love poem to Alice, *Lifting Belly,* a major Majorcan piece, which was posthumously published.

Alice was not only cook, gardener, and keeper of the house they rented, high on a hill. She continued as Gertrude's copyist, critic, and soul supporter. (With Alice as a friend, one had the sense of having God on one's side.) During the sultry afternoons she knitted, as she had been taught by Madame Matisse, pullovers and stockings for French soldiers, while Gertrude read aloud from one or another book, reserving the cooler evenings and nights for her writing.

Alice is "baby" in *Lifting Belly* ("Baby is so good to baby") and "pussy" ("Pussy how pretty you are")—and "pussy" she will be for Gertrude the rest of Gertrude's life; Alice called her "lovey." Alice is also "darling wifie" and Gertrude "little hubbie" in Gertrude's poem. But this is child's play compared to the eroticism of the lyrics repeating the title (one reason, at least, for publication after Gertrude's death). Witness the lines, as if written to the crescendo of Ravel's *Bolero* rising to sexual climax:

> I say lifting belly and then I say lifting belly and Caesars. I say lifting belly gently and Caesars gently. I say lifting belly again and Caesars again. I say lifting belly and I say Caesars and I say lifting belly Caesars and cow come out. I say lifting belly and Caesars and cow come out.[67]

When one realizes that Gertrude often played with the phrase "seize her" to arrive at "Caesar," who is also herself (Alice's "Roman emperor") and the equivalent of "maleness,"[68] and that the "cow" coming out is sexual explosion, then allusion to Antony and Cleopatra ceases to be pure, capricious fantasy.

The phrases lilt along, bold and unashamed:

> Lifting belly. Are you. Lifting.
> Oh dear I said I was tender, fierce and tender.
>
> I do not like bites.
> How lift it.
> Not so high.

Is this Alice to Gertrude or Gertrude to Alice?

> Lifting belly is so strong. I love cherish idolise adore and worship you. You are so sweet so tender and so perfect.
>
> Kiss my lips.
> She did.
> Kiss my lips again she did.
> Kiss my lips over and over and over again she did.

Is Alice "the levelheaded fattuski," who replies, "I do not wish to be Polish"? She was rather plump at this time. But "Mount Fatty" can only be Gertrude, and the following can refer only (and heavily) to Alice:

"Say how do you do to the lady. Which lady. The jew lady. How do you do. She is my wife." Granted, it is a kind of scratchy fun-poking at Toklas's particular semitic anti-Semitic flights, but this is rapidly left behind (and Alice, too, will have her day). "Lifting belly is a miracle" and "precious" and "Caesars do their duty."

> In the midst of writing.
> In the midst of writing there is merriment.[69]

There was not always merriment. Alice did have her day, as the Majorcan pieces record. She could be angry: "I am often angry. Sometimes I cry. Not from anger. I only cry from heat and other things."[70] Gertrude could shout, then apologize: "What is shouting./It is a disease."[71] More important, Alice could be very pressing, driving Gertrude in the direction she, Gertrude, wished to go—toward success.

Merriment, a rented house, terrace and garden, good food, excursions to Barcelona, and bullfights cost money. Since the separation from Leo, Gertrude's funds were diminished by that much. Alice's small income from an inheritance, moreover, was dwindling. The alternatives for the two were for Gertrude either to sell a painting or to make some money from her writing (*Three Lives* had been printed at Gertrude's expense). What, then, was Alice's role? The conventional, the traditional one of the writer's wife. "Success is what she was supposed to favor," Gertrude herself expressed it. "How was she supposed to favor success? She was supposed to favor success by being fond of money."[72] And Alice was indeed fond of money, nay, of luxury. (She left tips so large, one was certain she was confusing old with new francs.) One can feel Alice's pressure in Gertrude's solemn pledge: "I am going to conquer. I am going to be flourishing. I am going to be industrious. Please forgive me everything."[73]

Gertrude almost desperately wanted to be successful. "Only the successful are interesting," she once remarked, and one thought it cold and calculating until one recalled the sour smell of failure. She wanted to be rich, if that meant remaining independent, but she always insisted, "I never want to do what there is to do to get rich."[74]

Funds low, Gertrude and Alice began to tell each other that perhaps they could do better in Paris, a sentiment strengthened by a small sense of guilt. The war news that reached them was bad; the fighting at Verdun was indeed bloody. Their prayers now included Pétain. When, finally, the forces he led stopped the Germans, they decided to return and do something for their adopted country.

In Paris they discovered an American woman in uniform who drove a Ford for the American Fund for French Wounded. That was their ticket, too, Gertrude and Alice decided. They signed up, ordered a Ford from a cousin of Gertrude's in America, had it converted into a truck after it arrived, and took off for the military hospital at Perpignan, which was about as far from the front as France permitted. Gertrude drove (always forward; she never learned to back up) and Alice navigated, maps in hand. Gertrude would do the cranking, Alice the negotiating with the military for gas. They always found someone to help them change and repair a flat tire.

After delivering thermometers, bandages, X-ray equipment, and other medical supplies, the pair returned to Paris to restock, then went south again to Nîmes. Here they met an American doughboy who was the kind of handyman they were always looking for and finding and who would become an enduring friend (for us all), William "the Kiddie" Rogers. His description of the two at this time is quite priceless. He spent a ten-day furlough as their assistant—rather, as the assistant of Gertrude Stein's assistant, who informed him, the Kiddie says, that he was to fix anything that went wrong with the Ford, that he "must not get in the way," and thus must sit on a pillow on the floor with his feet on the running board. "I agreed happily . . . I crowded Miss Toklas but not Miss Stein." Miss Toklas, he would discover, ". . . devoted practically all her life to the prevention of any crowding of Gertrude Stein."[75]

In time the Kiddie learned to appreciate the weight, the wit, the "tonic acidity" of Alice Toklas and even dared to wonder "whose light was being hidden under whose bushel"—a remark he often repeated after Gertrude died and Alice had emerged into her own light.

When the war was over, the two were still at Nîmes. From there the American Fund sent them to Alsace, to help care for the refugees. They did not get back to Paris before the following May 1919. "The city, like us," says Alice without explanation, "was sadder than when we left it."[76] Because of the war dead, the change, the end of a kind of youth, "the heroic age of cubism"? Paris of the twenties would produce its own kind of youth.

In the meantime, within weeks of their return to the rue de Fleurus, someone showed up from Alice's past—Lilyanna Hansen. It is not certain who was the more troubled, Alice or Gertrude. "A photograph which Alice took of Lily in the Luxembourg Gardens was kept by her until after Gertrude's death"[77]—twenty-seven years later. Gertrude's response was slow to happen, but no less deep for that. She respected true feelings. She had too much self-respect not to, and she took a justified pride in lucidity. She knew of Alice's past with Nelly, Lily, and the others; she and Alice had agreed to tell each other all before deciding to live together. She loved Alice; she wanted to keep Alice. Gertrude could be jealous *and* generous: "The Steinian tone is never vindictive"[78]—rarely enough, that is, to say never. Frequently she reviewed her life with Alice and Alice's life before they loved. In 1922 it occurs directly in "Didn't Nelly and Lilly Love You"; in 1925 it arrives, belated and more troubled, in "A Third."

"Credit me understanding," begins "Didn't Nelly and Lilly Love You," and Gertrude early asks, "Do you think you are going to be true," almost immediately replying, "You did stay." "Marry me again," she pleads. "I am a husband who is very very good I have a character that covers me like a hood . . ."[79] Gertrude consistently requested domestic tranquility, the serenity and security she needed for her writing, her concentration. "A Third" is more puzzling and harrowing. Has Lilyanna again appeared in flesh or in spirit in 1925? Or is there another third party? Who has managed "to change two to two and a third"? Is it she who "prefers Bourbons to Jews, wives to weddings"—or is that Alice herself? Sadly Gertrude isolates a line: "Yesterday was the day there were only two." Today there are three. Anxiously she asks, "Do you like silver [a woman], do you like weeks [Mabel Weeks], do you like dear me do you like do you who has had you. Who has had you here. You." Gertrude tries to reassure herself: "She needs me. She needs me too," as she is needed. One cannot love and allow jealousy to destroy the love and the loved one; what does one gain by losing? "After all she [Alice] has another another set of ear-rings and after all she has another another way of holding grapes and after all she has another another way of saying it with corals. My only wife and mother." Why could not Alice have another "friend"? However, all was resolved: "When she heard of three she preferred two. When she heard of me she preferred me." Now "our mind can linger on the subject of cows and fishes in abundance . . ."[80]

Alice, threatened, would secure her love differently.

The twenties brought young American writers to Paris and to Stein's studio door, not least of them Ernest Hemingway in 1921, at the age of twenty-two. He carried a letter of introduction from novelist Sherwood Anderson, an admirer of Stein's writing and a recent visitor. Hemingway came to France as a correspondent for the *Toronto Daily Star;* a good first stage, he calculated, for a writing career. "An extraordinarily good-looking young man," remarked Gertrude after meeting him.[81] "We love Gertrude Stein," wrote Hemingway to Anderson, speaking for his young wife as well.[82] In fact, Gertrude, who was then forty-eight, and Hemingway, who was less than half her age, were strongly attracted to each other. For Hemingway it was frankly erotic beyond the usual pupil-teacher relationship: he wanted to make love to Stein (as he wrote to William Rogers, the Kiddie).[83]

"She had beautiful eyes," a wonderful head, Hemingway would recall in *A Moveable Feast,* reminding him "of a northern Italian peasant woman with her clothes, her mobile face and her lovely thick, alive, immigrant hair." Alice, he thought, was "frightening."[84] More frightened than frightening, he would discover. How quickly Alice had perceived the "danger" cannot be ascertained, but Hemingway was sure she had become his enemy very early. Picasso and the others whose hearts and tastes went conspicuously elsewhere never represented the same threat for Alice.

Hemingway showed Stein his opening pages of the "inevitable" first novel. Too much description, she told him, "and not particularly good description. Begin over again and concentrate."[85] He did. They walked and talked and worked together on his writing. "It used to be easy before I met you," Hemingway wrote to Stein after two years of tutelage. "I certainly was bad, gosh, I'm awfully bad now but it's a different kind of bad."[86] Alice remained convinced that he had learned his lean, crisp style from having prepared and proofread the first fifty pages of *The Making of Americans* for serialization in a Parisian, expatriate magazine.

Gertrude Stein's lessons, Hemingway would reveal forty years later and after a frigid break with her, included "instructing me about sex." By then, "we liked each other very much." He confesses to "certain prejudices against homosexuality," to begin with, and recounts that as a boy he had carried a knife when he sought the company of tramps and hobos and would have used it, if one turned "wolf" on him. "You had to be prepared to kill a man," said Hemingway stoutly to Stein, then you'd be left alone. More recently, he went on, an "old man with beautiful manners and a great name" had tried to seduce him as he lay wounded in an Italian hospital during World War I. "Those people are sick," he reports Stein as responding, ". . . you should pity them." Hemingway then continues with this fascinating exchange in *A Moveable Feast:*

> "You know nothing about any of this really, Hemingway," she said. "You've met known criminals and sick people and vicious people. The main thing is that the act male homosexuals commit is ugly and repugnant and afterwards they are disgusted with themselves. They drink and take drugs, to palliate this, but they

are disgusted with the act and they are always changing partners and cannot be really happy."

"I see."

"In women it is the opposite. They do nothing that they are disgusted by and nothing that is repulsive and afterwards they are happy and they can lead happy lives together."

"I see," I said. "But what about so and so?"

"She's vicious," Miss Stein said, ". . . she can never be happy except with new people . . ."

"I understand."

"You're sure you understand?"[87]

The reader gathers that Hemingway wasn't sure *Gertrude* understood. There is, moreover, a good deal of "reconstruction" in *A Moveable Feast,* about which one is forewarned by Hemingway himself in the preface. "If the reader prefers," he writes, "this book may be regarded as fiction." Including his story about the knife he carried as a boy, or should that be considered psychological fact? As for Gertrude's recorded attitude toward male homosexuality, to what extent is it hers and to what extent Hemingway's? Granted, her earlier writing refers to sexuality itself as "dirty," but even that must be put into a larger context. Witness this—to me, beautiful—paragraph that appears in the latter part of *The Making of Americans,* which Stein had written after she had met Alice Toklas and they had loved:

> . . . a great many have prejudices about people being loving. Some say alright all but one way of loving, another says alright all but another way of loving, some say all ways of loving are really ways of having loving feeling. I like loving . . . Slowly it has come to be in me that any way of being a loving one is interesting and not unpleasant to me. That came very slowly to be in me.[88]

Item: One winter afternoon Gertrude had me accompany an aging gentleman visitor back to his apartment, because of the icy sidewalks. The next day I said (whimsically, I thought), "How come you exposed me to one of Paris's most notorious homosexuals?" "Sink or swim," said Gertrude, shrugging her shoulders indifferently.

Other than dropping acid remarks, Alice could do little about Gertrude's initial fondness for Hemingway, but fortunately for her, separate trips provided spaces in their intimacy. She and Gertrude made a journey south to Saint-Rémy in the late summer of 1922, and they sent the Hemingways to Pamplona in 1923 for the bullfights ("We *all* sent Hemingway to Pamplona," said Robert McAlmon to a friend). Running with the bulls in the streets of Pamplona presumably tested the manhood of Hemingway and prepared him for his first and best novel, *The Sun Also Rises.* (One tends to set aside his previous, ungracious parody of his sponsor, Sherwood Anderson, *The Torrents of Spring.*)

The testing of Alice Toklas at St.-Rémy was of another order, though as typical. The two stayed in Provence from late summer until midwinter. The mistral blew and their hotel was freezing cold, and Alice suffered. One day they sat on the hard ploughed ground to get away from the incessant wind, but it didn't work. Then Alice discovered, when they rose, that she could not even walk on the ploughed field. "Suddenly I found myself crying. Gertrude said, What is the matter? The weather, I said, can we go back to Paris? She said, Tomorrow. But Gertrude had written so well there, and so happily and so much"—twenty pieces in the one year—"that I made up my mind I would behave and not complain."[89] As usual, Gertrude's writing came first for Alice; since that was also true for Gertrude, they had a good deal in common—priorities, love, gratitude, and the need to be needed.

Hemingway's gratuitous—and nasty—parody of Anderson, written in ten days, not only offended his "friend" and sponsor, but affected his relationship with Stein. She was not given to ingratitude, and Sherwood Anderson had been *publicly* supportive of her avant-garde work. However, she did not break with Hemingway, who was still the sedulous pupil; he used a remark Stein had addressed to him as the epigraph of his first novel—"You are all a lost generation"—and toyed with the idea of using *The Lost Generation* as its title instead of *The Sun Also Rises.*[90] Such gestures softened Gertrude's feelings for Hemingway. She often confessed a "weakness" for him, which she explained by saying, "He was such a good pupil." Hearing this, Alice would always protest, "He was a rotten pupil," not wishing to grant him even that. Over the years Gertrude and Hemingway met less and less often; *The Making of Americans* had finally been published and Hemingway was making a success of his career as *the* writer of his generation. Once, when Gertrude and Alice heard that he was back in Paris after a long trip, and telling people how much he wanted to see Gertrude, Alice warned her: "Don't you come home with Hemingway on your arm after one of your walks." Sure enough, one day she did. Then, says Alice, she didn't.[91]

Hemingway's account, in a chapter entitled "A Strange-Enough Ending" in *A Moveable Feast,* is a strange one indeed, and more revealing than he may have wished. Ostensibly the revelation is his shock at discovering that Gertrude and Alice were—he doesn't bring himself to say it, but it is there—lesbians! Perhaps the surprising thing is that one is still taken aback by Hemingway's shock rather than by his scarcely believable naïveté (assuming it is real, not the mask of the bluff male).

He had had the run of the studio at the rue de Fleurus, writes Hemingway, and had arrived late one morning unexpected and unannounced. The maid told him to wait in the studio; Miss Stein would be right down. While sipping an eau-de-vie served him by the maid, Hemingway continues:

> I heard someone speaking to Miss Stein as I had never heard one person speak to another; never, anywhere, ever.
>
> Then Miss Stein's voice came pleading and begging, saying, "Don't, pussy. Don't. Don't, please don't. I'll do anything, pussy, but please don't do it. Please don't. Please don't, pussy.

Hemingway left immediately. "That was the way it finished for me," he says. He would meet Stein again, but it would never be the same. "I could never make friends again truly, neither in my heart nor in my head."[92]

Nor could Gertrude Stein. One day toward the end of World War II, she told me that Hemingway had come by. "Gertrude," he had said, "I'm old and I'm rich; let's stop fighting." "Hem," she said she had replied, "I am not old and I am not rich; let's keep on fighting."

The real break arrived with Stein's first popular book, in 1933, *The Autobiography of Alice B. Toklas,* in which she flatly called Hemingway "yellow," a coward in the skin of the white hunter. Worse, she said he was a writer of small talent, and, devastatingly, she quoted him to this effect: "Hemingway said once, 'I turn my flame which is a small one down and down and then suddenly there is a big explosion.' "[93] After reading *The Autobiography,* Sherwood Anderson wrote to Stein that she "took such big patches of skin off Hemmy," he felt sorry for him. Several times Hemingway struck back, but never so strongly as in *A Moveable Feast.* And he struck at Alice even more fiercely than at Gertrude, for who else but Alice is that "someone" who spoke to Stein as Hemingway—who had seen life at its lowest, rawest, most brutal, as he would have had us believe—had "never, anywhere, ever" heard the like of? But if the writing is simply poor Hemingway, the attitude toward women in love is no less than deplorable.

In a very short Hemingway story titled *The Sea Change,* Alice Toklas's biographer aptly points out, the attitude is directly expressed. The Hemingway hero is suddenly confronted with a situation in which his girl friend informs him that she is quitting him *for another woman.* "I'll kill her," he cries. "I swear to God I will." (With his Boy Scout knife?) "Couldn't you just be good to me and let me go?" his girl friend pleads, but he could neither be good to her, let her go, nor understand her. To Hemingway's hero, a woman loving a woman was a vice.[94]

Alice never doubted that she had been right in ridding Gertrude and herself of Hemingway. One can even imagine her "screaming" at Gertrude that if she persisted in seeing him, she, Alice, would leave her, and that that might have been the basis of what Hemingway had overheard. "And when you are old," Gertrude would write, ". . . you can get your way by being angry."[95]

A more enduring problem troubled the two throughout the twenties. Despite Stein's growing reputation, her pile of manuscripts was not being greatly reduced. Little magazines, such as *transition* and the *Transatlantic Review,* and publishers of small editions, such as Leonard and Virginia Woolf, who brought out Stein's *Composition As Explanation,* were of help, but the audience she sought still escaped her. At this time Alice decided to undertake the publishing of Gertrude's work, calling her venture the Plain Edition. The first book to appear with that imprint was *Lucy Church Amiably;* the cost of bringing out one thousand copies was met by selling off Picasso's *Girl with a Fan.* (Gertrude once remarked that Cézanne had similarly "paid for the heating system.") There were still mounds of *Lucy Church* in the cupboards of the apartment on the rue Christine in the mid-forties, but the sight of her book in store windows gave Gertrude "a childish delight amounting almost to ecstasy."[96]

From typist to publisher, Alice seems inextricable from Gertrude's work. However, when asked once about her influence upon it, she had replied, "Not as much as landscape."[97] Almost as great as the modesty of the remark is its truth. From 1923 Gertrude and Alice had been summering in Savoy. Soon they rented a great house in Bilignin, a minuscule suburb of Belley, from which they could occasionally glimpse the Alps. Here Alice learned to weed, to garden vegetables and flowers, and to preserve fruit, while Gertrude ruminated and constructed phrases to the rhythm of cows munching grass. Several dogs were added to the scene: Basket I, a royal-size white poodle with a classical lion-cut, and Pépé, a tiny Chihuahua given to Alice by the painter Picabia. It all entered Gertrude's writing as a kind of collage, sometimes as the subject matter. For instance, the poem "To Basket": "A lion. Can be. A dog./Or. A lion. Can be. A lamb./ . . . Or a dog."[98]

The poem, like so much of her work, was posthumously published. The problem of contemporary publication remained very real. There were a few admirers, but there were more scoffers. One American critic gave Stein's morale a boost, though he qualified his comment. "Whenever we pick up her writings, however unintelligible we may find them," wrote Edmund Wilson, "we are aware of a literary personality of unmistakable originality and distinction."[99] That made Gertrude begin to feel "historic," but it was still insufficient. Alice read, validated, criticized, typed, and above all approved—and shoved. "Shove," Gertrude would shortly write, "is a proof of love."[100]

Nineteen thirty-two proved the critical year and turning point. Not until spring of that year did Alice Toklas know about Stein's unpublished novel of 1903, *Q.E.D.* Not, that is, until Gertrude "happened" to "discover" the manuscript and show it to Alice at the same time that she was showing it to an influential writer, Louis Bromfield, who thought its subject matter did not allow much chance of publication. Alice was furious when she learned from Gertrude about May Bookstaver. Violently she demanded the letters upon which Stein had based a great part of *Q.E.D.,* and "in a passion" (Alice's phrase[101]) she destroyed them. Had not she and Gertrude supposedly told each other about all others before joining their lives? *Now* she was told the story of this love affair! Not Bromfield, but rather Alice, determined the fate of the manuscript. She took charge of it. She saw to its not being published before Gertrude's death, and even then (1950) profoundly regretted having authorized its printing, though that was limited to 516 copies.[102]

"Some of the people in it," Alice gave as her reason, "are still alive." In fact, it was because her hurt was still very much alive. Alice, as she liked to say, could more easily forget than forgive, and she had forgotten nothing.

The *Autobiography of Alice B. Toklas* was Gertrude's payoff to Alice.[103]

Was it a direct demand for a payoff? Gertrude was self-driven, as well; her courage in plodding her own lonely road, save for Alice and a few strangers, is clear evidence of it. Continually she wondered not only about why she wrote as she did, but why she wrote at all. She posed the problem in a narrative poem, "Winning His Way" (actually, *her* way):

> The problem resolves itself. Into this.
> Does a poem. Continue. Because of. A Kiss.
> Or because. Of future greatness.
> Or because. There is no cause. Why.[104]

Was she writing for Alice ("a kiss"), Gertrude asked herself, for *la gloire* ("future greatness"), or for the compulsive need to write and for no other reason or cause? Even for Alice it was never merely the case of "a kiss," but often of forceful demanding. "Who is winning," writes Gertrude in *Stanzas in Meditation* (1932), "why the answer of course is she is."[105] Alice was winning by putting pressure on Gertrude to write a book that would bring fame and, with it, money—a popular book.

Thus Gertrude Stein wrote *The Autobiography of Alice B. Toklas* with the clear, sometimes rasping voice of Alice Toklas. Though the experience would shake Stein with a sense of making some betrayal of herself, it would not be the first time she had spoken in her work with Alice's voice. "Do I sound like Alice," she asked in *A Circular Play* (1920) after a few lines of dialogue. She did. *The Autobiography,* however, would be the first and unique work in which she would sustain that alter ego voice for the length of a book.

It was not easy. Despite Stein's assertion in the last paragraph of the last page of *The Autobiography* (where she first discloses that she is the author), the writing did not take six weeks, but, rather, six months, which is prodigious enough. There were "several false starts," as a notebook at Yale records, before Stein found Alice's voice and the writing began to flow more smoothly.[106] But even as she wrote Alice's "autobiography" by day, in the evening and sometimes at night Gertrude worked on her own *Stanzas in Meditation!* "This is her autobiography, one of two," she writes in *Stanzas.* "But which it is no one, which it is, can know" (my punctuation).[107] But one does. Throughout *Stanzas* there is a nocturnal debate about what she is writing—with Alice's aid, advice, and occasional correction of a date or citation—during the day:

> It is not easy to turn away from delight in moon-light.
> She asked could I be taught . . .
> And I said yes oh yes . . .
> How I wish I were able to say what I think
> In the meantime I can not doubt.
>
> I wish to say
> That it is her day.[108]

The day was indeed Alice's, and part of the night. What is still to be established is how often, thanks to her "paranoid" insistence, the word "may" in *Stanzas* was changed to "can," even if it made no sense, because "may" recalled May Bookstaver![109]

Stein's *Autobiography of Alice B. Toklas*—a rich, witty, stinging account of the Paris of the 1900s to 1932, a work that "still stands up to any amount of re-reading"[110]—won the fame, audience, success, and money, notably in America, that had been hoped for. It also brought a crisis of identity for Stein and, briefly, a writing block. She whom I had so often heard say, "Whatever happens, do not be seduced by your audience," she who had always written for herself and "strangers," as she also frequently repeated, had now deliberately written for an audience—and it greatly bothered her.

Perhaps Stein's return to America as the prodigal, triumphant daughter, following the success of *The Autobiography,* did most to reassure and restore the writer. She was lionized as she went from the east coast to the west coast on a lecture tour, and she loved it. To become a prophet in one's own country may be the supreme gratification. Old friends flocked to see her—rather, tried to see her—but more often than not were held off by Alice, who was still tense because of May Bookstaver.[111] Possibly the most critical moment occurred in California, when Alice flatly turned down a request by Mabel Dodge to renew contact with Gertrude. Did Gertrude threaten to leave Alice in midtour and Alice Gertrude? *Gertrude leave Alice?* Scarcely credible, but even if true, beyond doubt was their return to France together, to remain together until death ruled otherwise. And while in America, Alice, for all the world, convincingly played the devoted, self-effacing St. Teresa herself, as Gertrude persuades us in *Everybody's Biography.*

Asked by a photographer to strike a pose while he took her picture, Gertrude had replied, "All right, what do you want me to do?" He suggested that she unpack her airplane bag, to begin with:

> Oh I said Miss Toklas always does that oh no I could not do that, well he said there is the telephone suppose you telephone well I said yes but I never do Miss Toklas always does that, well he said what can you do, well I said I can put my hat on and take my hat off and I can put my coat on and I can take it off and I like water I can drink a glass of water all right he said do that and he photographed while I did that . . .[112]

Back in Paris, Alice, as usual, unpacked their bags and the possessions they had accumulated, and prepared, as usual, for the summer of 1935 in Bilignin. Here life was "quieter and lovelier" than they even remembered it, and here "we" planted the vegetables and American corn and got to work again on the garden.[113] In other words, life on a daily basis had resumed. An American publisher had promised Gertrude Stein regular publication, beginning with her *Lectures in America.* All was well with the world. Or was it?

Not that Nazism had taken over in Germany or that people were increasingly aware of being prewar. That was not Gertrude's case, nor Alice's. Neither was by character brightly optimistic, despite their practice of cheering up friends, neighbors, and each other. Their "bottom nature," to borrow Stein's phrase, was a pessimistic stoicism. "It is very meritorious to work very hard in a garden," she was writing in Bilignin, and see "green things." But when she shut her eyes and fell asleep, she saw them differently. "The green things then have black roots and the black roots have red stems and then she is exhausted."[114]

One may read conscious or unconscious symbolism in the black and red. After World War II, and shortly before her death, Gertrude remarked, "We are probably entering another Dark Ages, when the only question will be whether we will be bothered by the right or by the left."

Although both Gertrude and Alice were conservative politically, neither was very political in the ordinary sense. "Government is the least interesting thing in human life," Stein told a university dean in America, who had just expressed the contrary opinion,

> creation and the expression of that creation is a damn sight more interesting. . . . The real ideas are not the relation of human beings as a group but a human being to himself inside him and that is an idea that is more interesting than humanity in groups, after all the minute that there are a lot of them they do not do it for themselves but somebody does it for them.[115]

The dark side of Gertrude was turned away from the public—insofar as her writings to herself may be considered private. And that darkness is literal in the ending she chose for her *Doctor Faustus Lights the Lights* (1938). Just before the curtain falls, Faustus "sinks into the darkness and it is all dark and the little boy and the little girl sing Please Mr. Viper listen to me . . ."[116] Gertrude's darkness went back to childhood, and if it was lightened, it was not erased, by Alice Toklas, who joined her intellectually in pessimism and stoicism. Fundamentally they disagreed on nothing of importance—Alice could well have been the "she" who saw the black roots with the red stems at Bilignin; it may be the moral of their endurance as a couple. Each was a union of light and dark.

Gertrude expressed this chiaroscuro aspect when she turned to a portrait of Picasso, the only center, other than herself, of her lifelong speculation about genius and creation. Concluding her portrait—written first in French, with Alice's aid, then in English—Gertrude noted how happy she was to have his paintings back; they had been loaned for a Petit Palais exhibition. They were "more splendid" than she remembered. Then, characteristically, she considers splendor and the contemporary world:

> The twentieth century is more splendid than the nineteenth century. . . . The twentieth century has much less reasonableness in its existence than the nineteenth century but reasonableness does not make for splendor. . . . The twentieth century . . . is a time when everything cracks, where everything is destroyed, everything isolates itself, it is a more splendid thing than a period where everything follows itself.[117]

Oddly, the portrait, with its tribute to Picasso—or perhaps not so oddly—follows close upon their most serious quarrel (demonstrating that it is not quarreling with one's intimates that is fatal, but rather what one does with one's quarrels). Gertrude had heard from Picasso's dealer, Daniel-Henri Kahnweiler, that he had stopped painting in order to write poetry. She had a "funny feeling," Gertrude says, when she heard it. "One does you know. Things belong to you and writing belonged to me," as painting belonged to Picasso. They met soon afterward. Gertrude did not shake him—as the story has come down in its most succinct form—saying, "I write, you paint! I write, you paint!" Rather, Picasso invited Gertrude, Alice, and their friend Thornton Wilder to his apartment and read them his poetry, in French and Spanish. What did Gertrude think of it? Picasso asked with some uneasiness. "Very interesting," she said. And Wilder? "Yes, it is very interesting," he said. On their way back, Stein said to Wilder, "The poetry was not poetry."[118] Picasso recovered from the shock he was then experiencing of separation from his wife Olga, and, of course, resumed painting. (Alice seems never to be recorded by Gertrude in a three- or more-sided conversation, but it is not without reason. Alice normally was either silent or sat apart with the wives of geniuses being talked to by Gertrude—or, when at home, poured tea and served cookies to the guests. She reserved her more acrid remarks for Gertrude's hearing.)

What might have proved a considerable shock for Gertrude and Alice was the forced move from the rue de Fleurus. A bit bluntly, the proprietor of the studio and pavilion announced to them, late in 1937, that he was taking possession for his son, who was about to be married.

"We thought it would be difficult to leave," says Alice, "but it was not. We found a new place at [5,] rue Christine." The dull, dark, short little street made them hesitate, "but when we saw the apartment we were thrilled."[119] They particularly liked the terrace on the roof of an adjoining workshop, to which they had ready access through a ceiling-to-floor window of the salon—ideal for them to look at the stars or to let out the dogs.

If, as Alice declares, it was not difficult to leave the rue de Fleurus, to move to the rue Christine was something else. About one hundred and thirty paintings were involved, plus the furniture, furnishings, linens, silver, books, objects, manuscripts, and the like, of three decades. The chore "naturally" fell to Alice. Poor Alice, wrote Gertrude to the Kiddie, had quite forgotten how to sit "and just went on being on her feet." Natalie Barney, who lived in their new quarter near the Seine, observed the scene and wrote her dear friend Romaine Brooks, "Alice T. is withering away under the stress. . . . I am afraid 'the bigger one,' who gets fatter and fatter and fatter, will sooner or later devour her. She looks so thin . . ."[120] (Natalie Barney's pen, in private, could be particularly sharp.)

Gertrude and Alice settled in at 5, rue Christine, but not for long. Despite Gertrude's wishful attitude toward the "illogicality" of war, she agreed with the "forethoughtful" Alice that typing copies of all her manuscripts and sending them to America for safekeeping at Yale University would be a good idea, in case . . . "In case" arrived in September 1939, and war found them at Bilignin. Rather than taking refuge in the United States, as friends urged, they decided to stick it out in France, where they felt at home. A hurried trip was made back to Paris, in order to pick up their passports and take care of the paintings. At the rue Christine, however, the only identity paper they could lay their hands on was Basket II's pedigree (Basket I had died the year previous). Finding that paper, nonetheless, was fortunate, says Alice, "as it enabled us to obtain a ration for Basket II during the Occupation." As for the paintings, Gertrude and Alice commenced by taking them from the walls and placing them on the floor to protect them from bomb concussion. "But we found that there was less room on the floor than on the walls, so the idea was abandoned."[121] They could bring back only two paintings to Bilignin. The choice was significant: Picasso's portrait of Gertrude and Cézanne's of his wife—the work of the two painters who had the greatest meaning for Gertrude's own work.

The war years were marked by the civilian's preoccupation—procuring food. Happily, there was the large vegetable garden at Bilignin, which Alice exploited fully, and the black market, where Gertrude did the negotiating, since she had the "personality" for it—a cheerful authority. Paramount was the protection of a close friend, Bernard Faÿ, wartime Director of the Bibliothèque Nationale and extremely influential with the Vichy government. He personally persuaded Marshal Pétain to have the local prefect receive special instructions to watch over them. Once, when Faÿ was told that German officers were about to pick up the "degenerate" paintings at the rue Christine, he arranged to have a seal placed on the apartment door, which saved the collection. (The wax seal, with a faintly visible swastika stamped on it, could still be seen by visitors after the Liberation. Gertrude had simply refused to notice it or the fact that Germans had been in the apartment and rifled through some of their possessions.)

The presence of Germans—after all, France had been occupied—was similarly ignored, to the extent possible. At this time, Gertrude and Alice were in Culoz, in another house, the one at nearby Bilignin having been retaken by its owner for his family. Gertrude had spent the first year of the war writing a nostalgic *Paris France;* the second year composing a novel as well as stories for children; and in 1942, as a gesture of gratitude, she undertook a translation of Pétain's speeches, intended for American publication, which is still in manuscript at Yale University. Alice, much of this time, gardened, cooked, typed, and dreamed of food, reading cookbooks far into the night—and eventually would write a superb one of her own. During one night she had had the fantasy of a "long silver dish, floating on air" with three large slices of ham lying upon it, a dream that haunted her "for months."[122] In 1940 Alice had, even then, prepared the ingredients for a "Liberation Fruit Cake," filling pots and jars with kilos of lemons, lemon peel, pineapple, cherries, sugared oranges, and raisins, and then carefully put them out of sight. In September 1944 Alice joyfully baked the cake for General Patch, commander of the U.S. forces, which had come up from the south to liberate Gertrude, Alice, and Savoy. An American correspondent flying to New York took with him Gertrude's manuscript of *Wars I Have Seen;* it would appear, with the peace, as a book, signaling that all was well with Gertrude Stein and Alice B. Toklas.

Not before December, however, were the two able to pack their things for the return to Paris, taking only one painting with them—Picasso's portrait of Gertrude. Badly in need of money in 1943, they had driven to Switzerland to sell the Cézanne portrait and had then *driven back* to France, refusing Swiss residence for the rest of the war (to their friends' astonishment). "We ate the Cézanne," I can still hear Alice saying. On the road back to Paris in a truck they had hired (their car had been given to the Red Cross), the two were stopped at the break of day by two men and a woman in the Resistance. Who are you and what do you have there? they were asked. The men and woman leaned over the painting, says Alice, "and I said, Take care, that is a painting by Picasso, don't disturb it. And they said, We congratulate you, madame, you may go on."[123] Gertrude and Alice reached Paris while it was still daylight.

The next morning, Alice recalled, she scrounged in the kitchen to find what she could to make coffee, "and then Picasso came in. He and Gertrude embraced, and all of us rejoiced that the treasures of our youth, the pictures, the drawings, were safe."[124]

My memory is somewhat different.[125] Early that winter I was walking with Stein on a street in Paris, when someone called, "Gertrude! Gertrude!" The *g* was soft, the cry unforgettably affectionate. "Pablo!" said Gertrude. They embraced. They had not seen each other since the war, I was led to understand. Gertrude presented me as her "adopted nephew." Picasso looked at both of us suspiciously. "He is always Spanish-suspicious," she said afterward. They saw each other occasionally; Picasso showed her what he had done during their long separation. I do not know what she said to him, but during a walk she spoke of his war paintings, saying, "You know, Joe, I'm getting tired of the maltreated human figure." She spoke almost in a whisper, half turning as if to see who might be overhearing. The last memory before Picasso returned to the Mediterranean: Alice was in the kitchen. Somehow Gertrude and Picasso had begun to argue about who was the taller. They stood stiffly back to back, stretching upward, as I measured them. "Don't count the hair," said Picasso. "I won't," I said, pressing down on their heads with the spine of a book. They were exactly the same height.

Gertrude had begun her play *Yes Is For A Very Young Man* (also called *In Savoy*) before she and Alice left Culoz for Paris. Here she reworked it, asking for help to make it into a classical, three-act play. She then rejected the advice of a Broadway director (Josh Logan) and of a Hollywood screenwriter (Alan Campbell), both in American uniforms, who had been brought to her. She was right; she usually was. She was not a "classical" writer; that way would have lain oblivion. In the case of *Yes,* one can easily see Gertrude as Constance (she said she had thought of Clare Boothe Luce, seen at Bilignin with her husband, Henry, the summer before the war). The middle-aged American woman sagely listening to a divided French family and ambiguously appealing to its postadolescent son recreates the scene of Gertrude and the young Hemingway, Gertrude and all her young men. Now, as GIs in Paris, they flocked to the rue Christine, drawn by the legendary figure and held by a physical magnetism and a provocative word. Few of them have forgotten their passage through that salon, how Gertrude talked and how she had *listened.* It is all there in *Brewsie and Willie,* the book the GIs in camps throughout western Europe, where she toured, had asked her to write for them—Gertrude's and their worries and concerns about jobs and industrialism and declining individualism in America. "Find out the reason why," admonishes Stein, "look the facts in the face, not just what they all say . . . find out the reason why of the depression, find it out each and every one of you . . ." Gertrude ended her peroration in the manuscript with "I am an American."

I told her I liked the work, except for the ending—too flag-waving and personal. "Don't worry," said Alice, in an aside. "It will be changed in the typing." It was, and now the last line reads, "We are Americans."[126] Alice had had the last word. How many times had that been true? One wonders.

When she began her last composition, Gertrude was already ill, but neither she nor Alice knew how fatally sick she was. Certainly Gertrude did not think of *The Mother of Us All*—a libretto for Virgil Thomson's musical setting, with America's nineteenth-century suffragette as its heroine—as her last statement. But never had she spoken so forthrightly on men, women, feminism, and marriage as in her last, moving work. Without intending to, Gertrude painted a self-portrait in Susan B. Anthony as a woman who courageously faced ridicule in the struggle for the vote, as had Gertrude to write according to her principles, and ultimately won. She even placed Alice at her side, as Susan B.'s good companion Anne. Various friends also appear in the opera, including this author as Jo the Loiterer.[127]

"My father's name was Daniel," says Gertrude Stein, introducing Daniel Webster, Susan B. Anthony's male antagonist and the epitome of male pretentiousness. He had been accused of sleeping while a fellow senator orated. "The right to sleep is given to no woman," sings Susan B. She hoists an American flag. "I say fight for the right [to vote], be a martyr and live, be a coward and die . . ." Men, says Susan B., are conservative, selfish, boresome, ugly, gullible, monotonous bullies. "Yes," says Anne, "they are poor things." Susan B.: "Men want to be half slave half free. Women want to be all slave or all free." Yet, let women marry so that they can tell men that "two and two make four." Otherwise men would never know it. Anne: "I will never marry." Susan B.: "I am not married and the reason why is that I have had to do what I have had to do, I have had to be what I have had to be . . ."

Men are afraid, declares Susan B.: "They fear women, they fear each other, they fear their neighbor, they fear other countries and then they hearten themselves in their fear by crowding together and following each other, and when they crowd together and follow each other they are brutes . . ." Anne: "You will win." "Win what?" "The vote for women." Susan B.: "By that time it will do them no good because . . . they will become like men."[128]

Victory is won; women can vote—after Susan B. Anthony's death. And thereafter in the closing scene of *The Mother of Us All,* Susan B. sings from behind a statue of herself. "All my long life of strength and strife, all my long life . . ." she intones. The male chorus now bows and smiles to the statue. Was it worth it? Was there an alternative to her struggle? "We cannot retrace our steps," Susan B. tiredly replies to herself. (There is no second act in American lives, said F. Scott Fitzgerald.) One must go forward, even if "going forward may be the same as going backwards," says Susan B. And now "we are here, in marble and gold." But where is here, where is where? Long silence. "Do I want what we have got, has it not gone, what made it live, has it not gone because now it is had." Silence. "My long life, my long life," sighs Susan B. Curtain.[129]

My last long ride with Gertrude and Alice was to Bernard Faÿ's country place in the Indre-et-Loire, in July 1946. Faÿ himself was in prison for having collaborated during the Occupation. It gave Gertrude much concern.[130] She was up front in the car, and in discomfort. Occasionally she pressed her stomach. She must do something about changing her corset, she said, as the doctor had advised. Alice was studying the map and giving directions from the rear seat. It was Gertrude's car, but I was driving. We reached our destination at Luceau. I was to stay a few days, then take the train back to Paris. In the meantime we went on a quick trip to see the château at Azay-le-Rideau. On the road there Gertrude clutched at her stomach, in great pain, and we stopped at the nearest inn and put her to bed. Frightened, Alice hastily sent for a doctor. He came. He examined Gertrude and told Alice, "Your friend must be cared for by a specialist, at once!" Gertrude's nephew Allan was phoned and told of the situation. It was arranged to have him meet the two at the train station the next day. (I was to pick up our things at Luceau and drive the car back to Paris.) Aboard the train, Gertrude refused to have a nurse, and went from one side of the train to the other to look at the passing landscape. At the station in Paris, they were startled to find an ambulance waiting to take

Gertrude to the American Hospital, but "she put up with it," thanked Allan, "and went to bed . . ."[131]

A group of doctors was consulted at the hospital. They agreed that Gertrude had cancer of the stomach, but decided she was too weak then to be operated upon. Days of delay did not improve her condition or alleviate her pain. She sent for the director of the hospital and told him to send her a "younger surgeon," who would do what she asked of him. He arrived. She said, "I order you to operate. I was not made to suffer." The other doctors disputed Gertrude's demand, but the young surgeon replied that he had given his word of honor to operate, and a promise given to "a woman of her character" was meant to be kept. He would operate.[132]

The last words belong to Gertrude and Alice, written, this time, for Gertrude by Alice:

> [By now Gertrude] was in a sad state of indecision and worry. I sat next to her and she said to me early in the afternoon, What is the answer? I was silent. In that case, she said, what is the question? Then the whole afternoon was troubled, confused and very uncertain, and later in the afternoon they took her away on a wheeled stretcher to the operating room and I never saw her again.[133]

· Epilogue ·

On March 11, 1967, the little coffin—so like the sad little coffins of children—was lowered next to the older, larger coffin of Gertrude Stein at the Père Lachaise cemetery. Gertrude and Alice were together again in the earth of Paris, as they had been in life.[134]

Between Gertrude's death twenty and a half years before and her own death at eighty-nine, Alice Toklas had known moments of success and years of hardship. The success was her own work as she came forth from her widowhood; the hardship, ironically, was Gertrude Stein's will (there was no automatic protection for an unmarried companion).

The will had been made out by Gertrude as she lay waiting for her operation at the American Hospital. It would give Alice Toklas many of her problems, though Alice said not a word about it in her memoirs; nor did I hear her complain of it during her lifetime. Stein had bequeathed her Picasso portrait to New York's Metropolitan Museum (where it now is). She had authorized payment from her estate of all sums "necessary for the publication of my unpublished manuscripts"—and Alice saw to it that she lived to witness that wish, fulfilled by the eight-volume Yale University edition of the *Unpublished Writings of Gertrude Stein* (1951–1958).

No sacrifice was too much on Alice's part for this publication, though Stein had left "the rest and residue" of her estate "to my friend Alice B. Toklas . . . for her use for life and . . . proper maintenance," authorizing for that purpose the sale of "any paintings or other personal property belonging to my Estate." (The paintings alone would be valued at well over $6 million.) In the same will, however, and in gratitude for Michael's support, Stein had also left the estate, on Alice's death, to her brother's descendants—to his son Allan and, on *his* death, to his children. The final complication was Stein's having her will probated in the State of Maryland, because, to serve this end, she had established herself as a U.S. citizen legally domiciled in Baltimore.[135]

To sell a painting for her "proper maintenance," Alice Toklas had to go through the Baltimore executors of Stein's will, who were far away and distant indeed. In fact, Alice did not want to sell off *any* of the paintings. She hoped to keep them together, to have them bought by a museum and preserved as the Gertrude Stein Collection, "as Gertrude would have wished," she said. Thus a situation resulted as tangled as Stein's 1924 piece, entitled *Which One Will,* which prophetically concludes: ". . . which one will be seizing it as property which one will which one will have it at the start and which one will fairly well.[136] That is, which one will fare well? Certainly not Alice. Wherefore the irony that her hardship was due to Gertrude's "will," for that surely was not Gertrude's intention.

Alice lived on a small allowance from Gertrude's estate, agreed to by the heirs, which was slow to arrive and increasingly inadequate. There were monies as well from a few articles, and the royalties from her cookbook (1954) and her memoirs (1963). *The Alice B. Toklas Cook Book* is, to be sure, about cooking—and *Moby-Dick* is the story of a whale hunt. But in it are the comments of a richly provisioned life, of a cool and witty temperament found only at the highest attitudes. Alice's *What Is Remembered* tells anyone who never experienced it exactly what a conversation with Alice was like. And since conversation is the essence of companionship and her way with stories was the quintessence of Alice Toklas, her memoirs record for us that vital aspect of her twinship with Gertrude Stein (the most germinal conversationalist I have known). Slightly past the midpoint in the writing of her memoirs, Alice had to *talk* the rest to a secretary, since her declining vision allowed no alternative.

Almost blind, at the age of eighty-eight Alice Toklas insisted on an eye operation to remove one of two cataracts, so that she might read rather than be read to. Back home, the bandage removed, she picked up Henry James's *Tragic Muse* and commenced rereading it.

Home, the last home, was on the rue de la Convention, which is about as far as you can get from the Latin Quarter and still be on the Left Bank. It was from there that the little coffin was taken a hundred meters to the local church, followed by a few friends. Alice had been forced to move from the rue Christine, and someday there may be a plaque on the house at number 5 (as there is at 27, rue de Fleurus), which, if forthright, would read:

> Here lived Gertrude Stein, famous American writer, and Alice B. Toklas, her lifelong companion, from 1938 until Miss Stein's death in 1946 and Miss Toklas's expulsion in 1964.

It would be one of Paris's less delightful landmarks.

In 1964, the process server had come to the apartment on the rue Christine and found Alice in bed with a broken hip. Politely he read her the expulsion order (she could not read then), and carefully noted her reply: "I was born in 1877. If I leave this apartment, it will be to go to Père Lachaise." As eventually she did, via the rue de la Convention.

Trying to recover from pneumonia and broken bones and cope with arthritis, in 1960 Alice had gone to the baths at Acqui and a convent in Rome. She was away from the apartment on the rue Christine for about seven months. According to the law, a rented apartment could not be left vacant for more than four months in one year without a legitimate reason, so the owner of Alice's apartment sued for repossession. The reason offered the court was Alice's health. The court replied that perhaps she should move permanently south for her health, and she was expelled.

That trip to Rome also stripped the walls of the apartment of Stein's collection of paintings. The heirs (on Alice's death)—Michael Stein's grown grandchildren, since Allan had died—declared the paintings "endangered" by Alice's absence. The day before her return from Rome, they had been taken away by the Seine tribunal and cached in the vault of a Paris bank. Alice had almost lost them once before, having sold several Picasso drawings through Kahnweiler for her "proper maintenance." She had sold them, the heirs objected, without authorization from the estate's executors. She replied that she had had Picasso's authorization.

During the last years of her life, Alice lived largely on the charity of friends. For three of those years she lay in bed between the bare stucco walls of the rue de la Convention apartment. She took it with her customary stoicism, saying she could not see very well and in any case the paintings were alive in her memory. But she missed them very much. Gertrude's presence was in the paintings. So Alice lay on her bed and waited.

Not long before her coffin was lowered next to Gertrude's the Spanish maid, Jacinta, asked Alice if she wanted something to eat. She shook her head. Jacinta asked her if she wanted something to drink. She shook her head. She asked her if she wanted to die. Alice nodded. Yes.

9

THE REINVENTION OF ROMANTIC LOVE: JEAN COCTEAU AND JEAN MARAIS

> Instead of adopting as gospel Rimbaud's line, "Ours is the time of assassins," youth would do better to retain his phrase, "Love is to be reinvented."
>
> —Jean Cocteau, *Le Livre blanc*

PLAYFULLY, Aristophanes suggested during Plato's famous banquet that the origin of love was an imperfect human being's longing for completion; that originally we were double, but having become impious, we were punished by Zeus. We were split into two, and ever since, our bereaved halves have wandered in search of each other so that we may become whole again. It is sometimes forgotten that Aristophanes' originally intact beings were of *three* kinds; namely, all-male, all-female, and androgynous (half male and half female). Thus the divided male sought the missing male half, the female the missing female half, and the divided androgynous being the one or the other—the male half seeking the female half, or the female the missing male half.

Since the male pursuing the female, and the female the male, represent the plurality of the human experience, it might be argued that normally androgyny is wholeness.

In ancient Greece, however, at least among the privileged élite, it was so often the older male half in search of a younger, as if seeking rejuvenation by amorous grafting, that normality was, let us put it, statistically different. The classic Greek story is that of an older man loving a youth until the youth, at twenty-eight or thereabout, becomes a man and seeks, in his turn, usually after marriage, a younger lad. It is the handsome Alcibiades, as a mature, respected general, who brings Plato's banquet to a close, speaking admiringly of Socrates as the spiritual leader and lover of his youth. In the playful spirit of Aristophanes, then, one might suggest that a strain of the Platonic heritage —from feasting to civilized discourse and attitudes toward love and other politics—persists in French culture, and most insistently in homosexual culture, since the rebirth of classical culture.

TWO youths counted most in Jean Cocteau's life, and he in theirs—Raymond Radiguet and Jean Marais.

"It was Radiguet," says Marais, "who counted most." But he was in Cocteau's life so briefly, one objects.[1]

Raymond Radiguet was ten days short of his sixteenth birthday when he met and intrigued Jean Cocteau, fourteen years older, on June 8, 1919. Yet he was not the beautiful youth who would have brought feasting Athenians to a breathless silence upon his entry. "He was small, pale, and nearsighted," Cocteau tells us.[2] Nor did Radiguet favor older—or younger—men. He was preternaturally "normal." *At fourteen* he had fathered a child with a twenty-seven-year-old teacher, whose husband was away at the front. Nevertheless his meeting with Cocteau has been aptly described as comparable to that of Rimbaud with Verlaine. He had published some poetry and drawings; he immediately intimidated Cocteau with his high adolescent scorn even as he impressed him with signs of prodigal genius. Yet Cocteau himself had known adulation and fame for more than a decade!

COCTEAU came, he relates, like "all" writers and artists of his time, from a bourgeois family. ("Set aside your Baudelairean prejudices," he advises. "Baudelaire was a bourgeois." It gave him his "foundation," as that side of Cocteau would lead him to the French Academy.[3]) He was born on July 5, 1889, in Maisons-Laffitte, a kind of aristocratic Southhampton of Paris, sixteen miles west of the capital. "Here the racehorse and the bicycle reigned. Here we played tennis on each other's tennis courts in a bourgeois world torn by the Dreyfus affair."[4]

Jean's family on his mother's side was wealthy, cultivated, and very well connected; on his father's side, just cultivated. The Cocteaus spent most of the year in their Paris residence below Montmartre (when the butte was noted for its gardens rather than for seedy nightclubs). Jean's father was more subdued, more withdrawn than his mother, we are informed by the son, very likely because of a covert homosexuality—

and he killed himself, as a consequence, before Jean was ten. He had been a "sad, charming man"—sad, Cocteau says, because he failed to come to terms with himself. "Undoubtedly he was unaware of his tendency," but he committed suicide as a result; "in his time people killed themselves for less."[5]

An elegant, polished bachelor uncle—his mother's brother, and a distinguished career diplomat—became somewhat of a model for Jean's life style as a dandy, but not for his "singular" way of life. That choice or direction was clearly indicated to him, Cocteau says, when he fainted in a kind of ecstasy at the sight of a nude peasant boy astride a work horse in the family park. "As far back as I can remember. . . . I have always loved the stronger sex, which I think can be legitimately called the beautiful sex." And sexuality, one might assert with at least equal legitimacy, whether in fairy-tale costume or stark naked, was the core of Cocteau's writing (in a letter to a friend, he said, "It gives my work its strength"). With little surprise, then, one reads his description of the classroom at the Lycée Condorcet, where he entered as a third-year student and discovered masturbatory sexuality rampant: "The class smelled of gas, chalk, and sperm. The mixture made me want to throw up."[6]

One can believe Cocteau. He was essentially fastidious and essentially, if imaginatively, honest about himself. ("The lie that tells the truth," he liked to say, claiming the poet's privilege.) Young Jean, he tells us, was smitten by the comely, bullying Dargelos, and even then understood his emotion for what it was—love. The Dargelos figure recurs in Cocteau's work, in film and in fiction, where he is shown striking down a fellow student with a rock-hardened snowball—the shock of beauty felt by the young Cocteau. It was not simply that Jean wished to be loved by the strong, beautiful ones; he desperately wanted to be one of them, instead of the frail, small, gangly, ill-favored *odd one.* ("I never had a beautiful face." Body, hair, teeth went "in all directions." "My one desire is to overcome the embarrassment I feel and to show myself as I really am."[7])

Expelled from the Condorcet because he did not apply himself, Jean would also fail at another lycée and never obtain a baccalaureate. Jean was bourgeois and anarchic, heir to a culture and self-taught. At fifteen, he says, he ran off to the great port city of Marseilles, and claims, "It set me free!"[8] He seems to have lived with a "beautiful" Arab young man of twenty, besides having a brief affair with a prostitute. Both experiences presumably confirmed his predilection for the male and the beautiful, allowing for an emotional, but passing, liaison with a woman. "Two women," he would write a year before his death, "momentarily made me a misogynist by having abortions and depriving me of sons, forcing me to [adopt] adults."[9] The last of the two liaisons occurred in the early thirties (during Cocteau's forties) with an actress, Princess Natalie Pailey. A woman who was a friend of both had this to say about the affair to Cocteau's most searching biographer:

> Cocteau was all *esprit*—and later, of course, drugs. Even from the beginning almost everything was in his head, and later there was too much opium for sex anyway. Certainly he was no Oscar Wilde of bisexual capabilities. You will not find that women speak very well of Cocteau—they do not have very good memories of him.[10]

One of Cocteau's "adopted" young men, Jean Bourgoint, who became Brother Pascal, clergyman, wrote upon Cocteau's death in 1963, completing the above portrait by the Vicomtesse de Noailles: "He was profoundly chaste. Just as he smoked his opium chastely, like the Chinese sages, so in his loves he was of a delicacy and temperance of heart seldom found in the commonalty of men, and seldom even in poets."[11]

For Cocteau, the homosexuality he would openly affirm—a bold gesture at the time—was "strength loving strength." "The beautiful man is an *objet d'art.* The beautiful woman is a utensil . . . for making children."[12] His attitude was more than momentary misogeny. The theme is pounded like a nail that homosexuality between men is the true virility—"the conjugation of manly strengths"—since only men are involved![13] Strength, as we have already noted, is what Cocteau admired, *envied,* not finding it physically in himself. His passivity, furthermore, has been clearly delineated *by himself,* and signally, in his autobiographical novel, *Le Livre blanc* (The White Book), so frankly homophile that it was originally published anonymously to avoid giving pain to his mother. The setting is a Turkish bath. Young men are being offered to him at a price (Cocteau himself may have been twenty). He refuses them, and explains himself: "I must have been an enigma for these youth, accustomed to special demands from their clients. They looked at me incomprehensively, for I prefer chats with them to acts."[14]

RETURNING now to the younger Cocteau in Marseilles: after he spent perhaps the better part of a year there, his family had him fetched home, he says, by two gendarmes. However, because of his audacity, he had won a large measure of freedom and independence, recognized by his family. When, shortly thereafter, he met and kept intimate company with a flamboyant actor, Edouard de Max, soon a star of the Comédie Française—about whom mothers said to one another, "What, your son associates with de Max? He is lost!" as they would say it of the adult Cocteau—Jean's mother seems to have said not a word ("she had confidence in me, she was perfect"[15]). Had she not given him the "red-and-gold fever" of the theater as a child?

Cocteau's very conception of life was as a stage upon which he never ceased to perform, and he pleaded with his public, "Play along with me!" One memory of him involves a late-afternoon cocktail at the Vicomtesse de Noailles's apartment, where he was choosing her jewelry for the evening. His *rivière* of phrases, his famous hands, so like an anatomical drawing of da Vinci and long as those of the ancient Pharaohs, flash in my memory as much as the diamonds.[16]

As for young Cocteau's associating with actor de Max, his mother's permissiveness left him free to experience his first public fiasco. Costumed, bewigged, and made up to his painted toenails as Emperor Heliogabalus, Jean had gone with de Max and two other youth, all extravagantly costumed, to a theater ball. "People laughed in our faces. Sarah Bernhardt dispatched her maid Mlle. Seylor with this message for me: 'If I were your mother, I would send you straight to bed.' I sniffled back my tears. My mascara ran, burning my face." De Max, seeing his blunder, took the youth home.[17]

Nevertheless, it was de Max who gave eighteen-year-old Jean Cocteau his earliest moment of glory. The actor rented a theater on the Champs-Elysées and organized a matinee, when he and other celebrated performers assembled by him read out to a chic Parisian audience from Jean's poetry. It was the beginning of a spectacular career —"that afternoon marked my point of departure."[18] (There would be many "points of departure" in Cocteau's career.) Three slim volumes of verse would be published within three years—*La Lampe d'Aladin, Le Prince frivole,* and *La Danse de Sophocle.* All three would be dismissed by the mature Cocteau as "three silly nothings." He would not include them in his *Collected Works,* but they brought the young poet the adulation of duchesses, evenings in the salons, and acquaintance with the literary, including André Gide, who turned hostile, and Marcel Proust, who kept his distance but remained friendly.

These were the years that also brought an escapade in Venice, where a close companion committed suicide and scandal became a permanent fixture in the Cocteau saga. A la Byron and the Romantics, Jean believed, he had first to live what he would write. But by far the most important event was Cocteau's meeting, at the age of twenty-one, Serge de Diaghilev, gifted, sardonic director of the Ballets Russes. "From that moment I became a member of the troupe." Encouraged by Diaghilev and especially Léon Bakst, the company's designer, Cocteau turned his hand to painting the company's posters. The first (a collector's item) featured a dramatic and colorful drawing of Nijinsky in *Le Spectre de la rose.* Others followed. Thus painting and drawing joined poetry among Cocteau's accomplishments. His talent would be to have many talents, and he now went on to write the libretto of an unsuccessful ballet, *Le Dieu bleu,* although it was danced by Nijinsky. Nonetheless it was another beginning, at the age of twenty-two, and not long afterward came yet another turning point in his life—"the first sound of a bell signaling the opening of a period beginning in 1912, which will not close before my death." That bell was sounded by Diaghilev, one night on the Place de la Concorde.

> We were returning from supper after a performance. Nijinsky was sulking, as usual, and walking ahead of us. Diaghilev was mildly amused by my absurdities. When I asked him why he seemed so reserved (I was more accustomed to praise), he stopped, adjusted his monocle, and said, *"Etonne-moi,* Jean. Astound me." The idea of surprise, so dear to Apollinaire, had never before occurred to me.
>
> In 1917, on the opening night of *Parade,* I astounded him.[19]

Stravinsky, Stein, and a world war, however, were to intervene. A year or two before Diaghilev's ringing command, Cocteau had met the Russian composer, then in his late twenties and newly arrived in Paris; but only after the Ballets Russes performed Stravinsky's *Rite of Spring* in 1913 did he really understand, he says, what Diaghilev had meant.[20] The same year he began what he called his "serious" work, with a protosurrealist novel, *Le Potomak,* whose inspiration he variously attributed to Stravinsky's *Rite of Spring* and to Gertrude Stein's *Tender Buttons.* Why not to both? It was a single phrase in *Tender Buttons*—"Dining is west"—so striking it seemed to stick out in the middle of a blank page, that pointed him in the new direction, he declared, like "an arrow on a road sign," setting him free to transcribe his dreams.[21]

World War I saw Cocteau doing ambulance service with the Red Cross, having been found physically unfit—to his vexation—for army duty. He soon became an observer for Roland Garros, a young but already talked-about aviator (eventually shot down and taken prisoner when Jean was not with him). Actually Cocteau spent a good deal of the war in Paris, making it possible for him, at last, to meet Picasso—the "great encounter" of his life. It would lead to their collaboration on the project already taking shape in Cocteau's mind. So in 1916 he abruptly—and somewhat mysteriously—chose to "leave the war" for the "real front"—Montparnasse, Paris—and the "great battle" of realizing his dream of himself, Picasso, composer Erik Satie, Diaghilev, and his dancers combining in the creation and production of the first cubist ballet, the now-historical burlesque sideshow, *Parade.*[22]

The salesmanship involved in getting so many egos to work together as a team was on the order of *diplomatic* genius; to present a libretto and story line that would grip them all with enthusiasm was *pure* genius. Designing costumes and scenery for the first time, Picasso worked closely with Cocteau, which meant that both went down to Rome, where Diaghilev and his troupe were wintering. Cocteau called it a wedding trip. Before going, he suggested their dropping in on Gertrude Stein and telling her about it. Stein: "One day Picasso came in and with him and leaning on his shoulder was a slim elegant youth. It is Jean, announced Pablo, Jean Cocteau and we are leaving for Italy . . . He was very lively at the prospect of going to Rome."[23] The idea of going on to something new and leaving his followers behind delighted Picasso.

Parade opened on May 18, 1917, and had the instant success of *scandale,* reminiscent of the premiere of Stravinsky's *Rite of Spring.* Cocteau's story and characters—a country fair in Paris; an itinerant theater; a Chinese conjurer, an American girl, two acrobats, and three barker-managers—did indeed "astound." Surround them with Picasso's splendid front curtain, scenery, wild costumes, and cubist horse; animate them with Satie's dry, crackling music-hall themes and Massine's saucy choreography; and one can almost feel the impact on the first-night audience and ballet critics—an impact so strong that Diaghilev was obliged to *withdraw Parade* after the critics counterattacked! No matter. With *Parade* Cocteau opened the great festive ball that would be Paris, beginning with the closing of World War I and ending with the start of the Great Depression in the late twenties.

Following *Parade,* Cocteau assembled his war poetry, which he had first read in the salons of Paris, under the title, *Le Cap de Bonne-Espérance (Cape of Good Hope),* then swiftly became the spokesman for modern music with a manifesto, *Le Coq et l'arlequin (The Cock* [as in *Coc-*teau] *and the Harlequin).*

Thus, the twenty-nine-year-old Jean Cocteau whom the fifteen-year-old Raymond Radiguet now met, in 1919, was not so much the "notorious" corrupter of youth as the prodigious *artiste-*personality of his time. And the Radiguet whom Cocteau encountered was not one of the golden-haired boys who brought his heart to a stop, then to pounding, but rather the phenomenal adolescent, who had *already* fathered a child at fourteen with a twenty-seven-year-old instructress—and would soon transcribe that love affair into a first novel that would propel him into the front ranks of French literature.

The influence of the one upon the other, then, despite the widespread difference in their ages, was remarkably reciprocal. In truth, Radiguet's was the more profound, if only because of Cocteau's unparalleled capacity for absorption, digestion, and recreative *projection.*

One day when she felt annoyed with him, Chanel called Cocteau "an insect that knows how to get all excited." It was an unintended compliment. (On another day she said he was "a poem, but not a poet.")[24] Cocteau had his sensitive antennae out, catching the significant vibrations. He made few aesthetic mistakes; he made the right choices, and his work wears well. That is what to be "avant-garde" really means: the individual who understands his own time is a prophet.

Cocteau admired Radiguet before he loved him; it explains his modesty, his humbleness. "Erik Satie was my schoolmaster, Radiguet my examiner."[25] The boy made the man reexamine the classics and revalue them—if their contemporaries were all trying to astound by being absolutely original and novel, then novelty lost its originality. In this fashion, Radiguet set up the seventeenth century's masterpiece, *La Princesse de Clèves,* as his model, while writing his own, *Le Diable au corps (The Devil in the Flesh).* Do not aim at modernism, he admonished his elder; be sufficiently confident simply to create it. And as Radiguet wrote, under the critical eye and locked-door duress of Cocteau, his astonishingly mature first novel and then went on to *Le Bal du Comte d'Orgel,* Cocteau wrote some of his most durable poetry in *Plain-Chant* (expressing desire and longing for the *sleeping* Radiguet) and prose in *Le Grand Ecart*[26] and *Thomas l'Imposteur* (a still-powerful war novel).

Recalling his several years with Radiguet, Cocteau would write, "Working together is a permanent way of making love."[27] Further extending the idea, it suggests that the essential ingredient of the creative twenties was collective friction of so many artists in Paris rubbing against one another socially and in teamwork. "We were constantly with each other," said Cocteau, "at certain times in my life, talking, discussing the same things, trying out our work before presenting it." And when his mother reproached him for the constant "presence" of young Radiguet in his life, Cocteau asked a woman friend to plead his case. "She doesn't see that this child is a guardian for my work. She cannot understand that two weeks with him are a cure for a year at home."[28]

The time together was tragically short. Stricken by typhoid, erroneously diagnosed as pneumonia, Radiguet died at the age of twenty, December 12, 1923. Cocteau was neither at his side in the hospital nor at the lowering of his coffin in the cemetery. "I did not want to see him on his deathbed," he tried to explain much later. "All the dead resemble each other and do not resemble themselves. They are recumbent figures of wax, their faces are triply locked."[29] For weeks Cocteau lay in bed, then fled to Monte Carlo and took to using opium.

Diaghilev and his company were also at Monte Carlo, but it was some time before Cocteau could bring himself to concentrate on a ballet. It would be the last for Diaghilev—*Le Train bleu*— and it would fail—although the music was by Milhaud, the costumes by Chanel, the stage curtain by Picasso. It was "too slight," Cocteau would recognize. Briefly he returned to the Church (with a public exchange of letters with Jacques Maritain) and underwent a six-week cure for drug addiction (paid for by Chanel), only to return, not too long afterward, to the smoking of opium. The play *Orphée,* an oratorio for Stravinsky's *Oedipus Rex* (which Cocteau would also turn into a play), a revival of yet another play, *Antigone,* and the writing of *Le Livre blanc* were livelier signs of Cocteau's recovery and return to normalcy. Finally, with *Les Enfants terribles,* his ever-popular novel and scripture for several generations of French youth, Cocteau brought the twenties to their close.

The year 1930 was the year of minor miracles and, of course, a major "turning point." Let us quickly place *La Voix humaine*—the pathetic monologue of a woman telephoning her lover, which rivals *Camille* in perpetuity—among the minor miracles; and go on to the major turning point, *Le Sang d'un poète (The Blood of a Poet),* the first modern film *d'auteur,* where the true hero of the film is its film maker, though offscreen.

If the characteristic of Cocteau is this polymorphous activity, his métier, business, *trademark* as that of *the poet,* he has credibly insisted, remained the same. Only the expressive means changed, from verse, to novel, drama, painting, ballet, and now *"poésie cinématographique."* "I did not think of making a movie," he says of *The Blood of a Poet.* "I thought of expressing myself through a medium poets of another age had never used." When the Vicomte de Noailles had proposed financing the film venture, originally to be an animated cartoon with music by Georges Auric, Cocteau had jumped at the prospect. "I knew nothing about cinematic art. I invented it for myself and employed it like a draftsman who dips his finger for the first time into India ink and tracks a sheet of paper with it." He would accept all interpretations of *Blood of a Poet,* including Freud's—"it's looking through the keyhole at a man washing himself" (in Cocteau's self-deprecating summary). He preferred to think of himself as a cabinetmaker who had produced a table, leaving it to others to make it turn and talk.[30] (For this spectator, it is Cocteau's mirror that is unforgettable, surely the most poetic since, at the least, Lewis Carroll's looking glass.)

The next *complete* film by Jean Cocteau—written and directed by "the poet"—would be *La Belle et la Bête (Beauty and the Beast),* which means a giant leap to the year 1946, embracing, along the way, Jean Marais, the film's other begetter.

"It is I who sought Cocteau," Jean Marais says candidly. "I was nothing but a *petit arriviste* ('ambitious squirt')." Cocteau: "Marais always recounts things accurately."[31] And Marais always adds, "I owe him everything."[32]

In the spring of 1937, Jean Marais's first efforts to seek out Jean Cocteau were fruitless. Typically, he left their meeting somewhat to chance. As a part-time student actor in Charles Dullin's atelier-theater, Jean Marais had had a few bit roles on the stage and in the cinema. What he now sought from Cocteau was a modest part as an understudy in a new Cocteau play. What chance would bring was the opportunity to audition for a role in an older Cocteau play, *Oedipus Rex,* which a young troupe had easily persuaded the playwright to allow them to produce.

On the scheduled day for his audition with Cocteau, Jean Marais showed up at precisely 4:00 P.M. No Cocteau. At five Marais left for his class with Dullin. He returned at seven to the theater where he was to be auditioned and discovered Cocteau, patiently listening to aspiring actors and actresses.

"He was less young than I had imagined him," recalls Marais. (To one of twenty-three, a man of forty-seven is on the far edge of middle age.) "Astonishing thinness," Marais continues, "very elegant . . . Long, strange, triangular face, topped by a disorderly mass of hair further lengthening the face. Lively, intelligent, slanting eyes."[33]

What Cocteau saw before him was one of the most beautiful young men of his generation, a mythological "blue-eyed Hyperborean," whose Apollonian profile and physique Cocteau had been idly sketching since *his* youth. Marais was given the role of Oedipus himself. The troupe, to which Marais was temporarily attached, protested! Marais's role was changed; he became the Greek Chorus (of one). More important for the *petit arriviste,* Cocteau offered him the part of Sir Galahad in his new play, *Les Chevaliers de la Table Ronde (Knights of the Round Table),* in which he had craved to be but the understudy. Would he accept? Would he indeed!

"I must read you the play," said Cocteau. At the Hôtel de Castille, where Cocteau was residing (with Coco Chanel paying the bill), Marais found a world of long-stemmed pipes and the acrid-sweet odor of opium; Cocteau's drawings covered the walls; scattered on the tables were jade rings, books, copybooks, gold boxes, and a hand sculpted of wood. And sitting on the bed, where Cocteau was lying in a white, opium-stained, cigarette-burned hotel bathrobe, were the black fighter Al Brown and the brown-skinned North African Marcel Khill. "Gently" Cocteau dismissed them and invited Marais to sit beside him. He then read aloud from his play, until, tired, he sent Marais off, but not before asking him to return another evening.[34]

On a second night Cocteau read Marais the second act; on a third, the third. Marais appeared as the Chorus in *Oedipus* and prepared for the role of Sir Galahad, the knight in white armor. Abruptly Cocteau disappeared from Paris, apparently with Khill and Al Brown, although for two months Marais had no word from him. Then the phone rang and he heard Cocteau's voice: "Come quickly, there's a catastrophe!" Marais hurried to the Hôtel de Castille. "There *is* a catastrophe," Cocteau told him. "I am in love with you."

Marais hesitated. "I too am in love with you," he lied.

He lied, Marais says, for a number of reasons, some of which he still doesn't understand, and for which he still hasn't pardoned himself. He was flattered; he was an actor; he wanted to give some measure of happiness to a man he greatly admired; and, "of course, you mustn't forget the *arriviste,* ready to do anything to reach his goal."[35]

Before commencing rehearsals for *Les Chevaliers de la Table Ronde,* Cocteau took Marais to Toulon, in the south of France. In the sleeping car he smoked his customary pipes of opium (upward of sixty a day, he once claimed). Napkins were stuffed in the cracks of the door to keep the fumes from escaping. Marais helped Cocteau prepare the opium, cooking it over an oil lamp with a silver needle, but he vowed to himself, he says, to break Cocteau from the habit. He had seen him too often at the hotel in Paris heavily under its influence. One morning Cocteau had awakened and, still drugged, told him he wanted to die; when he saw the tears in Marais's eyes, he had taken him into his arms and had asked his forgiveness.

The trip south was courtship and honeymoon. "All the landscapes, views, and cities seen with him," recalls Marais, "were incomparable. I discovered beauty I never dreamed existed, thanks to him." So it was at Toulon. "I was happy. I was no longer acting. I loved Jean."[36]

Directed by Cocteau, *Les Chevaliers* had a moderate success. Marais, nonetheless, considered himself "frankly awful." A critic wrote of him, "He is *beau.* Period." Marais did not even agree with that. He has always thought of himself as too flawed: "One eye larger than the other, one ear higher than the other ear, the nose too bulbous at the point, etc., etc." As for his studio photos, they still look to him like so much "chocolate melting in the mouth." He swore to overcome the "obstacle" of his beauty by hard work and discipline. Cocteau encouraged him, but in this he was insufficiently critical—and Marais became wary of his stage direction, on occasion rejecting it.

Once more Cocteau disappeared from Paris, again without a word for two months. Then, suddenly, he reappeared during the last days of the play's run—in Marais's dressing room. Marais asked no questions. Later, at the hotel, Cocteau recounted that he had left with Al Brown and Marcel Khill, "because he was afraid of the proportions our friendship had assumed." It was, rather, Cocteau's fear of a deepening attachment, of an ultimate dependence upon one too young, too vital, perhaps too beautiful. Marais tried to reassure him, failed. After the play closed, he came to Cocteau's hotel room and stayed for three days. They had meals sent up.

The following weeks they worked on their first play together, *Les Parents terribles,* perhaps Cocteau's best. They worked together in the sense that Galatea worked with Pygmalion on his statue of her. Cocteau had installed them in the kind of small town and small, comfortable hotel he favored. Unfortunately it was too close to Paris. Friends came and went freely. Cocteau smoked his pipes. ("He felt perpetually ill at ease. Opium alone gave him the equilibrium he needed"—Marais.) But for almost two months he did not write, and Marais worried. To stimulate Cocteau, he told him stories about his own mother, whom he called "Rosalie"—and something of her, as well as something of Cocteau's mother, would be in the play's *parent terrible.* Asked the part he himself would like, Marais responded: "A modern role, lively and extravagant, in which I cry, I laugh, and I am not *beau.*" Then, before dawn one night, Marais saw Cocteau rise from bed, go to the table, and write. "His face was frightening to see." Night and day he wrote during the entire week, until the play was finished.[37]

During the summer of 1938 there was almost as much talk of war as of the theater, even among theater people. It was then, too, that Marais heard of the arrest of his mother for petty theft. (Rosalie was a kleptomaniac who had used to "disappear" regularly during Marais's childhood; later he discovered she had been going to prison for short spells.) Sharing this part of his life for the first time with Cocteau, who found the words to console him, Marais says, strengthened and deepened their relationship—which troubled his mother.

Rosalie was increasingly jealous of Cocteau, who, she felt—quite rightly, from her point of view—was removing her son from her. She had sensed it even before the rehearsals for *Les Chevaliers* and the trip to Toulon. Previously Jean and she had been *les inséparables.* Once

Marais had even reproached her for acting as if she were his mistress rather than his mother. Actually, he acknowledges, he had encouraged it. Since his infancy, she had been both his parents for him. His father—if indeed he had been his father; Marais would never be sure, Rosalie saw to that—had left for the war in 1914, before Jean was one year old. He had returned when Jean was five, and had slapped him for an insolent remark, according to Rosalie, who promptly quit him, departing with Jean and an "uncle." Jean had adored her as he grew up, snuggling in her bed, going hand in hand to the movies with her in his adolescence, exulting when he was mistaken for her young lover. Now she witnessed his happiness with Cocteau. "And she," says Marais, *"she* suffered because I was happy without her." ("She would have been truly happy," he said on another occasion, "if I had been an abandoned wreck, sick, so she could take me into her arms and care for me.")[38]

Marais's known intimacy with Cocteau did not, however, make things easier for him during rehearsals for *Les Parents terribles.* To the contrary, ice formed between him and his fellow professionals. It was not broken before opening night of the play, when Marais won the audience with his first line. As an adolescent in the drama, he had spent a night away from home and had returned to face outraged parents. Entering the living room onstage, he cried: *"Ecoutez, mes enfants!"* Listen, kids! It brought down the house; from that moment, the public was his and he was part of the troupe. Each night, with each act, he improved. The play was a sellout. Marais was able to give his mother a hundred francs a day. He hoped it would keep Rosalie from "working."

Les Parents terribles was *too* successful for several of the city's elders, who accused Cocteau in the *Journal officiel des conseillers municipaux de Paris* of "inciting adolescents to debauchery," indeed, to incest. Cocteau replied in *Ce Soir:* "I do not allow collectors of pornographic postcards to judge my play."[39] The theater, owned by the city, was closed to the troupe, which now had to find—and immediately did—another place to perform. But it is exemplary of the scandal trailing Cocteau and, by association, Marais. For the two men to decide, at this time, openly to share an apartment and to live together was a further act of fairly unprecedented courage. It provoked a scene of jealousy with Rosalie, who would be long in pardoning Cocteau—"though it was really I who made the decision," says Marais stoutly.[40]

What with the play and the apartment, says Marais further, the year 1939 was one of the happiest he had ever known. "I loved Jean." To prove it to himself, he put this question *to* himself: "What are you capable of doing for Jean?" Without hesitation, he replied (Marais says): "Everything! I would give my life for him." He had asked the same thing with regard to others. "Never had I responded the same way."[41] Early in the year Marais suffered a sudden attack of otitis, which induced such nosebleeds when he was onstage that front-row spectators offered him their handkerchiefs. A doctor ordered two months of rest, whereupon he motored with Cocteau to Le Piquey and the Hôtel Chantecler. The small Mediterranean town and hotel were Cocteau's choice: here he had stayed with Raymond Radiguet a decade and a half before. Marais was aware of it. For him, he affirms, it was a demonstrative gesture on the part of Cocteau of the place he shared with Radiguet in Cocteau's heart. As if to record it, Cocteau wrote *La Fin du Potomak (The End of Le Potomak),* and Marais, in homage to and in imitation of his companion, took up the paintbrush.

The two returned to Paris, resuming life, love, and work. Marais: "Work was our principal distraction." One morning after he had begun Cocteau's portrait in oils, Jeannot (as he was now called) discovered a poem that Cocteau had slipped under his bedroom door during the night.

Il le faut d'amour trait par trait
Il le faut plus vrai que ma vie
Te poser est ma seule envie:
Je veux devenir ton portrait . . .
Je veux n'être de moi que ce qu'il imagine
Le peintre, l'acteur, le choeur, le pur, l'ange Michel.

("It must be, stroke by stroke, of love/It must be truer than my life/To pose for you is my sole desire:/I would become your portrait . . ./I would naught of myself save what he imagines/The painter, the actor, the chorus, the pure [Galahad], the angel Michael.")

Other nights, other poems. "We must reinvent love," once wrote Cocteau, echoing Rimbaud.[42] For him it was with words, with poetry, invoking ancient Greeks and marble, phallic columns, but at times with a prosaic, quotidien touch skirting the scatological. What did he mean in one poem, Jeannot asked, by the phrase about the cock strutting on the "dunghill of gold"? "Of course, I recognize the cock [*coq,* as in Cocteau], but the rest?" "You," said Cocteau, "are the 'dunghill of gold.' "

Each night had its poem on a sheet folded into a paper flower or a star. One night there were two; the second read:

Je dis: Tu n'auras qu'un poème
Et voilà que j'en glisse deux
L'un pour te répéter: "Je t'aime"
L'autre: "Je suis ton amoureux."

(I say: You will have but one poem / And here I am slipping you two / One to repeat: "I love you" / The other: "I am your loving one.")

And then the concluding couplet, as if written by Montaigne to La Boëtie:

Mon coeur trouve réponse à l'éternel problème
Toi c'est moi—moi c'est toi—nous c'est nous—Eux c'est eux.

(My heart has found the answer to the eternal problem / You are I—I am you—we are we—They are they.)

But there was another equally eternal problem nestling in another poem of love, whose last quatrains read:

Ah! Jeannot je chante, je chante
Pour t'avoir le même demain
Car la vie a l'air trop méchante
Sans la caresse de ta main.

Que me veulent toutes ces pieuvres
Qui fouillent jusque sous mon toit?
Dix-neuf cent trente-neuf: mon unique chef-d'oeuvre
C'est d'être un jour pareil au Jean aimé de toi.[43]

("Ah, Jeannot I sing, I sing / To have you the same tomorrow / For life seems all too wretched / Without the caress of your hand. / What do they want, these octopi / Who nose about under my very roof? / Nineteen hundred and thirty-nine: my unique chef d'oeuvre / Is to be like the Jean you love.")

What *"pieuvres"?* The image itself of the young men courting Jean Marais as "octopi" gives one pause. In his disarmingly frank memoirs Marais says, "I loved Jean," then immediately speaks of Denham Foots, one of the very young men—nineteen and "sort of a picture of Dorian Gray," writes Marais—whom Cocteau saw "nosing about." But it was not really the presence of Foots and his friends in the apartment that rendered Cocteau uneasy. Rather, it was their *absence,* for they were taking Jeannot away with them for long nights.

Thus, late one morning, instead of a poem Marais found a letter from Cocteau slipped under his door, addressed to *"Mon Jeannot adoré."* If ever he met and fell in love with someone his own age, Cocteau implored in his letter, would he please consider him, Jean Cocteau, his father, *more* than his father, and take him into his confidence? He would not, he promised, be jealous. (In a poem without a date, Cocteau says sadly to Marais, "If you love me, I will be your age."[44])

Several days later, in a second letter, Cocteau repeated his promise not to be jealous, *but* he warned Jeannot that "the little band you are going out with is a band of worldly cheats, kept idlers, people say, unworthy of you. . . . I ask you to exercise the same reserve as I once did when I frequented such types." Think of our work, he pleaded, our projects, "our purity." Poor Cocteau, conscious of his age, was jealous of Denham Foots, while protesting—too much—to the contrary. "You are free," he wrote Marais (what else could he write?), and spoiled the beau geste by adding that he himself was suffering. But, realizing it, he played the game at a higher level: "My suffering is but poor animal reflex. The idea of you in the arms of another or of holding another in your arms tortures me." Cocteau, perhaps fearfully, did not ask Marais to choose between Denham Foots and himself, but rather "to make the situation tolerable" for him. *"Bref,"* he writes, "I should like to become a kind of saint." Marais replied that he had "sincerely" thought Cocteau indifferent to his liaison with Denham, but, knowing now how Cocteau felt, he was breaking with him. He *indifferent?* responded Cocteau. Stupidly, he had pretended to be, in order to make Jeannot happy, but when he heard from him that he had broken with D., "I thought I would die from gratitude and *tendresse."* Now "I will work with a thousand times more spirit."[45]

When I mentioned to Marais that an insuperable problem of the couple is often that one loves more than the other, he softly recited the opening lines of a poem by Cocteau:

> Ainsi que le roi Marc aimait le beau Tristan
> Je t'aime et mon amour m'égaye en m'attristant . . .

("As King Mark loved the beau Tristan / So I love you and my love makes me gay as it makes me sad . . .")

He might have quoted one more direct, proving that Cocteau was all too conscious of his predicament:

> L'un aime plus—toujours—quand même
> C'est la dure, la sombre loi . . .

("One loves more—always—nevertheless / It is the hard, dark law . . .")

"There was a panic in his poetry," said Marais.

"Did you make him suffer?" I asked.

"Love always makes one suffer. Did he make me suffer? No. Did I, him? A bit—the thoughtlessness of youth . . . I have loved a great deal in my life." He laughed. "I prefer loving to being loved." He paused to reflect. "I always wanted to please. So I hid my faults. I still do. Cocteau taught me to like simplicity, singularity, that which is unique, alone. I taught him how to be happy. *'A Jeannot,'* he wrote, *'qui a mis en échec le malheur, ami des poètes.'* ('To Jeannot, who checkmated unhappiness, the poet's companion.') I liked to please. I like to please."[46]

In celebration, the two went down to Saint-Tropez on the Côte d'Azur, then the romantic seaport of artists, writers, and yachtsmen. Marais: "My most beautiful holiday." Cocteau may have written his love poem here. It could also have been written in Paris after their reconciliation.

> Quand nous faisons l'amour ensemble
> Entre le ciel et l'enfer
> Je pense que cela resemble
> A de l'or pénétrant du fer
>
> Or dur, or mou, hélas . . . que sais-je?
> C'est froid, c'est chaud, c'est de la neige
> La neige on peut sculpter avec
> La colonne d'un temple grec.[47]

("When we make love together / Between heaven and hell / I think of it as resembling / Gold penetrating iron / Hard gold, soft gold, alas . . . what do I know? / It is cold, it is warm, it is snow / The snow with which one can sculpt / The column of a Greek temple.")

In Saint-Tropez, one morning, they learned that war had been declared.

Jean Marais was mobilized. He went off to the *drôle de guerre,* carrying poems, letters, and a bronze bust of Cocteau with him (none of them would be lost). "Tell yourself repeatedly that my heart beats in your chest," Cocteau wrote to him. "That your blood flows in my veins and that I am far less alone than others, because you and I are one, despite the space between us." "I am happy I love you," Marais replied.[48]

Ill, Cocteau moved from their apartment on the Place de la Madeleine to a room in the Hôtel Ritz. Here Mademoiselle Chanel, whose sensible idea it was and who had a suite under the roof, could more easily care for Cocteau. But not completely: somehow he procured opium, and despite the stuffed door, the smell was often perceptible in the hallway.[49] After the fall of France and in the face of advancing Germans, Cocteau fled to Perpignan, where he found refuge with friends. Demobilized, Marais joined him there, but they soon returned to occupied Paris and a small apartment, close to Colette's, overlooking the Palais-Royal gardens. Theaters had reopened, and a project to revive *Les Parents terribles* had brought them back.

Supported—or inspired—by the moralistic Pétain government, however, the Germans forbade revival of the Cocteau play. Profiting from the interim, Marais persuaded Cocteau to enter a clinic and undergo the long-promised, often-postponed cure of his opium habit. Almost as miraculously, Cocteau abided by the rules, kicked the habit, and put away his pipes for virtually the duration of the war. Marais, in the meantime, wanted to prove to his critics—and to himself—that, at the age of twenty-five, he could fly on his own. Deliberately keeping Cocteau apart from it, he produced, directed, costumed, stage-designed, and performed in Racine's *Britannicus.* It was a triumph; Marais was ecstatic, Cocteau content. He, however, had to confront another problem.

As the forbidden revival of *Les Parents* demonstrated, Cocteau's moral attitudes and behavior made him a marked man for Vichy and the Nazis. Moreover, early during the Occupation (in December 1940), he boldly spoke out in one of the few publications permitting free expression. He praised the now-damned prewar writers, such as André Gide, and the decried avant-garde art, such as his own *Parade.* He addressed himself to young writers unambiguously: "Do not say, 'It is too hard. I will go into hiding!' . . . Reflect, write, love, destroy. Launch little magazines. Produce plays. Trample on us, if you can."[50] How, then, to explain Cocteau's more debatable conduct during the remainder of the long years of the Occupation? By the friends he found among the few German aesthetes in Paris, notably Ernst Jünger and Hitler's favorite sculptor, Arno Breker (whom Cocteau had met in the twenties)? Breker would be of indisputable aid during one dangerous moment.

A French collaborationist critic had been particularly scurrilous in his personal remarks about Cocteau, when he "reviewed" his play, *La Machine à écrire* (in which Marais had two roles). Marais met him in a fashionable restaurant, waited for him outside, and smashed his face when he emerged.[51] There was no small audience for it. (Marais's act, wrote Simone de Beauvoir in *La Force de l'âge,* "made us very happy."[52]) Only Breker's influence kept Marais from prison or deportation to Germany. In return, though perhaps no less sincerely for that, Cocteau penned a "Salute to Arno Breker" during a Paris exhibition of his sculpture in 1943.

Far more memorably, earlier the same year, Cocteau had written a film script expressly for Marais, *L'Eternel Retour (The Eternal Return).* "Furious" when he read the scenarios French and Italian movie makers were now urging upon Marais (says Marais), Cocteau had decided to write one specifically tailored to his talents. "You need a hero's role and a great love story," Cocteau had said. "Since literature has existed, there have been only two great love stories—*Romeo and Juliet* and *Tristan and Isolde.* You should be, you *are*, Tristan."[53]

Not since *The Blood of a Poet* (1930) had Cocteau returned to film making in a major fashion. Now, in 1943, at the age of fifty-four, stimulated by the idea of working directly with Marais, he would resume his most congenial medium, and perhaps poetically his most enduring. It would give a kind of immortality to a most mortal relationship—playwright and actor, artist and model. (Apropos Cocteau's "working together is a permanent way of making love," it was remarked to Marais that he and Cocteau had made superb films together. "It was he who made them," Marais replied.)

The Eternal Return was not yet an entirely Cocteau movie. He wrote the scenario and dialogue; Jean Delannoy is credited with the direction. "I assisted, I aided Delannoy," Cocteau has repeatedly stated, though his hand in the direction is actually greater.[54] For the public, however, Marais as a modern-dress Tristan was the great discovery—a new romantic screen star—who moreover disclosed Cocteau to his first popular audience. ("I played it too romantically," Marais says now. "A fairy tale is fantasy and romance enough.")

This, to be sure, was occurring in occupied Paris, but likely because of the challenge *that* represented, there was an astonishing vitality, particularly in the performing arts—cinema and theater. Overt resistance themes were obviously *verboten;* classical subjects, though sometimes as subversive as Antigone, often passed the censor. The story of Tristan and Isolde presented no difficulty; Wagner was pure Aryan. Neither Marais nor Cocteau took part in the Resistance. Marais had offered to do so, only to be told by fellow actor Louis Jourdan, "I spoke of you. They said you were living with someone who talked too much."[55]

Had that been the only reproach made concerning Cocteau, he would not have been as uneasy when the Liberation came and the *épuration,* or purge, of collaborators ensued. Once again he hid out with Chanel at the Hôtel Ritz, until he was reassured that nothing important was held against him. Although he had one too many friends among the German occupiers, he had also suffered too much already from the French "moralists" of the Occupation. Once, on the Champs Elysées, he had been beaten for not saluting the country's flag, being carried by volunteers for the Russian front as they marched past with German soldiers. Even *Andromaque* had finally been forbidden, because of Marais's presence in the play. As for Marais, he would join in the liberation of Paris and go on with General Leclerc's division until the end of the war.

Within four months of the war's end, after a year's preparation, Cocteau was shooting *Beauty and the Beast,* his poetic masterpiece. The film idea had come from Marais, who would play the bewitched Prince changed by sorcery into a fanged, furred Beast, complete with claws. And it was as the monstrous Beast that he would be seen until the end, when he would become, although only briefly, the Prince, restored by the love of Beauty *for the Beast.* Marais had suggested the tale for that very reason—he yearned to prove that his acting could overcome the "handicap" of his handsomeness. His last performances as Nero in *Britannicus* and Orestes in *Andromaque* had public and critic still talking of his striking looks, not of his ability. Even Cocteau (in his unpublished Occupation diary) speaks of Marais's "beauty" first among his qualities in the role of Orestes, followed by "his nobility, ardor, and humanity."[56] Later Cocteau would realize that he had greatly helped create the "handicap" of Marais's *belle tournure* by stressing it when he directed him as the Chorus in *Oedipus:* "From that moment dated the obstacle that his physique was to oppose to his talent—the obstacle he hurdled blindfolded in *Les Parents terribles."*[57]

So effective, so moving is Jean Marais as the fanged, hairy Beast—only the haunted eyes are his in the lion's awesome mask—that one regrets his transformation at the close into Prince Charming, as called for by the eighteenth-century tale. The film becomes a dream—"by general consent one of the most enchanting pictures ever made."[58] It was Marais, said Cocteau generously,

> who achieved this miracle. By means of that beast that so dismayed the producers, he seduced the young women spectators. They all had the eyes of Beauty . . . Only Marais foresaw it. He detested the role of the Prince. He recognized himself more fully in a role where he was unrecognizable, and charged it with so much love that he died enacting it."[59]

The miracle, said Marais with a flatness that invited no hypocritical demurrer, was Cocteau's doing. He refashioned a fairy tale and made it a movie, he directed the performers, he brought out of designer Christian Bérard a combination of Vermeer and Gustave Doré costumes and settings, and he put together scenes as if he were the three painter brothers Le Nain. He succeeded in stirring the child that still abides in us, although "a hundred obstacles sprang up to defeat his masterpiece." There were up to seven electricity cuts or failures a day, unannounced, during the making of the movie, ruining or threatening the film (already scarce and unreliable in postwar France) in the developer, "obliging us often to work at night." Marais's makeup took four hours: three for the intricate fur mask and an additional one to make his hands into claws. Fangs were attached to his teeth; he was fed a kind of porridge at mealtimes. He developed a carbuncle on the inside of his thigh but forced himself to ride and rear his horse as scheduled (uncomplaining, noted Cocteau). But, said Marais,

> The hardest hit was Jean. For months he suffered all the skin ailments there are. At practically the same time he had impetigo, hives, eczema, boils, carbuncles, and an inflammation of the neck. The hot spotlights were murder for his face. He couldn't shave. He had to work with a black paper covering his face, with two holes for his eyes, fastened to his hat by clothespins. Yet, he directed us with a patience and courtesy I've never seen. He even made jokes . . . to put us into a good mood!"[60]

Cocteau's condition worsened when they moved from location to the Saint-Maurice studio outside Paris. There were nights he could not sleep for the pain, and would rise to jot down the day's events and his reflections in the journal he kept of the making of *Beauty and the Beast* (now on the bookshelf of every young *cinéaste*). Even then, one night, an electricity failure prevented him from writing! "Without the devotion, the goodness of soul of Jean Marais," he noted, "who, himself sick, takes care of me, coming to Saint-Maurice to give me insulin shots, I don't know what I would do." For two weeks, however, the film was held up while Cocteau lay ill in bed at the hospital of the Institut Pasteur; and when Marais visited him, Cocteau worried about *Marais's* health! "I found Jeannot had a yellow complexion and was coughing." He sent him to see a doctor. Yet, when Cocteau returned to the studio, he was exhilarated. "I felt happy, buoyed up by an indescribable elation. Nothing is more wonderful than writing a poem with people, faces, hands, lights, stage props you arrange as your fancy guides you." Cocteau infected the entire crew with a sense of camaraderie and relished it, recalling his youth with Diaghilev's company. "All I ask is to be able to go on working with people who accept me as I am and love me." "The only shadow is to observe how the film is advancing and the minute approaching when we will no longer be living together." On December 11, 1945, the crew brought Jean Marais a *corbeille* of roses for his birthday (the thirty-second). *"A notre bonne Bête,"* their card read, "To our nice Beast!" Cocteau's journal, January 4, 1946: "We shall work tonight. The last night. I do not know anything sadder than the end of a film, the breaking up of a team working affectionately." But it was not quite the end. There were still the cutting and editing—"among the most arousing tasks there are . . . one corrects the life one has created." Nor was that the ending. On Friday, May 31, 1946, Cocteau showed the finished film to the first group to see it—the crew; their work schedules were arranged so each would be free. "The reaction of that audience of workers was unforgettable. That constituted my reward. Whatever happens, I will never again find the same grace of the ceremony so very simply organized by the little village of artisans whose métier is the canning of dreams." That, at least, was the ending of the journal of the making of *Beauty and the Beast.*[61]

The beard Cocteau could not shave during the film making emerged gray, to his chagrin. An aging poet was an anachronism, he felt; an aging Cocteau a contradiction in terms. *The Two-Headed Eagle,* which was first produced as a play in 1946, then as a film in 1947, was authentic Cocteau, but not of his best year. Jean Marais was cast as a young, doomed poet caught in a love conflict with Edwige Feuillère's destructive Austrian queen. For one critic, the play was memorable only for Marais's dying fall down the length of a grand staircase. But that feat led to one of Marais's most popular films, an athletic *Ruy Blas* (adaptation and dialogues by Cocteau), typecasting him for cloak-and-dagger roles for much of his cinematic career. The exception, which quickly followed, though intended by Cocteau to provide Marais with a vehicle for escape, ironically confirmed the new direction of Marais's career. The screen version of *Les Parents terribles,* though a fine film, proved an embarrassment. Again Marais played the adolescent, but he was now thirty-five, and the close-ups revealed him looking rather like his own parent.

Did it make Cocteau feel—to his distaste—like a grandparent? Frequently he referred to Marais as his son. Indeed one day, Marais recalls, Cocteau had very seriously told him that he thought of marrying Rosalie, so that "I would really be his son. 'Don't ever do anything like that,' I said to him. 'If Rosalie ever has a ring on her finger, she will become the Venus d'Isle—like that statue of Mérimée, she will crush you!' "[62] Marais, in time, would also seek and eventually adopt a son. His one sense of frustration (according to Cocteau) derived from his not having one and from his fear that a woman who agreed to mother "his" child "would take it from him."[63] As for Cocteau, he himself recognized that his *"rage* for friendship came from not having sons. Failing that, I invent them. I want to educate them . . . [Of course] it is they who educate me." "I know better how to make friends than to make love."[64]

Once, Cocteau expressed their *mutual* frustration in not having a son together. The poem he wrote to Marais is moving and explicit:

> De notre bonheur large ouvert
> Jamais d'enfants! C'est trop injuste!
> Mais non, je mets au monde vers,
> Pièces, lettres, dessins et buste.[65]

("Of our embracing happiness / No children ever came! It's too unjust! / No, I give birth to verses, / Plays, letters, sketches, busts.")

Perhaps one speaks most of posterity when the past feels heavy and the present fleeting. During the years immediately after the war, says Marais, "Cocteau began to live like a monk. He believed that at his age certain 'exchanges,' certain relations, were nothing but a kind of depravity that easily became ridiculous."[66]

The words come almost directly from Cocteau's last important book, *La Difficulté d'être (The Difficulty of Being).* "I am old," he wrote in the Postface, dated July 5, 1946—his fifty-seventh birthday. A la Montaigne, he had been engaged in a series of self-probing essays—on his childhood, his style, his *"évasions";* on Raymond Radiguet, Serge de

Diaghilev, death, frivolity, morals. We have quoted some of the fragments in their time and place, such as, "I never had a beautiful face. Youth substituted for beauty." Others indicate the mood of his late middle age, as he saw it: "Friendship preserves me from that anguish men feel when they grow old." "Living disconcerts me more than death." "It must be a dream to live at ease in one's skin. From birth I have carried a badly stowed cargo. I have never been in balance. And in that lamentable state, instead of keeping to my room, I have knocked about everywhere. I haven't stopped a minute since I was fifteen."[67]

"Writing," begins Cocteau's essay on morals, "is an act of love. Else, it is nothing but scribbling."[68]

At a critical, delicate point in the story of his life, Marais reaches into the most personal pages of Cocteau's work to help him, swiftly and as gracefully as possible, describe their living together until their lives separated. "Reading *The Difficulty of Being,*" he says,

> overwhelmed me with its interior suffering. As he wrote it, he was living like a lay saint. And I? I was young . . . younger. I wanted to live. The act of love counted for me. It still does. But I am seventy now, and I am no longer young for the others. Perhaps only now do I understand Cocteau then.[69]

Now was 1984. *Then* was 1946 going into 1947.

The theme of loneliness runs like a gray thread throughout *The Difficulty of Being.* In part it is the natural letdown after the exhilaration —and exhaustion—of making *Beauty and the Beast.* But in larger part, I believe, the cause can be traced to a third person. Paul Morihien, a young man whom Marais had encountered toward the war's end on the movie set of a Marcel Carné film in which he was performing, had now become a factor in Marais's intimate life. He would also soon become Cocteau's secretary and publisher. It was a mark of Cocteau's understanding and acceptance, though it did not reduce his sadness. Cocteau never preached what he had never practiced—and he had had many younger lovers in his life. There is no overt expression of jealousy in the journal of *Beauty and the Beast,* and the only anxiety shown, concerns his health and the making of the movie. But the series of skin ailments may speak where Cocteau is silent, having interiorized the emotional suffering. Even Marais's carbuncle may be telling us of an internal stress about which *his* memoirs are more than discreet. His love for Cocteau and Cocteau's for him were a concurrent, underlying reality.

Early in 1947, while still maintaining the Palais-Royal apartment, Marais and Cocteau jointly bought a country house in Milly-la-Forêt, thirty miles southeast of Paris—"This house that I love," writes Cocteau in March, "that I occupy alone."[70] Cocteau was not made for solitude. In July he met Edouard Dermit, twenty-two, a miner in Lorraine since he was eighteen, gentle, well built, and with the profile of a Cocteau drawing. They met in a Paris art gallery that Dermit, a Sunday painter, happened to be visiting. Why the bandaged thumb? Cocteau had asked. A mine accident, replied Dermit, explaining. Wouldn't he rather do something else? Cocteau asked. Anything else, Dermit had answered.[71] In November, after settling his affairs in Lorraine, Dermit came to live at Milly-la-Forêt as gardener. He learned to drive and became Cocteau's chauffeur as well. (Dermit would also become Cocteau's legal heir and be considered his "adopted son." He is now married and lives in the house at Milly-la-Forêt. One of his three children is named Jean.)

Dermit was, moreover, installed in the Palais-Royal apartment and given a walk-on part in *The Two-Headed Eagle.* The small apartment was fine for two, but crowded for three. (Morihien was living elsewhere, close to his bookshop and publishing office, Marais insists, contradicting biographer Jacques Kihm, who maintains that Morihien was living with the other three in the Palais-Royal flat.)

Marais offered to exchange his corner of the flat for Cocteau's smaller one. "But he never wanted to bother me," Marais recalls in his memoirs,

> and gently refused my offer. I tried to find a way to make his life more comfortable. If I moved, Jean would be hurt. So I used the pretext of wanting some sun and air . . . I thought a houseboat would look like a temporary caprice. I found one, bought it, and tied it up in a quiet branch of the Seine, in Neuilly. My departure did not look like a departure.[72]

Nor was their separation a divorce.

Their story remains that of essentially gentle people, among the gentlest I have ever met. Marais: "I was happy Doudou [Dermit] made Jean happy. Jean wanted people to be happy. He taught me that." (Alice Toklas: "Cocteau kept the unfashionable virtues of generosity and loyalty."[73]) The affection, the friendship between them was effectively undiminished. Cocteau and Marais had several other *chefs-d'oeuvre* to do together, even as they went their separate ways—that of the "lay saint and monk" and that of the younger man for whom "the act of love counts." The film *Orphée* may be the most memorable. Marais regards this refreshed, modernized version of the classic Orpheus and Eurydice legend as Cocteau's "most important cinematographic work."[74] Certainly it is among the most magical, and for a long, long time—one almost risks saying forever—it will bring its creator and protagonist back to life. A theme he had played "with one finger" in making *The Blood of a Poet,* Cocteau liked to say, he fully "orchestrated," at the age of sixty, in *Orphée.*[75] "The grandeur of Orpheus depends on that of his performer. Once again, Marais lights up the film."[76] The praise, too, is Cocteau's, but when Marais received the same plaudit from the critics for his acting in *Orphée,* he replied, "It is the film that enacts our roles."[77]

From the Riviera, where he had gone to recuperate after the movie's triumphant but tiring reception, Cocteau sent Marais this poem:

Noël 1950

Mon Jeannot! mon nomade
Le ciel nous réunisse!
L'avenir est malade
Sous le soleil de Nice

Tâchons d'y vivre ensemble
Sous un ciel guérisseur
La beauté te ressemble
Et la bonté, sa soeur.[78]

("My Jeannot, my nomad! / The heavens unite us! / The future is sick / Under the sun of Nice / Let us try to live together / Under a healing sky / Beauty resembles you / And Goodness, its sister.")

The relations among the three men—Jean, Jeannot, and Doudou—remained almost classically Greek. Now the fully mature, aging adult, Marais sought younger men, as had Cocteau, without turning from the man who had been his lover or having the slightest rancor for the young man who had succeeded but not replaced him. As for Dermit, Cocteau's friends, he says, have always been "faithful and devoted" to him. "Particularly Jean Marais, who has really remained a brother, a presence, upon whom I can always depend."[79]

All lovers are brothers or sisters. Nothing may become the act of loving so much as its ending in neither indifference nor hostility, but rather in comradeship. "Our destinies," Cocteau wrote in his diary, four years after separating from Marais, "continue side by side."[80]

Perhaps this is quintessentially the story of the two Jeans. It is intrinsic in Cocteau's portrait, written in 1951 and titled *Jean Marais.* It is the heart of Marais's one-man tribute, titled *Marais Cocteau,* which he staged in 1983, twenty years after Jean's death.

10

THE SEXISM OF A "LIBERATED" COUPLE: JEAN-PAUL SARTRE AND SIMONE DE BEAUVOIR

> I sincerely and profoundly consider myself a bastard.
>
> —Sartre, Letter to Simone de Beauvoir, 1940.

> Love can be a trap that makes women accept many things.
>
> —Simone de Beauvoir, Interview, 1976.

JEAN-PAUL Sartre lay in a double coffin, April 19, 1980, in a small room off the large amphitheater of Paris's Hôpital Broussais. The inner coffin was for his cremation four days later. "The entire staff of *Les Temps modernes* was there. No one spoke." Simone de Beauvoir had collapsed into a chair. Someone close to her was nervously snapping pictures of Sartre's corpse. The camera slipped from his hands, rebounded with a hollow sound from the outer coffin, and hit the tiled floor. "Simone de Beauvoir had wanted a last photograph." Before the coffins were sealed, she rose painfully, bent over Sartre's body, and kissed him on the mouth. Outside the hospital, a crowd of photographers was waiting, and 40,000 would follow the hearse to the Montparnasse cemetery.[1]

Everything seems to be in the scene: Beauvoir's photographic memoirs of their couple, the last volume of which clinically details the last ten year of Sartre's decline; the kiss on the cold, stilled mouth, as if symbolizing the greater love of the one for the other; and the immense numbers paying homage to the man Francois Mauriac, who was neither his friend nor his admirer, had called "the most brilliant of his generation." The photographers, too, amateur and professional, who tried to catch the agonized face of the surviving member of possibly the world's most famous couple of the twentieth century, gracelessly underlined the "transparency" the two had sought in their lives and open relationship.

"All will be made known," Sartre promised, but heirs and heiresses sometimes have the last word about inherited papers. Sartre's adopted daughter, who had been briefly his mistress, Arlette Elkaïm-Sartre, has insisted on changed names and unidentified cuts in some posthumously published notes and letters—and it may be years before all will indeed be known.[2] However, what has been revealed and what can be firmly deduced are considerable.

"It is ridiculous to take us as models," Beauvoir said. "Sartre and I were very lucky, and our situation was special and very exceptional . . . We were formed in a similar way in our youth. Our childhoods were very solid and made us feel very secure."[3]

But were the childhoods of Sartre and Beauvoir really *"solides"* and *"sécurisantes"?*

JEAN-PAUL Sartre was born on June 21, 1905. Simone de Beauvoir followed two and a half years later, on January 9, 1908, as she would, quite literally, after they met in July 1929. One might say of their couple, along with a woman critic, "Sartre and she walked the same road but at a distance,"[4] Sartre leading, Beauvoir following. But to conclude, like the critic, that this distancing meant "solitude" for Simone de Beauvoir would be wrong. Rather, it meant the emotional torsion of conflicting drives as she passionately sought autonomy and, at the same time, "union with another."[5] She soon chose union, but with one not "made" for monogamy ("I never imagined a woman who would be the unique woman of my life"—Sartre[6]), although she certainly was. Their attitudes began in their infancy and childhood. "One is not cured of oneself," Sartre has written, ". . . all the traits of the child remain in the man in his fifties."[7]

Sartre's father had died before he was two, which was fine for little Jean-Paul ("Poulou"). "There is no such thing as a good father. . . . Had he lived, my father would have laid his full length upon me and crushed me . . . One must die at the right time . . . I was delighted."[8] Poulou now had his young, slim, pretty mother all to himself (she is "Anne-Marie" more often than "Mother" in Sartre's memoirs), and he would sleep in her bedroom, in an adjacent twin bed, until he was eleven.[9] "In my [sic] bedroom, one had put the bed of a young maid.

The young maid sleeps alone and wakes chastely. I am still asleep when she takes her bath. She returns entirely dressed; how could I have been born of her? She tells me her troubles and I listen with compassion; later I will marry her in order to protect her." ("She would have liked, when I was eight, for me to remain forever portable."[10]) When he was eleven, however, his mother remarried—and Poulou never recovered.[11]

Almost sixty years later, Sartre would recall to Simone de Beauvoir, "Before, I was a prince in relation to my mother"; now "there was this man who lived with her and had the principal role." His wish was to be cremated, Sartre also remarked, because "above all"—Beauvoir reports—"he did not want to find himself in the Père-Lachaise cemetery between his mother and his stepfather."[12] (When Sartre was twenty-nine, he had had an attack of asthma "toward two in the morning," because he had been put in a bedroom next to theirs, whose "walls were as thin as paper."[13])

During her first widowhood, Anne-Marie Sartre and Poulou had lived in the household of her father, Karl Schweitzer, uncle of the more famous Albert. (The Schweitzers were Alsatian and Protestant; Anne-Marie's husband had been Catholic, and their son had been thus baptized.) Karl resumed teaching in order to support the additional charge. Anne-Marie returned to her childhood and adolescence, once again the *jeune fille* of the family, who had to ask permission if she wanted to go out. Karl Schweitzer was the patriarch *par excellence.*

In an interview, Sartre ascribed his own "polygamous" and "macho" conduct to the "*machiste* education I was given, the *machiste* atmosphere that surrounded me" and particularly, in this connection, to the example of his grandfather, Karl, who hadn't had sexual relations for years with his grandmother, "because she detested them," and so "had relations with the elderly women students of his German class."[14]

Sartre's grandfather did, in fact, have a great influence upon his grandson, but for reasons other than his having bedded several of his women students. Karl was God the Grandfather, tall, handsome, and bearded, who took it upon himself to have seven-year-old Poulou's golden, shoulder-length curls cut off, exposing the poor lad as an ugly duckling with a right eye (which would go blind) out of focus with the left. And from this grandfatherly act, too, Sartre would never recover. "Each of my characters is a disabled person," he wrote at thirty-four. And again: "Roquentin, Mathieu . . . [heroes of two different novels] are myself, decapitated."[15]

Would it be too easy to add a castration complex to an unresolved Oedipus complex? A Freudian and French psychoanalyst has been, one might say, harsher. After dissecting Sartre's early life and later writing—his complete submissiveness to his grandfather, his playacting as the child genius for his elders' approval, his recurrent use of the image of Aeneas carrying his father, his lengthy obsession with Flaubert's unconscious homosexuality, and his admiration (he who said he admired no one) for Jean Genet's assumption of *his* homosexuality (Sartre, Genet has said, was the woman of the Sartre-Beauvoir couple) and more of the like—she has concluded that Sartre remained at the anal stage (never going on to the genital) and had marked tendencies and drives toward "anal eroticism," which is sadomasochistic, and "latent homosexuality."[16]

If anyone or anything commanded Sartre's becoming a writer—as if "stitching" the commandment under his skin (the image is Sartre's)—that "neurosis of writing" he imputed to Baudelaire, as to Flaubert, was fathered and mothered by his grandfather and Anne-Marie. He would write books, the child determined. He would *become* a book! It was more than metaphor: "I am taken, I am opened, I am spread on the table, flattened by the palm of a hand, and sometimes I am made to crack."[17]

Sartre had ambiguous feelings about his childhood. "Poulou hasn't understood anything about it," his mother said after reading his single book of memoirs, *Les Mots (Words),* which stops short of puberty, with his mother's remarriage.[18] Anne-Marie, one can safely comment, understood even less. "I detest my childhood," Sartre wrote, but he also recalled his having been "a little king" (before his curls were cut off), the spoiled darling of an old man and two women who told him he was a genius, and so "a little boy sure of himself, who had profound certainties because, during his first years, he has had all the love a child needs to become an individual and to constitute an ego that dares assert itself—and that little child was I."[19]

On the surface, then (a surface going down to the doubting core), Sartre's childhood was indeed *"sécurisante"*—until his mother's remarriage, when he was eleven.

Need one add that one's analysis of Sartre's childhood, whatever it discloses, does not reduce the writer who would receive, and merit, but refuse, the Nobel Prize; any more than Baudelaire or Flaubert are reduced as writers by Sartre's analysis of their "neuroses"? Nonetheless, this was the formative childhood of the man who would meet and love and form a lifelong couple with Simone de Beauvoir.

THE childhood of Simone de Beauvoir seems, in comparison with Sartre's, conventional, ordinary, and dull. "The state of the child to be was laid out in advance," says Beauvoir, "French, bourgeois, and Catholic; only its sex was unforeseen." Simone was the oldest child; a younger sister was born shortly afterward. Had her sister been a boy, she said, "I would probably have suffered the consequences." Instead, Simone remained the center of her parents' attention. "A large family fussed around my cradle. I looked out upon the world with confidence." Having a younger sister "helped me to assert myself. I invented the mixture of authority and *tendresse* that characterized my relations with her . . . I taught her how to read, write, and count. It was I who decided our games and our living relationship."[20]

Sister Hélène has since recalled those games and that relationship for a documentary film on Beauvoir. "In life, you did dominate me," she says to Simone. "However, in our games, you who always triumphed in our real life and had what you wished always chose the martyr's role, playing a heroic, saintly woman whom I martyrized." Of course, Simone would end unscathed and triumphant, which Hélène called her return to normalcy. But Beauvoir's sister recollected that the worst moment in her own childhood was the arrival of Zaza in Simone's life. "Abruptly, you dropped me." Beauvoir: "Yes, I was very brutal at that moment. Besides, I *am* a bit of a brute in life generally."[21]

Zaza, whom Simone had met when both were ten, "had counted enormously," she acknowledged to Hélène. Her feeling for Zaza had clouded everything. She had loved Zaza, Beauvoir says unabashedly in *Mémoires d'une jeune fille rangée (Memoirs of a Dutiful Daughter),* but she intended to marry and live forever with Jacques, her slightly older cousin—which she states with equal firmness. What else, then, was thinkable? She was French, bourgeois, and Catholic—a well-ordered, dutiful daughter. Yet, the suffering and death of Zaza compose the most harrowing pages of Beauvoir's earliest memoirs, whose last lines intone: "Together we had fought the abject fate that awaited us and for a long time I believed that I had paid for my freedom with her death."[22]

Another memory of the past seems to have struck Beauvoir's sister at almost the same time, for she immediately followed the reminiscence of Zaza with the recollection of something less painful to herself.

HÉLÈNE DE BEAUVOIR: At fourteen, you became quite ugly, you who had been such a pretty little girl . . . And Papa was very brutal toward you.

SIMONE DE BEAUVOIR: I think what went wrong was precisely *that* —Papa's brutality. [The effect has been noted.]

HELENE: All day long he told you, "How ugly you are, my poor child, how ugly you are!"

SIMONE: You had the good fortune of remaining very nice and very pretty. And besides, at that time Papa took it into his head to play actor and you playacted with him . . . I wouldn't have dared; I was very embarrassed by my body . . . I really abandoned everything, during those years, for my studies and reading.[23]

Simone would escape to the reading room of the Bibliothèque Nationale, but to be away from home during lunch hour, she had to ask her parents' permission. Her mother was still opening and censoring letters to her when she was twenty, the age when she passed the competitive entrance examination for the Ecole Normale Supérieure, France's preeminent teachers' college—where Sartre had preceded her.

The effect of cousin Jacques Laiguillon had faded from her life by this time. He was too middle class. She had an affection for him still, "but I was afraid my affection would lead to my becoming his wife," Beauvoir tells us with thirty years of hindsight, "and I fiercely refused the life that awaited me as the future Madame Laiguillon." At twenty? Perhaps. In any event, when she heard, considerably later, that he had taken a mistress, she said to herself with surely unfeigned indifference, "So be it, Jacques. It is the other I pity."[24]

As for cousin Jacques, there is little doubt that he sensed Simone's attitude from the start. Her early standards and demands concerning the "man of her life" were set even higher for him than for herself, since they embodied the image of her father. No man, she thought in her youth, was so intelligent, charming, or handsome as he; she could imagine no one less for herself. In fact, to be her equal, her man had to be her superior! "The chosen one must impose himself upon me . . . I would love the day a man subjugated me by his intelligence, his culture, his authority."

"Why did I insist that he should be superior to me?" Beauvoir asked, then tried to explain, admitting that, in part, it was because of her feelings for her father. The rationalization she finally offered, however, was not that of the fifteen-year-old Simone, but of the mature Beauvoir: "If, in the absolute sense, a man who was a member of a privileged species benefiting from a big advance start didn't count more than I, then I had to consider him relatively as counting less than I. In order to recognize him as my equal, I must be convinced of his superiority."[25]

Beauvoir arrived at the Ecole Normale Supérieure armed with a *certificat de mathématiques générales,* a *licence ès lettres* (bachelor's degree in literature), and a *certificat de philosophie.* No mean accreditations. She was striking, with her silky black hair, drawn tightly back; her devouring, light gray eyes in a delicate, oval face; her shapely, energetic figure. An unintimidated intellectual might have thought her beautiful.

Sartre, by this time, was the intellectual supreme, sure of himself to the point of arrogance, and, moreover, sexually sophisticated. He had already published a short story and several chapters of an unfinished novel, and he had clearly established dominance over his classmates at the Ecole Normale Supérieure, who included Raymond Aron, future leading sociologist of France; René Maheu, future director of UNESCO; and Paul Nizan, briefly political leader of his generation's leftist youth. ("I am atrociously terrorizing [my fellow conscripts]," Sartre would write Beauvoir in 1940, "as I terrorized [my fellow students] . . . at the Ecole Normale, in Berlin and so on."[26])

Sartre had courted, seduced, and was still occasionally seeing an older, sensual blonde, soon to be an actress, Simone Jolivet (called "Camille" in Beauvoir's memoirs). Sartre was nineteen, she twenty-two, when they met, in the provinces, at the burial of a common cousin. They spent nights together at Toulouse and in Paris, then separated amicably before Beauvoir's arrival at the Ecole Normale. Sartre's letters to Simone Jolivet, posthumously published, speak of himself as being "extremely ambitious" as well as "stupidly sentimental, cowardly, and soft," of a novel he plans to write, of living "too much, at the moment, in the admiration others have for me," and of Jolivet as "my *petite fille*" whom "I love" and in whose love "I want to be not the first, but *the only one.*"[27] He was not then, or afterward.

First of the small clan surrounding Sartre who approached Simone de Beauvoir was René Maheu, who was already married—which affected him not a whit. *Nothing* inhibited this clan, whose core was Sartre, Nizan, and Maheu. To the contrary, it intellectually terrorized —to use Sartre's strong term—the others at the Ecole Normale. Its members, Beauvoir observed, "mixed with no outsiders, only attended classes they chose to and sat apart from the rest of the students." Their reputation was bad, and Sartre's was the worst, but in discussions he was dialectically "unbeatable."[28] He certainly remarked the new student, but Maheu made the advances, as if blazing the way, before presenting Beauvoir to him. Offhandedly, Sartre sent her a drawing, titling it "Leibniz Bathing with the Monads," casually indicating he knew of her special studies of the German philosopher and mathematician. It was Maheu who gave Beauvoir the remarkably apt nickname that has since stuck—le Castor (Beauvoir=Beaver, which is *le castor* in French). And it was as Castor that she now entered the inner sanctum of the intimate trio, Sartre, Nizan, and Maheu (Aron was marginal), to work intensively together as a team in preparation for the final oral examination.

Sartre invited Beauvoir to spend an evening with him (Beauvoir: "Oh, you did notice me, you did notice me!"[29]), but Maheu asked her not to, and she sent her sister Hélène in her place (Simone was still the "dutiful" young woman). Sartre was polite; Hélène—as she told Simone—was unimpressed. Simone de Beauvoir felt differently, increasingly. In their study sessions, she lost every argument with Sartre—and was all admiration. "He's a marvelous intellectual coach," she noted at the time, just what she had sought "all" her life, and she was "overwhelmed by his generosity . . . his giving himself without counting the cost."[30]

At seventy, Beauvoir said she was fascinated by Sartre because, "Above all, he was more intelligent than I . . . and all the others. It was also his vitality, his generosity, his warmth, his drollery, well, something that made him, at least in my eyes, someone very fascinating."[31] Very special, one would say now.

They worked mostly in the mornings and took walks, all four, in the afternoon. Like her father, Sartre was an excellent mimic and enjoyed entertaining, rolling out "Old Man River" in a deep baritone. Finally they all passed the oral examination, except Maheu. Exit Maheu. "From now on," Sartre said to Beauvoir, "I'm taking you in hand." Beauvoir, aside to the reader: "He had a taste for feminine friendships."[32] He also told her his supreme ambition: "I want to be Spinoza and Stendhal."[33]

Nor did Sartre keep from Beauvoir his recent past with Simone Jolivet (or the fact that sporadically he still saw her?). The Beaver, by this time, was too full of the present, too young, too much in love to be greatly concerned about even the recent past. "It seemed to me at present that all the time I didn't spend with him was time lost."[34] She was even proud of having come second to Sartre, who was first, in the final philosophy examination![35] Sartre was indeed as ugly as Mirabeau (as Simone Jolivet had remarked), but as seductive when he paid court —when he began to talk and use his hands. ("I depended entirely on talking to seduce."[36])

"Here was a man," said a woman who had met sixty-year-old Sartre when she was twenty, "whom you felt loved women and listened to them—to you! Who took what you said and returned it to you as poetry. You felt wonderful—intelligent, brilliant, admired!" *And flattered.* Love, said Sartre, is a "courtly game of seduction," with the declaration of love, and lastly the act, as its goal. A frankly sensuous woman "would have disconcerted and shocked me."[37]

"We would talk about all kinds of things," Beauvoir recalled, "but especially about a subject that interested me most—myself." Never mind, for the moment, that Sartre let her know that "he would never be a family man or even a married man"; he was the most "superior" man she had ever hoped to meet: he knew more than she about *everything.* "It was the first time in my life that I ever felt intellectually dominated by someone." So much the better! "I preferred learning to dazzling." With Sartre's help and encouragement, she, too, would be a writer! "Suddenly, I was no longer alone." Jacques and other men were another species.

> Sartre corresponded exactly to my wish since I was fifteen: he was the double in whom I found all my obsessions brought to incandescence. With him, I could always share everything. When I left him at the beginning of August [1929], I knew that never again would he go out of my life.[38]

Adieu Jacques and the others.

In the fall Beauvoir rented a studio from her grandmother, and furnished and paid for it by giving private lessons at a lycée. With Sartre's return to Paris in mid-October, "my new life really began."[39] He had joined her that summer in the Limousin, where the Beauvoirs had a country home; Sartre stayed, unknown to her parents, in a neighboring hotel. They tried to keep their rendezvous hidden but were discovered by Beauvoir's very disapproving parents. Their love life proper, most likely, took place that October in Paris. For Beauvoir, it was intense and a "discovery." For Sartre, "the sexual act in the narrower sense did not have much interest, he preferred caressing."

This is Beauvoir speaking, September 1982. She continues: "I, on the other hand, was very passionate! For me, sexuality with Sartre the first two or three years was very, very important."[40] Questioned separately, Beauvoir and Sartre each remarked that frankness about their sexual life was most lacking in their autobiographical writings.[41] Beauvoir has since partially made up for the lack—and through her, Sartre. "Sexual relations with women," he told her in the summer and fall of 1974—that is, in the winter of their life—"were an obligation, because classically relations with women implied at some point sexual relations. But I didn't attach such importance to them, and, to be specific, they did not interest me as much as caressing. In other words, I was more a masturbator of women than a lover [*coïteur*] . . . The essential, emotional relationship is that I kiss, caress, run my lips over the body. But the sexual act—it took place, I performed it, I even performed it often, but with a certain indifference."[42]

But the young Sartre with whom Beauvoir was discovering sexuality could still provoke sexual jealousy, which Beauvoir, when she finally met the glamorous "Camille" (Simone Jolivet), sharply experienced. Worse, Sartre, who "lived to write," often teased her with Camille's example—*she* spent many nights writing, whereas the Beaver, drunk with her new freedom in Paris ("the multiple splendor of life"), was not. Beauvoir was further upset by the ease with which Camille went to bed with men without loving them before, during, or afterward. "Should I blame her casualness or my Puritanism?" Beauvoir asked herself. She would never resolve the question. Sartre, trying to help, in reality did not. He preached what he practiced (in his manner)—free and easy lovemaking—which was what Beauvoir felt she could not. Instructing Beauvoir in his preferred way of life, Sartre in fact *imposed* it: "Between us," he explained to her, using a vocabulary dear to him, "it's a matter of a necessary love. We should also have contingent love affairs."[43] It became the basis for their famous *pacte.*

Sartre was facing his own dilemmas: that of imminent military service and afterward a foreign teaching post in Japan; that of loving both Beauvoir and his freedom; and finally the understandable if egocentric desire to have his cake, eat, and preserve it. He proposed to Beauvoir that they sign a "two-year lease." She would arrange to stay that length of time in Paris and they would spend the period of his army leaves "in the closest possible intimacy." Then she, too, might seek a foreign post for several years—the extent of his term in Japan—and they would rejoin each other "to resume, for a more or less prolonged period, a more or less common life . . . But they must not allow their union to degenerate into constraint or habit."

"I agreed," said Beauvoir, ". . . I knew that nothing bad would ever happen to me because of him, except his dying before me."[44]

They added a codicil to their *pacte,* as precious to Sartre as ancillary love affairs: "Not only would neither of the two ever lie to the other, but they would also never conceal anything from each other." Accustomed to privacy, or prudishness, Beauvoir at first was uneasy with the practice of "transparency," but fairly soon Sartre educated her to it. Actually she felt relieved (she said) that she no longer had to put questions to Sartre about his "contingent" life, since he had now promised to hide nothing from her. However, "Later I realized, on two or three occasions, that it was the facile solution"—and a mistake. Still later, Beauvoir would wryly observe that a couple that "tells all" in the name of honesty (transparency?) can be engaged in the trickiest of hypocrisies:

> If the two persuade themselves mutually that they dominate events and the people about whom they are exchanging confidences, under the pretext of practicing honesty, then they are fooling themselves. There is a form of honesty that I have often remarked that is nothing but flagrant hypocrisy. If limited to sexuality, it doesn't at all aim at creating an intimate understanding between the man and the woman, but rather at providing one of the two —the man most frequently—with a tranquilizing ruse: he deludes himself into believing that in confessing his infidelities, he is redeeming himself, whereas, in fact, he is doubling the injury to his partner.[45]

Beauvoir insists, a bit too much, that she is speaking of other couples, which might have taken their own as exemplary, and *possibly* she believes it. There remains the extraordinary blindness—of love?—that marks so many passages of her memoirs. "Before even defining our relations, we had given them a name," she says blandly. Were it not Beauvoir, one would be tempted to write *sweetly.* " 'Ours is a morganatic marriage,' " they declared, and they called each other " 'Monsieur and Madame M. Organatique.' "[46]

How unaware was Beauvoir of the truth in the jest? A morganatic marriage is one in which a man of superior rank takes as his wife a woman of a lower station with the stipulation that neither she nor their issue, if any, shall have any claim to his rank or property. Or privileges? The unwitting aptness of "morganatic" to the Sartre-Beauvoir couple became increasingly manifest. Beauvoir would be the wife (and mother confessor) to whom Sartre would turn and return, because he very soon knew that he was indisputably first in her life, although more than once she anguishedly wondered whether she was first in *his.*[47] She would truly be faithful, even in his fashion, bringing to mind the terrible remark of Chamfort: "A woman depends, for her morals, on the man she loves."

"I accorded him such total confidence," says Beauvoir, at the time of the *pacte* with Sartre, "that he guaranteed me—as formerly my parents and God—a definitive security." How much more traditional or conventional could a marriage contract—their *pacte*—have been?[48] The "force" of her "beatific" love washed away even the grief over Zaza's death (Zaza's mother had forbidden her the man she loved). "That autumn . . . I belonged entirely to the present."[49]

An entire generation was to know and refer to the famous *pacte,* as described by Simone de Beauvoir. To what extent did *she* know Sartre's own thoughts and misgivings? In any event, they were withheld even from that generation until they exploded in the posthumously published intimate *Notebooks* of Sartre *(Les Carnets de la drôle de guerre, novembre 1939–mars 1940).*

In this wartime journal, Sartre examined the first period of his life, from adolescence to young manhood, which he dated from 1921 to 1929, the year of the *pacte* with Beauvoir. At the age of fifteen, he noted, he had already determined to become a "great writer." Women, such as Jolivet, were to be but milestones on the way to his destined *gloire.*

"I have always thought that a great man should hold on to his freedom . . . that he should pursue his way pitilessly." And, "as was natural at that age, I thought of asserting that freedom against women." In the several adventures he had had before the year of the *pacte,* Sartre had felt obliged, he writes, to warn a young woman he had seduced never to "infringe on my freedom." But being "naturally good," he continues, "I gave her the gift of this precious freedom, saying, 'It is the most beautiful present I can offer you.' "

It was a ploy, says Sartre, that had always succeeded. It made the young woman grateful, and one way or another he had always recuperated his freedom, to offer it grandly to another. Then: "I was caught in my own game. The Beaver accepted that freedom and kept it. In 1929, I had been stupid enough to have been affected by it: instead of realizing the extraordinary luck that was mine, I fell into a certain melancholy."[50]

The "luck" was the later realization that he had not lost his freedom with the *pacte* he had offered, but rather that the *pacte* had preserved it. However, what a "melancholic" beginning!

That autumn Sartre began his eighteen months of military service, most of it in the environs of Tours, one hundred and fifty miles southwest of Paris. As agreed, Beauvoir found a temporary post in Paris as a Latin teacher, so as to be in the capital when Sartre was on leave or be able to join him on weekends when he had to stay in camp. Sartre was learning to read wind drift and velocity as his military specialty, but was actually spending more time writing than soldiering. Beauvoir, too, now began to write—a novel—but "without conviction." It was an exercise primarily to satisfy Sartre's urging, and it would end with the third chapter. "Take care," said Sartre, "that you don't become a housewife."[51]

At least once Beauvoir went to Tours with great expectations. "I might have something to announce to you on my return," she wrote to their mutual friend Merleau-Ponty, "or perhaps not."[52] What she hoped to announce remains a mystery, even to Sartre when he heard of it nine years later from Merleau-Ponty.[53] A military wedding? One is free to speculate. But one thing is fairly certain: the sexuality Beauvoir discovered with Sartre did not find its fulfillment with him. She whose ambition had been to be an intellectual among intellectuals now discovered the aching imperatives of an awakened body. As Héloïse, she fought desire by day, "but in the evening, the obsession awoke, thousands of ants coursed my mouth; in the mirror I burst with health, yet a secret sickness rotted my bones . . . I was forced to admit a truth I had tried to mask since adolescence: those desires stronger than my will. . . . my lonely languor solicited no matter whom."

> At night, on the train *returning from Tours to Paris,* an anonymous hand could arouse the length of my leg a throbbing that overwhelmed me with frustration. I kept these shameful things to myself. Now that I was involved in telling everything, this silence seemed to be the touchstone: if I couldn't admit them, that meant they could not be talked about. Because of this silence it held me to, my body, instead of being a link, became an obstacle and I burned with resentment against it.[54] (Emphasis mine)

A burning resentment—against her own body! Not against Sartre, not even during the frustrating train rides back to Paris from Tours? "Everything conspired to fill me with a feeling of decadence and guilt." The resolution for Beauvoir, though she would deny it in these terms, was lifelong sublimation: "To recover, without cheating, my equilibrium, I had to have, I realized, a long-range work to do." It is surely more than coincidence that a page later in her memoirs Beauvoir recalls, "Sartre was again seeing, from time to time, a young woman to whom he had been very attached and whom I have been calling Camille." (Camille/Simone Jolivet was then living in a Montmartre apartment maintained by actor-director Charles Dullin.) Nine pages are needed thereafter for Beauvoir to exorcise "Camille" and finally accept her as a member of Sartre's circle of "feminine friendships." Beauvoir: "To the extent that I regained my self-esteem, I escaped the fascination she had initially had for me."[55]

In February 1931 Sartre terminated his military service. Told that the position in Japan would not be his, he gladly accepted a post teaching philosophy in Le Havre, a port city only a few hours by train from Paris. Beauvoir seems to have been informed rather than consulted. Remorsefully she jotted in her notebook: "I would like to learn how to be alone again. It is so long since I have been alone." But quickly she reconsidered: "I dread solitude more than I aspire to it."[56]

In her turn Beauvoir was named as a philosophy teacher in Marseilles, "more than five hundred miles from Paris"—and in the wrong direction. Sartre saw "my panic." He proposed revision of their *pacte.* "If we married," he said, "we could benefit from a double post and, all things considered, that formality wouldn't seriously affect our way of living." Hardly a romantic proposal of marriage! Beauvoir was not tempted "for an instant," she says.

> I could see how much it would cost Sartre to say good-bye to his travels, his freedom, his youth, in becoming a teacher somewhere in the provinces and settling down as an adult. To settle down as a married man would have been yet one more renunciation.[57]

Only the desire to have children, Beauvoir continues, might have made them really consider marriage, "but we didn't feel it." She had thought of having children when she had conceived marriage with cousin Jacques, but a child with Sartre (she says) would not have strengthened the bond between them. Moreover, it would have deprived her of the time and freedom needed to become a writer.

Sartre in 1977 offered a similar explanation for not having had a child, though acknowledging that "a great writer could have children," since obviously a goodly number of men writers have had them. He could conceivably have had a child and write (unlike the unmentioned Beauvoir, its mother), but, he insisted, he would not have been able to accord it the attention it would have needed (the classical role, of course, of the great writer's wife). And if he had had a child, Sartre was asked, what would he have preferred? "A daughter, certainly," he replied. "Undoubtedly because of the slightly incestuous feeling a father always has for his daughters."[58]

To Sartre's immense relief, Beauvoir said no to his "proposal" of marriage as a solution to their imminent separation. Their *pacte* was consequently reinforced, says Beauvoir. "We did not swear eternal fidelity to each other, but we cast into our distant thirties any possible dissipations." Thus "made calm again," Beauvoir went down to Marseilles and thought to herself, "The school year is only nine months long and trains are fast. A two-day leave, a convenient illness, and I can come to Paris," and there meet Sartre, arriving from Le Havre.[59]

Sartre disliked teaching, and settled down seriously to writing (an excellent first novel, *La Nausée [Nausea],* originally *Mélancholia,* would result). In Marseilles, Beauvoir experienced the exhilaration of the sight of the great city from its grand stairway, the delight of the walks in the woods of the surrounding hills, the heady liquor of her new independence. She, too, sat down to write, but she soon recognized that her first novel, built around the story of Zaza, was unpublishable, and she resolutely began again. Informed that she could have an assignment to Rouen for the next school year, she joyfully accepted. Her drive for independence, strong as it was, would always yield to her emotion for Sartre, who would now be less than a hour by train from her new post.

The next few years form one of Beauvoir's happiest memories. She and Sartre were together at least once every week of the school year and more lengthily during their extended summer vacations. Then Sartre applied for—and received—a research scholarship for 1933–34 in Berlin.

He was happy there at the French Institute, Beauvoir tells us, enjoying a freedom and comradeship he hadn't known since the Ecole Normale years. "Besides," she continues, "he knotted one of those feminine friendships to which he attached such a price." The woman with whom Sartre "knotted" this "friendship" was French (Sartre was not eloquent in German, which narrowed his field), and married to a fellow research scholar more passionately interested in philology (says Beauvoir) than in his wife. Beauvoir may have heard from Sartre about this "contingent affair" during his Christmas holidays in Paris. In any event she hurriedly arranged a two-week leave from the Lycée Jeanne d'Arc at Rouen, using the excuse of an impending nervous breakdown, and arrived in Berlin before the end of February. Not that she was jealous, she pauses to remark, or that she underestimated or was incapable of jealousy. The affair did not take her by surprise: "Sartre had prepared me for his adventures. I had accepted the principle and I accepted the fact, without difficulty."[60]

Beauvoir protests her nonconcern a bit too much and too often, though Sartre had promptly presented her "Marie Girard," whom she found "pretty," given to slow, lethargic smiles and *"stupeurs pensives,"* which had won Sartre's "lively sympathy." Moreover Sartre most likely spent the major part of Beauvoir's two weeks in Berlin with her rather than with Marie, whom he undoubtedly told, in time, of Beauvoir's priority in his life's affections.[61]

Sartre's "telling all," or virtually all, to Beauvoir recalls, to this writer's discomfort, the complicity of the intriguing pair, Valmont and the Marquise de Mertreuil, in that masterpiece of cynicism, *Les Liaisons dangereuses,* and rarely more than in the case of Olga Kosakiewicz, a teenager who had been Beauvoir's pupil.

It began not long after Sartre's return from Berlin and a trip the two took through Germany and Austria. Both, said each, were bored.

Sartre: "On returning I was repossessed by Le Havre, by my life as a teacher, more bitterly perhaps than before. I remember that in November [1934] the Beaver and I were sitting in a café called Les Mouettes, in Le Havre, facing the sea, deploring the fact that nothing new would happen to us."

Beauvoir: "Our lives were locked together, our friendships forever fixed, our careers laid out before us and the world pursuing its course. We were not yet thirty . . ."

Sartre: "We were tired of our meticulous intellectual examinations of our conscience, tired of the virtuous and orderly life we were leading, tired of what we then called 'the constructed.' Because we had 'constructed' our relationship on the basis of total sincerity, entire mutual devotion, and we were sacrificing our spirits and everything that could stir us up to that continuous, *supervised* love we had constructed. Fundamentally we [?] were nostalgic for a disorderly life, a troubled and demanding *laisser faire.* . . . We needed excess, because we had been reasonable so long."

Beauvoir: "Ordinarily I didn't take these complaints seriously. Sometimes, however, I fell from my lofty height. I would even weep buckets of tears when I had had a glass too many."

Sartre: "It all ended in a kind of funny black mood that turned into madness about the month of March [1935]—and, finally, by *my* meeting with O[lga], who was exactly what *we* were wanting and certainly showed us it was so."[62] (Emphasis mine)

Olga Kosakiewicz was slight, blond, pale, and eighteen, or nine years younger than her very recent teacher. (Beauvoir: "I had another concern—I was aging."[63]) She had "the woebegone look of a jellyfish washed up on dry sand,"[64] or exactly what appealed to Sartre ("vague, half-drowned women"[65]). Beauvoir (to change the metaphor) had quite literally taken the lame duckling under her wing while Sartre was in Berlin. Back in Le Havre, Sartre was undergoing his own difficulties, driving himself hard toward his "destiny." Turning thirty was proving a crisis for him. "I had a sort of depression . . . an identity crisis linked to this passage to adult life."[66] Beauvoir: "Sartre couldn't resign himself to passing . . . into full manhood."[67]

He was persuaded by someone to try mescaline to induce dream imagery as an aid to his writing. He had hallucinations. Once, when Beauvoir phoned him from Rouen, she heard Sartre say she had just rescued him from a losing battle with "devilfish." He had nightmares, even when awake, of "umbrellas becoming vultures . . . shoes becoming skeletons," visions of "swarming crabs and polyps." He fantasied houses with "leering faces," saw "eyes and jaws everywhere," and was absolutely convinced "a crawfish was trotting behind him." The menacing male-female figures suggest a sexually disturbed Sartre. Could it have been triggered by the encounter with Olga? He himself feared he was going mad. "Your only madness," a frightened Beauvoir said to him, "is your thinking that you're mad." "You'll see," replied Sartre gloomily.[68]

A trip together to the Italian lakes at Easter time had no effect. When they returned, Sartre would huddle in a corner, "silent, his face blank." He needed care. When Beauvoir was occupied with her school work in Rouen, she had Olga fill in as Sartre's nurse and companion. Not long afterward, Olga became his mistress, in the circumscribed sense of Sartre's particularity. Sartre: "In the story of O. I felt male . . . alas."[69] Nevertheless, or consequently, Sartre recovered as his story with Olga proceeded. She apparently told him she loved him. Sartre: "There is nothing more moving than the moment a confession of love is extracted from someone." He even went on a crash diet ("I began to have a deadly fear of becoming a fat little bald man"). Having won, he imposed his condition: absolute primacy in Olga's affection, though there was no question of subordinating his relationship with Beauvoir or his own freedom. Sartre: "The desire to be loved means affecting another's freedom." Beauvoir: "Sartre demanded exclusive rights [of Olga]." Beauvoir was privy to every twist and turn, she says, especially when Olga seemed to stray from Sartre to a young man of their circle ("We would discuss that for hours"). But better, for Beauvoir, was Sartre's obsession than his regression ("I preferred his fixation on the sentiments of Olga to a recurrence of his hallucinatory psychosis"). Finally, "instead of a couple, we would now be a trio."[70]

Both Beauvoir and Sartre were fascinated by what they called Olga's *"authenticité," "impétuosité," "extrémisme."* "Ours was the cult of youth . . . [which] Olga incarnated with éclat."[71] The physical attraction that Beauvoir felt for the eighteen-year-old has been frankly expressed by her in her first published novel, *L'Invitée* (appearing in English as *She Came to Stay*), which was based on the triangular affair. Its autobiographical content is not contested. "You tell more about yourself in your novels than in your memoirs," Beauvoir often heard—and has since confirmed as true.[72]

Xavière, who is Olga in the novel, kisses Françoise, who is Beauvoir, warmly on the mouth. Shortly before, Beauvoir writes, "Francoise, gazed with a lover's eyes at this woman whom Pierre [who is Sartre] loved." Was there not also the attraction of anyone loved by Pierre/Sartre? Surely, but when Françoise/Beauvoir danced with Xavière/Olga, the sensation was direct, if confused: "She felt Xavière's beautiful warm breasts against her, she inhaled her sweet breath. . . . [She felt] a confused need to keep this amorous face forever turned toward hers, and to be able to say with passion, 'She is mine.' " Eventually, however, inevitably, Françoise "began to feel stifled in this trio." Being Pierre's confidant, too, proved too much for her. As his jealousy of Xavière's own "contingent" affairs mounted, she felt as if she were a third person, set apart. Then, as inevitably, Pierre thrust Xavière aside. Pierre/Sartre: "I get a kick [only] out of the early stages"—not in the continuation.[73]

At the end of *She Came to Stay* (originally titled *Légitime défense*), a shaken Françoise, who weeps on every second page, kills Xavière, making it look like suicide or an accident. In life, Beauvoir would dedicate her novel to Olga, who remained a member of the "family" now grouping itself around Sartre. Beauvoir: "It is not by murder that one can surmont the difficulties brought on by coexistence."[74] As for Sartre: "I had other prospects, other hopes, other loves."[75] High among the other loves was Olga's younger sister, Wanda Kosakiewicz, similarly blond, slight, and wan. She entered Sartre's life as the liaison with Olga ended, in spring 1937.

It was indeed an ecstatic spring for Sartre. *La Nausée* had been accepted for publication by Gallimard; *"Le Mur"* ("The Wall"), an important short story, appeared in the leading literary magazine, *La Nouvelle revue française;* and, Sartre writes, "I knew"—in the Biblical sense—"T[ania, actually Wanda]; I was appointed to a teaching post in Paris. I suddenly felt permeated with profound, fantastic youthfulness."[76]

The following spring (1938) Sartre had another of what he called *"my* little springtime affairs," about which, of course, he wrote to Beauvoir, *"we* do not worry" (emphasis mine).[77] By this time both were teaching in Paris and living in the same Montparnasse hotel, one floor apart. Sartre's springtime affair was with a young student named Martine Bourdin. By July he was reporting to Beauvoir, on a walking tour in the French Alps, that the intrigue "is going too well: yesterday I kissed this girl of fire who sucked in my tongue with the power of a vacuum cleaner." (Beauvoir's letters in response have not yet appeared, assuming Sartre saved them or she kept a copy. But again there is the sulphurous smell of *Les Liaisons dangereuses.*) Sartre described this corner of the web of his "feminine friendships," even as he wove Beauvoir into it: he informed her that he had told Martine Bourdin he loved her, but added, "I spoke to her not only about you but about [Wanda]."[78]

Sartre's letter covers three days, three nights, and seven printed pages: he and Martine, he resumes, spent the following night together.

"Except for penetration, I did *everything*" (emphasis his). An odd remark ensued: "This is the first time I have gone to bed with a brunette" —where did that leave Beauvoir? "Or rather"—Sartre may have been catching himself—"with a *black,* Provencal as the devil, full of smells, and curiously hairy." The next night resulted in a similar experience. "Two wonderful tragic nights," but "there is no place for her in my life. She wanted to give me her virginity. I don't know whether I took it or not." By the way, he had just seen Olga, who had seen him with Martine, but he had reassured her that Wanda remained "the apple of my eye"! Would she tell her sister that, because it seemed Wanda had heard about Martine? Olga would, and did. All this to Beauvoir, "because," Sartre closed his letter, "I believe you are fonder of my love stories than declarations of love . . . I love you, good little Beaver." Finally Sartre deflowered the insistent Martine. He was sure this time, he told Beauvoir, since "I found traces of blood on my sheets."[79]

The anticlimax of the shoddy affair (which would drag on, as usual) was Sartre's writing a nasty, open letter to Martine, which he gave to Wanda to read and post, so that she might be made easy on the score of Martine's standing in his eyes. A copy of the letter went to Beauvoir for comment! Truly Sartre surpassed even himself. To Beauvoir, ever his mother confessor:

> I have never known how to lead my sexual life or my sentimental life properly; I sincerely and profoundly consider myself a bastard. And a two-bit bastard at that, a kind of university sadist and civil-service Don Juan who makes you want to throw up.[80]

But he did not give up Martine.

HOW about the others in these "contingent" love affairs—Olga, Wanda, and others, one of whom would kill herself after World War II? Sartre: "They weren't very content . . . They had to be made to swallow the *'pacte.'* " How would Sartre have liked to have been "contingent"? "It didn't happen to me at the time. . . . I would not have liked it at all."[81] Similarly queried, Beauvoir replied: "There was certainly a great deal of egotism on the part of Sartre and of myself to make our pact and involve third persons in these adventures." There is no reason to be proud of this, is there? Beauvoir: "No, far from it."[82]

These were largely the apolitical prewar years, when Beauvoir and Sartre noted Nazism by turning their back to it in their travels through Germany and central Europe. "We remained spectators," said Beauvoir, when the Popular Front was formed in France, and were scarcely more than that when the Spanish Civil War broke out, though she claimed "it dominated our life for two and a half years." Actually the preoccupation of both Beauvoir and Sartre was primarily Sartre. Beauvoir: "As Rilke wrote with regard to Rodin, Sartre was 'his own heaven,' " and thus Beauvoir's—"for me his existence justified the world that nothing justified in his eyes." And so wrote Milton of Adam and Eve: "He for God and she for God in him."[83]

The two voyaged together in Belgium and Italy, skied in the Alps. Beauvoir liked energetic hikes in the countryside, but Sartre was allergic to greenery, preferring tailored stone to trees, towns to landscapes, and generally scorning the world of plants and insects and uncooked foods. Shellfish were an absolute abhorrence. In Venice he was once again trailed by an imaginary crawfish. Beauvoir, as Sartre's Boswell, also wrote about his travels with his mother and stepfather in Norway, though made without her. The description was immediately preceded by a recording of a "family" (*their* family) get-together in Olga's hotel room, when "Sartre dressed as a woman." "Curiously," Beauvoir continued, "the disguise became him." Then: "During his cruise in Norway, on the occasion of a costume ball, he had put on a black velvet dress of his mother and a blond wig with long tresses." Throughout the ball and afterward, Beauvoir recounted blandly, Sartre, in drag, delighted in provoking "an American lesbian" to passionately court him and, the following morning, enjoyed her discomfiture.[84]

When the Munich Pact was signed in September 1938, Beauvoir celebrated. "I felt no scruple in rejoicing. It seemed to me that I had escaped death for an eternity."[85] On September 2, 1939, Sartre was mobilized. On September 3, war was declared.

Sartre went off to join the Seventieth Division at Nancy as a meteorologist, wearing Beauvoir's ski shoes. He wrote to her en route and continued his letter on arrival. The train trip, he said, was Kafkaesque, and he felt like a dwarf, in his oversize uniform. But the missive is a love letter, as well, speaking of his sadness at the sight of Beauvoir's "ravaged" face behind the gate at Gare de l'Est, Paris's railway station for trains to the east.

> If only you were lying on the straw mattress, next to me, how happy I would be. But you will not be lying there. It will be someone who snores, loudly. Oh, my love, how I love you, how I need you. Adieu . . . Now I'm going to write a little note to my parents and to Wanda [always printed as "T.," or "Tania"[86]]. I love you with all my strength.[87]

Sartre wrote Beauvoir and Wanda Kosakiewicz almost daily, besides working on a new novel, *L'Age de raison,* writing to his mother and others (his published correspondence is almost wholly with women), and soon filling notebook after notebook in journal form. His army task of sending up a weather balloon several times a day left him many hours to himself. From Nancy, six weeks later, he was trucked to Brumath, in Alsace, a small town less than ten miles from the Rhine. For days Beauvoir's and Sartre's letters had not reached each other; then they crossed in disorder. "My dear little wife," Sartre had written after receiving the first communication from Beauvoir. "I'm furious about the imbecilic remark of my mother [to you]."[88] Beauvoir: "She reprimanded my way of life."[89]

Sartre writes more easily of his tender memories of Olga and of his concern for Wanda. September 17: "At last a little letter from [Wanda] that stirred my heart . . . She seems terribly dejected. My love, do all you can to have her come to Paris (without ruining yourself) . . . And try to give a thousand francs a month to the two Z's [Kosakiewicz's]."[90] Sartre was making money from his writings and had given Beauvoir full power to draw upon it, as well as upon his military pay. (Beauvoir also had a salary as a lycée teacher.) Dutifully she would do what was expected—share an apartment with Olga and send for Wanda. September 28: Sartre announced he might soon have a leave. "If I have eight days . . . I'll spend six with you and two with [Wanda]. If I have six days, I will spend them all with you, so don't worry on this point."[91] On October 5 Beauvoir invented a sick sister living near Strasbourg, so that she could procure an official pass allowing her to see Sartre in Brumath, close by.

The visit became more urgent as she sensed Sartre's growing disquiet concerning Wanda. October 17, Sartre:

> What you tell me—that I will find her again after the war—is quite possible. . . . But—to keep nothing from you—that satisfies me little. I'm not thinking much about the postwar and really envisage, fundamentally, finding *you* then. But feeling her detaching herself progressively from me and falling into other hands . . . will be unpleasant for me. And that's what will fatally happen.[92]

But the five-day visit of Beauvoir with Sartre in early November did go well. They were indeed *one* when together (as Sartre wrote so often). Even the considerable time they spent talking of Sartre's *other*—or others—they spent as one. Immediately after her departure, Sartre wrote Beauvoir warmly of her visit, of her "stark naked presence, [her] little faces, tender smiles, and little arms around [his] neck." Sartre had a disconcerting (actually grandmotherly) habit of adding *petit* ("little") to his phrases. "My dear love, my little flower, we were one, were we not? . . . You were a little charm and you made me remember what real happiness was. I kiss you on your two little cheeks."[93] Several weeks later, however, Sartre was confiding his misgivings in a notebook. Beauvoir's arrival "had the effect of a delayed bomb," disturbing the equilibrium he had reached in his army life.[94] More likely he was upset because of what he was concurrently hearing. Olga was seeing a military man, and Wanda, which was worse, was going out with student-actor Roger Blin. Sartre was furious, with a jealousy he denied. His stratagem of self-deception was fairly typical. He wrote Beauvoir that he had "feigned" jealousy in a letter to Wanda, which had "the effect upon him of a pitiful little sacrilege" of a lie, but now "I am unburdening myself of it in telling it to you"![95]

Two months later, January 17, 1940, Sartre was telling Beauvoir about a letter from Martine Bourdin, which he was not forwarding because it was "not interesting." "I replied," Sartre said, "in the 'lover's' style, which you know."[96] But in February Sartre reached perhaps the lowest point in the highly complicated game he and Beauvoir were playing. In a letter to her, written exactly four days after his confession of having been a "bastard" in his relationship with Martine, Sartre wrote:

> I know: there is something ignoble in my relations with [Wanda]. It is ignoble that I should be obliged to tell her I don't love you anymore, ignoble that I should think I must write her, "I would walk over anyone's body, including the Beaver's . . . , for you." . . . I am not pretending when I do these things, as I used to pretend I was a "good little boy" once upon a time . . . I am in them . . . I believe that he who wants the end wants the means. And I want the end.[97]

Pursuing the same end, presumably, in May, Sartre offered to marry Wanda, when it seemed she might have become tubercular (she had not, he later wrote Beauvoir with relief), which did not prevent him from having his customary "little springtime affair" with "Charlotte" in June.[98]

In May, however, the German army had invaded Holland, and in June Marshal Pétain would ask for an armistice. On the twenty-first, Sartre was taken prisoner. In mid-June, meanwhile, Beauvoir had joined the exodus from Paris; then, hearing of the armistice, had returned to the capital, hoping for news of Sartre ("believing he was literally dying of hunger"[99]). In fact an unsuffering Sartre was finding new friends in the German stalag, going on with his writing, and even preparing a Christmas play for his fellow prisoners. Meantime Beauvoir, when not teaching, was trying to distract herself by reading Hegel's *Phenomenology of the Mind* in the Bibliothèque Nationale.

The Sartre she discovered when he finally returned, in March 1941, after his medical release from prison camp, "completely perplexed me: he arrived from another world." He was suddenly stiffly moralistic. She was wrong, he said, to buy on the black market (as did those who could). "I had done wrong in signing a paper certifying that I was neither a Free Mason nor a Jew"—so that she might continue teaching. But above all, Sartre declared, they must now abandon their former self-isolation. "We must break that seclusion, unite, organize the resistance."[100] Returning to the cafés of Paris from the German prison camp, Sartre, too, had the sensation of coming from another world:

> I had the strange impression that people were isolated from one another. It was simply that they were not touching each other, whereas in the prisoner-of-war camp we touched each other all the time . . . This sort of contact was, as it were, the superficial expression of a much more profound contact . . . which I first experienced there.[101]

Sartre was determined to retain that new sense of solidarity and *engagement,* social purpose and action. Beauvoir remained skeptical but compliant.

Rome, 1973. Interviewer: "Sartre, on your returning from the war, you said, 'Simone, we are going to be political.' And you, Simone, wrote, 'So we became political.'" Beauvoir: "It was not, I believe, because I am a woman that I reacted that way . . . Almost all our friends, the same age or younger, followed him then . . . But yes, I did have to agree with Sartre on everything—for the important things. . . ."[102]

Briefly Sartre went back to teaching (he never stopped writing) before going down by bicycle into the unoccupied zone of France with Beauvoir. The trip had a twofold purpose: to regularize his demobilization and, more important, to contact individuals on behalf of a new resistance movement that he hopefully baptized "Socialism and Freedom." On the Riviera, André Gide was noncommittal and André Malraux unencouraging—"he counted on Russian tanks and American planes . . ."[103] Daunted, Sartre set himself to writing a play with a

Greek theme, *Les Mouches (The Flies).* While he sat at a café and worked on the dialogue, Beauvoir continued cycling along the coast.

Back in Paris, Sartre renounced his resistance scheme as premature and Beauvoir learned to cook for the "family" on slim war rations and in a small hotel room. However, *L'Invitée* was finished and accepted, and *Les Mouches* performed (in occupied Paris). As Beauvoir worked on a new novel, Sartre undertook his massive philosophic tome, *L'Etre et le néant (Being and Nothingness).* When published in 1943, with a dedication "To the Beaver," it came to 724 printed pages. A line of Sartre was used on the wrapper around the 1945 reprint, as if to summarize the message: "What counts in a vase is the void in the middle." The work would establish Sartre among the leading philosophical thinkers of the postwar world, with the added label of "existentialist"—that is, a descendant of Kierkegaard via Husserl and Heidegger. That "existence precedes essence" is the essential doctrine.

"Existentialism," Sartre further explained to this author, then a young reporter, "is nothing else than an attempt to draw all the consequences of a coherent atheistic position. It declares that even if God did exist, that would change nothing, man has no excuses. He is free. He makes himself cowardly or heroic, what counts is total involvement."[104]

Beauvoir adopted Sartre's philosophy—its ethics, metaphysics, ontology, and *much of its sexism*—as her own. Paradoxically she would appropriate *macho* themes of *Being and Nothingness*—"which ends in an orgy of sexist remarks"—in the creation of her own pioneer work, *The Second Sex*—"which dynamized the women's movement in Europe and America."[105] This adoption of so many of Sartre's attitudes toward the relations between the sexes ("love is conflict"), and particularly toward Beauvoir's own sex (as we shall see), was critical for their couple. Wherefore the half-decade leap ahead at this point in citing comparable passages from both their major works.

From Sartre's *Being and Nothingness* (1943):

> To look upon is to *deflower* . . . . Knowledge is simultaneously *penetration* and a caress of the *surface*. . . .
>
> The For-itself is suddenly compromised. I open my hands, I want to let the slimy go and it sticks to me, it draws me, it sucks me . . . It is a soft, surrendering activity, moist and feminine in its sucking . . . it attracts me to it as the bottom of a precipice might attract me . . . Suddenly I seize the trap of the slimy . . . I cannot slide on this slime, all its suction cups retain me . . . it sticks like a leech . . . Slime is the revenge of the In-itself. A sickeningly

> sweet, feminine revenge that is symbolized at another level by the quality of the *sugary*. . . .
>
> The obscenity of the female sex organ is that of everything *gaping* . . . In herself a woman appeals to a foreign flesh that is to transform her into a plenitude of being by penetration and dilution. And conversely, woman senses her condition as an appeal precisely because she is a "hole." That is the true origin of the Adlerian complex. Without any doubt her sex organ is a mouth, and a voracious mouth, which devours the penis—which can well lead to the idea of castration: the act of love is the castration of man —but this is above all because the woman's organ is a hole (emphasis Sartre's).[106]

Knowledge as rape plus a few sexual fantasies . . . The "feminine" as a disparaging term . . . The vagina as a devouring threat. All that lacks is the *vagina dentata,* the vagina complete with teeth . . . Beauvoir must have been the most obtuse intelligent woman of her time.

From Beauvoir's *The Second Sex* (1949):

> The sex organ of man is clean and simple as a finger; it exhibits itself with innocence and often boys have shown it to their comrades with pride and rivalry; the feminine sex organ is mysterious to the woman herself, concealed, troubled, mucous, moist; it bleeds every month, it is often soiled with secretions, it has a secret and hazardous life . . . Whereas a man has an "erection," a woman becomes "wet"; in the word itself are memories of bedwetting, of guilty and involuntary yielding to the need of urinating . . . [For a man] projecting a liquid, urine or sperm, does not humiliate: it is an active operation; but it is humiliating when the liquid emerges passively . . . it is a process of decomposition that horrifies.
>
> Feminine sexual desire is the soft palpitation of a shellfish; whereas man is impetuous, woman is only impatient . . . man dives on his prey like the eagle and the falcon; she waits like a carnivorous plant, a boggy swamp in which insects and children are sucked down; she is suction, suction cup, humus, pitch, and glue, a passive attraction, insinuating and viscous . . . after her first coition, a woman is very often more in revolt against her sexual destiny than before.[107]

How often did Beauvoir speak—with more scorn than pity—of women who have swallowed whole a man's thinking?

By the end of the war and the liberation of France, both Beauvoir and Sartre were established writers, living from their work, sharing the royalties. Teaching was behind them; novels and plays sustained them. They founded a new political and cultural magazine, *Les Temps modernes (Modern Times).* Sartre's gift for polemics, for dominating his contemporaries with a dazzling brilliance, the sudden craze called "existentialism" that would seize postwar youth, were making them gurus of their time, famous beyond their coterie—Beauvoir somewhat by ricochet ("When they called me 'la grande Sartreuse' or 'Notre Dame de Sartre,' I simply laughed."[108])

Their emotional life may have briefly stabilized. In the aftermath of the Martine Bourdin liaison, Sartre had declared that Wanda thereafter would suffice for him "within the officially established relationship" with Beauvoir; that is, she would suffice as his "extramarital affair." As for Beauvoir, she, said Sartre, was "the only honesty in my life." If nothing else, "I will have loved a person with all my strength, without the passionate and without the marvelous, but *from within"* (emphasis Sartre's).[109] How did Beauvoir feel about being loved without passion or a sense of wonder? One might say she steeled herself to it. She quotes a furious young woman friend about this time (early in the war) who said to her: "You are a clock in a refrigerator!"[110]

More recently, apropos her relations with Sartre, Beauvoir said to another young friend, "There is something dark [mysterious, obscure] in sexuality. Between Sartre and me everything was transparent."

Albert Camus, Algerian-born author of *The Stranger* and *The Myth of Sisyphus,* whom Beauvoir found charming and seductive and Sartre talented and superficial, had become a fairly close friend, though their ties remained prickly. (Perhaps there was some professional jealousy on both sides; on Sartre's part it was more personal. Camus was considered handsome and irresistible. Sartre to Beauvoir: "[Wanda] is gentle as a lamb since her sister [Olga] has talked sense to her: why is she pursuing Camus? what does she want of him? am I not much better? and much nicer? She had better watch out."[111])

As director of the former resistance newspaper, *Combat,* Camus suggested to Sartre that he do a series of articles on America. Sartre gladly agreed, and flew to New York in January 1945 on a military plane, as a guest of the U.S. State Department. Eager to get away from a Paris without Sartre, Beauvoir managed to obtain an invitation to lecture in Portugal and write *her* series of articles on the Iberian peninsula. Within a few days of his arrival in New York, Sartre met Dolores V., whom Beauvoir calls "M" in her memoirs. On their third night together, he became Dolores's lover; he did not return to Paris before

May. Beauvoir had returned in April; she had few letters from Sartre, and they, she says laconically, were "lost."[112]

Sartre came back to discover that his stepfather (Joseph Mancy) had died and his mother wanted him to live with her. Apparently without hesitation, Sartre bought a large, easily divided apartment on the rue Bonaparte, which overlooked the eleventh-century church and square of St. Germain-des-Prés, and shortly afterward moved into it with his mother. "It's my third marriage!" Madame Mancy "gaily" told Beauvoir, who reports it less gaily. She had already heard Sartre's mother remark more than once, "I was twice married and a mother, but I am still virginal." (Beauvoir: "At eighty, her figure was still slim and elegant [and *coquette*]. . . . It even happened that men followed her in the street.")[113]

How soon or how fully Sartre spoke of Dolores to Beauvoir is still uncertain, but by the fall he had arranged to go back to New York to see her, *although they had agreed to end their affair in May.* It hit Beauvoir hard—understandably. The liaison with Dolores would last four more years, and four of Sartre's books would be dedicated to her. When he departed for America in December 1945, Beauvoir again desperately sought to get away from a Sartre-less Paris, a cold, lonely winter. Abruptly she tells us, "I had a carbuncle on one leg that immobilized me for several days," but characteristically she went skiing in Switzerland, and wrote sadly to Sartre of the memory it evoked.[114] Then she flew to North Africa, thanks to the Alliance Française, to lecture in Tunis and Algiers.

In the spring Sartre returned—overfull of talk about Dolores. "Their attachment was mutual and they envisaged spending three or four months every year together. So be it," says Beauvoir stiffly, "separations don't scare me."

> But he evoked with such gaiety the weeks he had spent with her in New York that I became worried . . . suddenly I asked myself whether M. [Dolores] did not mean more to him than I. . . . In a union that has endured more than fifteen years, what part is mere habit? What concessions does it imply? I knew my own answer, not Sartre's. . . . I found him more opaque; there were great differences between us; they didn't bother me, to the contrary, but him? According to what he said, M. shared exactly his reactions, his emotions, his restlessness, his desires . . . Perhaps this marked a profound harmony between them . . . which Sartre did not experience with me and which was more precious to him than our understanding. I wanted to know . . . I asked him, "Frankly, who

> means more to you, M. or I?" "M. counts enormously for me," Sartre replied, "but it is you I am with." I was breathless. I understood him to mean, "I respect our *pacte,* don't ask me anything more."[115]

It could have been the irritated reply of a husband resigned to his wife. "Such a reply put the whole future into question." Throughout the noon meal with friends, Sartre observed Beauvoir's uneasiness. Later he attempted to further explain. Had they not always placed more importance on actions than on words? "Instead of losing himself in words, he had invoked the proof of a fact. I believed him." Beauvoir thus closes *this* conversation. Then, as abruptly as she had mentioned her "carbuncle" upon Sartre's leaving her for New York and Dolores, she remarks: "Shortly afterward . . . Sartre had the mumps." To each *his* turn. Sartre, too, was deeply affected by their situation, though one might dwell on the difference of illness, on Sartre's virtual regression to childhood, or on Beauvoir's mention of Sartre's "mumps" as a kind of conscious or unconscious act of revenge for her deeply disturbed state, if not humiliation.[116]

But this, too, was absorbed. Together they traveled and lectured in Switzerland, Italy, and Holland. That winter Sartre began his break with Camus, who was too steadfastly anti-Communist, or rather anti-Stalinist, for Sartre's new political inclination. At about the same time Arthur Koestler, of *Darkness at Noon,* turbulently, hilariously, drunkenly, and transiently (some would add *erotically* for Simone de Beauvoir) entered their lives. But for them, he, even more than Camus, was "rabidly" anti-Soviet and, for most intellectuals of the French left, prematurely against the Communist Party, and he would disappear from the French scene.

Then, in January 1947, Beauvoir left France for a series of talks at American universities (on the moral problems of the postwar writer). She was scheduled to return late in May. In New York she met Dolores, about to depart for Paris to be with Sartre until Beauvoir's return. Dolores was "as charming as Sartre said she was," says Beauvoir, with "the prettiest smile in the world."[117] (These are recollections written in the tranquility of Sartre's ultimate rupture with Dolores.) In February, while in Chicago, Beauvoir met novelist Nelson Algren, was intrigued, returned several weeks later, and fell in love with him.

Beauvoir's falling in love was not a free fall (nor was it accidental that her liaison with Algren would last four years, or roughly the length of Sartre's liaison with Dolores; Chamfort has previously provided the commentary on *that*). She was having an unsatisfactory affair with a married man in New York, when, unexpectedly, she received a letter from Sartre early in May, asking her to postpone her return to Paris, "because [Dolores] was extending her stay for about ten days." Her emotional reaction, Beauvoir says carefully, was a kind of "nostalgia." "I too wanted to walk with a man who, for the time, would be mine." She phoned Algren to come to New York. He could not. She flew to Chicago. At first there were "embarrassment, impatience, misunderstanding, fatigue" between them, "then, finally, the dazzling sensation of deep understanding."[118] The physical encounter is rapturously, *hungrily,* described in *The Mandarins,* an autobiographical novel:

> He was already pressing me to him, a furnace of flesh imprisoning my lips, a tongue was probing my mouth, and my body was rising from the dead . . .
>
> Suddenly, he was no longer either awkward or modest. His desire transformed me. I who for so long a time had been without taste, without form, again possessed breasts, a belly, flesh; I was as nourishing as bread, as fragrant as earth. It was so miraculous that I didn't think of measuring my time or my pleasure; I know only that before we fell asleep I could hear the gentle chirpings of dawn . . . Lewis handed me a glass and in one gulp I drank the orange juice that had, that morning, a convalescent taste—as if voluptuousness were a sickness, or as if my whole life had been one long illness from which I was just beginning to recover.[119]

"My body was rising from the dead . . . my whole life had been one long illness . . ." One wants to say, "Poor Beauvoir, poor Sartre," such is the frustrated life revealed. However, one also applies their own philosophy of existentialist responsibility for their acts to each other as well as to *"l'autre"*—the other. Beauvoir, when she fell in love, sharply posed the problem: "Between fidelity and freedom is there a possible conciliation? At what price? . . . How would a third person accommodate himself or herself to our arrangement [the *pacte*]?"[120] The case was acutely presented now with Nelson Algren (Lewis Brogan in *The Mandarins*). When Beauvoir told him, just before leaving for New York and France, that her life was in Paris and with Sartre, he was very taken aback—even though she had told Algren (as Sartre had informed Dolores) that they could arrange to be together three or four months every year. "Why waste three quarters of our lives waiting?" Lewis Brogan would reply in the novel. "Because love is not everything," Anne Dubreuilh/Beauvoir would counter. The greater part of her life consisted of being with Sartre and working in France.

Anne and Lewis would try their "three–four month" arrangement for several years; it would not work. "You can't love someone who isn't all yours the same way as someone who is," Lewis would finally say. Anne, of course, would remain with her *husband* (Robert Dubreuilh/ Sartre), for she was indeed all *his;* Lewis would go back to his former wife. Neither in life nor in *The Mandarins* would the ending be happy. " 'For God's sake, don't yawn!' I said, bursting into tears. 'For God's sake, don't cry!' he said."[121]

Beauvoir would return again and again in her writing to her love liaison with Algren—"Would I be punished someday for having dared to love without giving my whole life?" Anne asks[122]—in *America Day by Day, The Mandarins* (dedicated "To Nelson Algren"), *Force of Circumstance, All Said and Done,* and many interviews. Nelson Algren, who had kept his silence, finally responded, or rather, exploded, when *Force of Circumstance* appeared in 1963 (in French). He was then fifty-four, Beauvoir fifty-five. To expose the relationship between two people as Beauvoir had, Algren said bluntly (there was no philosophical nod to the notion of "transparency" dear to the existentialist lovers), was to diminish it.

> It shows the relationship could never have meant a great deal in the first place, if its ultimate use has so little to do with love. It becomes something else. See, the big thing about sexual love is it lets you become her and lets her become you, but when you share the relationship with everybody who can afford a book, you reduce it.[123]

Algren would have more cutting things to say as their affair attained international notoriety, thus sharing, despite himself, in the reduction process he decried.

In the meantime, however, sixteen years before *Force of Circumstance* appeared . . .

Still shaken by the first passionate encounter with Algren, in May 1947 Beauvoir came back to Paris and an embarrassed Sartre. She recounts it with the relentless compulsion of her memoirs: Before embarking for Paris, Dolores had written to Sartre, "I am arriving determined to do everything to get you to ask me to stay." He had not. Dolores, nonetheless, chose to stay on until July. To avoid friction, Beauvoir *and* Sartre moved into a hotel in the suburbs. From there Sartre would go several evenings during the week to Paris to be with Dolores. That would have suited Beauvoir (she says), but it did not suit Dolores. The nights Sartre stayed in the suburbs, she telephoned him *"dramatiquement." She* was not resigned to going back to New York, as they had once agreed. Like Algren, she simply did not understand how one could say one loved someone and not want to be with that person "for months and months." Sartre, says Beauvoir, "felt guilty." Indeed he *was* guilty, as Beauvoir proceeds to prove and then attempts to disprove—or rather, to *excuse* (is she not also examining the contradiction of her declaration of love to Algren and her departure from him?):

> Of course, he had warned her . . . but by saying he loved her he denied his warning; for—especially in the eyes of women [!]—love triumphs over all barriers. M. [Dolores] was not entirely in the wrong . . . the truth of the present imperiously sweeps away all former words . . . Her error was to regard as mere verbal precautions what were, for Sartre, less a decision than a certainty . . . His excuse is that, while refusing to alter his relations with me, he cared for her violently and had wanted to believe a compromise possible.
>
> . . . I spent two painful months.[124]

With Dolores finally gone (until the following summer), Beauvoir and Sartre moved back to Paris and their lives somewhat as before (somewhat, because a distressed Beauvoir made a quick, two-week trip to Chicago to see Algren). The "family" had enlarged to include Boris Vian, young jazzman and writer, and his blond, willowy wife, Michelle. On Sartre's suggestion, Beauvoir now undertook *The Second Sex,* which was eventually two volumes and the historical starting point of modern feminism. Meanwhile Sartre completed his political play *Les Mains sales (Red Gloves* or *Crime Passionnel).* When not writing, it was the editing of *Les Temps modernes,* and particularly the growing involvement in politics, that preoccupied both, especially Sartre. To the end of his days he would vainly hope for a working relationship with the Communist Party, which responded with suspicion, scorn, or occasional opportunism, but always with distrust. The period coincided with the Manichaeism of the Cold War, which offered false alternatives to an already confused situation on the intellectual left. Beauvoir's *Mandarins* describes the scene and the players—Sartre, Camus, Koestler, et al.—with the predictable perspective of her key player.

For the third time, Beauvoir went to Algren in Chicago. It was the annual rendezvous. They were to spend four months together, while Dolores passed the same length of time with Sartre in Europe. Dolores, or Sartre, or both, proved difficult; their period of togetherness was cut to two months and Beauvoir informed. Unfortunately she failed to tell Algren of a change in plans—she was returning sooner than expected to Paris—until the end of their trip down the Mississippi and through Central America. Algren was bitter and upset. Beauvoir wept. In New York, before she flew back to France, Algren "proposed marriage." She refused, but "what a nightmare, that return," she says sadly. In Paris she prepared to leave with Sartre on *their* vacation, when suddenly he had a phone call from New York. It was Dolores, in tears. She pleaded for another month with him. "He yielded." When they went south to the Mediterranean coast, Beauvoir cabled Algren, proposing a month with him in Chicago. *He* refused: "Too much work." Beauvoir: "I was pained; work was only a pretext; but I was also relieved: these meetings, partings, rebuffs, and sudden élans were too much for me." Perhaps Beauvoir was really "relieved," but more assuredly that famous "liberating" pact of fidelity and contingent love had proved a terrible burden. There would be another voyage with Algren—to Italy and North Africa—then a fifth and last trip to see him in America in October 1951—when he told her he was going to remarry his former wife. Beauvoir offered friendship; Algren replied that he could never offer less than love. "All the past clutched my heart, my defeat was unbearable; in the taxi, on the train, in the plane, that evening in New York . . . I did not stop crying. . . . Never again would I sleep in the warmth of another's body. Never. What a death bell!"[125]

For three years Beauvoir had been living in a studio on the rue de la Bûcherie, near the cathedral of Notre Dame. Here she had established the habit of working in the morning, then going in the afternoon to work with Sartre in his apartment on the rue Bonaparte. Here, too, a year after the break with Algren, Beauvoir would begin life with Claude Lanzmann, but, as ever, within the constraints of the *pacte* with Sartre, who had meanwhile broken with Dolores and was intimately, if contingently, enjoying the company of Michelle Vian, now separated from her husband. The carrousel continued. Sartre always preferred the company of women, pretty women, he underlined, to that of men *—and there were "a great number of them" in his life, Beauvoir reminded him when he was seventy.*[126] When younger, Sartre had noted that he probably sought their company "to lighten the burden of my ugliness," at the same time remarking, "I always chose good-looking men as my friends."[127] Young or old, he relished saying, "Fundamentally I enjoy the company of a woman because I don't like conversations about ideas."[128] (Most Socratic and scarcely flattering for his women friends, one might suppose.)

"I was forty-four," said Beauvoir, "and I was relegated to the land of shadows."[129] It was 1952, the year she met Claude Lanzmann, twenty-seven. "I felt available and wanted something to happen. . . . Our differences in age and the circumstances brought the story to an end . . . to give way to a deep friendship. In this case, too, the end was inevitable."[130] There is a certain lucidity in this (written twenty years afterward) that implies a sang-froid that in fact did not then exist, certainly not on the part of Beauvoir, for whom the body's death bell was still tolling in "the land of shadows."

Claude Lanzmann was a young, emotive, left-wing journalist who had joined the staff of *Les Temps modernes* and become a member of the "family." Women found him attractive, says Beauvoir, "I also." He could toss off the most extravagant remarks with a boyish nonchalance, "and his turn of mind was like Sartre's." He had called one morning to invite her to the cinema. "What film?" she had asked. "Any film," he had replied. She had accepted. "When I hung up, I burst into tears." They became lovers. "I found my body again." After a trip together to Holland, they decided to live together (but "there was no question of replacing my entente with Sartre"). Lanzmann "accepted me with my past and my present." She would spend summers as usual with Sartre; "Lanzmann would join us for ten days." He moved his things into the studio on the rue de la Bûcherie. "His presence next to me relieved me of my age . . . it removed my anxieties." She saw Sartre "as often as before," but there were new practical arrangements. The "family" still preferred meeting in twos—that is, tête-à-tête—coming all together for fiestas, such as the New Year's celebration of the passing of 1952. "As I, Sartre especially liked the intimate circle I gathered at the rue de la Bûcherie—Olga and Bost, Wanda, Michelle, and Lanzmann."[131]

After receiving the Prix Goncourt, France's leading literary award, for *The Mandarins* and profiting from the sales that followed, Beauvoir bought a more commodious duplex on the rue Schoelcher, which faced the gray wall of the Montparnasse cemetery. She was aided by Lanzmann in furnishing it. The first night she slept in the new bedroom, she said to herself, *"Voilà,* my deathbed." "Sometimes," she wrote, "I repeat it to myself." The two would travel as a pair, then join Sartre and Michelle Vian, or Olga and Bost, or all four. But every summer, at the least, Sartre and Beauvoir spent weeks alone to themselves, usually in Rome. *They* were still the couple, whatever the variations on that theme.

Shared affections, memories, and politics, a kind of mysticism about the messianic role of the working class and "its Party," held the "family" together throughout the Cold War and the war in Indo-China, as it would throughout the war in Algeria. The splits with former friends, such as Camus and, earlier, Raymond Aron, simply made them a tighter *bande à part,* with Sartre as its uncontested *chef.* Here the "family" was far from alone. Ideologically, Sartre dominated—"terrorized," to use his term again—an entire generation of intellectuals leaning sentimentally to the left, with his debater's brilliance. (Because his peers deemed he had lost, Camus was so shaken by his conflict with Sartre that he was virtually paralyzed as a writer for some time.) "Little by little," Beauvoir has written, as if the unwitting spokesperson of that generation of intellectuals, "I liquidated my idealistic moralism and ended by considering as my own, Sartre's point of view."[132]

In the spring or early summer of 1956, Sartre met Arlette Elkaïm, an eighteen-year-old student, born in Algeria, who was preparing for a teachers' college in the suburbs of Paris. She had written Sartre apropos a term paper she had done whose debt to his work had drawn the discontent of her philosophy professor. She and Sartre became lovers. "There was some sexuality for a few years," she says, "then we settled down as father and daughter. One can have a full life without the 'sentimental' side. My life with him *was* my life."[133] (According to one account, Arlette had become pregnant during those first years, Sartre had shown a willingness to marry her, Beauvoir had made a scene, and the marriage proposal had been dropped.[134]) In 1965 Sartre adopted Arlette Elkaïm, despite Beauvoir's strong protest and the "family's" expression of unhappiness (particularly his "spiritual sons' "). On vacation in Rome with Arlette, Sartre had heard a woman refer to her as his daughter. It had stuck in his mind. "So, what if we adopted each other?" Sartre had suggested one day to Arlette. In the last years, when he was growing blind, Sartre said to her, "You will be my Antigone. You will push my little cart."[135]

May 13, 1958. A coup by the French army brought de Gaulle to power. June 18. Sartre and Beauvoir, vacationing in Italy, read about the execution of Nagy in Hungary. Poor Sartre (!), said Beauvoir, "who had wanted to forget politics for a few days." Lanzmann was away on a long journalistic mission to the Far East. Mid-August. Before returning to Paris, Beauvoir accompanied Sartre to Pisa, where he waited for Michelle to join him. Beauvoir's diary, August 17: "Sign of old age: the anguish of all departures, of all separations. And the sadness of all memories, because I sense they are condemned to death." September 9. Beauvoir participates with Bost and Lanzmann, back from China, in a mass demonstration against de Gaulle's referendum on a new constitution. September 16. Sartre returns, "exhausted, feverish, *vacant.*" De Gaulle wins his referendum. Beauvoir weeps and experiences nightmares. Writing articles against deadlines, Sartre "stuffs himself, one after another, with optalidon, belladénal, and corydrane" to relieve himself of dizzy spells and blinding headaches. Beauvoir: "Henceforth death possessed me. The possession had a name—old age." The much younger women—currently twenty-year-old Arlette—appealing to the ailing, aging Sartre; the explosive, gap-widening youth of an impulsive Lanzmann; did not help—they seem to have spelled out in Beauvoir's eyes her inexorable decline. "My relations with Lanzmann were falling apart. It was normal, fatal, and even to be wished for. . . . The business of separating, however, was difficult for me; for him, too, even if the initiative came from him . . . It was with a leaden heart that I came to the end of that oppressive year"—1958.[136] And Beauvoir was not yet fifty.

The paradox of Beauvoir and Sartre at this time was that the peak of their public influence occurred at a low point in their private lives, and in that of France—the years of the *sale guerre* (dirty war) in Algeria. By dramatizing resistance to the French colonial effort they provided a turning point in public opinion. The occasion occurred while they were in Brazil. There they read, signed, and promoted the now-historic Manifesto of the 121—the number of leading artists and writers supporting it—condemning the gangrenous war. And they defied authority by openly preaching disobedience to young conscripts.

No one who witnessed Sartre and Beauvoir during those demoralizing years, when they challenged the *sale guerre,* General de Gaulle (before he granted Algeria independence), and what they viewed as the endemic degradation of France, is likely to forget it. There was, for instance, the summoning of reporters to Beauvoir's Montparnasse studio, where Sartre vainly tried to oblige a reluctant government to indict him, as it had lesser-known signers of the antiwar manifesto. He talked passionately and eloquently as Beauvoir sat beside him, in the silence of complete rapport.

"This war is absurd," he said, "and it dishonors France. Not prosecuting me, the government attempts to discredit my act by putting me in the privileged position of those who do not have to bear the moral responsibility of their writings."[137] ("One does not put Voltaire into prison," de Gaulle is said to have declared. Louis XV, as we have seen, did.)

Equally memorable was the demonstration near Place Maubert in the winter of 1961. Shortly before noon the small Left Bank group began its walk from a secret rendezvous toward the Place, Sartre and Beauvoir taking the lead. From time to time she put her hand lightly on his shoulder. The group was stopped by the police short of the square and split into manageable pockets, Sartre in one, Beauvoir in another. As they were herded apart, a plastic bomb exploded in the square, at the foot of the monument where Sartre had been scheduled to speak. Beauvoir and her companions turned back to see the damage. Sartre and a few others continued walking, past a wall on which someone, most likely Communist, had scornfully written, "The Don Quixotes of peace!" Underneath someone else had added: "The more useless the *geste* [gesture], the more *beau.*"

The war and the *beaux gestes* ended less than a year later, but Beauvoir and Sartre never quite recovered. Their wounds were deeper than many produced by the war. One midnight at about this time, in Montparnasse, they could be seen hurrying up the Boulevard Raspail. He was unusually silent, leaning slightly forward, hunched against the drizzle, shorter, squatter, more "aggressively ugly" (Beauvoir's phrase for him thirty-six years earlier) than ever. She was leaning slightly toward him, distant but still handsome, taller, and protective. She walked heavily and was dressed with more than usual negligence.

Perhaps Beauvoir was walking Sartre to his new two-room flat above the Boulevard Montparnasse, to which he had moved after being bombed at the rue Bonaparte by ultrarightists late in the Algerian War (after first removing his mother). Or perhaps he was accompanying Beauvoir to hers, around the corner, where it faced the gray cemetery wall.

They looked old, they looked sad—they who in their younger years were looked upon as the loveliest couple on the Left Bank since Abelard and Heloise. Now the café talk was about their visible descent together to the bottom of despair—literary, political, personal. The descent, the disillusionment of the most celebrated dyad of all the world's Latin Quarters had become as public as their private *pacte,* thanks to their compulsive literateness.

For decades they had represented the liberated couple; Beauvoir, more specifically since *The Second Sex,* the emancipated Frenchwoman. When *The Mandarins* appeared, two Frenchwomen—a school director and a mathematician—had each, separately, referred me to the novel for an explanation of themselves. Simone de Beauvoir had symbolized for them the fulfillment of the free woman. Now, suddenly, with *La Force des choses (Force of Circumstance),* from which we have been extracting Beauvoir's dilemmas, the symbol had come crashing down. An older Beauvoir, who had asked herself, What have I done with my freedom? had concluded, "With stupor I realize to what extent I have been duped, cheated, *had* [*flouée*]." ("All Sartre's women were *flouées*" —Arlette Elkaïm-Sartre.) Such were the last words of the last chapter, which began, "There has been one absolutely certain success in my life —my relationship with Sartre."[138]

Was it so successful after all, women have been asking themselves, that *pacte* between the two from the beginning—she, the striking, undutiful daughter of a modest bourgeois family; and he, the "false bastard" (his term for Baudelaire because he, too, had had a stepfather) of another, both disdaining bourgeois marriage? So often Beauvoir has remarked—as if to convince *herself*—that Sartre was not made for monogamy, nor she for children. Yet there are her incessant tears, *tristesse,* and *resentment* whenever she touches upon Sartre's liaisons (a good number of which are omitted) in her memoirs—and more than one friendly feminist has been profoundly troubled by Beauvoir's submissiveness, subordination, *wifeliness.* "Surely in her dreams they were married," says a woman painter who knew her for twenty years. "Did she not marry them in *The Mandarins,* complete with a daughter?"

Sartre's own slim volume of memoirs, *Les Mots (Words),* published in 1963, as was *Force of Circumstance,* provoked the most acute discussion since Zola's *J'accuse,* for this was Sartre's *Je m'accuse (I Accuse Myself).* Dedicated "To Madame Z." (Zazoulich, as he often referred to the Kosakiewicz?), it deals with his infancy and childhood and stops with his adolescence—wherefore, he explained lamely, his never mentioning Beauvoir. He would never go deeply into what he called "the worst years of my life"—from age eleven to fifteen—the year commencing with the remarriage of his mother through the years with his stepfather at La Rochelle.[139]

To a visitor in the spring of 1964, Sartre attempted to explain the new pessimism that he simultaneously sought to deny. He was, as usual, in fluent possession of all his faults. He struck at the "neurosis," the obsession since childhood to be a writer, at the value of literature itself, which he downgraded to absolute zero or thereabouts. "Balanced against a dying child," Sartre said, as the non sequitur of the literary season, "*Nausea* [his first novel] has no weight."[140] But no statement so startled French literary life—and the great circle eddying from it— as Sartre's conclusion of *Words:*

> I was happy. I changed. Later I will tell about the acids that ate at the deforming transparencies that enveloped me [he never would] . . . by what reasoning I was led to think systematically against myself to the point of valuing an idea by the displeasure it caused me . . . I see clearly, I am disenchanted [*"flouée,"* wrote Beauvoir] . . . since about ten years ago, I am a man awakening from a sleep, cured of a long, bittersweet madness from which he has not recov-

> ered and which he cannot recall without laughing at his former mistaken ways, and who no longer knows what to do with his life.[141]

The "awakening," Sartre told his visitor, actually took place in 1954, when he knotted—or rather slipknotted—relations with the Communist Party. "Suddenly I saw clearly the kind of neurosis that dominated my past work." But "in the meantime I realized that [social] action, too, has its difficulties, and that one can be led to it by neurosis. One is no more saved by politics than by literature."

By what, then, are we saved? "By nothing," said Sartre; "there is no salvation anywhere." There remain simply things to be done, and "literature is not the most privileged among them." It was in this sense, he said, that he had written, "I no longer know what to do with my life," which critics wrongly saw as a cry of despair, as was Simone de Beauvoir's "I was duped, cheated, *flouée*." It was not, Sartre insisted.[142]

It was, of course, but Sartre was recoiling from the right-wing delight in his self-deprecation. Friends, members of the "family," indicated their upset; staff members of *Les Temps modernes,* their discouragement. "Sartre comes to our meetings," said one of the latter,

> when he does come, declaring nothing can be done about anything in France. In reality, Sartre and Beauvoir have always been defeatists, "anguished." At the Liberation, he thought literature had impact. He no longer thinks so. Note that in his last play [*The Condemned of Altona*] the two principals commit suicide as the only thing left to do. He tried a rapprochement with the Communists in 1956 with his play *Nekrassov.* It was a failure, politically and as a play. He has always been despised by the "Party." He was torn by its attitude vis-à-vis the Algerian revolt as nothing but a petit-bourgeois nationalist movement. He had thought it would create a revolution in France. It did not, obviously. Not once did the French working class go on strike in favor of the Algerians.

The failure of the French "proletariat" was most crushing for Sartre, but he was not talking about it publicly any more than he was assimilating it privately; after the student-worker uprising in May 1968 and its failure, he would attempt to rejuvenate his political life and illusions through the young Maoists (to Beauvoir's distress). There had been, it was being discovered, a dishonesty in Sartre of possibly the sincerest kind. He was true to his principles, but political truth was not among them. "If you begin by saying, 'Thou shalt not lie,' " he once remarked, "there is no longer any possibility of political action. What matters above all else is the liberation of man."[143] Thus for Sartre, in contrast to Camus, truth might be readily sacrificed for the "greater" truth of the morrow's revolution. ("The workers must not be made to despair" —*Nekrassov.* Sartre accurately assumed that the workers did not read his work, for it contains little to encourage them.)

The pessimism is unrelieved during the years remaining. "I no longer have the feeling of going toward a goal," Beauvoir wrote in 1972, "but only that of sliding ineluctably to my grave."[144] There is much talk of death in *Tout compte fait (All Said and Done)*—of Sartre's mother, of others, but little of the death of one of Sartre's lovers by suicide, actress Evelyne Rey, Lanzmann's younger sister. Though it was only that death among the others that had deeply moved her, says Beauvoir in a painfully short and isolated passage, "I have no desire to talk about it."[145] (That story is not among the nicer stories one might tell about Sartre, though it is implied in what he himself has said: "I have always tried to surround myself with women who are at least good to look at . . . I prefer their company to that of men . . . [Moreover] women have qualities that come from their situation, the fact that they are, at the same time, slave and accomplice."[146]) Beauvoir also offers her dreams for the delectation of the psychoanalyst, lay or professional: the eroticism of "flying," of joining Sartre in an oasis called Ouargla (Olga?); the frustrations of "missed trains, empty stations, lost baggage." "Sartre," she says, "has always been [in my dreams] either the companion he was in my life or a man with a heart of stone whom my reproaches or prayers, my tears or my fainting leave indifferent"! Yet . . . "on the whole it is with pleasure I go to sleep, anticipating my nightly adventures, and it is with regret that I tell them adieu in the morning."[147] Who has spoken more harshly, more intimately, of the abusive self-centeredness of Sartre? One wants to repeat Beauvoir's remark about the "trap of love," but one wants, at the same time, to cite the observation of Henry James that worse than the tyrant is the tyrant's victim, who is "slave and accomplice."

Is there—one continues one's searching questions—more than a touch of the "widow's revenge" in the last volume of Beauvoir's memoirs, "the first of my books"—she addresses the absent Sartre—"that you will not have read before it was printed"?[148] That book is *La Cérémonie des adieux* (published in English as *A Farewell to Sartre*).

It was 1970. Sartre had just celebrated his sixty-sixth birthday in June with the "family." He was about to go to southern France for three weeks with Arlette, as usual, then spend two weeks in Italy with Wanda, as usual, before joining Beauvoir in Rome. She, meanwhile, would be voyaging as usual with Sylvie Le Bon, a student she had met ten years before, who was now a teacher, Beauvoir's closest friend, and, to fill in a detail, thirty-three years younger. Beauvoir was having lunch with Sartre at the Coupole brasserie, "anguished at the thought of leaving him . . . He smiled in an indefinable way and said, *'Alors,* this is the *cérémonie des adieux!'* "[149] Thus the title of Beauvoir's account of the last ten years of Sartre's life and of hers with him. Sartre himself had written, as if from beyond the tomb: "In a life that has ended, it is the end that tells us the truth of the beginning."[150]

The physical ending, with its implications for Sartre's faculties, had begun well before 1970: hospitalization in 1954 due to hypertension; the intake of amphetamines (up to twenty a day) from 1957 onward, leading to hallucinations of shellfish in 1958; dizzy spells, which terrified Beauvoir, in 1968; and so on. Some have been signaled already. From 1970 to the last year, Beauvoir seems to leave nothing unnoted: her portrait of a long-dying Sartre is a litany of illnesses and decline.

However, there is the anguish of the portraitist as well: "Every morning, when I went to wake him, I hastened to reassure myself he was still breathing," such was the state of his "large and small arteries." (Five nights a week Sartre was sleeping on the balcony of Beauvoir's studio, the other two nights at Arlette's place, also in Montparnasse.) The last decade of Sartre's life, nevertheless, and of Beauvoir's with him, was not *all* black. "We chatted, we listened to music; I assembled a large collection of records that I added to every month." (At Arlette's studio, Sartre played a piano, and rather well—at least until he was quite blind—while she played the flute or sang.)[151]

1971: ". . . great difficulty in the circulation of the blood in the left hemisphere of the brain . . ." Beauvoir played a recording of Verdi's *Requiem,* "which Sartre liked very much. . . . 'It's appropriate,' he murmured." But he worked on the proofs of the third volume of his never-to-be finished study of Flaubert (and at this time reminded Beauvoir that he did not want to be buried next to his stepfather). 1972: Beauvoir noted that Sartre could no longer hold back his urine: he had left "a damp spot on his armchair." (In *The Second Sex,* one recalls, Beauvoir had spoken of the shamefulness of such uncontrolled urination, so like a woman's monthly bleeding.) 1973: Sartre insisted on two forbidden drinks of Scotch, then fell apart. "I sent him to bed . . . and lay down, dressed, on my sofa." Cigarettes, too, were forbidden, but friends smuggled them in as well as a bottle of Scotch. ("She will see it," said Sartre glumly.[152]) Most serious: Sartre had a hemorrhage in his good, right eye and could no longer read or write. Beauvoir read to him, but "he accepted badly my helping him to cut the meat on his plate." From time to time his mind wandered. He was moved to an apartment with two bedrooms, so that Arlette or Beauvoir could always sleep adjacent to him when he could not go to them. "You are a good wife!" said Sartre to Beauvoir one morning after she gave him his medicine. Lanzmann came to visit, and embraced Sartre on leaving. "I don't know whether you are embracing part of a tomb or a living man," Sartre said. Beauvoir: "We were petrified . . . I cried all night."[153]

1974: Sartre could no longer control certain functions or safely walk the streets alone. Nevertheless he insisted on a "normal" life. He, Beauvoir, and Sylvie Le Bon vacationed in Italy, returned to Paris, and "celebrated" Sartre's sixty-ninth birthday in June. "He had only one concern: his Greek friend [Melina] seemed . . . to be going mad, in the full sense of the word." (Melina, an admiring student, had been met on a recent trip in Greece and invited by Sartre to continue her studies in Paris at his expense. In almost every country they visited together, or where he went alone, Beauvoir once recalled to Sartre, he would incorporate into his visit and his life one woman who was "the incarnation of the country," such as "M. [Dolores] in America, Christina in Brazil, and others"—Marie Girard in Germany, and now Melina of Greece.[154]) 1975: Another trip to Greece—Sartre, Beauvoir, and Sylvie—where they saw a recovered, "still-beautiful" Melina, with whom "Sartre enjoyed himself . . . while I went for walks with Sylvie in Athens." Back in Paris, "Sartre's blood pressure rose from 14 to 20, then to 21.5." Otherwise life resumed as before, with the women of the "family" caring for him or taking their usual vacation turns with him during the summer of 1976, which included a week of Sartre and Beauvoir in Athens with Melina. "He spent the days with me, the evenings with her." But in 1977, Beauvoir broke off the relationship between Sartre and Michelle Vian for a time, because Michelle had encouraged Sartre to polish off half a bottle of whiskey. Sartre, in fact, was worsening, and Beauvoir was terribly worried, and taking tranquilizers. Sartre said *au revoir*—not quite *adieu*—to Melina, but there were "newcomers." " 'Never have I been so surrounded by women,' " he exclaimed "joyously" to Beauvoir. In 1978 she would shed furious tears when relatively newly come Françoise Sagan, hoping to give Sartre his last, if forbidden, pleasures, "made" him eat too much when they lunched together, and conspicuously held hands.[155]

1980, the last days: Women continued to bring Sartre whiskey surreptitiously. He drank immoderately. "Reduced to the present, he regarded himself as already dead." March 20: Sartre could scarcely breathe—edema of the lungs. Distraught, Beauvoir called for an ambulance, which took him to the hospital. He was bled. His case was hopeless—uremia, then gangrene, took hold. April 14: When Beauvoir arrived, Sartre was asleep. He awoke but kept his eyes closed. "I kissed him on the mouth, on the cheek." April 15: Arlette phoned Beauvoir from the hospital, telling her Sartre was dead. Beauvoir came to watch over the body. "At one moment I asked to be left alone with Sartre. I wanted to lie next to him under the sheet. A nurse stopped me, saying, *"Non. Attention . . . la gangrène."* Beauvoir lay, instead, on the covers and slept a bit.[156]

Jean-Paul Sartre was incinerated; his ashes were buried in the Montparnasse cemetery. On the other side of the cemetery wall, Simone de Beauvoir penned the last words of her *Farewell to Sartre:* "His death separates us. My death will not reunite us." Death came on April 14, 1986.

NOTES

Chapter 1

1. Algernon Charles Swinburne, *Hymn to Proserpine.*

2. Amaury de Riencourt, *Sex and Power in History* (New York: Delta Books, 1975), p. 83.

3. Cf. René Nelli, *L'Erotique des troubadours,* 2 vols. (Paris: Edition 10/18, 1974). We shall return at length to courtly love in Chapter 2.

4. There are thirty-seven variations of the spelling of Abélard. His works in the Bibliothèque Nationale of Paris are listed under Abaillard.

5. Henry Adams, *Mont-Saint-Michel and Chartres* (New York: Anchor Press, 1959), p. 321.

6. Peter Abélard and Héloise, *Historia Calamitatum and Letters 1–7,* ed. J. T. Muckle and T. P. McLaughlin, *Mediaeval Studies,* Vols. 12, 15, 17, 18 (Toronto: Pontifical Institute of Mediaeval Studies, 1950, 1953, 1955, 1956). All quotations from Abelard's autobiography *Historia Calamitatum* and the Heloise-Abelard correspondence are from this source. The accents have been dropped from their two names for convenience. The translation has been arrived at from the original Latin in conjunction with various English and French translations. A useful English translation of the *Historia* and the correspondence of Heloise and Abelard, as well as other important items, such as the letters of Peter the Venerable and that of Heloise to him, is provided by *The Letters of Abelard and Heloise,* translated and with an introduction by Betty Radice (New York: Penguin Books, 1974).

7. Michel Foucault, *Histoire de la sexualité,* Vol. 1, *La Volonté de savoir,* (Paris: 1976) p. 27. For an English translation, see *History of Sexuality* (New York: Pantheon Books, 1979).

8. Ovid, *Art of Love* (London: 1735).

9. Régine Pernoud, *Héloïse et Abélard* (Paris: 1970), p. 12.

10. Frederick B. Artz, *The Mind of the Middle Ages* (New York: 1953), p. 257.

11. D. W. Robertson, Jr., *Abelard and Heloise* (London: 1974), p. 38.

12. Charlotte Charrier, "Héloise dans l'histoire et dans la légende" (Ph.D. diss., Paris, 1933), p. 51.

13. *Notice historique sur les sépultures d'Héloise et d'Abélard* (Paris: 1815), p. 4, note 2.

14. For Heloise's letters, see Note 6.

15. Adams, *Mont-Saint-Michel,* p. 321.

16. Robertson, *Abelard and Heloise,* p. 42.

17. Étienne Gilson, *Heloise and Abelard* (Ann Arbor: 1960), pp. 33–34. Originally published as *Héloïse et Abélard* (Paris: 1948).

18. Cf. Edward Shorter, *The Making of the Modern Family* (Glasgow: Fontana, 1977), p. 171. "It was the pioneer social historian Philippe Ariès who first argued that maternal indifference to infants characterized traditional society." See Ariès, *Centuries of Childhood* (New York: Vintage Books, c. 1962), originally published in French as *L'Enfant et la vie familiale sous l'ancien régime* (1960).

19. Denis de Rougemont, *L'Amour et l'occident* (Paris: Édition 10/18, c. 1939). The fundamental theme is "Western preoccupation with love and death" as based on the Tristan and Iseult legend, and viewed from a romantic, Wagnerian perspective, which distorts the medieval original. Historically unsound (see Moshé Lazar, *Amour courtois et "fin'amours" dans la littérature du xiiè siècle* [Paris: 1964] and male-contoured (see Evelyne Sullerot, *Histoire et mythologie de l'amour* [Paris: 1974], pp. 18–19). The book has been translated into English as *Love in the Western World* (New York: 1956).

20. Mark Twain, *Innocents Abroad* (1869). Twain had just made a pilgrimage to the tomb of Abelard and Heloise in Paris's Père Lachaise cemetery.

21. There is a critical rundown of the history of the controversy concerning the Abelard-Heloise correspondence in the appendix of Gilson, *Heloise and Abelard.* He too finds the arguments for forgery unconvincing. For more on the pros and cons of the correspondence's authenticity, see the papers presented at a colloquy concerning *Pierre Abélard et Pierre le Vénérable,* held at the Cluny Abbey, July 2–9, 1972 (Paris: CNRS, 1975).

22. Gilson, *Heloise and Abelard,* p. 105.

23. Mary Martin McLaughlin, "Abelard and the Dignity of Women," paper presented at the Cluny colloquy (see Note 21).

24. As quoted in Norbert Elias, *La Civilisation des moeurs* (Paris: 1973), p. 351. Originally published as *Über den Prozess der Zivilisation* (1969).

25. C. B. A. Behrens, *New York Review of Books,* June 14, 1979.

26. McLaughlin, "Abelard," p. 313.

27. As quoted in Pernoud, *Héloise et Abélard,* p. 232.

28. Ibid., p. 246.

29. Betty Radice, Introduction, *The Letters of Abelard and Heloise,* (New York: Penguin Books, 1974), p. 44.

30. Enid McLeod, *Héloïse* (London: 1971), pp. 216–19.

Chapter 2

1. Chrétien de Troyes, "Lancelot," in *Arthurian Romances,* trans. W. Wistar Comfort (London: Everyman, 1975), p. 270.

2. Heinrich Zimmer, *The King and the Corpse, Tales of the Soul's Conquest of Evil* (Princeton, N.J.: Princeton University Press, 1973), p. 133.

3. This quotation and those that follow are based on the W. W. Comfort translation of Chrétien de Troyes's *Arthurian Romances.* The reader might be amused by Comfort's own complaint about Chrétien's "threatened, if not actual, indelicacy" (p. x).

4. Zimmer, *King and Corpse,* p. 167.

5. F. X. Newman, ed., *The Meaning of Courtly Love* (Albany: 1968), p. vi.

6. Cf. C. S. Lewis, *The Allegory of Love: A Study in Medieval Tradition* (London: 1938), p. 12.

7. Cf. Georges Duby, *Le Chevalier, la femme et le prêtre* (Paris: 1981), pp. 334–36.

8. Cf. Herbert Moller, "The Social Causation of the Courtly Love Complex," *Comparative Studies in Society and History* 1, no. 2 (January 1959): 137–63. Also Georges Duby, "Au xiiè siècle: les 'Jeunes' dans la société aristocratique," *Annales, économies, sociétés, civilizations* 19ème année, no. 5 (September–October 1964): 835–46.

9. Andrée Lehmann, *Le Rôle de la femme dans l'histoire de la France au moyen âge* (Paris: 1952), p. 223.

10. François-Pierre-Guillaume Guizot, *Histoire de la civilization en France, depuis la chute de l'Empire romain,* 4 vols. (Paris: 1840), 3:6.

11. As quoted in Nina Epton, *Love and the French* (London: 1959), p. 10.

12. Henri-Irénée Marrou, Les Troubadours (Paris: 1971), p. 18.

13. Cf. Arnold Hauser, *The Social History of Art,* 4 vols. (New York: Vintage, 1951), 1: 195–232.

14. Cf. John C. Moore, " 'Courtly Love': A Problem of Terminology," *Journal of the History of Ideas* (October 1979), pp. 40–51. For a literate sweep of the subject, see also Moore's *Love in Twelfth-Century France* (Philadelphia: 1972). Courtly love, or *l'amour courtois* (first coined as such in 1883; in the Middle Ages the terms *fin'amors* and *cortez'amors* were used), was little less than a revolution in human relations. But it remains a kind of medieval miracle, so much of a miracle that several modern historians have put into doubt its actual existence and have put down its literary manifestations as irony or parody. See the contributions of D. W. Robertson, Jr., and John F. Benton in Newman, *Courtly Love.* What, then, one might ask, were the some 460 troubadour poets, who are known by name and who have left behind several thousand poems, some of them thousands of verses long, being ironical about or parodying? Something "inexistent?" Cf. Jean Frappier, "Sur un procès fait à l'amour courtois," *Romania* 93 (1972), p. 149. See also, regarding the adulterous aspect of courtly love, Duby, *Chevalier, femme et prêtre* pp. 230, 234.

15. Simone de Beauvoir, *The Second Sex* (New York: Vintage, 1974), p. 113.

16. Frederick Engels, "The Origin of the Family," in *A Handbook of Marxism* (New York: 1935), p. 306.

17. As quoted in Jacques Lafitte-Houssat, *Troubadours et cours d'amour* (Paris: 1971), p. 13.

18. As quoted by John F. Benton in Newman, *Courtly Love,* p. 24.

19. Ibid., p. 39.

20. Ibid., pp. 25–26.

21. Emmanuel Le Roy Ladurie, *Montaillou, village occitan de 1294 à 1324* (Paris: 1975), pp. 229–41.

22. René Nelli, *L'Erotique des troubadours,* 2 vols. (Paris: Edition 10/18, 1974), 1: 391.

23. In Jules Véran, *Les Poétesses provençales du moyen âge et de nos jours* (Paris: 1946), p. 169.

24. As quoted in Charles Sallefranque, *Périples de l'amour en orient et en occident* (Paris: 1947), p. 98. As does Nelli in *L'Erotique,* Sallefranque examines the Arabic and other Islamic influences in courtly love poetry.

25. Andreas Capellanus, *The Art of Courtly Love,* intro. trans., and notes by John Jay Parry (New York: 1969). All quotations from Andreas's *De Arte Honesti Amandi* are based on this translation.

26. Marie had married Count Henry of Champagne, called *le Libéral,* in 1159, when their court in Troyes became a center of the new poetry. She had ruled in his stead when he went on the Crusades from 1177 to 1178, then from spring 1179 until his return in 1781, to die.

27. Andreas, *Art of Courtly Love,* p. 23.

28. John F. Benton in Newman, *Courtly Love,* p. 36.

29. Geoffrey La Tour Landry, *The Book of the Knight of La Tour Landry for the Instruction of his Daughters,* trans. G. S. Taylor (London: 1930).

30. Eileen Power, *Medieval Women* (London: 1975), p. 11.

31. *La Mort le roi Artu, roman du xiiiè siècle,* ed. Jean Frappier (Geneva: 1964), p. x. Less than a century after Chrétien de Troyes had recorded the love story of Lancelot and the queen, its consequences as catastrophe for King Arthur and his court are related in *La Mort le roi Artu,* circa 1230, attributed to "Gautier Map, archdeacon of Oxford." The punishment for their adultery was, to quote Ferdinand Lot, "to be in the late autumn of their lives the involuntary cause of the final conflicts that rend Arthur's court and bring about the downfall of the companions of the Round Table in a fratricidal struggle in which succumbs their sovereign as well, the incomparable Arthur."

32. Johan Huizinga, *The Waning of the Middle Ages* (New York: Anchor Books, 1954), p. 115.

33. Pierre de Bourdeilles Brantôme, seigneur de, *Les Dames Galantes* (Paris: 1962), p. 129.

34. Marie-Joseph Pinet, *Christine de Pisan* (Paris: 1927).

35. Christine de Pisan, *Oeuvres poétiques,* ed. Maurice Roy (Paris: 1886–1896). See "La Vision de Christine" (1405).

Chapter 3

1. Philippe Erlanger, *Diane de Poitiers* (Paris: 1955), p. 35.
2. *Journal d'un Bourgeois de Paris sous François Ier, 1515–1536* (Paris: 1854), p. 192.
3. Armand Baschet, *La Diplomatie vénitienne. Les Princes de l'Europe au xviè siècle* (Paris: 1862), p. 438.
4. Ruth Kelso, *Doctrine for the Lady of the Renaissance* (Urbana, Ill.: University of Illinois Press, 1956), pp. 129–30.
5. Pierre de Bourdeilles Brantôme, seigneur de, *Les dames galantes* (Paris: 1962), p. 289.
6. Lucien Romier, *Les Origines politiques des guerres de religion,* 2 vols. (Paris: 1913–14), 2: 247.
7. Erlanger, *Diane de Poitiers,* pp. 136–37.
8. Diane de Poitiers, *Lettres inédites de Diane de Poytiers* (Paris: Georges Guiffrey, 1866), p. 228.
9. Ibid., p. 227.
10. Ibid., p. 228.
11. Ibid., Introduction, p. lix.
12. Nina Epton, *Love and the French* (London: 1959), p. 87.
13. Brantôme, *Dames galantes,* p. 174.
14. Ambassador Julio Alvarotti, in a dispatch to the Duke of Ferare, November 18, 1558, as quoted in Lucien Romier, *Guerres de religion,* 2: 313–15.
15. Erlanger, *Diane de Poitiers,* p. 319.
16. Brantôme, *Dames galantes,* p. 217.
17. Michel de Montaigne, *Oeuvres complètes* (Paris: Seuil, 1967), Book 3, p. 352. This is the edition of reference for Montaigne's *Essays.* Translations are by the author of this work.
18. Donald M. Frame, *Montaigne: A Biography* (New York: 1965), p. 100.
19. Montaigne, *Oeuvres complètes,* Book 2, p. 166.
20. Christine de Pisan, *Le Livre de la cité des dames,* written in 1404. Cf. Kelso, *Lady of the Renaissance,* p. 5.
21. Kelso, *Lady of the Renaissance,* p. 281.
22. Montaigne, *Oeuvres complètes,* Book 3, pp. 344–45.
23. Ibid., Book 3, p. 442.
24. Ibid., Book 1, p. 91.
25. Ibid., Book 3, p. 334.
26. Ibid., Book 3, p. 355.
27. Ibid., Book 1, p. 88.
28. Ibid., p. 89.
29. Etienne de La Boëtie, *Oeuvres complètes* (Paris: 1892), p. 225.

30. André Gide, *Montaigne* (London: 1929), pp. 32–33. Gide believed that Montaigne was fortunate in not having been too long exposed to La Boëtie's moralizing: "Once La Boëtie is gone, Montaigne will strive less and less to fight against himself." It was Montaigne's drive to realize himself completely, at least as a thinker, that Gide most admired in him.

31. Montaigne, *Oeuvres Complètes,* Book 1, p. 89.

32. Gide, *Montaigne,* p. 31.

33. Montaigne, *Oeuvres Complètes,* Book 1, p. 91.

34. Ibid., Book 2, p. 166.

35. Ibid.

36. Ibid., Book 1, p. 97.

37. Ibid., Book 3, p. 338.

38. Ibid., p. 393.

39. Ibid., Book 1, p. 71.

40. Kelso, *Lady of the Renaissance,* pp. 50, 60, 69, 81.

41. Montaigne, *Oeuvres Complètes,* Book 1, p. 97.

42. Alain M. Boase, "Montaigne annoté par Florimond de Raemond," *Revue du seizième siècle* 15 (1928): 239–40.

43. Kelso, *Lady of the Renaissance,* pp. 87–88. Ms. Kelso cites as her authorities here Bouchet, Gouge, Lesnauderie, Tasso, Tillier, and Vives.

44. Ibid.

45. Montaigne, *Oeuvres Complètes,* Book 2, p. 179; Book 3, pp. 441, 344.

46. Ibid., Book 1, p. 97.

47. Ibid., Book 1, p. 352.

48. Théophile Malvezin, *Michel de Montaigne, son origine, sa famille* (Bordeaux: 1875), p. 300.

49. Cf. Maurice Rat, "Le Ménage de Montaigne," *Bulletin de la Société des Amis de Montaigne,* no. 15 (1949–52), pp. 14–23. See also Alexandre Nicolaï, *Montaigne intime* (Paris: 1947), pp. 75–78.

50. Montaigne, *Oeuvres Complètes,* Book 3, p. 352.

51. Ibid., Book 2, p. 162.

52. Ibid., Book 1, p. 133.

53. Ibid., p. 112.

54. Ibid.

55. Ibid., Book 3, pp. 335–36.

56. Ibid., pp. 383, 384, 393.

57. Ibid., p. 436.

58. Ibid., Book 1, p. 40.

59. Ibid., Book 2, p. 169.

60. Ibid., p. 168.

61. Ibid., p. 163.

62. Edith Sichel, *Michel de Montaigne* (London: 1911), pp. 42–43. For Marguerite of France, timidity was the principal defect of women.

63. Montaigne, *Oeuvres Complètes,* Book 3, p. 346.

64. Ibid., Book 3, pp. 333–34.

65. Kelso, *Lady of the Renaissance,* pp. 25, 36, 3–4, 78.

66. Marjorie Henry Ilsley, *A Daughter of the Renaissance: Marie le Jars de Gournay, Her Life and Works* (The Hague: 1963), pp. 17–18, 21; also Marie de Gournay, *Advis ou Presens de la Damoiselle de Gournay . . .* (Paris: 1634). Some of these pages are in Nicolaï, *Montaigne intime.*

67. Montaigne, Oeuvres Complètes, Book 3, p. 363.

68. Ibid., Book 1, p. 40.

69. Michel de Montaigne, *Essais,* ed. with preface, Marie le Jars de Gournay (Paris: 1635), p. 517. The passage quoted, which first appeared, at greater length, in the 1595 edition of Montaigne's *Essays,* was shortened for this edition of 1635 and is accepted by most scholars as essentially Montaigne's opinion of his *fille d'alliance* (who was also editor of the 1595 edition, as Montaigne's literary executor).

70. Montaigne, *Oeuvres complètes,* Book 3, p. 396.

Chapter 4

1. Georges Bordonove, *Molière, génial et familier* (Paris: 1967), pp. 61, 64, 517.

2. Georges Mongrédien, ed., *Recueil des textes et des documents du xviiè siècle relatifs à Molière,* 2 vols. (Paris: 1965), p. 64. A collection of texts and documents of the seventeenth century that relate to Molière.

3. Ibid., pp. 91–92.

4. Scene 4.

5. Dorothy Anne Liot Backer, *Precious Women* (New York: 1974), p. 10.

6. Grimarest, "Vie de Molière," in Molière, *Oeuvres complètes* (Paris: Seuil, 1962), p. 16.

7. Jacques Scherer, "Adventures des Précieuses," *Revue d'histoire littéraire de la France* 72, no. 5–6 (September–December 1972): 862.

8. Mongrédien, *Recueil des textes,* p. 143.

9. Act I, Scenes 2 and 4.

10. Mongrédien, *Recueil des textes,* p. 193.

11. Ibid., pp. 515–16.

12. Grimarest, "Vie de Molière," p. 19.

13. Mongrédien, *Recueil des textes,* pp. 108–109.

14. Act I, Scene 4.

15. Act I, Scene 1; Act V, Scene 4; Act III, Scene 2; Act IV, Scene 8.

16. Scenes 1, 4, 1, and 5.

17. Cf. Joseph Barry, *Passions and Politics, A Biography of Versailles* (New York: 1972), pp 98–99. This author pleads guilty as well.

18. Grimarest, "Vie de Molière," p. 19.

19. Anonymous, *La Fameuse Comédienne ou Histoire de la Guérin, auparavant femme et veuve de Molière (1688)* (Paris: 1870), p. 17.

20. Grimarest, "Vie de Molière," pp. 21–22.

21. Ibid.

22. Georges Mongrédien, *La vie privée de Molière* (Paris: 1950), pp. 150–51.

23. Molière, *Le Mariage forcé,* Scene 4.

24. *La Fameuse Comédienne,* pp. 17–21.

25. Act II, Scene 1; Act I, Scene 1; Act II, Scene 1; Act III, Scene 4; Act IV, Scene 3; Act V, Scene 4.

26. Act III, Scene 10.

27. Act III, Scene 8.

28. Act II, Scene 2.

29. "She was small, but had an engaging air," a contemporary describes Armande, known from childhood. "Though her eyes were very small, her mouth large and flat, she did everything with gracefulness, down to the smallest movement." Angélique Ducroisy, quoted by Sylvie Chevalley, "Armande Béjart, comédienne," *Revue d'histoire littéraire de la France* 72 (1972): 1,035.

30. Act III, Scene 9.

31. Mongrédien, *Recueil des textes,* p. 219.

32. Act I, Scene 1.

33. Act I, Scene 2.

34. Act I, Scene 3; Act II, Scene 7.

35. Act III, Scene 2.

36. Act IV, Scene 3.

37. Act V, Scene 4.

38. Marcel Aymé, "Philaminte avait raison" ("Philaminte Was Right") in *Chronique de la Comédie-Française* (September–December 1965), ed. Sylvie Chevalley.

39. Grimarest, "Vie de Molière," p. 30.

40. Mongrédien, *Recueil des textes,* p. 444.

41. Quoted in Chevalley, "Armande Béjart," p. 1,036.

Chapter 5

1. Léon Abensour, *La femme et le féminisme avant la révolution* (Paris: 1923), p. 75.

2. Madame Louise d'Epinay, *Mémoires,* 2 vols. (Paris: 1863), 1: 17–18.

3. Nancy Mitford, *Voltaire in Love* (London: 1957), p. 20.

4. Jean-Frédéric Maurepas, *Mémoires,* 4 vols. (Paris: 1792), 4: 173.

5. Quoted in René Vaillot, *Madame du Châtelet* (Paris: 1978), p. 53.

6. Quoted in Jean Orieux, *Voltaire ou la royauté de l'esprit* (Paris: 1966), p. 112.

7. Cf. Mitford, *Voltaire,* p. 48.

8. Voltaire, *Correspondance,* ed. Theodore Besterman (Geneva: 1955–1965), D85, July 1719. There are over one hundred volumes of this correspondence of Voltaire and his circle. *Hereafter references with D and a number, as well as (usually) a date, indicate letters in this collection.*

9. D607, May 6, 1733.

10. D649, August 29, 1733.

11. D645, August 14, 1733.

12. D651, September 10, 1733.

13. D698, 700, 701, 703, 705, 707, January 1734.

14. Quoted in Vaillot, *du Châtelet,* p. 85.

15. Quoted in Theodore Besterman, *Voltaire* (New York: 1969), p. 177.

16. Madame du Châtelet, *Lettres,* ed. Theodore Besterman, 2 vols. (Geneva: 1958), 1: 37.

17. D738, May 8, 1734.

18. Du Châtelet, *Lettres,* 1: 41–42.

19. D793, October 1734.

20. D805, December 1734.

21. Mitford, *Voltaire,* p. 65.

22. D795, October 1734.

23. D848, March 2, 1735.

24. Cf. Vaillot, *du Châtelet,* p. 106.

25. Ibid.

26. Du Châtelet, *Lettres,* 1: 61–63.

27. Ibid., pp. 65, 68–69.

28. He would go in 1736 to Lapland, accompanied by Clairaut, confident he could prove by his measurements that the earth was flatter at the poles, as Newton maintained and the academicians denied. He would succeed, and thereafter Voltaire would refer to him as Maupertuis "the earth-flattener."

29. Du Châtelet, *Lettres,* 1:75.

30. Voltaire, *Mémoires* (1759) in *Oeuvres complètes,* ed. Beuchot, 1: 7.

31. Quoted in Vaillot, *du Châtelet,* p. 114.

32. Du Châtelet, *Lettres,* 1: 80.

33. Ibid., p. 91.

34. Ibid., p. 82.

35. The demonstration is in Ira O. Wade, *With Some Unpublished Papers of Mme. du Châtelet* (Princeton, N.J.: Princeton University Press, 1947), pp. 70–74.

36. Ira O. Wade, *Voltaire and Mme. du Châtelet: An Essay on the Intellectual Activity at Cirey* (Princeton, N.J.: Princeton University Press, 1941), p. 232.

37. D1173, October 18, 1736.

38. Wade, *Papers of du Châtelet,* pp. 231–32.

39. Condorcet almost forty years later: "When Voltaire published this work, Jean Bernouilli, the greatest mathematician in Europe, still opposed Newtonianism; more than half of the Academy of Sciences was Cartesian." Quoted in Besterman, *Voltaire* p. 195.

40. Wade, *Papers of du Châtelet,* pp. vi, 191–93.

41. D1220, December 8, 1736.

42. D1126, August 8, 1736.

43. D1294, March 6, 1737.
44. D1290, July 6, 1737.
45. D1221, December 9, 1736.
46. Du Châtelet, *Lettres,* 1: 129–30.
47. D1462, February 22, 1738.
48. D1498, May 10, 1738.
49. Madame de Graffigny, *Vie privée de Voltaire et Mme du Châtelet, ou six mois de séjour à Cirey* (Paris: 1820).
50. Madame du Châtelet, *Institutions de physique* (Paris: 1740), Preface.
51. D2175, March 2, 1740.
52. D2278, July 29, 1740.
53. D2317, September 24, 1740.
54. D2377, December 1, 1740 (approximate).
55. D2378, December 1, 1740 (approximate).
56. Madame du Châtelet, *Lettres,* 1: 91.
57. Ibid., 2: 38.
58. Ibid., 38, 33.
59. D2394, January 6, 1741.
60. D2399, January 7, 1741.
61. Voltaire, *Commentaire historique sur les oeuvres de l'auteur de la Henriade* (1775–76?) in Besterman, *Voltaire,* p. 557.
62. Mitford, *Voltaire,* p. 163.
63. Ibid., pp. 163–64.
64. D2875, November 4, 1743.
65. Du Châtelet, *Lettres,* 2: 107.
66. Madame du Châtelet, *Discours sur le bonheur* (Paris: 1961), p. 26.
67. Voltaire, *Lettres d'amour à sa nièce,* ed. Theodore Besterman (Paris: 1957), p. 33.
68. Besterman, *Voltaire,* pp. 261–62.
69. D2789, July 9, 1744.
70. Voltaire, *Lettres d'amour,* pp. 53, 59, and 146.
71. Ibid., pp. 39, 44, and 129.
72. Madame du Deffand, *Correspondance complète* (Paris: 1865), 1: 93–94.
73. Du Châtelet, *Discours,* pp. 20, 28, 31–34, 17, 25.
74. Du Châtelet, *Lettres,* 2: 168–69, 170–71.
75. Du Châtelet, *Discours,* pp. 19, 30, 35–36.
76. Du Châtelet, *Lettres,* 2: 173, 178, 196.
77. Ibid., p. 175.
78. Voltaire, *Lettres d'amour,* p. 146.
79. Longchamp, *Voltaire et Mme du Châtelet* (Paris: 1863), pp. 200–204.
80. Du Châtelet, *Lettres,* 2: 247–48.
81. Ibid., pp. 267–74.
82. Ibid., p. 284.
83. Ibid., p. 288–89.

84. Ibid., p. 294.
85. Ibid., p. 306.
86. Longchamp, *Voltaire et Mme du Châtelet,* p. 251.
87. Voltaire, *Lettres d'amour,* p. 193.
88. Ibid., p. 194.
89. Longchamp, *Voltaire et Mme du Châtelet,* p. 262.

Chapter 6

1. Geoffrey Gorer, *The Life and Ideas of the Marquis de Sade* (London: 1953), p. 36.
2. Donatien-Alphonse-Francois de Sade, Marquis, *Oeuvres complètes,* 12 vols. (Paris: 1966–80), 4 *(Aline et Valcour):* 16.
3. As quoted in Gilbert Lely's *Vie du Marquis de Sade,* which constitutes the first two volumes of *Oeuvres,* 1: 62.
4. Ibid., 1: 64–65.
5. Ibid., 12: *(Correspondance),* 13–16. The entire letter can be read in English in *Justine . . . and Other Writings* (New York: Grove Press, 1966), pp. 121–24.
6. Sade, *Oeuvres,* 1: 84.
7. Ibid., p. 88.
8. Ibid., pp. 103, 107.
9. Ibid., p. 138.
10. Ibid., p. 110.
11. Ibid., p. 115.
12. Ibid., pp. 119–20.
13. Ibid., pp. 128–29.
14. Ibid., p. 138.
15. Ibid., p. 144.
16. Ibid., p. 173. Based on Rose Keller's testimony.
17. Ibid., p. 196.
18. Ibid., p. 242.
19. Ibid.
20. Ibid., p. 251.
21. Ibid., p. 254.
22. Cf. Sigmund Freud, *Civilization and Its Discontents* (London: 1973), pp. xii, 54–56.
23. Simone de Beauvoir, *Faut-il brûler Sade?* (Paris: 1955), p. 77.
24. Sade, *Oeuvres* 1: 341, 441.
25. Ibid., pp. 430, 435.
26. Ibid., p. 470.
27. Ibid., supplementary volume *(Lettres et mélanges littéraires écrits à Vincennes et à la Bastille avec des lettres de madame de Sade . . .),* i: 12.
28. Sade, *The 120 Days of Sodom . . .* (New York: 1967), p. 192.

29. Sade, *Justine . . .*, p. 378.
30. Sade, *Oeuvres,* 1: 561; and Paul Bourdin, ed., *Correspondance inédite du marquis de Sade, de ses proches . . .* (Paris: 1929), p. 160.
31. Sade, *L'Aigle, Mademoiselle . . .* (Paris: 1949), p. 43.
32. Sade, *Oeuvres,* 1: 550–51.
33. Bourdin, *Correspondance,* p. 31.
34. Ibid., p. 32.
35. Sade, *Lettres,* ii: 1, 137.
36. Sade, *Oeuvres,* 1: 597.
37. Sade, *Le Carillon de Vincennes* (Paris: 1953), pp. 9–11.
38. Sade, *Oeuvres,* 1: 603–604.
39. Sade, *Lettres,* ii: 108–10.
40. Sade, *Oeuvres,* 1: 624–25.
41. Gorer, *Life and Ideas,* p. 42.
42. Bourdin, *Correspondance,* p. 109.
43. Ibid., p. 114.
44. Ibid., pp. 117–16, 114.
45. Ibid., p. 98.
46. Ibid., p. 125.
47. Sade, *Oeuvres,* 2: 20.
48. Ibid.
49. Ibid., 2: 36.
50. Sade, *Lettres,* iii: 71.
51. Bourdin, *Correspondance,* p. 160.
52. Sade, *Oeuvres,* 2: 78–79.
53. Ibid., 2: 79.
54. Sade, *Lettres,* iii: 92; i: 277.
55. Ibid., iii: 340.
56. Ibid., pp. 344–45.
57. Sade, *Oeuvres,* 12: 327–28.
58. Ibid., 2: 94.
59. Ibid., 12: 331–33.
60. Ibid., 2: 96.
61. Sade, *Lettres,* ii: 290, 297.
62. Sade, *Oeuvres,* 2: 122–23.
63. Ibid., 2: 132.
64. Sade, *Lettres,* ii: 335.
65. Sade, *Oeuvres,* 2: 161–62, 163.
66. Sade, *Lettres,* ii: 368.
67. Ibid., iii: 197.
68. Sade, *Oeuvres,* 2: 177.
69. Sade, *Lettres,* ii: 369.
70. Ibid., p. 370.
71. Ibid., i: 110.
72. Ibid., ii: 371–72.

73. Ibid., i: 114, 119, 123–24, 127–28.
74. Ibid., ii: 374–77.
75. Sade, *Oeuvres,* 2: 190.
76. Bourdin, *Correspondance,* p. 269.
77. Sade, *Oeuvres,* 2: 278.
78. Ibid., p. 538.

Chapter 7

1. Bernard Gavoty, *Liszt* (Paris: 1980), p. 122.
2. Marie d'Agoult, Countess, *Mémoires, 1833–1854* (Paris: 1927), p. 21.
3. Ibid., pp. 21–22.
4. The anti-Semitism of Cosima, daughter-to-be of Liszt and Marie d'Agoult, may be in part explained by the concealed family origin on the maternal side, added to her sense of injury from her mother's neglect. Her revered future husband, Richard Wagner, on the other hand, contributing his own animus, accounts for a larger part. Cf. Eleanor Perényi, *Liszt—The Artist as Romantic Hero* (Boston: 1974), pp. 90–93.
5. Marie d'Agoult, *Mes Souvenirs, 1806–1833* (Paris: 1877), p. 349.
6. Jacques Vier, *La Comtesse d'Agoult et son temps,* 6 vols. (Paris: 1955–1963), 1: 26.
7. Agoult, *Souvenirs,* pp. 85–86.
8. Quoted in Vier, *d'Agoult,* p. 348, note 15.
9. Ibid., p. 87.
10. Agoult, *Mémoires,* p. 81.
11. Agoult, *Souvenirs,* pp. 220–22.
12. Agoult, *Mémoires,* pp. 13, 16.
13. Perényi, *Artist as Hero,* pp. 16–18.
14. *Correspondance de Liszt et de la comtesse d'Agoult,* 2 vols. (Paris: 1933—34), 1: 95.
15. Quoted in Gavoty, *Liszt,* pp. 107–108.
16. Agoult, *Mémoires,* pp. 24–26, 29.
17. Ibid., pp. 77–78.
18. Ibid., p. 29.
19. Ibid., pp. 30–31.
20. Liszt and d'Agoult, *Correspondance,* pp. 47, 49.
21. Ibid., p. 76.
22. Ibid., p. 70.
23. Ibid., pp. 88–89.
24. Ibid., p. 98.
25. Ibid., p. 99.
26. Ibid., p. 100.
27. Félicité de Lamennais, Abbé, *De l'art et du beau* (Paris: n.d.), p. 149.
28. Heinrich Heine, "Lettres confidentielles," in *Revue et Gazette Municipale de Paris* 5 (1838): 42.

29. George Sand, "Journal intime," in *Oeuvres autobiographiques,* 2 vols. (Paris: 1970–71), 2: 959.

30. George Sand, "Lettres d'un voyageur, VII," *Oeuvres,* 2: 846. This "Lettre" is addressed to Franz Liszt.

31. Quoted in Samuel Rocheblave, "Une amitié romanesque, George Sand et Madame d'Agoult," *Revue de Paris,* Dec. 15, 1894, p. 819.

32. George Sand, *Correspondance,* 21 vols., ed. Georges Lubin (Paris: 1964–86), 3: 44–45. Cf. Joseph Barry, *Infamous Woman, the Life of George Sand* (New York: 1977), pp. 200–202.

33. Liszt and d'Agoult, *Correspondance,* pp. 132–33.

34. Agoult, *Mémoires,* p. 200.

35. Vier, *d'Agoult,* pp. 176, 179.

36. Liszt and d'Agoult, *Correspondance,* p. 136.

37. Perényi, *Artist as Hero,* pp. 127, 124.

38. Agoult, *Mémoires,* p. 42.

39. Gavoty, *Liszt,* p. 162.

40. Agoult, *Mémoires,* pp. 52–53.

41. Ibid., pp. 55–56.

42. Quoted in Vier, *d'Agoult,* p. 393, note 33.

43. Agoult, *Mémoires,* pp. 64–66.

44. Ibid., pp. 67–68.

45. Quoted in Vier, *d'Agoult,* p. 394, note 55; p. 396, note 71.

46. Perényi, *Artist as Hero,* p. 135.

47. Quoted in Vier, *d'Agoult,* p. 393, note 50.

48. Ibid., pp. 393–94, note 50.

49. Agoult, *Mémoires,* p. 69.

50. Liszt and d'Agoult, *Correspondance,* pp. 193–97.

51. Sand, *Correspondance,* 3: 290.

52. Ibid., pp. 223–24, 226. For George Sand's brief but passionate liaison with actress Marie Dorval, see Barry, *Infamous Woman,* pp. 143–51.

53. Ibid., p. 397, footnote.

54. Liszt and d'Agoult, *Correspondance,* p. 156.

55. Sand, *Correspondance,* 3: 370–2.

56. Liszt and d'Agoult, *Correspondance,* p. 178.

57. Cf. Barry, *Infamous Woman,* pp. 217–18.

58. Wladimir Karénine (pseud. of Varvara Dmitrievna Komarova), *George Sand: sa vie et ses oeuvres,* 2 vols. (Paris: 1899–1926), 2: 329–30.

59. Perényi, *Artist as Hero,* p. 145.

60. Adolphe Pictet, *Une course à Chamonix* (Paris: 1838), pp. 20, 77.

61. Ibid., p. 30.

62. Quoted in Rocheblave, "Amitié romanesque," p. 800.

63. Agoult, *Mémoires,* p. 90.

64. Sand, *Correspondance,* 3: 570 (both letters).

65. Quoted in Vier, *d'Agoult,* p. 233.

66. Thérèse Marix-Spire, *Les romantiques et la musique. Le cas de George Sand, 1804–1838* (Paris: 1954), pp. 508–509.
67. Quoted in Rocheblave, "Amitié Romanesque," p. 828.
68. Sand, *Correspondance,* 3: 569.
69. Agoult, *Mémoires,* pp. 89–90.
70. Sand, *Correspondance,* 3: 716.
71. Marix-Spire, *Les romantiques,* p. 555.
72. Quoted in Rocheblave, "Amitié romanesque," p. 819.
73. Quoted in Perényi, *Artist as Hero,* p. 163.
74. Quoted in Vier, *d'Agoult,* p. 249.
75. Sand, *Correspondance,* 3: 765.
76. Quoted in Vier, *d'Agoult,* p. 258.
77. Sand, *Correspondance,* 4: 86–87.
78. Agoult, *Mémoires,* pp. 75–76.
79. Sand, "Entretiens journaliers," in *Oeuvres,* 2: 980–81.
80. Quoted in Rocheblave, *"Amitié romanesque,"* p. 819.
81. Thérèse Marix-Spire, "Bataille de dames, George Sand et Madame d'Agoult," in *Revue des Sciences Humaines,* Lille (April–Sept. 1951), p. 229.
82. Sand, *Correspondance,* 2: 980.
83. Karénine, *George Sand,* 2: p. 362.
84. Agoult, *Mémoires,* p. 97.
85. Karénine, *George Sand,* 2: 370.
86. Agoult, *Mémoires,* p. 98.
87. Quoted in Vier, *d'Agoult,* p. 296.
88. Ibid., p. 420, note 212; p. 218.
89. Quoted in Gavoty, *Liszt,* p. 203.
90. Agoult, *Mémoires,* p. 140.
91. Ibid., pp. 143–44.
92. Liszt and d'Agoult, *Correspondance,* p. 218.
93. Agoult, *Mémoires,* pp. 145–46.
94. Ibid., pp. 146–47 (includes preceding paragraph).
95. Ibid., pp. 147–50.
96. Liszt and d'Agoult, *Correspondance,* pp. 234–35.
97. Agoult, *Mémoires,* p. 157.
98. Ibid., pp. 174–75.
99. Liszt and d'Agoult, *Correspondance,* pp. 238–39.
100. Agoult, *Mémoires,* p. 179.
101. Quoted in Vier, *d'Agoult,* pp. 317–18.
102. Liszt and d'Agoult, *Correspondance,* p. 399.
103. Agoult, *Mémoires,* p. 168.
104. Ibid., pp. 166–67.
105. Liszt and d'Agoult, *Correspondance,* pp. 262–64.
106. Vier, *d'Agoult,* p. 319.
107. The Anna Karenina image derives from a line in a book review by

Susan Jacoby for *The Washington Post,* reprinted in the *International Herald Tribune,* November 27–28, 1982. The book reviewed was a novel having nothing to do with Marie d'Agoult; the comment was on the behavior of the heroine, so unlike Tolstoy's.

Chapter 8

1. Gertrude Stein, "An American and France," in *What are Masterpieces* (Los Angeles: 1940), pp. 62–70.
2. Maurice Sachs, *The Decade of Illusion, Paris 1918–1928* (New York: 1935), p. 10.
3. Gertrude Stein, *Everybody's Autobiography* (New York: 1937), pp. 115, 134.
4. Stein, *The Making of Americans, Being a History of a Family's Progress* (Paris: 1925), p. 398.
5. Ibid., p. 412.
6. Stein, *Everybody's Autobiography,* p. 142.
7. Gertrude Stein, *Wars I Have Seen* (New York: 1945), p. 14.
8. Stein, *Making of Americans,* pp. 412–13.
9. Donald Gallup, ed., *The Flowers of Friendship: Letters Written to Gertrude Stein* (New York: 1953), p. 132.
10. Cf. Richard Bridgman, *Gertrude Stein in Pieces* (New York: 1970), pp. 11–12. A consummate and generally dependable exegesis of Gertrude Stein's writings from Radcliffe College to her death.
11. Stein, *Making of Americans,* p. 432.
12. Gertrude Stein, *A Primer for the Gradual Understanding of Gertrude Stein,* ed. Robert Bartlett Haas (Los Angeles: 1971), p. 34.
13. Stein, *A Primer,* p. 34.
14. Stein, *Making of Americans,* pp. 388, 424.
15. Elizabeth Sprigge, *Gertrude Stein: Her Life and Work* (New York: 1957), p. 39.
16. Leon Katz relates the details, including often intense interviews with Alice Toklas, in "The First Making of *The Making of Americans:* A Study Based on Gertrude Stein's Notebooks and Early Versions of Her Novel (1902–1908)" (Ph.D. diss., Columbia University, 1963). He has since discussed Stein, Toklas, and the notebooks with this author, as will be noted. If anyone could, and should, write *The Autobiography of Gertrude Stein,* as Stein wrote that of Toklas, it is Mr. Katz. If not, it should be Ms. Ulla Dydo, whose knowledge of the Stein correspondence, notebooks, and other papers at Yale University, derived as she researches Stein's *Stanzas in Meditation* in preparation for a book on Gertrude Stein during this period, can only be compared to Mr. Katz's. Ms. Dydo, too, will be referred to in subsequent notes.
17. Gertrude Stein, *Fernhurst, Q.E.D., and Other Early Writings* (New York: 1971), pp. 54–60. *Q.E.D.* was originally published as *Things As They Are*

(Pawlet, Vt.: Banyon Press, 1950). See Leon Katz's introduction to *Fernhurst* for autobiographical connections.

18. Stein, *Fernhurst,* pp. xiii–xiv.

19. Ibid., pp. 60–63.

20. Ibid., pp. 66, 75, 78, 82.

21. Ibid., pp. 97–133.

22. Jane Rule, *Lesbian Images* (New York: Pocket Books, 1976), p. 65.

23. Ibid.

24. Gertrude Stein, *The Autobiography of Alice B. Toklas,* in *Selected Writings,* ed., with intro. and notes, Carl Van Vechten (New York: 1946), p. 3.

25. Roland E. Duncan, "An Interview with Alice Toklas in Paris on 28–29 November 1952," quoted in Bridgman, *Stein in Pieces,* p. 12.

26. Alice B. Toklas, *What Is Remembered* (New York: 1963), p. 3.

27. Ibid., p. 12.

28. Linda Simon, *The Biography of Alice B. Toklas* (New York: 1977), pp. 22, 27.

29. Toklas, *Remembered,* p. 13.

30. Ibid., p. 17.

31. Ibid., p. 23.

32. Ibid., pp. 23–24.

33. Ibid., p. 24.

34. Katz, "First Making," p. 235.

35. Conversation with Leon Katz.

36. Stein, *Making of Americans,* pp. 385, 401–402, 606.

37. Gertrude Stein, "A Third," in *As Fine As Melanctha (1914–1930)* (New Haven: Yale University Press, 1954), p. 347.

38. Toklas, *Remembered,* p. 27.

39. "My attack on Alice is like Grant on Lee," that of "the unaggressive complete egotist, always a forward pressure"—Gertrude Stein, Notebook C-46, Yale University Collection.

40. Toklas, *Remembered,* p. 44.

41. Alice Toklas, Stein noted months earlier, has a good deal "of self-righteousness and un-self-consciousness," but her "sexual base is May [Bookstaver], the elusive, finer purer flame of the prostitute"—Notebook B-5. Here Stein is adopting the vocabulary and categories of Otto Weininger's *Sex and Character,* in which the female prostitute is near the extreme end of "total femaleness"; for Weininger, that is all bad, but not for Stein. (See Katz, "The First Making," p. 276.)

42. Gertrude Stein, "First Page," in *Stanzas in Meditation and Other Poems (1929–1933)* (New Haven: Yale University Press, 1956), p. 285.

43. Toklas, *Remembered,* pp. 48, 50–51.

44. Ibid., p. 54.

45. Stein, *Making of Americans,* pp. 348, 459 and 485.

46. The term *validated* was used by Ulla Dydo in conversation.

47. Gertrude Stein, *Two: Gertrude Stein and Her Brother and Other Early*

Portraits (1908–1912) (New Haven: Yale University Press, 1951), pp. 45, 47, 57, 99, 124, 126.

48. Stein, *Autobiography of Toklas,* p. 4.

49. Ibid., p. 95.

50. Stein, "Ada," in *A Primer* pp. 45–47.

51. Toklas, *Remembered,* p. 68.

52. Ibid., p. 71.

53. Simon, *Biography,* p. 82.

54. Mabel Dodge Luhan, *European Experiences* (New York: 1935), p. 332, quoted in Ibid., p. 85.

55. Stein, "Portrait of Mabel Dodge at the Villa Curonia," in *Selected Writings,* pp. 465–68.

56. Gertrude Stein, *Lectures in America* (New York: 1935), p. 150.

57. Stein, *Autobiography of Toklas,* pp. 98–99.

58. Stein, "Preciosilla," in *Selected Writings,* p. 486.

59. Stein, Interview, *A Primer,* p. 18.

60. Leo Stein, *Journey Into the Self* (New York: 1950), p. 53, quoted in Bridgman, *Stein in Pieces,* p. 121.

61. Stein, *Everybody's Autobiography,* p. 77.

62. Quoted in Sprigge, *Life and Work,* p. 84.

63. Alice B. Toklas, *Staying On Alone: Letters of Alice B. Toklas,* ed. Edward Burns (New York: 1973), p. 195.

64. Toklas, *Remembered,* p. 84.

65. Katz, "First Making," p. 73.

66. Stein, "A Sonatina Followed by Another," in *Bee Time Vine, and Other Pieces (1913–1927)* (New Haven, 1953), p. 12.

67. Stein, *Lifting Belly,* in *Bee Time Vine,* pp. 78, 110, 91.

68. In one of her notebooks, Stein jotted: "Pablo [Picasso] & Matisse have a maleness that belongs to genius. Moi aussi [sic] perhaps." Gertrude Stein, *Gertrude Stein on Picasso,* ed. Edward Burns (New York: 1970), p. 97. Yet she would also write that "the only real thinking has been done by a woman," herself. Gertrude Stein, *The Geographical History of America* (New York: 1936), p. 182.

69. Stein, "Lifting Belly," in *Bee Time Vine,* pp. 96–115.

70. Gertrude Stein, "This One Is Serious," in *Painted Lace and Other Pieces (1914–1937)* (New Haven: Yale University Press, 1955), p. 20.

71. Gertrude Stein, "Farragut or A Husband's Recompense," in *Useful Knowledge* (New York: 1928), p. 9.

72. Ibid., p. 11.

73. Gertrude Stein, *Geography and Plays* (Boston: 1922), p. 346.

74. Stein, *Everybody's Autobiography,* p. 128.

75. William G. Rogers, *When This You See Remember Me: Gertrude Stein in Person* (New York: 1948), pp. 13–14.

76. Toklas, *Remembered,* p. 104.

77. Simon, *Biography,* p. 116.

78. Bridgman, *Stein in Pieces,* p. 153.

79. Stein, "Didn't Nelly and Lilly Love You," in *Fine As Melanctha,* pp. 221, 226–27, 245.

80. Stein, "A Third," in *Fine As Melanctha,* pp. 347, 335, 340, 343, 346, 348, 350–51, 356.

81. Stein, *Autobiography of Toklas,* p. 175.

82. Quoted in Simon, *Biography,* p. 117.

83. "In his letter [to William Rogers], Hemingway paid Gertrude the ultimate masculine compliment, saying that he had always had an urge to fuck her." James R. Mellow, *Charmed Circle: Gertrude Stein and Company* (New York: 1974), p. 458.

84. Ernest Hemingway, *A Moveable Feast* (New York: Penguin Books, 1966), p. 17.

85. Stein, *Autobiography of Toklas,* p. 176.

86. Donald Gallup, *Flowers of Friendship,* p. 165.

87. Hemingway, *Moveable Feast,* pp. 20–23.

88. Stein, *Making of Americans,* p. 606.

89. Toklas, *Remembered,* pp. 121–22.

90. Hemingway, *Moveable Feast,* p. 28; and Mellow, *Charmed Circle,* p. 273.

91. Stein *Autobiography of Toklas,* pp. 178–79, 182.

92. Hemingway, *Moveable Feast,* pp. 88–89.

93. Stein *Autobiography of Toklas,* p. 182.

94. Simon, *Biography,* pp. 122–23.

95. Stein, "First Page," in *Stanzas in Meditation,* p. 285.

96. Stein *Autobiography of Toklas,* p. 201.

97. Toklas, *Staying On Alone,* p. 205.

98. Stein, "To Basket," *Stanzas in Meditation,* p. 232.

99. Edmund Wilson, *Axel's Castle* (New York: 1931), p. 253.

100. Stein, *Stanzas in Meditation,* p. 142.

101. Katz, "First Making," p. 16.

102. Stein, *Fernhurst, Q.E.D.,* p. vii.

103. The blunt statement is that of scholar Ulla Dydo, who is preparing a book demonstrating, *inter alia,* its likely truth. The bluntness is that of conversation as well as conviction. Ms. Dydo has also used the term *peace offering* elsewhere. Ulla Dydo, *Stanzas in Meditation: The Other Autobiography,* unpublished manuscript, p. 37.

104. Stein, "Winning His Way," in *Stanzas in Meditation,* p. 164. Cf. Bridgman, *Stein in Pieces,* pp. 205–206.

105. Ibid., p. 90.

106. Bridgman, *Stein in Pieces,* p. 212.

107. Stein, *Stanzas in Meditation,* p. 77.

108. Ibid., pp. 116, 80, 79, 134.

109. The book by Ms. Dydo should tell us. Alice herself said she was "paranoid about the name May." Dydo, "Other Autobiography," p. 30.

110. Cyril Connolly, *Previous Convictions* (New York: 1963), p. 283, quoted in Bridgman, *Stein in Pieces,* p. 218.

111. Cf. Dydo, "Other Autobiography," pp. 30–31.

112. Stein, *Everybody's Autobiography,* pp. 218–19.

113. Toklas, *Remembered,* p. 156.

114. Gertrude Stein, "What Does She See When She Shuts Her Eyes," in *Mrs. Reynolds and Five Earlier Novelettes* (New Haven: Yale University Press, 1952), p. 375.

115. Stein, *Everybody's Autobiography,* pp. 206–207.

116. Gertrude Stein, *Doctor Faustus Lights the Lights,* in *Last Operas and Plays* (New York: 1949), p. 118.

117. Gertrude Stein, *Picasso* (London: 1939), pp. 48–49.

118. Stein, *Everybody's Autobiography,* pp. 15–17.

119. Toklas, *Remembered,* p. 161.

120. Both are quoted in Simon, *Biography,* p. 179.

121. Toklas, *Remembered,* p. 162.

122. Ibid., p. 164.

123. Ibid., p. 167.

124. Ibid., p. 168.

125. Cf. Joseph Barry, *The People of Paris* (New York: 1966), pp. vi and viii.

126. Gertrude Stein, *Brewsie and Willie* (New York: 1946), p. 114.

127. Cf. Carl Van Vechten's introduction to Stein, *Last Operas,* pp. x–xi. A letter from this author to Van Vechten on Stein's practice as well as the explanation for "Jo[e] the Loiterer" can be found on these pages.

128. Stein, *The Mother of Us All,* in *Last Operas,* pp. 53, 57–58, 60, 72–73, 75, 80–81.

129. Ibid., pp. 83, 87–88. Cf. Bridgman, *Stein in Pieces,* pp. 341–45.

130. In 1952 Alice would help Faÿ to escape to Switzerland, eventually to be amnestied by the French government.

131. Toklas, *Remembered,* p. 172.

132. Conversation with Alice Toklas. Cf. Toklas, *Remembered,* pp. 172–73; and Virgil Thomson, *Virgil Thomson* (New York: 1966), p. 377.

133. Toklas, *Remembered,* p. 173.

134. Cf. Joseph Barry, "Alice B. Toklas," in *The Village Voice,* March 16, 1967; and Barry, "A Tribute to Alice B. Toklas," in *People of Paris,* pp. 154–62.

135. Mellow, *Charmed Circle,* pp. 467–68. For details of Stein's will.

136. Stein, "Which One Will," in *Fine As Melanctha,* p. 386.

Chapter 9

1. Conversation with Jean Marais.

2. Jean Cocteau, *La Difficulté d'être* (Paris: 1978), p. 21.

3. Jean Cocteau, *Le Rappel à l'ordre,* quoted in "Cocteau," *Libération,* Numéro hors-série, October 1983.

4. Cocteau, *La Difficulté,* p. 10.

5. Cocteau, *Le Livre blanc,* (Paris: 1981), pp. 32–33.

6. Ibid., pp. 26, 29, 34.

7. Cocteau, *La Difficulté,* pp. 7, 24–25.

8. Jean Cocteau, *Entretiens avec Roger Stéphane* (Paris: 1964), p. 66.

9. Quoted in "Cocteau."

10. Francis Steegmuller, *Cocteau: A Biography* (Boston: 1970), pp. 20, 413. Princess Pailey is unnamed. See, however, p. 40 in "Cocteau."

11. Quoted in Steegmuller, *Cocteau,* p. 498.

12. Cocteau, "Textes érotiques inédits," *Le Livre blanc,* p. 141.

13. Cocteau, letter to Jean-Jacques Kihm, quoted in *Cahiers Jean Cocteau* 8 (1979), p. 133. Compare Gore Vidal, reviewing the memoirs of Christopher Isherwood in the *New York Review of Books* (December 6, 1976):

> A beautiful irony never to be understood by United Statesmen given to the joys of the sexual majority is that a homosexualist like Isherwood cannot with any ease enjoy a satisfactory sexual relationship with a woman because he himself is so entirely masculine that the woman presents no challenge, no masculine hardness, no exciting *agon.*

Gore Vidal then quotes Isherwood:

> "Why do I prefer boys? Because of their shape and their voices and their smell and the way they move. And boys can be romantic. I can put them into my myth and fall in love with them. Girls can be absolutely beautiful but never romantic. In fact, their utter lack of romance is what I find most likeable about them."

Vidal adds: "There is a clear-eyed normality (if not great accuracy) about all this."

14. Cocteau, *Le Livre blanc,* p. 63.

15. Jean Cocteau, *Portraits-souvenir, 1900–1914* (Paris: 1977), p. 153.

16. Ibid., p. 210. Cf. Maurice Sachs, *The Decade of Illusion, Paris 1918–1928* (New York: 1933), p. 177.

17. Cocteau, *Portraits-souvenir,* p. 158.

18. Ibid., p. 159.

19. Cocteau, *La Difficulté,* pp. 31–32.

20. Cf. Steegmuller, *Cocteau,* p. 87.

21. Quoted in Ibid., p. 92.

22. Cf. Ibid., p. 160.

23. Gertrude Stein, *The Autobiography of Alice B. Toklas* in *Selected Writings* (New York: 1946), p. 143.

24. Conversations with Mlle. Chanel.

25. Cocteau, *La Difficulté,* p. 18.

26. "Poor Gide," wrote Cocteau, "thought *Le Grand Ecart* was a camouflage à la Proust [a man in the fictional guise of a woman; that is, Albertine for Albert], whereas it is the literal account of my love affair with Madeleine Carlier"—when he was twenty and she a thirty-two-year-old actress.

27. A line from Cocteau's play, *L'Aigle à deux têtes (The Two-Headed Eagle).*

28. Quoted in Steegmuller, *Cocteau,* pp. 267, 272.

29. Cocteau, *Entretiens avec Stéphane,* pp. 93–94.

30. Jean Cocteau, *Entretiens sur le cinématographe* (Paris: 1973), pp. 43, 15.

31. Cocteau, *Jean Marais* (Paris: 1951), p. 68.

32. Conversation with Marais.

33. Jean Marais, *Histoires de ma vie, avec une suite poétique composée de cent quinze poèmes inédits de Jean Cocteau* (Paris: 1975), p. 56.

34. Ibid., pp. 57–58.

35. Ibid., pp. 62–63.

36. Ibid., p. 68.

37. Conversation with Marais. Also, Marais, *Histoires,* pp. 74–75.

38. Marais, *Histoires,* pp. 67, 218.

39. Ibid., pp. 83–84.

40. Ibid., p. 85.

41. Ibid., p. 95.

42. Cocteau, *Le Livre blanc,* p. 94.

43. Quoted in Marais, *Histoires,* pp. 91–94.

44. Ibid., p. 286.

45. Ibid., pp. 95–99.

46. Conversation with Marais. Poems quoted in Ibid., pp. 273, 258.

47. Quoted in Marais, *Histoires,* p. 268.

48. Marais, *Histoires,* p. 115.

49. Conversation with Chanel.

50. In *La Gerbe,* December 5, 1940, quoted in Steegmuller, *Cocteau,* pp. 441–42.

51. Marais, *Histoires,* p. 141. Marais was remarkably nonviolent, otherwise. One night as he was performing, there was an air raid. The play went on. During intermission Marais and several others watched "the monstrous fireworks" from the roof. He thought of the war, the dead, the wounded, "but I was incapable of bringing myself to hate. I felt like a cripple."

52. Simone de Beauvoir, *La Force de l'age* (Paris: 1960), p. 498.

53. Marais, *Histoires,* p. 144.

54. Cocteau, *Entretiens sur le cinématographe,* p. 157.

55. Marais, *Histoires,* p. 161.

56. Quoted in Ibid., p. 162.

57. Jean Cocteau, *Jean Marais* (Paris: 1951), p. 105.

58. Steegmuller, *Cocteau,* p. 457.

59. Cocteau, *Jean Marais,* pp. 110–11.

60. Marais, *Histoires,* p. 175.

61. Jean Cocteau, *La Belle et la Bête, journal d'un film* (Monaco: 1958), p. 127 and passim. Cf. Steegmuller, *Cocteau,* pp. 457–61.

62. Marais, *Histoires,* p. 216.

63. Cocteau, *Jean Marais,* p. 66.

64. Cocteau, *La Difficulté,* pp. 54–55.

65. Marais, *Histoires,* p. 275.

66. Conversation with Marais. Cf. Ibid., p. 177; and Cocteau, *La Difficulté,* p. 152.

67. Cocteau, Ibid., pp. 177, 24, 56, 88, 128.

68. Ibid., p. 151.

69. Conversation with Marais. Cf. Marais, *Histoires,* p. 177; and Cocteau, *La Difficulté* p. 152.

70. Cocteau, Ibid., Preface, p. 6.

71. Jean-Jacques Kihm, Elizabeth Sprigge, and Henri C. Béhar, *Jean Cocteau, l'homme et les miroirs* (Paris: 1968), p. 308.

72. Marais, *Histoires,* p. 184.

73. Alice B. Toklas, *Staying on Alone: Letters of Alice B. Toklas* (New York: 1973), p. 129.

74. Marais, *Histoires,* p. 188.

75. Jean Cocteau, *Du cinématographe* (Paris: 1973), p. 127.

76. Ibid.

77. Cocteau, *Jean Marais,* p. 117.

78. Quoted in Marais, *Histoires,* p. 189.

79. Interview with Edouard Dermit, "Jean Cocteau," *Masques,* September 1983, p. 55.

80. Jean Cocteau, *Le Passé défini, I, 1951–1952, journal* (Paris: 1983), pp. 93–94.

Chapter 10

1. Georges Michel, *Mes Années Sartre* (Paris: 1981), pp. 31–35.

2. Sartre's manuscripts are to be deposited at the Bibliothèque National and made available at a future time.

3. Claude Francis and Fernande Gontier, *Les Ecrits de Simone de Beauvoir* (Paris: 1979), p. 563.

4. Suzanne Lilar, *Le Malentendu du "Deuxième sexe"* (Paris: 1969), p. 319.

5. Dorothy MacCall, "Existentialisme ou féminisme," *Obliques,* special issue: "Sartre," 1979, p. 320.

6. Jean-Paul Sartre, "Interview," *Le Nouvel observateur,* January 31, 1977.

7. Jean-Paul Sartre, *Les Mots* (Paris: 1964), pp. 211–12.

8. Ibid., p. 11.

9. "When his father died, Baudelaire was six, living in the adoration of his mother. . . . He lost himself in the sweet warmth of their mutual love; theirs was . . . an incestuous couple." Jean-Paul Sartre, *Baudelaire* (Paris: 1947), p. 18.

10. Sartre, *Les Mots,* pp. 13, 111.

11. "In November 1828 that woman, so loved, is remarried to a soldier; Baudelaire is sent to a boarding school. His famous 'crack' dates from that time." "It has been easy to attribute to him a badly resolved Oedipus complex. But it matters little whether he actually desired his mother, or

not" (Sartre, *Baudelaire,* pp. 19, 67). To be added: "Fire and ice, delights mixed with frustration, incest pleased me when it remained Platonic" (Sartre, *Les Mots,* p. 42). A badly resolved Oedipus complex?

12. Simone de Beauvoir, *La Cérémonie des adieux suivi d'entretiens avec Jean-Paul Sartre, août–septembre 1974* (Paris: 1981), pp. 444, 38.

13. Jean-Paul Sartre, *Lettres au Castor et à quelques autres,* edited, presented and annotated by Simone de Beauvoir, 2 vols., (Paris, 1983) 1, p. 54.

14. Sartre, "Interview," *Nouvel Observateur,* January 31, 1977.

15. Jean-Paul Sartre, *Les Carnets de la drôle de guerre, novembre 1939–mars 1940* (Paris: 1983), pp. 409–11.

16. Josette Pacaly, *Sartre au miroir, une lecture psychanalytique de ses écrits biographiques* (Paris: 1980), pp. 429–52.

17. Sartre *Les Mots,* pp. 136, 161.

18. Simone de Beauvoir, *Tout compte fait,* Folio ed. (Paris: 1972), p. 132. Published in English as *All Said and Done* (New York: 1974).

19. Sartre, *Les Mots,* p. 137; Sartre, *Les Carnets,* p. 320; Sartre, *Situations, X* (Paris: 1976), p. 97.

20. Beauvoir, *Tout compte,* pp. 14–15, 18.

21. Beauvoir, *Simone de Beauvoir, un film de Josée Dayan et Malka Ribowska* (Paris: 1979), pp. 35–36.

22. Ibid., p. 36. Simone de Beauvoir, *Mémoires d'une jeune fille rangée* (Paris: 1958), pp. 208, 359. Published in English as *Memoirs of a Dutiful Daughter.*

23. *Beauvoir, un film de Josée Dayan,* pp. 36–37.

24. Beauvoir, *Fille rangée,* pp. 231, 316.

25. Ibid., pp. 145–46. This call for a superior male who would "subjugate" her by his "intelligence, culture and authority" was written ten years *after* Beauvoir's *Le Deuxième sexe (The Second Sex)*—the feminist Bible, certainly the Old Testament, of the women's liberation movement—which appeared in 1949.

26. Sartre, *Lettres,* 2: 53.

27. Ibid., 1:9–10, 13, 16–17.

28. Beauvoir, *Fille rangée,* p. 310; Madeleine Chapsal, *Les Ecrivains en personne* (Paris: 1960), p. 2.

29. Sartre *Lettres,* 1:40.

30. Beauvoir, *Fille rangée,* p. 334.

31. *Beauvoir, un film de Josée Dayan,* p. 20.

32. Beauvoir, *Fille rangée,* p. 338.

33. Beauvoir, *Cérémonie des adieux,* p. 184.

34. Beauvoir, *Fille rangée,* p. 338.

35. "It is hard to imagine Colette, had she attended the Sorbonne, getting any kind of buzz out of coming second to Sartre . . . or to anybody. After all these years, de Beauvoir still appears to be proud that only Sartre achieved higher marks in those [final] exams than she. What would have happened, one wonders, if she had come top? What would it have done to Sartre? Merely to think of it makes the mind reel. Only love can make you

proud to be an also-ran." Angela Carter, review of Michèle Sarde, *Colette,* in the *London Review of Books,* October 2–16, 1980.

36. Sartre, *Les Carnets,* p. 345.

37. Ibid.

38. Beauvoir, *Fille rangée,* pp. 339–43.

39. Simone de Beauvoir, *La Force de l'âge* (Paris: 1960), pp. 17–18. Published in English as *The Prime of Life* (New York: 1962).

40. Interview with Alice Schwarzer, recorded in September 1982, and published in *Die Zeit* 2 (January 7, 1983). The translation is from the German. Cf. Schwarzer, *Simone de Beauvoir aujourd'hui* (Paris, 1984), p. 113. The statement of Beauvoir about her being "very passionate," in contrast to Sartre, has been eliminated in the French edition of Ms. Schwarzer's book.

41. Cf. Sartre interview with Michel Contat in Sartre, *Situations, X,* p. 146; and Beauvoir interview with Alice Schwarzer, *Marie Claire,* June 1978 (also, Schwarzer, *Beauvoir aujourd'hui,* p. 89).

42. Beauvoir, *Cérémonie des adieux,* p. 385.

43. Beauvoir, *La Force de l'âge,* pp. 19, 76, 26.

44. Ibid., pp. 26–28.

45. Ibid., pp. 28–29.

46. Ibid., p. 24.

47. Schwarzer, *Beauvoir aujourd'hui,* p. 112.

48. "Such a *pacte* most often simply regularizes and legitimizes masculine infidelity. In accepting it, a woman simply loses her right to complain or to protest"—Suzanne Lilar, *Le Couple* (Paris: 1963), p. 286.

49. Beauvoir, *La Force de l'âge,* p. 31.

50. Sartre, *Les Carnets,* pp. 96–99.

51. Beauvoir, *La Force de l'âge,* pp. 65–66.

52. Sartre, *Lettres,* 1:192.

53. Ibid.

54. Beauvoir, *La Force de l'âge,* p. 68.

55. Ibid., pp. 69–80.

56. Ibid., p. 81.

57. Ibid., pp. 81–82.

58. Jean-Paul Sartre, "Interview," *Le Nouvel observateur,* February 7, 1977.

59. Beauvoir, *La Force de l'âge,* pp. 81–83.

60. Ibid., pp. 190–91.

61. Ibid.

62. Sartre, *Les Carnets,* pp. 100–101; Beauvoir, *La Force de l'âge,* pp. 214–15.

63. Beauvoir, *La Force de l'âge,* p. 215.

64. Beauvoir, *She Came to Stay* (Cleveland: 1954), p. 33. Originally published as *L'Invitée* (Paris: 1943).

65. Sartre, *Les Carnets,* p. 83.

66. Sartre, *Situations, X,* p. 177.

67. Beauvoir, *La Force de l'âge,* p. 218.

68. Ibid., pp. 216–18.

69. Sartre, *Les Carnets,* p. 337.

70. Ibid., pp. 325, 156, 312; Beauvoir, *La Force de l'âge,* pp. 248, 250.

71. Beauvoir, *La Force de l'âge,* p. 250.

72. Simone de Beauvoir, *La Force des choses* (Paris: 1963), p. 7. Published in English as *Force of Circumstance* (New York: 1964).

73. Beauvoir, *She Came to Stay,* pp. 210, 237, 247, 25.

74. Beauvoir, *La Force de l'âge,* p. 622.

75. Sartre, *Les Carnets,* p. 15. Sartre has since said that he "chivalrously" left Olga to Jacques-Laurent Bost when he saw that they loved each other (conversation with Arlette Elkaïm-Sartre).

76. Sartre, *Les Carnets,* p. 102.

77. Sartre, *Lettres,* 1:192.

78. Ibid., pp. 184, 187.

79. Ibid., pp. 188, 190, 193, 200.

80. Ibid, 2: 88–90, 94.

81. Sartre, "Interview," *Nouvel Observateur,* January 31, 1977.

82. *Beauvoir, un film de Josée Dayan,* p. 75.

83. Beauvoir, *La Force de l'âge,* pp. 224, 283, 219–20.

84. Ibid., p. 255.

85. Sartre, *Lettres,* 1:345.

86. Sartre's letters to Wanda Kosakiewicz have been promised by her for publication. They will cast a colder light on the Sartre-Beauvoir couple.

87. Sartre, *Lettres,* 1:275–76.

88. Ibid., p. 290.

89. Beauvoir, *Tout compte,* p. 129.

90. Sartre, *Lettres,* 1:301.

91. Ibid., p. 321.

92. Ibid., p. 358.

93. Ibid., pp. 390–91.

94. Sartre, *Les Carnets,* p. 174.

95. Sartre, *Lettres,* 1:427.

96. Ibid., 2: 43.

97. Ibid., p. 105. Has Beauvoir brought out this letter to demonstrate that Sartre had told her *everything,* thus anticipating revelations in his letters to Wanda when they finally appear?

98. Ibid., p. 264.

99. Beauvoir, *La Force de l'âge,* p. 465.

100. Ibid., pp. 492–94.

101. Jean-Paul Sartre, Interview, in James D. Wilkinson, *The Intellectual Resistance in Europe* (Cambridge, Mass.: Harvard University Press, 1981), p. 36.

102. Schwarzer, *Beauvoir aujourd'hui,* p. 65.

103. Beauvoir, *La Force de l'âge,* p. 509.

104. Sartre, Interview, in Joseph Barry, *Left Bank, Right Bank* (New York: 1951), pp. 102–103.

105. Michele Le Doeuff, "Operative Philosophy, Simone de Beauvoir and Existentialism" (Paper delivered at the conference "*The Second Sex*—Thirty Years later," New York University, New York, September 1979).

106. Jean-Paul Sartre, *L'Etre et le néant* (Paris: 1943), pp. 638–39, 671, 676. Cf. Margery L. Collins and Christine Pierce, "Holes and Slime: Sexism in Sartre's Psychoanalysis," in Carol G. Gould and Marx W. Wartofsky, eds., *Women and Philosophy* (New York: 1976), pp. 112–25. See also Le Doeuff, "Operative Philosophy."

107. Simone de Beauvoir, *Le Deuxième sexe,* 2 vols. (Paris: 1949), 1:456–57. Published in English as *The Second Sex.*

108. Beauvoir, *La Force des choses,* p. 58.

109. Sartre, *Lettres,* 2: 110–11, 184.

110. Beauvoir, *La Force de l'âge,* p. 490.

111. Sartre, *Lettres,* 2: 320.

112. Ibid., p. 323.

113. Beauvoir, *Tout compte,* pp. 130, 129, 128.

114. Beauvoir, *La Force des choses,* p. 64.

115. Ibid., pp. 81–82.

116. Ibid.

117. Ibid., p. 137.

118. Ibid., p. 141.

119. Simone de Beauvoir, *The Mandarins* (London: Fontana Books, 1960), pp. 303–31. Originally published in French as *Les Mandarins* (Paris: 1954).

120. Beauvoir, *La Force des choses,* p. 140.

121. Beauvoir, *Mandarins,* pp. 574, 581, 696.

122. Ibid., p. 562.

123. H. E. F. Donohue, *Conversations with Nelson Algren* (New York: 1963), quoted in Axel Madsen, *Hearts and Minds, the Common Journey of Simone de Beauvoir and Jean-Paul Sartre* (New York: 1977), p. 140.

124. Beauvoir, *La Force des choses,* pp. 141–42.

125. Ibid., pp. 176, 179, 269, 274.

126. Francis and Gontier, *Les Ecrits,* p. 534.

127. Sartre, *Les Carnets,* p. 342.

128. Jean-Paul Sartre, *Sartre, un film réalisé par Alexandre Astruc et Michel Contat, texte intégral* (Paris: 1977), p. 116.

129. Beauvoir, *La Force des choses,* p. 301.

130. Beauvoir, *Tout compte,* p. 42.

131. Ibid., p. 42; Beauvoir, *La Force des choses,* pp. 271, 301–302, 306–308.

132. Beauvoir, *La Force des choses,* pp. 366 and 312.

133. Conversation with Arlette Elkaïm-Sartre.

134. Madsen, *Hearts and Minds,* p. 206.

135. Conversation with Arlette Elkaïm-Sartre.

136. Beauvoir, *La Force des choses,* pp. 438, 458, 466, 476–77.

137. Joseph Barry, *The People of Paris* (New York: 1966), pp. 101–109.

138. Beauvoir, *La Force des choses,* pp. 686, 672.

139. Beauvoir, *Cérémonie des adieux,* p. 193.

140. Jean-Paul Sartre, Interview with Jacqueline Piatier, *Le Monde,* April 18, 1964. Following this dismissal of literature, Sartre's refusal of the Nobel Prize for Literature in 1964 was scarcely a surprise. The reason proferred was that he did not want to become "institutionalized."

141. Sartre, *Les Mots,* pp. 210–11.

142. Sartre, Interview, *Le Monde.*

143. Conversation with Sartre.

144. Beauvoir, *Tout compte,* p. 10.

145. Ibid., p. 138.

146. Jean-Paul Sartre, Interview with Madeleine Gobeil, *Playboy,* May 1965, quoted, and translated from the French, in Michel Contat and Michel Rybalka, *Les Ecrits de Sartre* (Paris: 1970), p. 415.

147. Beauvoir, *Tout compte,* pp. 139–61, especially pp. 160–61.

148. Beauvoir, *Cérémonie des adieux,* p. 14.

149. Ibid., p. 35.

150. Sartre, *Les Mots,* p. 166.

151. Beauvoir, *Cérémonie des adieux,* pp. 20–22.

152. Georges Michel, *Mes Années Sartre,* p. 158.

153. Beauvoir, *Cérémonie des adieux,* pp. 32, 51, 59, 75, 86–87.

154. Ibid., p. 386.

155. Ibid., pp. 89, 95, 111, 116, 123, 136. See also Francoise Sagan, "Lettre d'amour à Jean-Paul Sartre," in *Avec mon meilleur souvenir* (Paris: 1984), pp. 179–94.

156. Beauvoir, *Cérémonie des adieux,* pp. 151, 153, 155, 157.